MOO0309671

THE PHILOSOPHY OF MIND

A deep concern with consciousness and intentionality is one of the several things that has lately moved into the centre of the philosophy of mind. The issue of consciousness is often treated as something distinct from intentionality, but – as Tim Crane notes in his incisive new Foreword – there is now something of a sea-change. This classic volume may be at least partly responsible for the shift in how philosophy of mind is starting to be understood. Before its first appearance, discussions of consciousness and intentionality in the context of perception were in their infancy. The book was a departure from the way this part of philosophy was conceived. It pointed to new ways to look at the discipline, addressing both the epistemology of mind, and intentionality and consciousness, especially in connection with perception. Showcasing many leading figures in the field, it offers a splendid overview of the issues at stake.

ANTHONY O'HEAR, OBE, is Professor of Philosophy at the University of Buckingham. He is an Honorary Director of the Royal Institute of Philosophy and Editor of the Institute's journal Philosophy.

TIM CRANE is Professor of Philosophy at Central European University in Vienna. He was formerly (from 2009-17) Knightbridge Professor of Philosophy in the University of Cambridge and a Fellow of Peterhouse. His most recent book is *The Meaning of Belief: Religion from an Atheist's Point of View* (Harvard University Press, 2017). From 2012-20 he served as Philosophy Consultant Editor of the Times Literary Supplement.

TALKING PHILOSOPHY

General Editor: James Garvey

The Royal Institute of Philosophy has been, from the very start, a fundamentally outward-facing organization. In 1924, Sydney Hooper – main mover behind the establishment of the Institute – realized that outreach to a wide interested public was a vital part of the value (whether social, cultural or intellectual) that philosophy at its best can impart. The Institute's first executive committee actively promoted that broad pedagogical message through accessible civic talks, and included in its ranks many of the most eminent luminaries of the day: not just professional philosophers but also sociologists, physicians, politicians, evolutionary biologists and psychologists. The Institute, from its foundation, has thus been rooted in an egalitarian community of people devoted to the principles of learning, debating and teaching philosophical knowledge in the broader service of what Hooper called 'the most permanent interests of the human spirit'. Talking Philosophy maintains this noble tradition. A book series published under the joint auspices of the Institute and Cambridge University Press, it addresses some of the most pertinent topics of the day so as to show how philosophy can shed new light on their interpretation, as well as public understanding of them.

Books in the series:

Moral Philosophy
The Philosophy of Mind
Ethics

THE PHILOSOPHY OF
MIND

EDITED BY

ANTHONY O'HEAR
University of Buckingham

WITH A FOREWORD BY

TIM CRANE
Central European University, Budapest

CAMBRIDGE
UNIVERSITY PRESS

University Printing House, Cambridge CB2 8BS, United Kingdom

One Liberty Plaza, 20th Floor, New York, NY 10006, USA

477 Williamstown Road, Port Melbourne, VIC 3207, Australia

314–321, 3rd Floor, Plot 3, Splendor Forum, Jasola District Centre, New Delhi – 110025, India

103 Penang Road, #05-06/07, Visioncrest Commercial, Singapore 238467

Cambridge University Press is part of the University of Cambridge.

It furthers the University's mission by disseminating knowledge in the pursuit of education, learning, and research at the highest international levels of excellence.

www.cambridge.org
Information on this title: www.cambridge.org/9781009108638
DOI: 10.1017/9781009105262

First published as Royal Institute of Philosophy Supplement: 43, Current Issues in Philosophy of Mind, 1998, Paperback ISBN 9780521639279
This edition first published 2022

A catalogue record for this publication is available from the British Library.

ISBN 978-1-009-10863-8 Paperback

CONTENTS

vii

CONTENTS

TIM CRANE

When this volume came out in 1998, it accurately represented some of the dominant and emerging concerns of the philosophy of mind at that time. It is interesting to compare, twenty years on, how these topics look now, what has and has not changed and what this tells us about the state of the philosophy of mind today.

A notable feature of *Current Issues* is the relative lack of discussion of the traditional mind–body problem, and its various proposed solutions: dualism, idealism and the varieties of physicalism and functionalism. At the time this represented something of a departure from the way this part of philosophy is usually conceived. The leading student anthologies of the 1990s (e.g. W. G. Lycan's *Mind and Cognition* (1990) or David Rosenthal's *The Nature of Mind* (1991)[1]) put the mind–body problem at the centre of their story of the philosophy of mind, a tradition which continued into the 2000s with David Chalmers's *The Philosophy of Mind* (2002) and Timothy O'Connor and David Robb's

[1] W. G. Lycan (ed.), *Mind and Cognition*. Oxford: Blackwell, 1990; David Rosenthal, *The Nature of Mind*. Oxford: Oxford University Press, 1991.

The Philosophy of Mind (2003)[2]. This story typically begins with Cartesian dualism – perhaps because it is historically prior, or because it is thought to be closer to the reader's 'pre-philosophical' views – and then presents criticisms and alternative metaphysical visions: behaviourism, physicalism of reductive and non-reductive kinds, and functionalism.

Despite the familiar and almost mechanical way in which these ideas are introduced in these books, there is nonetheless something slightly odd about this roll-call of philosophical positions. For one thing, why is behaviourism treated so seriously? Behaviourism in psychology was historically important, but philosophical behaviourism is surely more of an argumentative stalking horse than a genuinely believable doctrine. After all, the only philosophers who are ever attributed behaviourist views, Gilbert Ryle and Ludwig Wittgenstein, both explicitly denied they were behaviourists. Another obscure aspect of this picture is why the problem is so often framed in terms of the Cartesian concept of substance, a concept which few philosophers these days employ elsewhere in their metaphysics. The somewhat wooden nature of this whole debate often arises from its participants neglecting or refusing to question the intelligibility of the categories in terms of which it is frequently framed.

Current Issues, by contrast, largely ignored this metaphysical straitjacket, and provided an alternative picture of the discipline. (The one exception is Jaegwon Kim's paper, to which I

---

[2] David Chalmers (ed.), *The Philosophy of Mind*. Oxford: Oxford University Press, 2002; Timothy O'Connor and David Robb, *The Philosophy of Mind*. London: Routledge, 2003.

will return later.) A number of distinct themes can be identified. One was the epistemology of mind – the papers by Martin Davies and (the late) Tony Stone, and by Jane Heal on other minds; Crispin Wright wrote on self-knowledge; and Quassim Cassam investigated more broadly some Kantian themes in the epistemology of mind. Among other themes, the papers by Cynthia Macdonald and Michael Morris investigated the 'normativity' of the mind and mental discourse, Andy Clark discussed embodiment, Jennifer Hornsby action and Christopher Peacocke freedom. The remaining papers – by Ned Block, Naomi Eilan, Ted Honderich, M.G.F. Martin, the late Gregory McCulloch and me – focus mainly on questions about consciousness and intentionality, especially in connection with perception.

A deep concern with consciousness and its relationship to intentionality is obviously one of the things that have moved into the centre of the philosophy of mind since 1998. This concern has expressed itself in two broad trends. One is the idea that consciousness itself should be understood in terms of intentionality: this is 'intentionalism' or 'representationalism'. The other is the idea of the phenomenology of thought or cognition, that thought has its own distinctive phenomenology.[3] Related to this 'cognitive phenomenology' is the distinct doctrine of phenomenal intentionality,[4] which attempts to explain intentionality in terms of consciousness.

[3] Tim Bayne and Michelle Montague (eds.), *Cognitive Phenomenology*. Oxford: Oxford University Press, 2011; Michelle Montague, *The Given*. Oxford: Oxford University Press, 2016.

[4] Uriah Kriegel (ed.), *Pheomenal Intentionality*. Oxford: Oxford University Press, 2013.

Each of these trends, in their different ways, attempts to break down the sharp distinction between consciousness (or 'phenomenal consciousness') and intentionality, which had dominated analytic philosophy of mind since at least the 1950s. This distinction has been formulated in a number of ways, but common to them all is the idea that intentionality has nothing essentially to do with consciousness, and that the core (or especially problematic) conscious phenomena have nothing essentially to do with intentionality. Here is a clear statement of the view by David Rosenthal in 1994:

> There are two broad categories of mental property. Mental states such as thoughts and desires, often called propositional attitudes, have content that can be described by 'that' clauses. For example, one can have a thought, or desire, that it will rain. These states are said to have intentional properties, or intentionality. Sensations, such as pains and sense impressions, lack intentional content, and have instead qualitative properties of various sorts. (349)[5]

Qualitative properties in this sense are sometimes known as 'qualia', and the problem of consciousness is often conceived as the problem of explaining how a physical system can have such properties.

This conception of the distinction between two kinds of mental properties and the associated conception

---

[5] David Rosenthal, 'Identity Theories' in Samuel Guttenplan (ed.) *A Companion to the Philosophy of Mind*. Oxford: Blackwell, 1994.

of the problem of consciousness is presupposed in Jaegwon Kim's 'The Mind–Body Problem after Fifty Years', the one paper in *Current Issues* which does address the traditional problem of mind and body directly. One of the conclusions of Kim's paper is that 'the two central problems in the philosophy of mind, the problem of consciousness and the problem of mental causation, come together'. This is because the only way to explain consciousness physically is to 'functionalize it in the physical domain': that is, give a complete functionalist or causal characterisation of consciousness. Kim then argues that doing this would also solve the problem of the causal powers of the mental. But he then argues that it cannot be done, for what are now familiar reasons. It is worth looking back at these reasons, not least because of what they show about how intentionality and consciousness have been conceived.

At the heart of Kim's argument is the view that there are no 'unsurmountable obstacles to a causal/functional account of intentionality', but 'the trouble comes from qualia. For, by contrast with the case of intentional phenomena, we seem able to conceive a physical duplicate of this world in which qualia are distributed differently or entirely absent (a "zombie world" as some call it)'. Kim supports this remark with a reference to David Chalmers's (1996) discussion in *The Conscious Mind*.[6] Kim's view, then, is that although intentionality can be functionalised, consciousness cannot: essentially because zombie worlds are possible.

---

[6] David Chalmers, *The Conscious Mind*. Oxford: Oxford University Press, 1996.

In other words, a subject or thinker could have all the intentional states it does without being conscious in the 'qualitative' or 'phenomenal' way. (The phenomenal way is sometimes contrasted with the 'access' way of being conscious: a distinction introduced by Ned Block, and discussed in detail in his contribution to *Current Issues*.)

In any case, Kim's line of argument relies on the sharp distinction between intentionality and consciousness which was challenged by intentionalism on the one hand (the view that consciousness is a form of intentionality) and cognitive phenomenology on the other (the view that some intentional states have their own distinctive form of conscious phenomenology). The rejection of this sharp distinction is also the focus of many of the essays in *Current Issues*. Gregory McCulloch rejects the idea that consciousness should be primarily conceived in terms of sensory states, and argues for a kind of cognitive phenomenology. The content of an intentional state 'can be as much a constituent of the stream of consciousness – whatever that means – as itches or patches of red'. McCulloch's emphasis is on the understanding of the meanings of words, rather like Galen Strawson and David Pitt in similar writings from the 1990s. 'Meanings' McCulloch argues, 'others' as well as our own, can figure as integral components of our conscious life'.

Unsurprisingly, McCulloch is on the side of those who reject the notion of qualia as a useful one in classifying mental phenomena. He would agree wholeheartedly with M. G. F. Martin's statement in 'Setting Things Before the Mind' that 'although many philosophers write as if it is simply obvious to us that there are qualia, and that we know what they are, I shall argue instead that this is all chimerical'. And in my own contribution to the volume, I argue that the notion of intentionality should not be understood in a way that rules out consciousness at the outset; and this means not construing consciousness in terms of qualia.

The attempts in these papers to break down the sharp distinction between consciousness (conceived of in terms of qualia) and intentionality is, strictly speaking, independent of the roles of these notions in formulating the mind–body problem. However, a connection can certainly be made if the mind–body problem is formulated in the way Kim does – in terms of whether qualia can be functionalised – or the way Chalmers does – in terms of hard and easy problems. For if the distinction between qualia and intentionality has been misconceived by the tradition, and if the distinction between hard and easy problems is not what Chalmers thinks it is, then the mind–body problem will start to look rather different. As Naomi Eilan argues in her contribution to the volume, 'while this bifurcation between easy and hard problems of consciousness is of some polemical value, it is fundamentally misguided, in my view, if it is treated as a resting place. Neither intentionality ... nor access-consciousness are easy concepts in the sense suggested, and phenomenal consciousness is not impenetrably hard in the sense suggested'. Eilan then explicitly makes a connection between the easy/hard distinction and the intentional/phenomenal distinction: 'a fundamental assumption in treating them as easy is that we can give an account of intentionality and accessibility wholly independently of an account of phe-nomenal aspects of experience'. Eilan's hope is that if we abandon this assumption then we will make progress with the so-called 'hard problem'.

This hope has not yet been realised: the problem of consciousness is still widely treated as something distinct from the problem of intentionality (see Goff 2019)[7]. But there have been some movements in the direction that Eilan favours in her essay. These days intentionalism or representationalism about consciousness and perception are more widespread, and are seen as a crucial part of the philosophical landscape. And together with the revival of interest in cognitive phenomenology, and the emerging research programme of phenomenal intentionality (Kriegel 2013; Mendelovici 2018; Pitt forthcoming[8]), the simplistic distinction between qualia and intentionality is beginning to break down. It would be nice to think that *Current Issues* has had something to do with these changes in direction in the philosophy of mind.

References

Bayne, Tim and Michelle Montague (eds.) *Cognitive Phenomenology*. Oxford: Oxford University Press, 2011.

---

[7] Philip Goff, *Galileo's Error*. New York: Random House, 2019.

[8] Uriah Kriegel (ed.), *Pheomenal Intentionality*. Oxford: Oxford University Press, 2013; Angela Mendelovici, *The Phenomenal Basis of Intentionality*. Oxford: Oxford University Press, 2018, David Pitt, *The Quality of Thought*. Oxford: Oxford University Press, forthcoming.

Chalmers, David. *The Conscious Mind*. Oxford: Oxford University Press, 1996.

Chalmers, David. (ed.) *The Philosophy of Mind*. Oxford: Oxford University Press, 2002.

Goff, Philip. *Galileo's Error*. New York: Random House, 2019.

Kriegel, Uriah (ed.)) *Pheomenal Intentionality*. Oxford: Blackwell, 2013.

Lycan, W. G. (ed.) *Mind and Cognition*. Oxford: Oxford University Press, 1990.

Mendelovici, Angela *The Phenomenal Basis of Intentionality*. Oxford: Oxford University Press, 2018.

Montague, Michelle *The Given*. Oxford: Oxford University Press, 2016.

O'Connor, Timothy and David Robb. *The Philosophy of Mind*. London: Routledge, 2003.

Pitt, David. *The Quality of Thought*. Oxford: Oxford University Press, forthcoming.

Rosenthal, David. *The Nature of Mind*. Oxford: Oxford University Press, 1991.

Rosenthal, David. 'Identity Theories' in Samuel Guttenplan (ed.) *A Companion to the Philosophy of Mind*. Oxford: Blackwell, 1994.

LIST OF CONTRIBUTORS

Jaegwon Kim

Ned Block

Andy Clark

Martin Davies

Tony Stone

Jane Heal

Crispin Wright

John Campbell

Ted Honderich

M. G. F. Martin

Naomi Eilan

Bill Brewer

Tim Crane

Gregory McCulloch

Cynthia Macdonald
Michael Morris

Quassim Cassam

Christopher Peacocke

Jennifer Hornsby

Introduction

ANTHONY O'HEAR

The philosophy of mind is one of the most exciting and innovative areas in philosophy at the current time. Necessarily, much of the work in the area is highly specialized, but as a consequence it is not widely available or accessible. By bringing together some of the leading figures in the field, we hope in this volume to fill what is often perceived both inside and outside philosophy to be a gap. Contributors have attempted in their papers to give an idea of their current concerns, to indicate the directions in which their work is taking them, and to suggest how it relates to other issues both in the philosophy of mind and in philosophy generally.

After a general review of work on the mind-body problem over the last 50 years, the collection focuses on various aspects of neural activity and embodiment, on mental simulation, on the first person, on consciousness (including a new approach to the topic), on intentionality, on perception, on the mind as generating norms, on its connection to the world outside, on free will and on action.

The papers in the volume are based on the lectures given in the Royal Institute of Philosophy's annual lecture series 1996–7. Thanks are due to all the contributors, and especially to Christopher Peacocke and Ted Honderich for their help in planning the series. I would also like to thank James Garvey for preparing the index, and for help with editing the volume.

The Mind–Body Problem after Fifty Years

JAEGWON KIM

I

It was about half a century ago that the mind–body problem, which like much else in serious metaphysics had been moribund for several decades, was resurrected as a mainstream philosophical problem. The first impetus came from Gilbert Ryle's *The Concept of Mind,* published in 1948, and Wittgenstein's well-known, if not well-understood, reflections on the nature of mentality and mental language, especially in his *Philosophical Investigations* which appeared in 1953. The primary concerns of Ryle and Wittgenstein, however, focused on the logic of mental discourse rather than the metaphysical issue of how our mentality is related to our bodily nature. In fact, Ryle and Wittgenstein would have regarded, each for different reasons, the metaphysical problem of the mind–body relation as arising out of deplorable linguistic confusions and not amenable to intelligible discussion. There was C. D. Broad's earlier and much neglected classic, *The Mind and Its Place in Nature*, which appeared in 1925, but this work, although robustly metaphysical, failed to

This paper derives in part from my 'The Mind-Body Problem: Taking Stock After 40 Years', forthcoming in *Philosophical Perspectives,* 1997.

connect with, and shape, the mind–body debate in the second half of this century. It is fair to say that the mind-body problem as we know it today had its proximate origins in a trio of papers published in the late 1950s: U. T. Place's 'Is Consciousness a Brain Process?',[1] in 1956, and J. J. C. Smart's 'Sensations and Brain Processes' and Herbert Feigl's 'The "Mental" and the "Physical"', published in 1958 and 1959 respectively.[2] In these papers, Place, Smart and Feigl proposed an approach to the status of mind that has been variously called 'the mind–body identity theory', 'central-state materialism', 'type physicalism', and 'the brain-state theory'. In particular, it was the papers by Smart and Feigl that had a major philosophical impact, launching the debate that has continued to this day.

---

[1] U. T. Place, 'Is Consciousness a Brain Process?', *British Journal of Psychology* 47/1 (1956), 44–50. There were even earlier modern statements of the identity approach: e.g. Samuel Alexander, *Space, Time, and Deity* (London: Macmillan, 1920), vol. II, p. 9, where he says, 'The mental process and its neural process are one and the same existence, not two existences'; the psychologist Edwin G. Boring states, 'If we were to find a perfect correlation between sensation *A* and neural process *a*, a precise correlation which we had reason to believe never failed, we should then identify *A* and *a* ... it is scientifically more useful to consider that all psychological data are of the same kind and that consciousness is a physiological event' (*The Physical Dimensions of Consciousness* (New York: Dover reprint, 1963), p. 14). Boring's book was first published in 1933.

[2] J. J. C. Smart, 'Sensations and Brain Processes', *Philosphical Review* 68 (1959), 141–56. Herbert Feigl, 'The "Mental" and the "Physical"', in *Minnesota Studies in the Philosophy of Science,* vol. II, eds. Herbert Feigl, Grover Maxewell and Michael Scriven (Minneapolis: University of Minnesota Press, 1958).

For those of us who came of age philosophically in the 1960s, the brain-state theory was our first encounter with the mind–body problem as a problem in systematic philosophy. We were impressed by its refreshing boldness, and it seemed in tune with the optimistic scientific temper of the times. Why can't mentality turn out to be brain processes just as heat turned out to be molecular motion and light turned out to be electromagnetic waves? But the brain-state theory was surprisingly short-lived – its precipitous decline began only several years after its initial promulgation – and by the late sixties and early seventies it had been abandoned by almost all philosophers working in philosophy of mind and psychology. This was more than the fading away of a bold and promising philosophical theory: the demise of the brain-state theory gave a bad name to all forms of reductionism, turning the term 'reductionist' into a distinctly negative, often disdainful, epithet. In most academic and intellectual circles these days, calling someone a reductionist has become more than saying that he or she holds an incorrect view; it is a thinly disguised putdown that labels the targeted person as intellectually backward and simplistic.

It is clear in retrospect, though, that in spite of its brief life, the Smart–Feigl physicalism made one crucial contribution that has outlived its reign as a theory of the mind. What I have in mind is the fact that the theory helped set the basic parameters for the debates that were to follow – a set of broadly physicalist assumptions and aspirations that still guide and constrain our thinking today. One indication of this is the fact that when the brain-state theory collapsed philosophers didn't lapse back into Cartesianism or other serious forms of dualism. Almost all the participants in the debate stayed within the physicalist framework, and even those who had a major hand in the demise of the Smart–Feigl materialism continued their allegiance to a physicalist worldview. And this fact has played a central role in defining our *Problematik*: through the seventies and eighties and down to the present, the mind–body problem – our mind–body problem – has been that of finding a place for the mind in a world that is fundamentally and essentially physical. If C. D. Broad were writing his 1925 book today, he might well have given it the title *The Mind and its Place in the Physical World*.

What made the demise of the brain-state theory so quick and seemingly painless, causing few regrets among philosophers, was the fact that the principal objection that spelled its doom, the so-called multiple (or 'variable', as they say in Britain) realization argument, first advanced by Hilary Putnam,[3] contained within it seeds for an attractive alternative approach, namely functionalism. The core thesis of functionalism, that mental kinds are 'functional kinds', not physical or biological kinds, was an appealing and eye-opening idea that seemed to help us make sense of 'cognitive science', which was being launched around then. The functionalist conception of the mind seemed tailor-made for the new science of mentality and cognition, for it appeared to posit a distinctive and autonomous domain of mental/cognitive properties that could be scientifically

---

[3] In 'Psychological Predicates' first published in 1968 and later reprinted with a new title, 'The Nature of Mental States', in Hilary Putnam, *Collected Papers* II (Cambridge: Cambridge University Press, 1975).

investigated independently of their physical/biological embodiments – an idea that promised both legitimacy and autonomy for psychology as a science. Functionalism made it possible for us to shed the restrictive constraints of physicalist reductionism without returning to the discredited dualisms of Descartes and others. Or so it seemed at the time. The functionalist conception of mentality still is 'the official story' about the nature and foundation of cognitive science.[4]

But functionalists, by and large, were not metaphysicians, and few of them were self-consciously concerned about just where functionism stood in regard to the mind–body problem. Some functionalists, like David Armstrong and David Lewis, thought that they were defending physicalism, whereas others, like Hilary Putnam and Jerry Fodor, claimed that functionalism delivered a decisive refutation of physicalism. The key term they used to describe the relation between mental properties (kinds, states, etc.) and physical properties was 'realization' (or sometimes 'implementation', 'execution', etc.): mental properties are 'realized' or 'implemented' by (or in) physical properties, though not identical with them or reducible to them. But the term 'realization' was introduced[5] and quickly gained currency, chiefly on the basis of computational analogies (in particular,

---

[4] See, e.g., Zenon Pylyshyn, *Computation and Cognition* (Cambridge, MA: MIT Press, 1985).

[5] The first philosophical use of this term, roughly in its current sense, that I know of occurs in Hilary Putnam's 'Minds and Machines', in *Dimensions of Mind,* ed. Sydney Hook (New York: New York University Press, 1960).

mathematically characterized computing machines being realized in physical computers), and few functionalists, especially in the early days, made an effort to explain what the realization relation consisted in – what this relation implied in terms of the traditional options on the mind–body problem.

I believe that the idea of 'supervenience' came to the fore in the seventies and eighties in part to fill this void. The doctrine that mental properties are supervenient on physical properties seemed nicely to meet the needs of the post-reductionist physicalist in search of a metaphysics of mind; for it promised to give a clear and sturdy sense to the primacy of the physical domain and its laws, thereby vindicating the physicalist commitments of most functionalists, while freeing them from the burdens of physical reductionism, thereby protecting the mental as an autonomous domain. Further, by allowing multiple physical bases for supervenient mental properties, it was able to accommodate the multiple realizability of mental properties as well. Many philosophers, especially those who for one reason or another had abandoned hopes for a physicalistic reduction of the mental, sought in mind–body supervenience a satisfying metaphysical statement of physicalism without reductionism. By the late seventies, what Ned Block has aptly called 'the antireductionist consensus',[6] was firmly in place. This has helped to enthrone 'nonreductive physicalism' as the new orthodoxy not only on the mind–body relation but,

---

[6] In his 'Antireductionism Slaps Back', forthcoming in *Philosophical Perspectives*, 1997.

more generally, on the relationship between 'higher-level' properties and underlying 'lower-level' properties in all other domains as well. Thus, the approach yielded as a bonus a principled general view about the relationship between the special sciences and basic physics.

One side effect of the entrenchment of the antireductionist consensus has been the return of emergentism – if not the full-fledged doctrine of classic emergentism of the 1920s and 30s, at least its characteristic vocabulary and slogans. When positivism and the idea of 'unity of science' ruled, emergentism was often regarded with undisguised suspicion, as a mysterious and possibly incoherent metaphysical doctrine. With reductionist physicalism out of favour, emergentism appears to be making a strong comeback,[7] and we now see an increasing and unapologetic use of terms like 'emergence', 'emergent characteristic', 'emergent phenomenon', 'emergent cause' and the like, roughly in the sense intended by the classic emergentists, not only in serious philosophical writings[8] but in primary scientific literature in many fields.[9]

---

[7] In addition to a number of recent journal titles, the signs of the return of emergentism include a recent collection of new essays on emergence, *Emergence or Reduction?* ed. A. Beckermann, H. Flohr and J. Kim (Berlin: de Gruyter, 1992), two volumes of essays on emergence being prepared in Europe as of this writing, and the 1997 Oberlin Philosophy Colloquium on the topic 'Reductionism and Emergence'.

[8] See e.g., John R. Searle, *The Rediscovery of the Mind* (Cambridge, MA: MIT Press, 1992).

[9] E.g., Francisco Varela, Evan Thompson and Eleanor Rosch, *The Embodied Mind* (Cambridge, MA: MIT Press, 1993). See especially Part IV entitled 'Varieties of Emergence'.

To sum up, then, three ideas have been prominently on the scene in recent discussions of the mind–body relation: the idea that the mental is 'realized' by the physical, the idea that the mental 'supervenes' on the physical, and the idea that the mental is 'emergent' from the physical. In this paper I want to explore the interplay of these three ideas, and the roles they play, in current debates over the mind–body problem, and, in the process, to indicate where I think we now stand with this problem.

II

Let us begin with supervenience. It is convenient to construe supervenience as a relation between two sets of properties, the supervenient properties and their 'base' properties. As is well known, a variety of supervenience relations is available, but for our present purposes fine-grained distinctions won't matter. The core idea of mind–body supervenience is that the mental properties or states of something are dependent on its physical, or bodily, properties, in the sense that once its physical properties are fixed, its mental properties are thereby fixed. This implies that if two things – organisms, persons or electromechanical systems – have identical physical properties, they must have identical mental natures as well; that is to say, exact physical twins are ipso facto exact mental twins. Mind–body supervenience can be equivalently formulated in the following useful way: if an organism instantiates a psychological property M (say, pain) at a time, it has at that time some physical property P on which M supervenes, in the sense that necessarily if anything has P, it has M. Thus, if you experience pain at a time, you must instantiate a certain physical property at the time (presumably, some neural property) on which pain supervenes. No mental property can be instantiated in an organism unless that organism instantiates some suitable physical property that serves as its physical base.

In this way, mind–body supervenience promised to give sense to the physicalist idea that the physical enjoys ontological primacy over the mental, and the idea that physics is the most basic, and most comprehensive, of our sciences, all other sciences being 'special sciences' over restricted domains. Moreover, and this was of crucial importance to the nonreductive physicalist, supervenience prima facie did not seem to commit us to reductionism: after all, many moral theorists, like G. E. Moore and R. M. Hare, believed in the supervenience of the moral on the nonmoral, but rejected the reducibility of the former to the latter. And accepting the idea that aesthetic properties of works of art are supervenient on their physical characters doesn't seem to lead to the position that aesthetic properties are reducible to physical properties. In mind–body supervenience, then, we seemed finally to have found a metaphysical basis for non-reductive physicalism; supervenience seemed to be just the metaphysical relation of dependence that would enable us to understand how the mental, in spite of its dependence on the physical, could still remain irreducible to it, forming its own autonomous domain.

Much of the discussion that followed the introduction of the supervenience idea into the mind–body debate was over the question whether supervenience was indeed free of reductionist implications. The question is still unsettled, but it has become clear that this was really a non-issue. The real issue, I believe, is whether or not the doctrine of mind–body supervenience itself can claim to be a distinctive position on the mind–body problem. The question, then, is this: do we have in mind–body supervenience an account of how our mentality is related to the physical nature of our being? That is, can we use supervenience itself to state a philosophical theory of the way minds are related to bodies?

Brief reflection shows that the answer is no, that mind–body supervenience by itself cannot constitute a theory of the mind–body relation. There are two related reasons for this. First, mind–body supervenience is consistent with a host of classic positions on the mind–body problem; it is in fact a shared commitment of many mutually exclusionary mind–body theories. Take emergentism, for example: emergentism is a dualistic theory that stresses the irreducibility of the emergents, including mental properties, to more basic physicochemical conditions, and yet it respects supervenience. On emergentism, the emergents necessarily emerge when, and only when, appropriate 'basal conditions' are present; when identical basal conditions are present, identical emergents must emerge. The functionalist view that the mental, when it is realized, must be physically realized, too, entails mind body supervenience: the same physical conditions, the same functional properties. What is more obvious, mind–body supervenience is a trivial consequence of type physicalism (for example, the brain-state theory), which reductively identifies mental properties with physical properties. Even epiphenomenalism is committed to supervenience; if two things differ in some mental respect, that must be because they differ in some physical respect – it must be because the physical cause of the mental respect involved is present in one and absent from the other. If mind–body supervenience is a commitment of each of these conflicting approaches to the mind–body problem, it cannot itself be a position on this issue alongside these classic alternatives.[10]

What this shows is that the mere fact (assuming it is a fact) of mind–body supervenience leaves open the question of what *grounds* or *accounts* for it – that is, why the supervenience relation obtains between the mental and the physical.[11] To see the general issue involved here, consider normative supervenience, the widely accepted doctrine that normative or evaluative properties supervene on nonnormative, nonevaluative properties. Various metaethical positions are committed to normative supervenience but offer differing accounts of its source. According to ethical naturalism, the supervenience holds because normative properties are definable in terms of nonnormative, naturalistic properties; that is, normative properties turn out to be naturalistic

---

[10] Mind–body supervenience is not excluded even by Cartesian substance dualism. See my 'Supervenience for Multiple Domains', reprinted in *Supervenience and Mind* (Cambridge: Cambridge University Press, 1993).

[11] On the need for explaining supervenience relations see Terence Horgan, 'Supervenience and Cosmic Hermeneutics', *Southern Journal of Philosophy* 22 (1984), Supplement, 19–38, and Terence Horgan and Mark Timmons, 'Troubles on Moral Twin Earth: Moral Queerness Revisited', *Synthese* 92 (1992), 221–60.

properties. Ethical intuitionists, like G. E. Moore, would see normative supervenience as a primitive synthetic *a priori* fact not susceptible to further explanation; it is something we directly apprehend through our moral sense. R. M. Hare, a noncognitivist, would attempt to explain it as a form of a consistency condition essential to the regulative character of the language of commending and prescribing. Still others may try to explain it as arising from the very idea of normative evaluation, maintaining that evaluative or normative properties must have descriptive criteria. It is clear, then, that the thesis of normative supervenience by itself does not serve to characterize a distinctive position in metaethics.

Similarly, it is useful to think of the diverse mind–body theories as offering competing explanations of mind–body supervenience: the explanation offered by type physicalism is parallel to the naturalistic explanation of normative supervenience: mind–body supervenience holds because mentality is physically reducible and mental properties turn out in the end to be physical properties. Emergentism, like ethical intuitionism, takes mind–body supervenience as a brute fact not amenable to explanation, something that should be accepted, as Samuel Alexander urged, with 'natural piety'. In contrast, epiphenomenalism invokes the causal relation (the 'same cause, same effect' principle) to explain supervenience, and on functionalism, as we will see, mind–body supervenience is a consequence of the view that mental properties are functional properties with physical properties as their realizers.

We must conclude, then, that mind–body supervenience itself is not an *explanatory theory;* it merely states a pattern of property covariation between the mental and the physical, and points to the existence of a dependency relation between the two. Yet it is wholly silent on the nature of the dependence relation that might explain why the mental supervenes on the physical. Supervenience is not a metaphysically deep, explanatory relation; it is merely a phenomenological relation about patterns of property covariation. Mind–body supervenience, therefore, *states* the mind–body problem – it is not a solution to it.

III

Cartesian substance dualism pictures the world as consisting of two independent spheres, the mental and the material, each with its own distinctive defining properties. There are causal interactions across the domains, but entities in each domain, being 'substances', are ontologically independent of those of the other, and it is metaphysically possible for one domain to exist in the total absence of the other. What has replaced this picture of a dichotomized world is the familiar multi-layered model that views the world as stratified into different 'levels', 'orders' or 'tiers', organized in a hierarchical structure. The bottom level is usually thought to consist of elementary particles, or whatever our best physics is going to tell us are the basic bits of matter out of which all material things are composed.[12] Higher up on the ladder, we find

---

[12] The layered model as such of course does not need to posit a bottom level; it is consistent with an infinitely descending series of levels.

atoms, molecules, cells, larger organisms and so on. The ordering relation that generates the hierarchical structure is the mereological relation: entities belonging to a given level, except those at the very bottom, have an exhaustive decomposition, without remainder, into entities belonging to the lower levels. Entities at the bottom level have no physically significant proper parts.

What then of *the properties* of these entities? It is part of this layered conception that at each level there are thought to be properties, activities and functions that make their first appearance at that level (we may call them the 'characteristic properties' of that level). Thus, among the characteristic properties of the molecular level are electrical conductivity, inflammability, density, viscosity and the like; activities and functions like metabolism and reproduction are among the characteristic properties of the cellular and higher biological levels; consciousness and other mental properties make their appearance at the level of higher organisms. For much of this century, a layered picture of the world like this has formed an omnipresent, if only implicit, background for debate over the mind–body problem, emergence, reductionism, the status of the special sciences and related issues, and has exerted a pervasive influence on the way we formulate philosophical problems and debate their solutions. Sometimes, the layered model is couched in terms of concepts and languages instead of entities in the world and their properties. Talk of levels of *descriptions,* levels of *analyses,* levels of *concepts,* levels of *explanations* and the like is rampant everywhere – it has thoroughly pervaded primary scientific literature as well as philosophical writings about science.[13]

Now we come to a critical question: how are the characteristic properties of a given level related to the properties at the adjacent levels – in particular, to those at the lower levels? How are biological ('vital') properties related to physicochemical properties? How are consciousness and intentionality related to biological/physical properties? How are social phenomena, phenomena characteristic of social groups, related to phenomena involving individual members? As you will agree, these are some of the central questions in philosophy of science, metaphysics and philosophy of mind. Possible answers to these questions define the classic philosophical options on the issues involved. Some of the well-known major alternatives include reductionism, antireductionism, methodological individualism, functionalism, emergentism, neo-vitalism and the like. You may attempt to give a single uniform answer applicable to all pairs of adjacent levels, or you may take different positions regarding different levels. For example, you might argue that

---

[13] In his work on vision David Marr famously distinguishes three levels of analysis: the computational, the algorithmic and the implementational. See his *Vision* (New York: Freeman Press, 1982). The emergentists, early in this century, appear to have been first to give an explicit formulation of the layered model; see, e.g., C. Lloyd Morgan, *Emergent Evolution* (London: Williams and Norgate, 1923). For a particularly clear and useful statement of the model, see Paul Oppenheim and Hilary Putnam, 'Unity of Science as a Working Hypothesis', *Minnesota Studies in the Philosophy of Science,* vol. II, ed. Feigl, Maxwell and Scriven.

properties at every level (higher than the bottom level) are reducible, in some clear and substantial sense, to lower-level properties, or you might restrict the reductionist claim to certain selected levels (say, biological properties in relation to physicochemical properties) and defend an antireductionist stance concerning properties at other levels (say, mental properties). Moreover, it isn't necessary to give a uniform answer in regard to all characteristic properties at a given level; concerning mental properties, for example, it is possible to hold – and some have done just that – that phenomenal or sensory properties, or qualia, are irreducible, while holding that intentional properties, including propositional attitudes, are reducible (say, functionally or biologically).

Let us now turn to the reductionist approach to the question of interlevel property relationships. As I said, reductionism, in particular mind–body reductionism, suffered massive defections during the 1970s and 1980s, with the result that there are hardly any reductionists left anywhere in sight in philosophy of mind.[14] This, I think, is generally true in all areas of philosophy; there may still be

---

[14] Andrew Melnyk writes: 'Indeed, it seems to be a little-known law governing the behavior of contemporary philosophers that whenever they profess faith in any form of materialism or physicalism they must make it absolutely clear that they are, of course, in no way endorsing anything as unsophisticated, reactionary, and generally intolerable as reductionism', in 'Two Cheers for Reductionism: Or, the Dim Prospects for Non-Reductive Materialism', *Philosophy of Science* 62 (1995), 370–88. According to Melnyk there are only two reductionists left on the scene; he says, 'The law holds *ceteris paribus;* for example, it does not apply if your name is Jaegwon Kim or Patricia Churchland.'

reductionisms or reductionist programmes (and I believe there are), but I don't know anyone who advertises him/ herself as a reductionist about anything. But what is reduction, to begin with? And what has made the reductionist a persona non grata in philosophy of mind?

The concept of reduction that has served as a shared background in the discussion of physical reductionism was derived from a model of reduction elaborated by Ernest Nagel in the 1950s.[15] Nagel was mainly interested in inter-theoretic reduction, as a relation between two scientific theories, and his principal focus was on the logical relationship between the theory to be reduced and the theory serving as the reduction base. According to Nagel, reduction is fundamentally a proof procedure, consisting in the logical/ mathematical derivation of the laws of the reduced theory from those of the base theory, taken in conjunction with 'bridge laws' connecting the predicates of the two theories. Nagel thought that these intertheoretic linkages were necessary to secure logical/derivational connections between the two theories, since the theories may be couched in entirely distinct descriptive vocabularies. Standardly, these bridge laws are taken to be biconditionals in form ('if and only if' statements), providing each property in the domain of the theory to be reduced with a nomologically coextensive property in the reduction base. For mind–body reduction, then,

[15] See *The Structure of Science* (New York: Harcourt, Brace & World, 1961), chapter 11. The model had been developed in Nagel's earlier papers published during the 1950s.

the Nagel model requires that each mental property be provided with a nomologically coextensive physical property; that is, a law of the following form must hold for every mental property M:

(BL) $M \leftrightarrow P$

where P is some physical property.

This bridge-law requirement made mind–body reductionism – in fact, all reductionisms – an easy target. As noted earlier, the most influential antireductionist argument, one that had a decisive role in establishing the antireductionist consensus, was the multiple realization argument based on the observation that, on account of their multiple realizability, mental properties fail to have coextensions in the physical domain, and that this makes mind–body bridge laws unavailable for Nagelian reduction. This argument was then extended in defence of a general antireductionist position in regard to all special sciences.[16] This has made bridge laws the focal point of debates on reduction and reductionism: for three decades the battles over reductionism have been fought on the question whether biconditional bridge laws are available to connect the mental with the physical domain.

But this is the wrong battlefield on which to contest the issue of reduction. The Nagel model is the wrong model of reduction for discussions of mind–body reduction, and bridge laws are linkages of the wrong kind to induce

[16] See J. A. Fodor, 'Special Sciences (or The Disunity of Science as a Working Hypothesis)', *Synthese* 28 (1974), 97–115.

reduction. My view is that *bridge laws are neither necessary nor sufficient for reduction.* I think it is easy to see that derivation via bridge laws is not sufficient for reduction. There are two reasons for this. The first has to do with the explanatory import of a reduction: a reduction must explain how, and why, the reduced phenomena ('higher-level' phenomena) arise from the processes at the level of the reduction base ('lower-level' phenomena), and this explanatory demand is not met when, as in Nagel reduction, the bridge laws are assumed as unexplained primitives of reductive derivations. A bridge law of the form (BL) only tells us that mental property M (say, pain) co-occurs, as a matter of nomic necessity, with a physical property P (say, C-fibre activation), and Nagel reduction simply does not address the question why this is so. Why is it that you experience a pain, rather than an itch or tickle, whenever your C-fibres are activated? Why don't you experience pain when your A-delta fibres are firing? Why does any conscious experience arise when these neural fibres are firing?

When the emergentists claimed that the properties of consciousness are irreducible emergent properties, it was because they despaired of ever answering these explanatory questions. They accepted both a fundamental physicalist ontology and the supervenience of higher-level properties on the lower-level ones; and they were not concerned about the multiple realizability of the former in relation to the latter. The *availability* of biconditional correlation laws was the least of their concerns. The *intelligibility* of these laws was what agitated the emergentists. It is the phenomena of emergence, codified in our bridge laws, that they advised us to accept as brute facts – 'with natural piety'. As far as the emergentists were concerned, we were welcome to help ourselves to as much Nagel reduction of the mental as we pleased, but this would only be so much logical exercise – it would not advance by an inch our understanding of why, and how, mentality makes its appearance when certain propitious configurations of biological conditions occur. Attaining such an understanding is exactly the same task as explaining the likes of (BL), that is, mind–body bridge laws.

A second reason that Nagelian derivation via bridge laws does not suffice for reduction is ontological: we expect our reductions to simplify – simplify our scheme of concepts or scheme of entities. But bridge laws are standardly taken as contingent and empirical, not analytic or *a priori,* and this means that the concepts M and P in (BL) remain distinct. Hence, Nagel derivation does nothing for conceptual simplification. Moreover, a bridge law expresses only nomic coextensivity of properties, not their identity, which means that M and P remain distinct properties. Hence, Nagel derivation via bridge laws doesn't do anything for ontological simplification either. It does give us some simplification of laws – the laws of the reduced theory have been absorbed into the reducer – but this, too, may be largely illusory, since we are forced to inflate our base theory by adding the bridge laws as new primitive laws. Introduction of these new laws can represent a significant expansion of both the ideology and the ontology of the base theory, since these laws bring with them concepts and properties alien to the original base theory.

At this point, the standard move we see in the philosophical discussion of theory reduction is to consider how, and under what conditions, correlations of the form (BL) can be enhanced into identities of the form:

(I) $M = P$

This strategy is proper as long as we work within the Nagelian paradigm. I believe, however, that the Nagelian conception of reduction should be jettisoned, and that our thinking about reduction needs to be reoriented if reduction is to remain a philosophically significant factor in our reflections on the mind–body problem and related issues concerning interlevel relationships of properties. For the philosophical poverty of Nagel reduction is easy to see. As I have already pointed out, there is nothing in emergentism that rules out a Nagel reduction of psychology to physical theory. Not even substance dualism needs to preclude Nagelian mind–body reduction. Furthermore, some forms of dualism *actually entail* the Nagel reducibility of psychology to physical theory: for example, the double-aspect theory and the doctrine of pre-established harmony each would provide us with mind–body bridge laws in abundant numbers to enable a Nagelian mind–body reduction (and reductions in the opposite direction as well!). It is clear, then, that any doctrine of mind–body reductionism couched in the Nagelian conception of reduction cannot be a significant claim about the status of the mind. If so, the refutation of mind–body reductionism in that sense of reduction cannot be regarded as a significant philosophical accomplishment either.

IV

I will now sketch a model of reduction that I believe is more appropriate for both science and philosophy. If M and P in bridge law (BL) are both intrinsic properties, the correlation between M and P must be taken as a brute fact about the two distinct intrinsic properties, and no amount of philosophical legerdemain can turn it into an identity. The only way we can go beyond such brute correlations is to interpret, or reinterpret, the reduction target, M, as an extrinsic/relational property. Let us look at some examples. Consider temperature: to reduce temperature, we first must think of it relationally and characterize it in terms of its relation to other properties. Temperature is that property of an object, or system, which is such that its magnitude increases when the object is in contact with another with a higher magnitude of it; when it is sufficiently high, it can cause wood and coal to burn; when it is extremely high, it can cause iron to turn into a molten state; when it is sufficiently low, it causes water to freeze – well, you get the idea. What is being done is to understand temperature as a property characterized in terms of its causal/nomological relations to other properties; that is, it is given an extrinsic characterization as a 'causal role'. Consider another example: the reduction of the gene. To get started we must construe the concept of a gene in terms of its causal function: the gene is that mechanism in an organism that is causally responsible for the transmission of heritable characteristics. Reduction of temperature is achieved when we can identify the property that fills the causal specification: for gases the property turns out to be the mean kinetic energy of the molecules; for solids and plasmas, and in vacuums, it turns out to be different properties. The reduction of the gene is accomplished when we identify the mechanism that fills the causal role specified: it turns out to be the DNA molecule – at least, for earthly organisms.

On this view of reduction,[17] then, the reduction of a property M consists in two steps: (i) the conceptual step of construing M in terms of its causal/nomological relations to other properties; and (ii) the empirical-theoretical step of identifying M's 'realizers' – that is, properties, or mechanisms, in the reduction base domain that have the specified causal/nomological characteristics. We can expect the second step to involve a theory that explains just how these realizers get to have these causal/nomological properties (such a theory will almost certainly be involved in the process of identifying the realizers of targeted functional properties). Step (i) is in effect the process of 'functionalizing' the target property, that is, defining it as a causal role.

---

[17] The ideas involved here go back to David Lewis, 'An Argument for the Identity Theory', *Journal of Philosophy* 63 (1966), 17–25 and David Armstrong's argument for central-state materialism in his *A Materialist Theory of Mind* (New York: Humanities Press, 1968). See also Robert Van Gulick, 'Nonreductive Materialism and the Nature of Intertheoretical Constraint', in *Emergence or Reduction?* ed. Beckermann, Flohr and Kim, and Joseph Levine, 'On Leaving What It Is Like', in *Consciousness*, ed. Glyn W. Humphreys and Martin Davies (Oxford: Blackwell, 1993). Relevant also are David Chalmers' discussion of 'reductive explanation' in *The Conscious Mind* (New York: Oxford University Press, 1996), and Frank Jackson's views on the role of conceptual analysis in metaphysics, in, e.g., 'Armchair Metaphysics', in *Philosophy in Mind,* ed. J. O'Leary Hawthorne and M. Michael (Dordrecht: Kluwer, 1993).

More specifically, it is useful to think of functionalization in terms of second-order properties: to have M is to have the second-order property of having some property, Q, meeting specification C. This is second-order in the sense that it involves quantification over first-order properties (that is, the properties already given). When the specification C involves causal/nomic relations, we can call the second-order property a 'functional' property.[18]

At step (ii), multiple realizers have to be expected as a rule. We now must face the following question: does the phenomenon of multiple realizability of the target property present difficulties to this account of reduction as well? Answering this question is a somewhat complicated affair that to some extent depends on a decision as to what we want to call 'reduction'. However, a persuasive case can be made for a negative answer: there is no need to fear multiple realization. Suppose that M has two realizers, Q_1 and Q_2. For something, x, to have M is for x to have Q_1 or Q_2. (Notice that this does not introduce a disjunctive property, having Q_1 or Q_2; the 'or' here is a sentence disjunction, not a predicate disjunction with disjunctive properties as semantic values.) That is to say, each

---

[18] The notion of a second-order property in the present sense is due to Hilary Putnam, 'On Properties', in *Essays in Honor of Carl G. Hempel*, ed. N. Rescher *et al.* (Dordrecht: Reidel, 1969). It's interesting to note that although the inventor of functionalism also introduced the concept of a second-order property, which is tailor-made for a perspicuous explanation of 'realization', no functionalist, to my knowledge, took advantage of it until Ned Block did so in his 'Can the Mind Change the World?', in *Meaning and Method*, ed. George Boolos (Cambridge: Cambridge University Press, 1990).

M-instance is either a Q_1-instance or Q_2-instance, and there are no M-instances over and above these Q-instances. Suppose M is instantiated on a given occasion in virtue of its realizer Q_1 being instantiated on that occasion. This M-instance, then, is identical with this Q_1 instance, and they have exactly identical causal powers: no new causal powers can magically accrue to the M-instance that are not had by the Q_1-instance. The realizers of M do all the work that M does, and M does not represent a net addition to the ontology or causal structure of the world.

But some might object: 'But what about M *itself*? M is identical with neither Q_1 nor Q_2, and therefore must be counted as a property distinct from each and every property in the reduction domain.' This is the same ontological challenge we posed for Nagel reduction: where is the ontological payoff as far as M is concerned? So does M still need to hang around in our ontology? I think we can handle M in one of two ways. One simple way is to identify M as the disjunctive property, $Q_1 \lor Q_2$. If the Qs are diverse realizers of M, their diversity must mean something, and the only thing it could mean is causal/nomological diversity. If they are causally and nomologically identical or quite similar, there would be no reason for counting them as distinct realizers. It is generally accepted that kinds in science are primarily individuated on the basis of causal powers. So M as a disjunction of causally diverse properties, will be a causally heterogeneous kind, and it will have only limited usefulness as a scientific kind.[19]

---

[19] I argue that such properties are not inductively projectible in 'Multiple Realization and the Metaphysics of Reduction', in *Supervenience and Mind* (Cambridge: Cambridge University Press, 1993).

The second way of handling M to view it only as a *concept,* not a property. By forming a second-order expression of the form 'having some property or other, Q such that $C(Q)$', we cannot literally bring a new entity into our ontology. All we are doing is to introduce a way of picking out certain first-order properties by specifying a condition they need to meet; we might say that a second-order expression of this form refers indifferently to members of a class of first-order properties, namely those that satisfy the specified condition. By mere linguistic operations like quantification we can neither expand nor contract our ontology; what we expand is our linguistic repertoire.

This, I believe, is a sufficient answer to the ontological question. It shows how a functional reduction gives us a simplified ontology. But how does the functional model of reduction meet the explanatory demands on reduction? In what way is a functional reduction an explanatory reduction? I believe that this question has a satisfying answer. Why is M instantiated in systems of kind S whenever Q_i is instantiated by these systems? Because having M just is having some property meeting causal specification C, and Q_i is a property that realizes M – that is, meets the specification C – in systems of kind S. Why does this particular system instantiate M on this occasion? Because it is instantiating Q_i, one of M's realizers. Why does this M-instance cause an effect of kind E? Because it is in fact a Q_i-instance. where Q_i is a realizer of M, and Q_i-instances have effects of kind E. Since the causal powers of M-instances are identified with those of their realizers, all questions about the causal relations involving M-instances are answerable at the level of

M's realizers. What more can we ask from an explanatory reduction of *M*?

When functionalism was introduced as an alternative to classic type physicalism, that is, the brain-state theory, it was thought, and is still widely thought, that it was a form of antireductionism – in fact, the principal version of antireductionism about the mental. What I am advocating is the exact opposite: *the functionalizability of mental properties is necessary and sufficient for reduction* (*sufficient pending successful scientific discovery of their realizers for domains of interest to us*). This is not merely a redefinition of the term 'reduction'; I hope I have persuaded you that the functional model points us toward the right way to think about reduction. On this model of reduction, then, emergent properties are easily characterized: a property *M* is emergent relative to a given domain *D* of properties just in case *M* is not functionalizable in terms of properties in *D*.

V

In assessing where we now are with the mind–body problem, therefore, we must know where we stand with the functionalist approach to the mental. It has been customary to distinguish between two broad categories of mental phenomena, the intentional and the phenomenal, without excluding those that have aspects of both (for example, emotions). Intentionality is particularly evident in propositional attitudes, like belief, desire and intention. There has been much scepticism about the viability of a functionalist account of intentionality; in particular, Hilary Putnam, the father of functionalism, has recently mounted sustained attacks on the causal/functionalist accounts of content and reference, and John Searle has also vigorously resisted the functionalization of intentionality.[20] However, I remain unconvinced by these arguments; I don't see unsurmountable obstacles to a causal/functional account of intentionality. Let me just say here that it seems to me inconceivable that a possible world exists that is an exact physical duplicate of this world but lacking wholly in intentionality.[21] Such a world must be identical with ours in all intentional-psychological aspects.[22]

The trouble comes from qualia. For, by contrast with the case of intentional phenomena, we seem able to conceive a physical duplicate of this world in which qualia are distributed differently or entirely absent (a 'zombie world' as some call it). To get to the point without fuss, it seems to me that the felt, phenomenal qualities of experiences, or qualia, are intrinsic properties if anything is. To be sure, we commonly refer to them using extrinsic/causal descriptions; e.g., 'the colour of jade', 'the smell of ammonia', 'the taste of avocado', and so on. However, this is entirely consistent with the claim that what these descriptions pick out are intrinsic qualities, not something extrinsic

---

[20] See Hilary Putnam, *Representation and Reality* (Cambridge, MA: MIT Press, 1988); Searle, *The Rediscovery of the Mind*.

[21] I believe others (perhaps Shoemaker and Block) have made a similar observation.

[22] A position like this is explicitly defended by David Chalmers in *The Conscious Mind*.

or relational. (Arguably it is because they are intrinsic and subjective that we need to resort to relational descriptions for intersubjective reference.) Compare our practice of ascribing intrinsic physical properties to material objects by the use of relational descriptions; e.g., 'two kilograms', '32 degrees Fahrenheit', etc. To say that an object has a mass of 2 kilograms is to say that it will balance, on an equal arm balance, two objects each of which would balance the Prototype Kilogram (an object stored somewhere in France). That is the linguistic meaning, the 'concept' if you prefer, of '2 kilograms'; however, the property it designates, having a mass of two kilograms, is an intrinsic property of material bodies.

If the qualitative properties of consciousness are intrinsic, they will resist functionalization and hence reduction. My doubts about the functionalist accounts of qualia are by and large based on the well-known, and not uncontested, arguments from qualia inversions and the familiar epistemic considerations. In any case, it seems to me that if emergentism is correct about anything, it is more likely to be correct about qualia than about anything else.[23]

This is what makes the stance you take on the problem of qualia a decisive choice point with respect to the mind–body problem. Let me close by noting how the question of reducibility relates to another central problem in the metaphysics of mind, namely the problem of mental

---

[23] This position on qualia and reductionism bears close similarity to the positions defended by a number of philosophers – in particular, Joseph Levine, Frank Jackson, David Chalmers and perhaps Ned Block.

causation. If mental property M is functionally reducible in our sense, there is an easy answer to the question how M can have causal powers in the physical domain. As we noted, the causal powers of any given M-instance are identical with the causal powers of the particular physical realizer of M on that occasion, there being no net addition of causal powers beyond those of physical properties. But if M is not functionally reducible it is difficult, in fact not possible, to see how M, or M-instances, can exercise causal powers in the physical domain if we assume, as I believe we should, that the physical domain is causally closed. Thus, the price we may have to pay – I believe it *is* the price we must pay – for the irreducibility of qualia is their causal powers: if they are irreducible, they are threatened with causal impotence – at least, in the physical domain.[24]

In this way, the two central problems in the philosophy of mind, the problem of consciousness and the problem of mental causation, come together in the same arena. The only visible way of explaining consciousness physically – that is, finding a place for it in the physical world – is to functionalize it in the physical domain. If that could be done, we could also solve the problem of its causal powers. If, as seems likely, it cannot be done, consciousness is threatened with epiphenomenalism. It seems, then, that we can preserve consciousness, or any other aspect of our mentality, as something distinctive and autonomous only if

[24] I believe the irreducibility leads to causal impotence *tout court*, but a detailed argument must await another occasion.

we are willing to accept their causal impotence. In short, the two problems make each other insoluble.[25]

Fifty years of debate have shown, I believe, that the central core of the mind–body problem is constituted by two great and deep puzzles, consciousness and mental causation. And these two puzzles turn out to be intimately intertwined – the key to both is the question whether phenomenal properties of consciousness can be functionalized. I believe that is where we now stand with the mind–body problem, half a century after its reintroduction into philosophy by Ryle, Smart, Feigl and others.

[25] This way of putting it was suggested by David Chalmers in conversation.

How to Find the Neural Correlate of Consciousness[*]

NED BLOCK

There are two concepts of consciousness that are easy to confuse with one another, access-consciousness and phenomenal consciousness. However, just as the concepts of water and H_2O are different concepts of the same thing, so the two concepts of consciousness may come to the same thing in the brain. The focus of this paper is on the problems that arise when these two concepts of consciousness are conflated. I will argue that John Searle's reasoning about the function of consciousness goes wrong because he conflates the two senses. And Francis Crick and Christof Koch fall afoul of the ambiguity in arguing that visual area V1 is not part of the neural correlate of consciousness. Crick and Koch's work raises issues that suggest that these two

[*] This is a substantially revised version of a paper in *Trends in Neuroscience* 19/2 (1996). I am grateful to audiences at the 1996 consciousness conference in Tucson, at the 1996 cognitive science conference at the University of Sienna, at the University of Oxford, Department of Experimental Psychology, at Union College Department of Philosophy and the Royal Institute of Philosophy. I am grateful to Susan Carey, Francis Crick, Martin Davies, Christof Koch, David Milner and to the editor of *Trends in Neuroscience* for comments on a previous draft.

concepts of consciousness may have different (though over-lapping) neural correlates – despite Crick and Koch's impli-cit rejection of this idea.

I will start with two quotations from Searle. You will see what appears to be a contradiction, and I will later claim that the appearance of contradiction can be explained if one realizes that he is using two different concepts of consciousness. I'm not going to explain yet what the two concepts of con-sciousness are. That will come later, after I've presented Searle's contradiction and Crick and Koch's surprising argument.

Searle's Contradiction

Searle discusses my claim that there are two concepts of consciousness, arguing that I have confused modes of one kind with two kinds:

> There are lots of different degrees of consciousness, but
> door knobs, bits of chalk, and shingles are not conscious
> at all ... These points, it seems to me, are misunderstood
> by Block. He refers to what he calls an 'access sense of
> consciousness'. On my account there is no such sense.
> I believe that he ... [confuses] what I would call
> peripheral consciousness or inattentiveness with total
> unconsciousness. It is true, for example, that when I am
> driving my car 'on automatic pilot' I am not paying much
> attention to the details of the road and the traffic. *But it is
> simply not true that I am totally unconscious of these
> phenomena. If I were, there would be a car crash.* We
> need therefore to make a distinction between the center
> of my attention, the focus of my consciousness on the

one hand, and the periphery on the other... [Italics added].[1]

Note that Searle claims that if I became unconscious of the road while driving, the car would crash. Now compare the next argument.

> ...[T]he epileptic seizure rendered the patient totally unconscious, yet the patient continued to exhibit what would normally be called goal-directed behavior ... In all these cases, we have complex forms of apparently goal-directed behavior without any consciousness. Now why could all behavior not be like that? Notice that in the cases, the patients were performing types of actions that were habitual, routine and memorized ... normal, human, conscious behavior has a degree of flexibility and creativity that is absent from the Penfield cases of the unconscious driver and the unconscious pianist. Consciousness adds powers of discrimination and flexibility even to memorized routine activities ... one of the evolutionary advantages conferred on us by consciousness is the much greater flexibility, sensitivity, and creativity we derive from being conscious.[2]

Note that according to the first quotation, if I were to become unconscious (and therefore unconscious of the road and traffic), my car would crash. But in the second quotation, he accepts Penfield's description 'totally unconsciously'

[1] John Searle, 'Who is Computing with the Brain?' Behavioral and Brain Sciences 13/4 (1990), 632–4.

[2] John Searle, The Rediscovery of the Mind (Cambridge, MA; MIT Press, 1992).

as applying to the case of the petit mal patient who drives home while having a seizure. Thus we have what looks like a contradiction.

Crick and Koch's Peculiar Argument

I will now shift to Crick and Koch's recent article in *Nature*[3] arguing that V1, the first major way station in the brain for processing visual signals, is not part of the neural correlate of consciousness (what they call the NCC). Crick and Koch say that V1 is not part of the neural correlate of consciousness because V1 does not directly project to the frontal cortex. (They extrapolate (tentatively) from the fact that no direct connections are known in macaques to no connections in humans.) Their reasoning makes use of the premise that part of the function of visual consciousness is to harness visual information in the service of the *direct* control of reasoning and decision-making that controls behaviour. On the hypothesis that the frontal areas are involved in these mental functions, they argue that a necessary condition of inclusion in the NCC is direct projection to frontal areas. Though something seems right about their argument, it has nonetheless puzzled many readers. The puzzle is this: why couldn't there be conscious activity in V1 despite its lack of direct connection to frontal cortex? This is Pollen's[4]

---

[3] F. Crick and C. Koch, 'Are We Aware of Neural Activity in Primary Visual Cortex?' *Nature* 375 (11 May 1995), 121-3.

[4] D. Pollen 'Cortical Areas in Visual Awareness', *Nature* 377 (28 September 1995), 293-4.

worry: 'I see no *a priori* necessity for neurons in perceptual space to communicate directly with those in decision space.' The possibility of conscious activity in V1 is especially salient in the light of Crick and Koch's suggestion that visual consciousness is reverberatory activity in pyramidal cells of the lower layers of the visual cortex involving connections to the thalamus.[5] For one wonders how they have ruled out the possibility that such activity *exists* in V1 despite the lack of direct connection between V1 and frontal cortex. They do not address this possibility at all. The overall air of paradox is deepened by their claim that 'Our hypothesis is thus rather subtle; if it [no direct connection] turns out to be true it [V1 is not part of the neural correlate of consciousness] will eventually come to be regarded as completely obvious' (p. 123). But the reader wonders why this is true at all, much less obviously true. When such accomplished researchers say such puzzling things, one has to wonder if one is understanding them properly.

I will argue that once the two concepts of consciousness are separated out, the argument turns out to be trivial on one reading and not clearly compelling on the other reading. That's the critical part of my comment on Crick and Koch, but I have two positive points as well. I argue that nonetheless their conclusion about V1 should be accepted, but for a different reason, one that they implicitly suggest and that deserves to be opened up to public scrutiny. Further, I argue that the considerations that they raise

[5] F. Crick, *The Astonishing Hypothesis* (New York: Scribners, 1994).

suggest that the two concepts of consciousness correspond to different neural correlates despite Crick and Koch's implicit rejection of this idea.

The Two Concepts

The two concepts of consciousness are *phenomenal* consciousness and *access*-consciousness[6]. Phenomenal consciousness is just *experience*; access-consciousness is a kind of direct control. More exactly, a representation is access-conscious if it is poised for direct control of reasoning, reporting and action.

One way to see the distinction between the two concepts is to consider the possibility of one without the other. Here is an illustration of access without phenomenal consciousness. In Anton's Syndrome, blind patients do not realize that they are blind (though implicit knowledge of blindness can often be elicited). Hartmann et al.[7] report a case of 'Reverse Anton's Syndrome' in which the patient does not realize that he is *not* really blind. The patient regards himself as blind, and he is at chance at telling whether a room is illuminated or dark. But he has a small preserved island of V1 which allows him to read single words and recognize faces and facial expressions if they are presented to the upper right part of the visual field. When asked

[6] N. Block, 'On a Confusion about a Function of Consciousness', *Behavioral and Brain Sciences* 18/2 (1995), 227–47.

[7] J. A, Hartmann et al., 'Denial of Visual Perception', *Brain and Cognition* 16 (1991), 29–40.

how he knows the word or the face, he says 'it clicks' and denies that he sees the stimuli. There is no obvious factor in his social situation that would favour lying or self-deception. In addition to the damage in V1, he has bilateral parietal damage, including damage to the left inferior parietal lobe. Milner and Goodale[8] have proposed that phenomenal consciousness requires ventral stream activity plus attention, and that the requisite attention can be blocked by parietal lesions. So perhaps this is a case of visual access without visual phenomenal consciousness. (Note that Milner and Goodale's account is not in conflict with Crick and Koch's claim that V1 is not part of the NCC if activity in V1 is not the object of attentional processes.)

So we see that access-consciousness without phenomenal consciousness makes sense and may even exist in a limited form. What about the converse, phenomenal consciousness without access? For an illustration at the conceptual level, consider the familiar phenomenon in which one notices that the refrigerator has just gone off. Sometimes one has the feeling that one has been hearing the noise all along, but without noticing it until it went off. One of the many possible explanations of what happens in such a case illustrates phenomenal consciousness without access-consciousness: before the refrigerator went off, you had the experience (phenomenal consciousness) of the noise (let us suppose) but there was insufficient attention directed towards it to allow direct control of speech, reasoning or

[8] A. D. Milner and M. A. Goodale, *The Visual Brain in Action* (Oxford: Oxford University Press, 1995).

action. There might have been *indirect* control (the volume of your voice increased to compensate for the noise) but not direct control of the sort that happens when a representation is poised for free use as a premise in reasoning and can be freely reported. (It is this free use that characterizes access-consciousness.) On this hypothesis, there is a period in which one has phenomenal consciousness of the noise without access-consciousness of it. Of course, there are alternative hypotheses, including more subtle ones in which there are degrees of access and degrees of phenomenality. One might have a moderate degree of both phenomenal consciousness of and access to the noise at first, then filters might reset the threshold for access, putting the stimulus below the threshold for direct control, until the refrigerator goes off and one notices the change. The degree of phenomenal consciousness and access consciousness may always match. Although phenomenal consciousness and access-consciousness differ conceptually (as do the concepts of water and H_2O) we don't know yet whether or not they really come to the same thing in the brain.

Once one sees the distinction, one sees many pure uses of both concepts. For example, the Freudian unconscious is *access*-unconscious. A repressed memory of torture in a red room could in principle be a phenomenally vivid image; what makes it unconscious in the Freudian sense is that it comes out in dreams, slips, fleeing from red rooms and the like rather than directly controlling behaviour. Thus in principle an image can be unconscious in one sense (not poised for access), yet experienced and therefore conscious in another sense (phenomenally).

Searle's contradiction

Let's go back to Searle's contradiction. You will recall that he says that if he were to become unconscious of the details of the road and traffic, the car would crash. 'When I am driving my car "on automatic pilot" I am not paying much attention to the details of the road and the traffic. But it is simply not true that I am totally unconscious of these phenomena. If I were, there would be a car crash.' But he also says that Penfield's famous unconscious driver is 'totally unconscious', yet manages to drive home. Note that there is no room for resolving the contradiction via appeal to the difference between 'conscious' and 'conscious of'. If Penfield's driver is 'totally unconscious', then he is not conscious *of* anything. And thus we have a conflict with the idea that if one were to become unconscious of the road and traffic, the car would crash. Can we resolve the contradiction by supposing that what Searle thinks is that *normally* if one were to become unconscious of the road the car would crash, but the Penfield case is an abnormal exception? Not likely, since Searle's explicit conclusion is that consciousness adds flexibility, creativity and sensitivity to action – suggesting that he thinks that consciousness is simply not necessary to routine activities like driving home.

I think that appeal to the access/phenomenal distinction does serve to resolve the contradiction. The resolution is that Searle is presupposing that the Penfield *petit mal* seizure case loses phenomenal consciousness but still has sufficient access-consciousness to drive. But when he says that if he were unconscious of the road the car would crash, he is thinking of loss of both phenomenal and access-consciousness – and it is the loss of the latter that would make the car crash.

I find that audiences I have talked to about this issue tend to divide roughly evenly. Some use 'conscious' to mean phenomenal consciousness – to the extent that they control their uses. Others use 'conscious' to mean either access-consciousness or some kind of self-consciousness. But Searle's error suggests that he – and I don't think he is alone – mixes the two concepts together.

How Crick and Koch's Argument Depends on a Conflation

Crick and Koch argue that V1 is not part of the neural correlate of consciousness because V1 does not project to frontal cortex. Visual consciousness is used in harnessing visual information for directly guiding reasoning and decision making and direct projection to frontal cortex is required for such a use. But what concept of consciousness are Crick and Koch deploying? They face a dilemma. If they mean phenomenal consciousness, then their argument is extremely interesting but unsound: their conclusion is *unjustified.* If they mean access-consciousness, their argument is *trivial.* Let me explain.

Let us look at their argument more closely. Here it is:

1. Neural machinery of visual consciousness harnesses visual information for *direct* control of reasoning and decision making.

43

2. Frontal areas subserve these functions.
3. V1 does not project *directly* to frontal cortex.
4. *So* V1 is not part of neural correlate of consciousness.

Note that the 'direct' in premise 1 is necessary to generate the conclusion. But what reason is there to suppose that there cannot be *some* neural machinery of visual consciousness – V1, for example – that is part of the machinery of control of reasoning and decision making, but only indirectly so? If by 'consciousness' we mean *phenomenal consciousness*, there is no such reason, and so premise 1 is unjustified. But suppose we take 'consciousness' to mean *access-consciousness*. Then premise 1 is *trivially* true. *Of course* the neural machinery of access-consciousness harnesses visual information for *direct* control since access consciousness just *is* direct control. But the trivial interpretation of premise I trivializes the argument. For to say that *if* V1 does not project directly to areas that control action, *then* V1 is not part of the neural correlate of *access*-consciousness is to say something that is very like the claim that *if* something is a sleeping pill, then it is dormitive. Once Crick and Koch tell us that V1 is not directly connected to centres of control, nothing is added by saying that V1 is not part of the neural correlate of consciousness in the *access* sense. For an access-conscious representation just *is* one that is poised for the direct control of reasoning and decision making.

On this reading, we can understand Crick and Koch's remark about their thesis that 'if it [V1 is not directly connected to centres of control] turns out to be true it [V1 is not part of the neural correlate of consciousness] will eventually come to be regarded as completely obvious'. On the access-consciousness interpretation, this remark is like saying that if it turns out to be true that barbiturates cause sleep, their dormitivity will eventually come to be regarded as completely obvious.

To avoid misunderstanding, I must emphasize that I am not saying that it is a triviality that neurons in V1 are not directly connected to frontal areas. That is an empirical claim, just as it is an empirical claim that barbiturates cause sleep. What is trivial is that if neurons in V1 are not directly connected to frontal areas, then neurons in V1 are not part of the neural correlate of access-consciousness. Similarly, it is trivial that if barbiturates cause sleep, then they are dormitive.

That was the 'access-consciousness' interpretation. Now let us turn to the phenomenal interpretation. On this interpretation, their claim is very significant, but not obviously true. How do we know whether activity in VI is phenomenally conscious without being access-conscious? As mentioned earlier, Crick and Koch's own hypothesis that phenomenal consciousness is reverberatory activity in the lower cortical layers makes this a real possibility. They can hardly rule out this consequence of their own view by fiat. Crick and Koch[9] say, 'We know of no case in which a person has lost the whole prefrontal and premotor cortex, on both sides (including Broca's area), and can still see.' But there are two concepts of seeing, just as there are two concepts of

---

[9] F. Crick and C. Koch, untitled response to Pollen, *Nature* 377 (28 September 1995), 294–5.

consciousness. If it is the phenomenal aspect of seeing that they are talking about, they are ignoring the real possibility that patients who have lost these frontal areas *can* see.

Crick and Koch attempt to justify the 'directly' by appeal to representations on the retina. These representations control but not directly; and they are not conscious either. Apparently, the idea is that if representations don't control directly, then they are not conscious. But this example cuts no ice. Retinal representations have *neither* phenomenal *nor* access-consciousness. So they do not address the issue of whether V1 representations might have phenomenal but not access-consciousness.

So Crick and Koch face a dilemma: their argument is either not substantive or not compelling.

Is the Point Verbal?

Crick and Koch often seem to have phenomenal consciousness in mind. For example, they orient themselves towards the problem of 'a full accounting of the manner in which subjective experience arises from these cerebral processes . . . Why do we experience anything at all? What leads to a particular conscious experience (such as the blueness of blue)? Why are some aspects of subjective experience impossible to convey to other people (in other words, why are they private)?'[10]

---

[10] F. Crick and C. Koch, 'Why Neuroscience May Be Able to Explain Consciousness', sidebar *in Scientific American,* December 1995, 92.

Crick and Koch often use 'aware' and 'conscious' as synonyms, as does Crick in *The Astonishing Hypothesis.* For example, the thesis of the paper in *Nature*[11] is that V1 is not part of the neural correlate of consciousness and also that V1 is not part of the neural correlate of visual awareness. But sometimes they appear to use 'awareness' to *mean* access-consciousness. For example, 'All we need to postulate is that, unless a visual area has a direct projection to at least one of [the frontal areas], the activities in that particular visual area will not enter visual *awareness* directly, because the activity of frontal areas is needed to allow a person to report *consciousness*' (p. 122, emphases added). What could 'consciousness' mean here? 'Consciousness' can't mean *access*-consciousness, since reporting is a kind of accessing, and there is no issue of *accessing* access-consciousness. Consciousness in the sense in which they mean it here is something that might conceivably exist even if it cannot be reported or otherwise accessed. And consciousness in this sense might exist in V1. Thus when they implicitly acknowledge an access/phenomenal consciousness distinction, the possibility of phenomenal without access consciousness looms large.

My point is not a verbal one. Whether we use 'consciousness' or 'phenomenal consciousness', 'awareness' or 'access-consciousness', the point is that there are two different concepts of the phenomenon or phenomena of interest. We have to acknowledge the possibility in principle

[11] Crick and Koch, 'Are We Aware?'

that these two concepts pick out different phenomena. Two vs. one: that is not a verbal issue.

Are the Neural Correlates of the Two Kinds of Consciousness Different?

Perhaps there is evidence that the neural correlate of phenomenal consciousness is exactly the same as the neural correlate of access-consciousness? The idea that this is a conceptual difference without a real difference would make sense both of much of what Crick and Koch say and of much of the empirical work on consciousness. But paradoxically, the idea that the neural correlates of the two concepts of consciousness coincide is one which Crick and Koch themselves actually give us reason to *reject*. Their hypothesis about the neural correlate of visual *phenomenal* consciousness is that it is localized in reverberatory circuits involving the thalamus and the lower layers of the visual cortex[12]. This is a daring and controversial hypothesis. But it entails a much less daring and controversial conclusion: that the localization of visual phenomenal consciousness *does not involve the frontal cortex.* However, Crick and Koch think that the neural correlate of *access*-consciousness *does* involve the frontal cortex. Even if they are wrong about this, it would not be surprising if the brain areas involved in visual control of reasoning and reporting are not exactly the same as those involved in visual phenomenality.

[12] Ibid.

One way for Crick and Koch to respond would be to include the neural correlates of *both* access- and phenomenal consciousness in the 'NCC'. To see what is wrong with this, consider an analogy. The first sustained empirical investigation of heat phenomena was conducted by the Florentine Experimenters in the seventeenth century. They didn't distinguish between temperature and heat, using a single word, roughly translatable as 'degree of heat', for both. This failure to make the distinction generated paradoxes. For example. when they measured degree of heat by the test 'Will it melt paraffin?' heat source A came out hotter than B, but when they measured degree of heat by how much ice a heat source could melt in a given time, B came out hotter than A.[13] The concept of degree of heat was *a mongrel* concept, one that lumps together things that are very different.[14]

The suggestion that the neural correlate of visual consciousness includes both the frontal lobes *and* the circuits involving the thalamus and the lower layers of the visual cortex would be like an advocate of the Florentine Experimenters' concept of degree of heat saying that the molecular correlate of degree of heat includes both *mean* molecular kinetic energy (temperature) and *total* molecular kinetic energy (heat). The right way to react to the discovery that a concept is a *mongrel* is to distinguish distinct tracks of

[13] M. Wiser and S. Carey, 'When Heat and Temperature Were One', in *Mental Models,* ed. D. Gentner and A. Stevens (Hillsdale, N.J.: Erlbaum, 1983).

[14] See N. Block, 'On a Confusion'.

scientific investigation corresponding to the distinct concepts, not to lump them together.

Another way for Crick and Koch to react would be to include both the frontal lobes and the circuits involving the thalamus and the lower layers of the visual cortex in the neural correlate of *phenomenal* consciousness. (Koch seems inclined in this direction in correspondence.) But this would be like saying that the molecular correlate of *heat* includes both mean and total molecular kinetic energy. The criteria that Crick and Koch apply in localizing visual phenomenal consciousness are very fine grained, allowing them to emphasize cortical layers 4, 5 and 6 in the visual areas. For example, they appeal to a difference in those layers between cats which are awake and cats which are in slow wave sleep, both exposed to the same visual stimuli. No doubt there are many differences between the sleeping and the waking cats in areas outside the visual cortex. But we would need a very good reason to include any of those other differences in the neural correlate of visual phenomenology as opposed, say, to the non-phenomenal cognitive processing of visual information.

A Better Reason for not Including V1 in the NCC

Though I find fault with one strand of Crick and Koch's reasoning about V1, I think there is another strand in the paper that does justify the conclusion, but for a reason that it would be good to have out in the open and to distinguish from the reasoning just discussed. (Koch tells me that what I say in this paragraph is close to what they had in mind.)

They note that it is thought that representations in V1 do not exhibit the Land effect (colour constancy). But our experience, our phenomenal consciousness, does exhibit the Land effect, or so we would all judge. We should accept the methodological principle: *at this early stage of inquiry,* accept what people say about their own experience. Following this principle and assuming that the claim that cells in V1 don't exhibit colour constancy is confirmed, then we should accept for the moment that representations in V1 are not on the whole phenomenally conscious. This methodological principle is implicitly accepted throughout Crick's and Koch's work.

An alternative route to the same conclusion would be the assumption that the neural correlate of phenomenal consciousness is 'part of' the neural correlate of access-consciousness (and so there can be no phenomenal without access-consciousness). Phenomenal consciousness is automatically 'broadcasted' in the brain, but perhaps there are other mechanisms of broadcasting. (Blindsight would be a weak example.) So even if the 'reverse Anton's syndrome' case turns out to be access- without phenomenal consciousness, Crick and Koch's conclusion might still stand. This is a weaker argument than the one just given because of the possibility that colour nonconstant information *is* actually broadcast in the brain but 'swamped' by colour constant information from higher visual areas.

Note that neither of the reasons given here make any use of the finding that V1 is not directly connected to frontal areas.

The assumption that phenomenal consciousness is part of access consciousness is very empirically risky.

One empirical phenomenon that favours taking phenomenal without access-consciousness seriously is the fact that phenomenal consciousness has a finer grain than access-consciousness based on memory representations. For example, normal people can recognize no more than 80 distinct pitches, but it appears that the number of distinct pitch-experiences is much greater. This is indicated (but not proven) by the fact that normal people can *discriminate* 1400 different frequencies from one another.[15] There are many more phenomenal experiences than there are concepts of them.

Despite these disagreements, I greatly admire Crick's and Koch's work on consciousness and have written a very positive review of Crick's book.[16] Crick has written 'No longer need one spend time ... [enduring] the tedium of philosophers perpetually disagreeing with each other. Consciousness is now largely a scientific problem.'[17] I think this conceptual issue shows that even if largely a scientific issue, it is not entirely one. There is still some value in a collaboration between philosophers and scientists on this topic.

---

[15] D. Raffman, 'On the Persistence of Phenomenology', in *Conscious Experience,* ed. T. Metzinger (Place: Schningh, 1995).

[16] N. Block, Review of Francis Crick, *The Astonishing Hypothesis, Contemporary Psychology,* May 1996, pp. 427–9.

[17] F. Crick, 'Visual Perception: Rivalry and Consciousness', *Nature* 379 (2 August 1996), 485–6.

Embodiment and the Philosophy of Mind

ANDY CLARK

I   Introduction: The Rediscovery of the Body and of the World

Cognitive science is in some sense the science of the mind. But an increasingly influential theme, in recent years, has been the role of the physical body, and of the local environment, in promoting adaptive success. No right-minded cognitive scientist, to be sure, ever claimed that body and world were completely irrelevant to the understanding of mind. But there was, nonetheless, an unmistakeable tendency to marginalize such factors: to dwell on inner complexity whilst simplifying or ignoring the complex inner–outer interplays that characterize the bulk of basic biological problem-solving.[1] This tendency was expressed in, for example, the

---

[1] Notable exceptions to this trend include work such as J. J. Gibson, *The Ecological Approach to Visual Perception* (Boston: Houghton-Mifflin, 1979) and, in a more philosophical key, Maurice Merleau-Ponty's, *La Structure du Comportment* (Paris: Presses Universitaires de France, 1942). Recent work in Animate Vision and ecological optics (see Section II below) is clearly influenced by Gibsonian ideas, while treatments such as F. Varela, E. Thompson and E. Rosch, *The Embodied Mind* (Cambridge, MA: MIT Press, 1991) explicitly acknowledge Merleau-Ponty. There is a brief discussion of these historical roots in chapter 8 of

development of planning algorithms that treated real-world action as merely a way of implementing solutions arrived at by pure cognition (more recent work, by contrast, allows such actions to play important computational and problem-solving roles[2]). It also surfaced in David Marr's[3] depiction of the task of vision as the construction of a detailed three-dimensional image of the visual scene. For possession of such a rich inner model effectively allows the system to 'throw away' the world and to focus subsequent computational activity on the inner model alone.[4] More generally, the whole vision of cognition as inner operations on internal world models reflects an explanatory strategy which might reasonably be dubbed isolationism:[5]

my own *Being There: Putting Brain, Body and World Together Again* (Cambridge, MA: MIT Press, 1997).

[2] See, e.g., P. Agre and S. Rosenschein (eds.) *Computational Theories of Interaction and Agency* (Cambridge, MA: MIT Press, 1996); D. Kirsh and P. Maglio 'On Distinguishing Epistemic from Pragmatic Action', *Cognitive Science* 18 (1995), 513–49; and E. Hutchins, *Cognition in the Wild* (Cambridge, MA: MIT Press, 1995).

[3] See D. Marr *Vision* (San Francisco, CA: W. H. Freeman, 1982).

[4] This tradition is nicely critiqued in P. S. Churchland, V. Ramachandran and T. Sejnowski, 'A Critique of Pure Vision' in C. Koch and J. Davies (eds.), *Large-Scale Neuronal Theories of the Brain* (Cambridge, MA: MIT Press, 1994).

[5] Roboticists refer (usually disparagingly) to this isolationist vision as the idea of a linear Sense–Think–Act Cycle, See, e.,g., C. Malcolm, T. Smithers and J. Hallam, 'An Emerging Paradigm in Robot Architecture', *Edinburgh University Department of Artificial Intelligence Technical Report*, 1989.

(Isolationism)
The world is (just) a source of inputs and an arena for outputs, and the body is (just) an organ for receiving the inputs and effecting the outputs (actions). The task of early processing is to render the inputs as an inner world-model of sufficient richness to allow the bulk of problem-solving activity to be defined over the inner model alone.

Isolationism, it is fair to say, is in increasing disrepute. But the precise shape of an alternative approach remains unclear. Anti-isolationist assertions range from the relatively innocent insistence that we won't achieve a balanced vision of what the brain does until we pay more heed to the complex roles of body and world, to the self-consciously revolutionary accusation that mind itself is not, after all, a special inner arena populated by internal models and repre- sentations but is rather the operation of a profoundly inter- woven system, incorporating aspects of brain, body and world – a system which resists informative analysis in terms of the old notions of inner models, representations and computation.[6] The most radical anti-isolationist vision thus depicts human beings as a species of (so-called)

[6] Major statements of this view include J. Haugeland, 'Mind Embodied and Embedded' in Y.-H. Houng and J.-C. Ho (eds.), *Mind and Cognition* (Tapei, Taiwan: Academia Sinica, 1995), pp. 3–38, and T. Van Gelder, 'What Might Cognition Be, If Not Computation?' *Journal of Philosophy* 92/7 (1995), 345–81. Closely related claims and arguments appear in T. Van Gelder and R. Port. 'It's About Time' Introduction to R. Port and T. Van Gelder (eds.), *Mind as Motion: Dynamics, Behavior, and Cognition* (Cambridge, MA: MIT Press, 1995). E. Thelen and L. Smith, *A Dynamic Systems Approach to the Development of Cognition*

post-*Cartesian agent*.[7] The post-Cartesian agent is a locus of knowledge, acts for reasons and has beliefs and desires. Yet she harbours no internal representations and resists analysis in terms of any cognitely important distinctions between inner and outer processes, between perception, cognition and action, or between mind, body and world.

I shall argue that the post-Cartesian vision is unconvincing and that a key move in the argument (a move I dub the 'cognitive-to-coping shift') is both dialectically suspect and empirically unsound. More positively, I shall argue for a much weaker but still anti-isolationist stance: one that nevertheless suggests the need for some deep revisions in our understanding of the nature of internal representations and inner world models. The foundational and conceptual challenges thus prove real enough, even when stripped of their radical post-Cartesian trimmings.

II   Inner Symbol Flight

The outright rejection of the notion of internal representation is just the extreme limiting case of a marked tendency that might be dubbed 'inner symbol flight'. This flight

and Action. (Cambridge, MA: MIT Press, 1994), and Varela, Thompson and Rosch, *The Embodied Mind.*

[7] This vision is clearly contemplated in Haugeland 'Mind Embodied' and in Van Gelder, 'What Might Cognition Be?' Both authors, however, recognize the large space of intermediate possibilities. The term 'post-Cartesian agent' is from Van Gelder, p. 381. See also Thelen and Smith, *A Dynamic Systems Approach,* p. 338, Van Gelder and Port, 'It's About Time', p. ix.

involves the progressive rejection of more and more of the apparatus and assumptions associated with the vision of cognition as the manipulation of chunky inner symbols. According to one simple (and historically important) vision, semantically sensible transitions between mental states are best explained in terms of syntactically constrained transitions between inner symbol strings. These symbol strings contained discrete elements corresponding rather closely to the semantic elements identified in sentential descriptions of the relevant mental states. Thus, the thought that John loves Mary is imagined to be realized as a complex inner symbol string that incorporates distinct and independently manipulable elements standing for 'John' 'loves' and 'Mary'.[8]

This vision of simple inner symbolic atoms (unstructured base items) corresponding rather closely to the familiar concepts and relations enshrined in daily discourse was challenged by the development of distributed connectionist[9] models. The sentential paradigm[10] was replaced, in this research, by a vision of internal representations as distributed patterns of activity across a whole array of simple processing units. Such distributed patterns were allowed to overlap in semantically significant ways, giving

---

[8] See J. Fodor and Z. Pylyshyn, 'Connectionism and Cognitive Architecture: A critical analysis', *Cognition* 28 (1988), p. 13.

[9] See D. Rumelhart, J. McClelland and the PDP Research Group, *Parallel Distributed Processing: Explorations in the Microstructure of Cognition*, Vols. I and II (Cambridge, MA: MIT Press, 1986).

[10] P. S. Churchland, *Neurophilosophy* (Cambridge, MA: MIT Press, 1986).

rise to a variety of computationally significant side-effects including free generalization, damage-resistance, etc.[11]

More recently still, we have witnessed increased attention to the temporal dynamics of the inner representational vehicles. The use of (for example) simple recurrent neural networks[12] allows information to be encoded not just in instantaneous patterns of activity but in temporally extended processing trajectories. In these networks, much of the information-processing power resides in the way a current state allows or restricts future change and evolution. The progression has thus been from a view of simple, atomistic inner symbols to a notion of spatially distributed patterns, to a notion of spatially *and temporally* distributed patterns. The inner vehicles of content, courtesy of this progression, have come to look less and less like simple inner *states* and more like increasingly complex inner *processes*.

This metamorphosis, moreover, is probably still incomplete. Future developments look set to include seeing many inner vehicles as multiply functional and seeing aspects of the inner architecture as dynamically reconfigurable. Multiple functionality would mean that one and the same inner resource may play a variety of content-bearing

---

[11] The details need not concern us here. But see e.g. my *Microcognition: Philosophy, Cognitive Science and Parallel Distributed Processing* (Cambridge, MA: MIT Press, 1989), for discussion.

[12] J. Elman, 'Representation and Structure in Connectionist Models', in G. Altman (ed.), *Cognitive Models of Speech Processing* (Cambridge, MA: MIT Press, 1991).

roles[13] (perhaps varying in accordance with local context). Dynamic reconfigurability would mean that the inner archi- tecture is itself subject to rapid change and reorganization, as when the release of a chemical neuromodulator causes two neural networks to temporarily fuse and behave as one.

The moral, then, is that our understanding of the nature of the (putative) inner vehicles of content is in a state of extreme flux, characterized by a rapid flight from the initial image of static, chunky unstructured inner symbols. This flight has a content-related aspect too. For as the inner vehicles have become more complex, so the characteristic contents seem to have become more partial and fragmen- tary. This is because the emphasis has shifted from isolation- ist forms of problem-solving towards iterated series of agentenvironment interactions. This shift is nicely exempli- fied by recent work in the field known as Animate Vision.[14]

Recall Marr's depiction[15] of the task of vision. The task, according to Marr, is to construct a rich inner model of the three-dimensional visual scene on the basis of the avail- able (two-dimensional) input information. Recent work in the field known as Animate Vision takes a very different tack. This work depicts the task as, simply, the use of visual strategies to control behaviour, in real-world contexts, at as

---

[13] For some hints of such content-sensitive complexity, see J. Knierim and D. Van Essen, 'Visual Cortex: Cartography, Connectivity and Concurrent Processing', *Current Opinion in Neurobiology* 2 (1992), 150–5.

[14] D. Ballard, 'Animate Vision', *Artificial Intelligence* 48 (1991), 57–86.

[15] D. Marr, *Vision* (San Francisco, CA: W. H. Freeman, 1982).

low a computational cost as possible. To this end, Animate Vision avails itself of three central ploys.

1. The use of task-specific cues and shortcuts.
2. The use of body-centred (egocentric) strategies.
3. The use of repeated environmental interactions.

Task-specific cues and shortcuts include, for example, the use of personalized idiosyncratic strategies such as searching for bright yellow (a cheap, easy visual cue) when searching for *my* coffee cup (which just happens to be canary yellow). Egocentric strategies include the use of so-called deictic pointers (explained below). Repeated environmental inter-actions include, for example, the use of repeated visual saccades to visit and re-visit different aspects of a scene retrieving specific information only as and when required.

The case of deictic pointers can serve as a general illustration. A pointer in classical Artificial Intelligence is an inner state which can function in self-contained com-putational routines but which can also point to other data structures.[16] This pointing allows the retrieval, when required, of more detailed information, and the effective binding of certain items of information to others. Such binding often needs to be temporary, as when we bind certain features (e.g. bright yellow) to certain current (but clearly temporary) visual locations (e.g. 'yellow detected at the top left of visual field').

---

[16] See, e,g., Z. Pylyshyn (ed.), *The Robot's Dilemma: The Frame Problem in Artificial Intelligence* (Norwood: Ablex, 1987).

Deictic pointers, however, are actual bodily orientations (such as saccadic eye movements) that play the same kind of functional role. The idea is that the system is set up so that the very act of fixating a particular aspect of a visual scene implements a kind of temporary variable binding in which the detected features are bound to a given spatial location. A related example concerns binding a 'reaching-and-grasping' routine to a target object. Here too the binding may be cheaply implemented using what is informally called a 'do-it-where-I'm-looking' strategy. Here, the system is set up so that the grasping routine is automatically directed to the currently fixated visual location. In all these cases, the authors comment:

> The external world is analogous to computer memory. When fixating a location, the neurons that are linked to the fovea refer to information computed from that location. Changing gaze is analogous to changing the memory reference in a silicon computer.[17]

One important thrust of the Animate Vision research, then, is that bodily actions (such as saccadic eye motions) can play vital computational roles. Another is that repeated agent-environment interactions obviate much of the need to create all-purpose, detailed internal world models. By visiting and re-visiting different aspects of the current scene as and when required, we allow the world to function as 'its own best

---

[17] D. Ballard, M. Hayhoe, P. Pook and R. Rao, 'Deictic Codes for the Embodiment of Cognition', *Behavioral and Brain Sciences,* forthcoming.

model'. The research programme is thus staunchly anti-isolationist. But it is not by any means 'post-Cartesian' – it does not reject the very ideas of internal models and representations, so much as reconfigure them in a sparser and more interactive image. We still read of 'inner databases' e.g. ones that associate small objects, such as my car keys, with larger, easily detectable locations, such as on the kitchen table), of 'internal featural representations' (of colour, shape, etc.), of 'indexical representations' that specify locations relative to bodily position and so on. What is being rejected is emphatically *not* the notion of inner content-bearing states per se, but rather the much more specific notion that we construct rich, memory-intensive internal representations of all aspects of the current visual scene.

A similar profile is presented by much actual research into real-world robotics. A good example is work[18] in real-world robotic navigation in which knowledge of location is directly encoded as a perceptuo-motor routine: a routine that actually specifies how to move the robot from its present position to the target location. In these models the inner map is *itself* the controller of the appropriate action. There is no need for a further system to access the map and to plan a route. The robot's knowledge is thus both

[18] M. Matraric, 'Navigating with a Rat Brain: A Neurobiologically Inspired Model for Robot Spatial Representation', in J.-A. Meyer and S. Wilson (eds.), *From Animals to Animals* 1 (Cambridge, MA, MIT Press, 1991). This work is further discussed in Clark, *Being There*, chapter 2.

descriptive and prescriptive[19] – a dual nature that affords great economies both in terms of response-time and computational effort. Once again, we see interesting work that is not so much anti-representational as sparsely representational. The crucial distinction, it seems to me, is not between representational and non-representational solutions so much as between rich and expensive forms of internal representation (which may increase flexibility but which often require additional computational work to specify a behavioural response) and sparser, more action-oriented forms of representation.

The most convincing work in Animate Vision and real-world robotics thus stops well short of the full 'post-Cartesian' rejection of inner models and representations. Why, then, have some theorists gone on to question the idea of internal representations and inner models *tout court*?

III   Radical Interactionism

The leading anti-representationalist argument[20] seems to turn on the impact of dense, reciprocal causal exchanges

---

[19] For more on this theme, see R. Millikan 'Pushmi-pullyu Representations', in L. May, M. Friedman and A. Clark (eds.), *Mind and Morals* (Cambridge, MA: MIT Press, 1996).

[20] This argument is the centrepiece of Van Gelder, 'What Might Cognition Be?' where we read, for example, that: 'The core dynamical hypothesis ... goes hand in hand with a conception of cognitive systems ... as complexes of continuous, simultaneous and mutually-determining change. [ ] In this vision, the cognitive system is not just the encapsulated brain; rather, since the nervous system, body, and

uniting agent and environment in a complex web of mutual influence. Under such conditions, it is argued, the kinds of representational decomposition and analysis that work so well for many contemporary computer models of intelligent processes simply get no foothold. The problem (it is argued) is that the notion of x representing y is too oneway and too simplistic to do justice to cases in which x is continuously affecting and being affected by y and vice versa. Yet typical agent–environment interactions, the argument continues, often present just such a complex and circular causal profile.

Consider ballroom dancing. As you dance, your motions (if you are a good dancer!) are both continuously influenced by and an influence upon, those of your partner: the two sets of motions 'coevolve' in a highly interdetermined way. Nor is the presence of two human agents essential to the phenomenon. The same complex relation obtains between (for example) an experienced windsurfer and her rig: the windsurfer constantly affects and is affected by the set of the rig. Van Gelder makes the same point using the extended example of the Watt (or centrifugal) governor – a device which maintains a steam engine at a steady speed by both affecting and being affected by the engine speed.[21]

environment are all constantly changing and simultaneously influencing each other, the true cognitive system is a single unified system embracing all three' (p. 373). The argument is also visible in Van Gelder and Port, 'It's About Time', pp. 23–5, in Thelen and Smith, *A Dynamic Systems Approach,* p. 27, and in Varela, Thompson and Rosch, *The Embodied Mind,* pp. 172–5.

[21] Here Van Gelder 'What Might Cognition Be?' (p. 353) notes that: 'arm angle and engine speed are at all times both determined by, and

Such episodes of mutual influence were much discussed both in early cybernetics[22] and in the work of the French phenomenologist Maurice Merleau-Ponty.[23]

Where such continuous, dense, circular causal influence obtains, it is argued, the tools of representational (and computational) analysis run aground. The idea of explaining the shape of these complex ongoing agent–environment interactions by depicting inner states as representing outer ones is rejected as coarse and unilluminating. Instead, inner and outer co-evolve in a mathematically precise way that is best captured (so the argument goes) by the use of coupled differential equations in which the current values of certain internal variables appear as parameter settings in the evolution equation for the external system and vice versa.[24] Fortunately, the details of such a dynamical systems model are unimportant for present purposes.[25] What matters is

determining, each other's behavior ... there is nothing mysterious about this relationship ... Yet it is much more subtle and complex than the standard concept of representation can handle.' This example is treated in detail in A. Clark and J. Toribio, 'Doing Without Representing?' *Synthese* 101 (1995), 401–31.

[22] For example, in W. Ross Ashby's *Introduction to Cybernetics* (New York: Wiley, 1956).

[23] Maurice Merleau-Ponty, *The Structure of Behavior* (New York: Beacon, 1963). Originally *La Structure du Comportment* (Paris: Presses Universitaire de France, 1942).

[24] For an accessible introduction to these dynamical approaches, see S. Kelso *Dynamic Patterns* (Cambridge, MA: MIT Press, 1995). A classic text is R. Abraham and C. Shaw *Dynamics – The Geometry of Behavior* (Redwood, CA: Addison-Wesley, 1992).

[25] For a fuller discussion, see Clark, *Being There*, chapters 5, 6 and 8.

rather the general shape of the argument. Van Gelder puts it well:

> The internal operation of a system interacting with an external world can be so subtle and complex as to defy description in representational terms. (p. 381.)

Before responding to this argument, it is worth pausing to clarify the challenge. For what is at issue is not the status of certain systems (ourselves, for example) as *representers*. That is a given. We surely do represent our world, our past, our possible futures, our absent friends and so on. We think of these things and states of affairs and to that extent we clearly represent them to ourselves. What is *not* a given (and what is at issue here) is that we use *internal representations* to do so. The point is that the scientific claim that cognition involves internal representations (and computations defined over them) is meant not as a simple rehearsal of the fact that we are thinkers, but as a substantial and explanatorily potent empirical hypothesis: the kind of thing that could indeed turn out to be false. The falsifiable claim, to a first approximation, is that there exist distinct, identifiable inner states or processes whose systemic or functional role is to stand in for specific features or states of affairs.

This notion of internal stand-ins is, however, itself ambiguous. It is ambiguous[26] between a weak notion in which x 'stands in' for y iff x is an inner resource that (a) carries information about y and (b) is used to control

[26] See A. Clark and R. Grush, 'Towards a Cognitive Robotics' (submitted).

behaviour, and a much stronger notion in which the inner resource must be capable of functioning as a genuine surrogate, i.e. be capable of systematically controlling appropriate behaviour *even if y is absent or non-existent.* A neural population[27] closely keyed to bodily orientation and used to control on-line skilled action may thus be counted as a system of weak stand-ins. And even here the representational gloss seems to tell us something useful about the purpose of the neuronal population. But such a population, though it engages in the information-based control of action, need not be capable of driving appropriate actions in the absence of the (weakly represented) state of affairs. It is this latter, and surely less common, capacity to act as an inner surrogate *in the absence of* direct environmental control that. I suggest, characterizes the strongest and most conceptually unequivocal cases of internal representation.[28]

The problem then is that the entire argument concerning the circular causal complexity of rich agent–environment interactions is vitiated by its failure to engage the real issue of strong representation. All the examples share (and must share) a certain problematic feature,

---

[27] For example, the posterior parietal neuronal population in the rat which encodes information about which way the rat's head is facing and which is exploited in radial maze running – see B. Naughton and L. Nadel, 'Hebb–Marr Networks and the Neurobiological Representation of Action in Space', in M. Gluck and D. Rumelhart (eds.), *Neuroscience and Connectionist Theory* (Erlbaum, 1990).

[28] David Israel 'Bogdan on Information', *Mind & Language* 3/2 (1988), 123–40 makes essentially the same point. See also Brian Cantwell Smith, *The Origin of Objects* (Cambridge, MA: MIT Press, 1996).

namely, they are all cases in which the target behaviour is *continuously driven and modified by* the relevant environmental parameter. Yet one major motivation for positing internal representations in the first place was to explain our puzzling capacity to go beyond such tightly coupled agent–world interactions and to coordinate our activities and choices with the distal, the modal and the non-existent. The original notion of internal representation is thus grounded in the notion of strong inner surrogates and is merely extended (perhaps problematically) to the case of (merely) information-bearing inner states used for the control of action. This helps to explain why the best cases for the argument-from-continuous-reciprocal-causation may well strike us as rather *poor* examples of traditionally cognitive phenomena. For they depend crucially on the constant presence of the relevant environmental factors and thus do not strike us as especially representation-hungry[29] in the first place. Properly representation-hungry scenarios would be, for example, planning next year's vacation, using mental imagery to count the number of windows in your old house (this example is from Dan Dennett, in conversation), doing mental arithmetic, dreaming, etc., etc.

The dialectical situation is, however, rather delicate. For the anti-representationalist may now reply that the point of her argument, in part, was to suggest that these traditional cases (of what might be termed 'environmentally de-coupled' reason) are in fact empirically marginal and

---

[29] The phrase is from Clark and Toribio, 'Doing Without Representing?'.

that the bulk of daily intelligent response displays *precisely* the richly interactive profile the argument highlights. Environmentally de-coupled reason, it is claimed, is at best a tip-of-the-iceberg phenomenon. What is being promoted is thus a shift of emphasis away from off-line cogitation and onto real-time interactive engagement[30] – a kind of cognitive-to-coping shift.

This shift in emphasis is in one sense welcome. From both an evolutionary and a developmental[31] point of view, real-world realtime responsiveness is clearly in some sense primary. But as we shall now see, the notion that the richly interactive case is in some way *biologically basic* is in fact perfectly compatible with the claim that off-line environmentally de-coupled reason is *not* the mere tip of the adaptive iceberg. Indeed, the way to forge a genuinely cognitive science of embodied, environmentally embedded agency is, I believe, precisely to target the relations between densely coupled and more strongly representationally mediated forms of adaptive success. This is the project that I dub Minimal Cartesianism, and to which we now turn.

IV Minimal Cartesianism

Minimal Cartesianism seeks to locate the roots of strongly representational reason in the richly interactive settings emphasized in work on embodied cognition. Thus consider

---

[30] This move is explicitly made in Haugeland, 'Mind Embodied' and is also clearly in evidence in van Gelder and Port, 'It's About Time'.
[31] See Thelen and Smith, *A Dynamic Systems Approach.*

the phenomenon of skilled reaching.[32] Smooth, skilled reaching involves the use of proprioceptive feedback – signals that tell the brain how the arm is oriented in space. But the timing of these signals poses a problem. The minimal delay between the onset and the use of such information looks to be between 200 and 500 milliseconds.[33] Yet we make essential trajectory corrections, that look to be governed by such feedback, within the first 70 milliseconds[34] of reaching. How does nature turn the trick?

This problem of requiring feedback before it is practically available crops up in industry too: in chemical plants, bioreactors and so forth.[35] One common solution, in these cases, is to add a forward model or emulator into the systems. This is a circuit that takes as input a specification of both the previous state of the system and the commands just

---

[32] I borrow this case from R. Grush, 'Emulation and Cognition' (Ph.D. Dissertation, University of California at San Diego, 1995). A further treatment is available in Clark and Grush, 'Towards a Cognitive Robotics'.

[33] This figure is established by, for example, using artificial vibrators strapped to the tendons to disrupt proprioceptive signals arriving from the muscle spindles, and timing the gap between such disruptive input and alterations to the arm motion itself (see C. Redon, L. Hay and J. L. Velay, 'Proprioceptive Control of Goal Directed Movements in Man, Studied by Means of Vibratory Muscle Tendon Stimulation', *Journal of Motor Control* 23/2 (1991), 101–8).

[34] See J. van der Meulen, R. Gooskens, J. J. Dennier van der Gon, C. C. A. M. Gielen and K. Wilhelm, 'Mechanisms Underlying Accuracy in Fast Goal-directed Arm Movements in Man', *Journal of Motor Behavior* 22/1 (1990), 67–84.

[35] See Grush, 'Emulation and Cognition' for a review.

issued, and that gives as output a *prediction* of the feedback that should later arrive. The emulator thus generates a kind of mock feedback signal available substantially in advance of the real thing.

Nature, it now seems, may deploy much the same strategy. There is a growing body of neuroscientific evidence[36] that suggests that neural circuitry spanning the cortico-spinal tract, the red nucleus, the inferior olive, the contralateral dentate and cerebellar cortex may be playing just such a role. Such circuitry looks to take a copy of the afferent motor command and to output a fast prediction of the feedback later due arrive by the slow 200–500 millisecond route.

The same trick has been replicated in a variety of neural network[37] models. What matters for our purposes, however, is an additional conjecture. It is the conjecture[38] that the biological emulator circuit plays a dual role. This dual role involves both the fine tuning of on-line reaching

---

[36] See M. Ito, *The Cerebellum and Neural Control* (New York: Raven Press, 1984), M. Kawato, K. Furukawa and R. Suzuki, 'A Hierarchical Neural Network Model for the Control and Learning of Voluntary Movement', *Biological Cybernetics* 57 (1987), 169–85, and D. Wolpert, Z. Ghahramani and M. Jordan, 'An Internal Model for Sensorimotor Integration', *Science* 269 (1995), 1880–2.

[37] E.g. M. Kawato, 'Computational Schemes and Neural Network Models for Formation and Control of Multijoint Arm Trajectory', in W. T. Miller III, R. Sutton and P. Werbos (eds.), *Neural Networks for Control* (Cambridge, MA: MIT Press, 1990), Wolpert *et al.,* 'An Internal Model'.

[38] Grush, 'Emulation and Cognition'.

(the normal case, in which the emulator circuit acts as an aid to smooth real-time reaching) and the production of visuo-motor imagery allowing the *off-line mental rehearsal* of motor routines. In the latter case, the emulator circuit is now running alone, de-coupled from the real-world action system. Such an additional role for the very same emulator circuitry implicated in daily skilled reaching looks evolution-arily plausible and helps to explain some otherwise puzzling results. These include the robust finding that mental rehearsal can actually improve sports skills[39] and the sur-prising activity of the cerebellum (generally thought of as a motor area) during mental imagery.[40]

Motor emulation circuitry, if this is correct, is both an aid to fluent, real-world action and a support for inde-pendent, environmentally decoupled mental rehearsal. It is thus a minimally Cartesian mental tool, but one that is parasitic upon adaptations closely geared to the promotion of smooth real-time agent–environment interactions. As a result, even the modestly Cartesian phenomenon of visual imagination remains closely tied to the biomechanics and action-taking profile of the agent.

Given this profile, we can see why isolationist meth-odologies and assumptions may prove inadequate even in

[39] See e.g., D. Fetz and D. Landers, 'The Effects of Mental Practice on Motor Skill Learning and Performance: A Meta-Analysis', *Journal of Sport Psychology* 5 (1983), 25–57.

[40] J. Decety, H. Sjoholm, E. Ryding, G. Stenberg and D. Ingvar, 'The Cerebellum Participates in Cognitive Activity', *Brain Research* 535 (1990), 313–17.

the case of certain kinds of environmentally decoupled cognitive skills. For such skills may remain action-oriented at one remove, courtesy of the constraints on the original endowment: an endowment that is now redeployed to serve 'off-line' 'Cartesian' ends. Crucially, this failure of isolationism should not be seen as an invitation to scepticism about internal representation and inner models. In the emulator case, at least, it is clearly apparent that we are now dealing with identifiable circuitry whose functional role is, at times, strongly representational. Yet the account is perfectly compatible with the various morals and emphases suggested by the action-oriented research discussed in section II above. The conciliatory position that I favour thus involves combining the stress on real-world, real-time action with a search for the biologically basic roots of more decoupled forms of thought and problem-solving. For it is only by confronting the latter class of cases that representationalism can be given a fair trial.

V   Scaling, Rationality and Complexity

Minimal Cartesianism aims to build bridges between the recent emphasis on richly interactive tasks and the more traditionally cognitive focus on decoupled reason. To that end it stresses the use of multiple, partial, action-oriented inner models and of deictic, idiosyncratic and action-oriented internal representations. The compelling question at this point becomes whether we can really hope to explain the full gamut of human cognition without at some point just reinventing the classical image of context-neutral, rich, actionindependent, highly manipulable inner symbolic structures. In short, can Minimal Cartesianism scale up so as to account for the full complexities of 'higher cognition'?

Such 'scaling up', if it is to have a reasonable chance of success, must give due credit to the way external structures, linguistic actions and cultural practices all conspire to effectively re-configure the shape of the computational spaces we must negotiate in order to solve more complex and abstract problems. Complex human cognition is best depicted as occurring at the fecund interface between a variety of action-oriented internal resources and a larger scaffolding of external structures, tools and practices: a supportive web that acts so as to substantially alter the computational spaces that can be explored by our form of basic, on-board biological reason. A classic example[41] is the use of pen and paper to do (e.g.) long multiplication: a trick that allows us to use an iterated sequence of simple inner computations (such as 7 x 7, 4 x 4) and a sequence of externally stored and manipulated inscriptions so as to solve much more complex problems (such as 777 x 444). Public language, I elsewhere argue, plays a wide variety of similar roles.[42]

---

[41] D. Rumelhart, J. McClelland, R. Smolensky and G. Hinton, 'Schemata and Sequential Thought Processes in PDP Models', in D. Rumelhart, J. McClelland and the PDP Research Group (eds.), *Parallel Distributed Processing: Explorations in the Microstructure of Cognition,* vol. II (Cambridge, MA: MIT Press, 1986), pp. 7–58.

[42] A. Clark, 'Magic Words: How Language Augments Human Cognition', in P. Carruthers and J. Boucher (eds.) *Thought and Language: Interdisciplinary Themes* (Cambridge: Cambridge University Press, forthcoming).

The mere act of labelling, as Dennett[43] points out, affords great economies of search and classification, while the capacity for linguistic rehearsal may, according to Ray Jackendoff,[44] be what enables us to attend to the details of our own thoughts – thus opening up vast new possibilities of reflection and analysis.[45] External artefacts and social organizations likewise alter and transform the tasks that individual brains need to perform. The cognitive anthropologist Ed Hutchins[46] offers, in this vein, a wonderfully detailed and persuasive account of the process of ship navigation in which it is the overall system comprised of multiple brains, bodies and instruments that solves the navigation problem. Each crew member within this larger nexus merely monitors and responds to certain simple environmental conditions. The responses alter a few aspects of the shared work space and thus promote and support similar forms of responsiveness among the others. The whole process constitutes an environmentally extended computational flow in which multiple agents, simple routines, and a variety of external props and artefacts (such as nautical slide rules) all combine to solve a complex problem.

---

[43] D. Dennett, 'Labelling and Learning', *Mind and Language* 8 (1994), 540–8. See also Chapter 13 of his *Darwin's Dangerous Idea* (New York: Simon & Schuster, 1995).

[44] R. Jackendoff, 'How Language Helps Us Think', *Pragmatics and Cognition* 4/1 (1996), pp. 1–34.

[45] Ibid., pp. 19–22.

[46] E. Hutchins, *Cognition in the Wild* (Cambridge, MA: MIT Press, 1995).

Even a minimally Cartesian treatment of basic bio-logical reason may thus hope to scale up so as to illuminate the full panoply of human thought and reason. The trick is to take the issue of external scaffolding very seriously indeed (and especially to recognize the computational virtues of public language: the one action-neutral symbolic code we already know ourselves to possess). One implication of this approach to the scaling problem is that we will need, at times, to study these larger systems (of multiple communi-cating brains and artefacts) as organized wholes and to recognize extended computational processes spanning the boundaries between brain, body and world. Such assertions can easily be mistaken for antipathy towards the study of inner resources and processes. But the real challenge, once again, is to interlock the two approaches and thus to relocate individual human reason in its proper ecological niche.

The project also raises questions about the notion of human rationality itself. Isolationist cognitive science tended to depict rationality in terms of semantically apt transitions between inner mental states. Turing's achievement, as repeatedly stressed by Jerry Fodor,[47] was to show how such transitions could be supported by a purely mechanical pro-cess. The environmentally extended approach just mooted need not reject that account. It may (and should)

[47] For example, see the comments on pp. 277–8 of his 'Replies to Critics', in B. Loewer and G. Rey (eds.), *Meaning in Mind: Fodor and his critics* (Oxford: Blackwell, 1991), pp. 255–319.

incorporate Turing's central idea of inner processes whose syntactic[48] properties preserve semantic relations. But this will be just part of a more encompassing theory that allows rational behaviour to supervene on wider webs of structure involving other agents, artefacts and aspects of the local environment.

There remains a worry about complexity. Even if the general project sketched in this paper proves attractive (the project of bridging between interaction-based models and more environmentally decoupled forms of reason), it could still turn out that the inner vehicles of content prove too spatially and temporally complex to figure in illuminating accounts of mental processes. Such a worry gains some force from recent demonstrations of the role of complex recurrent connections[49] in modulating the information-processing profile of neuronal populations and from the sheer difficulty of assigning specific content-bearing roles to tracts of neural machinery. These complexities and difficulties can lead to a subtly different kind of scepticism in which it is the complexity of the inner story itself (not the inner–outer interaction) that is supposed to make trouble for the representational analysis.

The issues here are more purely empirical and it is impossible, given the current state of research, to make any firm predictions. But one interesting possibility is that new

---

[48] Syntactic properties are any non-semantic properties that can be directly exploited by a physical system. Temporally extended processes, as described in section II, are in this sense syntactic too.

[49] Knierim and Van Essen, 'Visual Cortex', 150–5.

analytic tools may yet provide the means to identify functionally important patterns of activity. Dynamical systems analyses, of the kind sometimes promoted as an alternative to the representational approach, may in fact help us to identify tractable inner vehicles despite the presence of burgeoning spatial and temporal complexity. This possibility is clearly noted by van Gelder[50] himself, who allows that 'an exciting feature of the dynamical approach is that it offers opportunities for dramatically reconceiving the nature of representation in cognitive systems'. Internal representations, then, may be realized not as simple inner states but as dynamical patterns of just about any conceivable kind. Such patterns may, in addition, be transient entities that form only in response to the details of current context. We thus better appreciate the limits of the inner vehicle metaphor itself. Such vehicles need be neither simple nor static in order to play a representational role.

Van Gelder's observation is important. He does not take himself to have shown that there are no internal representations: just that there *might* not be any, and that if there *are* they may take a very different form to the one we once expected. I have tried to show that some of the more specific sceptical considerations he advances (concerning the potential complexity of agent–environment interactions) fail (and must fail) to make contact with the original pro-representationalist argument: an argument grounded directly in our capacities for *environmentally decoupled* reason.

[50] Van Gelder, 'What Might Cognition Be?'.

The revisionary representationalist option, however, remains open, appealing and increasingly in evidence in actual cognitive scientific applications.[51]

In sum, our vision of biological reason is rapidly changing. There is a growing emphasis on the computational economies afforded by real-world action and a growing appreciation of the way larger structures (of agents and artefacts) both scaffold and transform the space of individual reason. These twin forces converge on a rather more minimalist account of individual cognitive processing – an account that tends to eschew rich, all-purpose, action-neutral internal models and sentential forms of internal representation. Such minimalism, however, has its limits. Despite some rather ambitious arguments, there is currently no reason to doubt the guiding vision of individual agents as both loci of modest internal representations and users of a variety of inner world models. Rather than *opposing* representationalism against interactive dynamics, we should be embracing a broader vision of the inner representational realm and seeking the crucial continuities between tightly coupled behavioural strategies and the more 'Cartesian' space of environmentally decoupled reason. Our reward will be a better vision of rational agency itself.

---

[51] See papers in Port and Van Gelder (eds.), *Mind as Motion*.

Folk Psychology and Mental Simulation

MARTIN DAVIES AND TONY STONE

This paper is about the contemporary debate concerning folk psychology – the debate between the proponents of the *theory theory* of folk psychology and the friends of the *simulation alternative*.[1] At the outset, we need to ask: What should we mean by this term 'folk psychology'?

Some of the material in this paper was presented at the Pacific Division meeting of the American Philosophical Association and at the University of Michigan, as well as at seminars in Canberra, Melbourne, Oxford, Paris and Sydney. We are grateful to many friends and colleagues, including Ned Block, Greg Currie, Allan Gibbard, Robert Gordon, Paul Harris, Jane Heal, Frank Jackson, Janet Levin, Christopher Peacocke, Philip Pettit, Huw Price, Peter Railton, Ian Ravenscroft, Michael Smith, Dan Sperber, Stephen Stich and Kendall Walton, for comments and conversations. MD is pleased to acknowledge financial support from the Australian National University and the Humanities Research Board of the British Academy and is especially grateful to members of the Philosophy Department at the University of Michigan for the opportunity to visit as the James B. and Grace J. Nelson Philosopher in Residence.

[1] Much of the relevant literature is gathered in three collections: *Folk Psychology: The Theory of Mind Debate*, ed. M. Davies and T. Stone (Oxford: Blackwell Publishers, 1995); *Mental Simulation: Evaluations and Applications*, ed. M. Davies and T. Stone (Oxford: Blackwell Publishers, 1995); and *Theories of Theories of Mind*, ed. P. Carruthers and P. K. Smith (Cambridge: Cambridge University Press, 1996).

Shall we perhaps say that folk psychology is just what the folk know (or believe) about psychological matters? The problem with this putative definition is that, if folk psychology is a body of known or believed propositions about psychology, then it may be said that folk psychology is a psychological theory. This would threaten to render invisible even the possibility of an alternative to the theory theory of folk psychology.

Someone might respond to this problem by saying that not just any collection of propositions about psychology deserves to be called a *theory*. Only a set of propositions organized around generalizations that support counterfactuals and are appropriately objective will earn that title.[2] So, folk psychology will be a theory only if what the folk know or believe about psychology has something of the character of a science. This response has some plausibility. There is surely something to be said for this restrictive use of the term 'theory', and it will be important in Section III of this paper, when we consider explanation and understanding. But many of the participants in the debate between the theory theory and the simulation alternative have used the term 'theory' in an extremely inclusive way. For example, Stephen Stich and Shaun Nichols adopt a 'wide interpretation' of the term on which 'just about any internally stored body of information about a given domain [counts] as an

---

[2] T. Nagel, *The View from Nowhere* (Oxford: Oxford University Press, 1986), p. 5: 'A view or form of thought is more objective than another if it relies less on the specifics of the individual's makeup and position in the world, or on the character of the particular type of creature he is.'

internally represented theory of that domain'.[3] Our initial aim is to describe the debate – or at least one aspect of the debate – in a way that takes account of the use of the term 'theory' to include any body of knowledge, belief or information.

Instead of beginning with folk psychology as what the folk know or believe about psychology, we do better to start with folk psychological *practice* – a practice in which we all engage on an everyday basis. We *describe* people as bearers of psychological states. We *explain* people's behaviour (or decisions, or judgements or other psychological states) by appeal to their psychological states. We *predict* people's behaviour (or decisions, or judgements or other psychological states) by relying on assumptions about their psychological states. The debate between the theory theory and the simulation alternative can then be seen as a debate about this three-stranded practice.[4]

---

[3] S. Stich and S. Nichols, 'Folk Psychology: Simulation or Tacit Theory?' in *Folk Psychology,* ed. Davies and Stone, p. 133. See also S. Stich and S. Nichols, 'Second Thoughts on Simulation', in *Mental Simulation,* ed. Davies and Stone; S. Nichols, S. Stich, A. Leslie and D. Klein, 'Varieties of Off-Line Simulation', in *Theories of Theories of Mind,* ed. Carruthers and Smith.

[4] The debate (particularly in its early stages) seems to have been conducted under two assumptions. One is that there is a single question to be asked about folk psychology. The other is that the theory theory and the simulation alternative offer the only two viable approaches to answering that question. But both of these assumptions are flawed. As against the first assumption, we would say that there are many different, and fairly independent, questions to be asked about folk psychological practice, each one of which might be given a theory theory or a simulation theory style of answer. (See T. Stone and M. Davies,

Amongst the many questions that can be asked about folk psychological practice, one question that has been central in much of the recent literature is *the basis question*: What is the basis of our ability to engage in folk psychological practice?[5] Indeed, a great deal of attention has been focused on the basis question applied to just the prediction strand of folk psychological practice. The greater part of this paper shares this relatively narrow focus (sections I and II). Only in the final section do we move to consider explanation and understanding.

I   Prediction, Theory and Simulation

What would be the theory theory's account of folk psychological prediction, and what alternative account would the

'The Mental Simulation Debate: A Progress Report', in *Theories of Theories of Mind,* ed. Carruthers and Smith, pp. 119–20, for nine such questions. No doubt there are more.) As against the second assumption, we would make two brief points. One point is that we cannot simply assume that the two terms, 'theory theory' and 'simulation theory', even when quite generously construed, cover the whole space of possible answers to the questions that are at issue. The other point is that, even for a single question, and even when the theory theory and the simulation alternative are the only approaches in view, the correct answer might be a hybrid, drawing on both approaches.

[5] Elsewhere (Stone and Davies, 'The Mental Simulation Debate: A Progress Report', p. 120), we have put the question this way: 'What resources do mature adult humans draw upon as they go about the business of attributing mental states, and predicting and explaining one another's mental states and actions?' We called it the *explanatory question about normal adult folk psychological practice.* We have now opted to call it the basis question lest the term 'explanatory' suggest that the question relates only to the explanation strand of folk psychological practice.

simulation theory offer? We approach the question indirectly by considering first a case of prediction in a straightforwardly physical domain. How could someone predict the change in pressure of the gas in a cylinder when its temperature is raised?

Prediction in a physical domain

One possibility would be to use an empirical generalization about the way in which the pressure of a volume of gas increases as its temperature increases.[6] In this case, the predictor would be drawing on a body of information about gases, in line with a theory theory account. Another possibility would be to draw on a theory about the movement and energy of gas molecules. By considering the forces exerted on the walls of the cylinder, the predictor might arrive at a prediction of increased pressure without actually having antecedent knowledge of the temperature-pressure law. Or again, the predictor might not draw on any knowledge about gases in general, but simply make use of a formula relating the temperature and pressure of the gas in this particular cylinder. Given the inclusive notion of theory that is in play, this would count as use of a theory.

There is, of course, an alternative to these theory-based strategies for arriving at a prediction about the

[6] The general principle is that pressure is proportional to (absolute) temperature and inversely proportional to volume. In the present context, the volume is constant. If, instead, the temperature is regarded as constant then the resulting principle, that volume is inversely proportional to pressure, is known as Boyle's law.

pressure of the gas in a cylinder, A, after its temperature is raised. We could take another similar cylinder of gas, B, heat it to the temperature in question, and measure the pressure. Provided that the cylinder B really is relevantly similar to cylinder A, this method is liable to yield an accurate prediction. By using the behaviour of the second cylinder of gas as a *simulation* of the behaviour of the first cylinder, we can make a prediction about cylinder A in the absence of any antecedent empirical knowledge about changes in the behaviour of gases under increases in temperature.

In order to use simulation in this way to predict the pressure in gas cylinder A, we need to use another real gas cylinder and we need to raise its temperature in reality. This *simulation in reality* provides for prediction in the absence of antecedent empirical knowledge about the behaviour of gases. A predictor who did not have a second cylinder to hand could, of course, *imagine* having a second gas cylinder. Or a predictor who was armed with a second gas cylinder but did not want to heat it could imagine its temperature being raised. But in order for either of these imaginative strategies to yield a prediction about the pressure in cylinder A, the predictor would need to develop the imagined gas cylinder narrative beyond its starting point ('There is a cylinder of gas. It is heated up. And then...'); and to do this, the predictor would need to draw on some theory – some body of information – about the behaviour of gases.[7]

---

[7] This kind of prediction by simulation in imagination is closely connected with the use of thought experiments in science. Thought experiments are often important in the development of theory, and so it

As a strategy for predicting the pressure in cylinder A, *simulation in imagination* must deploy essentially the same resources as those that are used according to the theory theory account. So, in this case at least, simulation in imagination is *theory-driven* simulation.[8] It is only simulation in reality that constitutes a genuine alternative to the use of empirical theory in prediction.

Psychological prediction

In the folk psychological case, it is clear enough how knowledge of an empirical theory about psychological matters can yield predictions. The body of theory drawn on might consist of some relatively superficial generalizations about (personal level) psychological properties (cf. the laws relating temperature, pressure and volume of gases) or postulates about (subpersonal level) information processing apparatus (cf. postulates about the movement and energy of gas

---

may seem implausible to say that simulation in imagination draws on theory. We need to note, once again, that an inclusive notion of theory is in play, and that in some cases the propositions drawn on will simply be intuitive assumptions about what kinds of thing do, or do not, tend to happen in the physical world. See, for example, R. Sorenson, *Thought Experiments* (Oxford: Oxford University Press, 1992), pp. 52–4, for an account of Stevinus's use (in 1605) of a thought experiment to determine the force needed to keep a ball from moving down an inclined plane. One of the assumptions at work in this case was that perpetual motion does not happen.

[8] See A. I. Goldman, 'Interpretation Psychologized', in *Folk Psychology*, ed. Davies and Stone, p. 85, for the distinction between theory-driven and process-driven simulation.

molecules); or it might be information that is specifically about a particular individual (e.g. someone whom the predictor knows well; cf. a formula linking temperature and pressure in cylinder A).

It is also clear that, in the psychological case, simulation in reality can be an effective way of generating predictions without relying on knowledge of empirical theory. Suppose that I want to predict (i) how a person C will feel (or how soon C will fall over) after drinking a pint of whisky, or (ii) how the Müller-Lyer illusion will look to C, or (iii) how C will feel and what he will decide to do if he is suspended over a cliff on a rope and he cannot find a foothold and his hands are starting to slip, or (iv) whether C will draw the conclusion that something is white from his belief that snow is white.[9] In each case, I can use the strategy of placing another person, D, into the same situation and observing D's reactions. This may well yield a correct prediction about C, provided that C and D are relevantly similar

[9] The whisky example is discussed by Jane Heal, 'How to Think About Thinking', in *Mental Simulation,* ed. Davies and Stone, p. 48, and by Richard Moran, 'Interpretation Theory and the First Person', *Philosophical Quarterly,* 44 (1994), p. 163. The Müller-Lyer illusion is discussed by Robert Gordon, 'Reply to Stich and Nichols', in *Folk Psychology,* ed. Davies and Stone, pp. 175-6. The example of emotional response to a story is discussed by Kendall Walton, 'Spelunking, Simulation and Slime: On Being Moved by Fiction', in *Emotion and the Arts,* ed. M. Hjort and S. Laver (Oxford: Oxford University Press, 1997), and Ian Ravenscroft, 'What Is It Like to be Someone Else?: Simulation and Empathy', *Ratio,* 11 (1998). The case of inference is central in Heal's discussions. We take the example from Allan Gibbard, 'Brains, Thoughts, and Norms', unpublished manuscript.

((i) in the way that alcohol affects their bodily constitution; (ii) in the way that their visual systems work; (iii) in the way that they experience and act on emotions; (iv) in the way that they reason). To the extent that I, myself, am relevantly similar to C, I have an option that is not available to me in the case of gas cylinder simulation in reality; namely, I can place myself into those situations and observe my own reactions. I drink a pint of whisky, or look at the two lines, or dangle perilously over a cliff, or draw out some simple inferences from my belief that snow is white. Indeed, in discussions of mental simulation in reality, it is usually this option of using oneself in a simulation that is considered.[10]

[10] S. Stich and S. Nichols, 'Cognitive Penetrability, Rationality and Restricted Simulation', *Mind and Language,* 12 (1997), p. 302, call this 'actual-situation-simulation'. It is important to avoid a possible confusion here. In some important examples, a protagonist has a false belief about her situation: there is a difference between the situation as it actually is and the situation as the protagonist takes it to be. A subject who is asked to predict what the protagonist will think or do may make an incorrect prediction by focusing on the situation as it actually is rather than the situation as the protagonist takes it to be. (This is what very young children tend to do. There is a substantial empirical literature on the *false belief task.* See, for example, H. Wimmer and J. Perner, 'Beliefs About Beliefs: Representation and Constraining Function of Wrong Beliefs in Young Children's Understanding of Deception', *Cognition,* 13 (1983), pp. 103–28.) But this predictive strategy is not what Stich and Nichols mean by 'actual-situation-simulation' (and not what we mean by 'simulation in reality'). Rather, actual-situation-simulation would involve placing myself into the same situation as the protagonist and making myself (perhaps *per impossibile*) subject to the same false belief.

But it is *mental simulation in imagination* that is central for the simulation theory. We saw that gas cylinder simulation in imagination needs to be driven by empirical theory. Does the same go for mental simulation? It seems clear that if, with a view to making a prediction about C, I imagine placing another person D into the same situation, then I shall need to draw on theory in order to develop the simulation beyond this starting point. But if what I imagine is actually being in the situation,[11] then simulation in imagination might allow a prediction about C to be generated. What this prospect seems to depend on is the possibility that my imagining being in a situation engages the same psychological or mental processes in me as would be operative if I were really in that situation.

Consider, then, the conditions under which simulation in imagination would yield correct predictions in the four sample cases that we have mentioned, (i) If simulation in imagination is to yield a correct prediction about how C will feel after drinking a pint of whisky, then imagining drinking a pint of whisky must produce in me feelings of giddiness leading to a fall – or at least imagined feelings of giddiness leading to an imagined fall. (ii) In the case of the Müller-Lyer illusion, imagining the two lines and the arrowheads must lead to a visual experience – real or imagined – as of one line being longer than the other. (iii) When I imagine being suspended over a cliff on a rope, this act of imagination must lead to real or imagined feelings of fear

---

[11] B. A. O. Williams, 'Imagination and the Self', in *Problems of the Self* (Cambridge: Cambridge University Press, 1973).

and panic, (iv) When I imagine believing that snow is white (or, more to the point, when I imagine believing that, say, butter is white – something that I do not, in reality, believe), this must lead to the real or imagined act of judging that something is white.

We take it that the facts about these cases are roughly as follows.

(i) Imagining drinking a pint of whisky does not, in and of itself, produce real or imagined feelings of giddiness. The bodily processes that lead up to a feeling of giddiness are not engaged by the imagined consumption of alcohol in the same way that they would be engaged by the real consumption of alcohol. If my simulation in imagination does move forward from the drinking to the feelings, then this is because I am bringing to bear some empirical knowledge about how people typically feel – or about how I usually feel – after consuming large quantities of alcohol.

(ii) Imagining the lines and the arrowheads does not, in and of itself, generate the Müller-Lyer illusion in imagination. The visual processes that give rise to the illusion are not engaged by the imagined confrontation with that array of lines and arrowheads in the same way that they would be by the real presentation of the array,

(iii) On the other hand, imagining being in that dangerous situation, dangling at the end of a rope, may well lead to real feelings of fear or panic, without my drawing on any empirical theory about how people in that kind of situation typically feel. Imagined danger may engage a range of bodily and emotional processes in somewhat the same way that real danger does.

(iv) Finally, imagining believing the premises of an argument (that butter is white) certainly can lead me to an imagined judgement of the conclusion (that something is white), without my using any antecedently known empirical theory about how people typically reason. There is an important contrast between the case of reasoning from imagined beliefs and the case of emotional response to imagined danger. The bodily symptoms of fear or panic may well be real, even though the danger is only imagined. But in the case of reasoning, if my commitment to the premises is only an imagined commitment, then my judgement of the conclusion is similarly imagined rather than real. The process leading from one to the other is, however, real, and not merely imaginary, reasoning; and that real reasoning may also prompt a real judgement, namely, the conditional judgement that if the premises were true then so would be the conclusion.

What all this suggests is that the prospects for psychological prediction by simulation in imagination, without the use of empirical theory, are not utterly forlorn. It may also seem to suggest that we need to set about the task of cataloguing which psychological processes are engaged in the same way by imagined inputs as by real inputs. But while real interest and importance would attach to that cataloguing project, it is also important to note that it is not just a brute fact that imagining premises engages our reasoning abilities in the same way that really believing the premises does.[12] Rather, the explanation of this fact is that reason relations (such as entailment relations) obtain, and are known by any thinker to obtain, amongst imagined or hypothesized thought contents, in just the same way that they obtain amongst believed thought contents. When I simulate C's reasoning in imagination, a theory may well be used. But it is not an empirical theory about how people happen typically to reason. Rather, it is a normative theory about right reasoning; and it is the very same theory that I can use when I engage in reasoning from premises that I actually believe.[13]

Although the simulation of reasoning may involve deployment of normative principles, the simulation theory is not (even when restricted to reasoning) to be equated with what might be called the *normative theory theory*. It is possible to know normative principles relating to an activity in which one does not, oneself, engage. But the simulation theory is clearly not proposing that we make predictions by the disengaged use of a set of normative principles about reasoning.[14] Rather, normative principles may be used in

---

[12] This point is stressed, for example, by Goldman, 'Interpretation Psychologized', p. 85, and by Heal, 'How to Think About Thinking', pp. 34-5.

[13] See Stone and Davies, 'The Mental Simulation Debate: A Progress Report', pp. 136-7.

[14] See S. Blackburn, 'Theory, Observation and Drama', in *Folk Psychology*, ed. Davies and Stone, p. 283: 'Theorizing under a normative umbrella is still *theorizing*. It could, it seems, be done quite externally, in the light of a sufficient stock of principles telling what it would be right or wrong to think or feel in some situation. . .'. Janet Levin, 'Folk Psychology and

simulation because they are already available to us when we ourselves engage in reasoning. When we use those normative principles, our reasoning becomes what Tyler Burge describes as critical reasoning.

> Critical reasoning is reasoning that involves an ability to recognise and effectively employ reasonable criticism or support for reasons and reasoning. It is reasoning guided by an appreciation, use, and assessment of reasons and reasoning as such. As a critical reasoner, one not only reasons. One recognises reasons as reasons...
>
> Essential to carrying out critical reasoning is using one's knowledge of what constitutes good reasons to guide one's actual first-order reasoning.[15]

Not all reasoning is critical reasoning. But it is arguable that the possibility of critical reasoning is an essential part of normal adult reasoning as we know it.[16]

The point we have reached is that predicting the conclusions of another person's (theoretical or practical) reasoning appears to be a particularly favourable case for a simulation theory answer to the basis question about the

---

the Simulationist Challenge', *Acta Analytica,* 14 (1995), p. 91, also makes the point that if we use a normative theory to predict what inferences a person will make then this does not yet seem to involve anything that is 'in any serious sense *a simulation*'.

[15] T. Burge, 'Our Entitlement to Self-Knowledge', *Proceedings of the Aristotelian Society,* 96 (1996), pp. 98–9.

[16] Burge, 'Our Entitlement to Self-Knowledge', p. 99: 'A non-critical reasoner reasons blind, without appreciating reasons as reasons. Animals and children reason in this way.'

prediction strand of folk psychological practice. Of course, in order to reach a correct prediction about C's conclusions by simulating his reasoning in imagination, I need to take account of differences between C and myself. If C believes that butter is white, while I do not, then C may arrive at the judgement that butter and snow are the same colour, given that snow is white, whereas I would not myself draw that conclusion. But I can take account of this difference between C and me within the simulation, without needing to draw on any empirical information about how people who believe that butter is white tend to reason. Rather, in imagination I take on the belief that butter is white and then, given the premises that snow is white and that butter is white, I conclude that butter and snow are the same colour. That is what right reasoning requires.

Predicting how someone will feel after drinking a pint of whisky, in contrast, is a good case for a theory theory answer to the basis question. Consequently, predicting the conclusions that will be reached by someone reasoning after drinking a pint of whisky also depends on at least some contribution from empirical theory. If C has just drunk a pint of whisky and I have not, then I need to take account of this difference between him and me when I try to simulate his reasoning in imagination. Even if I correctly take on C's premises in imagination *and* imagine drinking a pint of whisky, still my predictions about C's conclusions are liable to be incorrect, unless I bring to bear some empirical information about how whisky affects (C's) reasoning. Here, correct prediction requires an intrusion of theory. But this is not to say that, in the case of the inebriated C, my prediction strategy must owe everything to empirical theory and nothing to mental simulation. The empirical information that I draw on might take the form of information about the ways in which someone in C's condition is liable to depart from right reasoning. In that case, I could first use my own reasoning ability to work out what would be a correct conclusion to draw from C's premises and then tweak my prediction in the light of that empirical information.

The epistemology of prediction by simulation

Let us now consider, in a little more detail, how prediction by simulation would work. We have already noted that, in the case of the gas cylinders, prediction by simulation in reality relies on some assumption of relevant similarity between cylinder B and cylinder A. One form that this assumption can take is that cylinder B is a typical member of a class, G, of gas cylinders of which A is also a member. Heating the gas in cylinder B and measuring its pressure can then be conceived as an *experiment*, licensing a general claim about temperature and pressure in gas cylinders in the class G. Since cylinder A is assumed to be a member of this class, the experimentally licensed generalization can be applied to it. Essentially the same kind of account could be given, in the psychological case, of the role of the assumption of relevant similarity between person D and person C. And if, in a case of mental simulation in reality, I use myself instead of another person D, then an assumption of relevant similarity between me and C plays the same role again.

Placing myself in the situation can be conceived as an experiment.

It would seem plausible, then, that there is no very deep difference between the epistemological status of predictions based on simulation and predictions that rely on experimentally licensed knowledge of empirical generalizations. Furthermore, it would appear that, in the case of mental simulation in imagination, much the same account would be given, but with an extra empirical assumption to the effect that the processes in me that are engaged by imagined inputs work in the same way as the processes in me, and in C, that are engaged by real inputs. The cataloguing project mentioned on p. 60 above would then be seen as the project of assessing the extent to which that empirical assumption is warranted.

However, the account that we have sketched of simulation of reasoning in imagination may open the possibility of a distinctive epistemology of psychological prediction. What the normative theory of right reasoning tells the simulator is that the conclusion – say, that something is white – is the right thing to think, given the premise – say, that snow is white, or that butter is white. This normative judgement about what is the thing to think does not, by itself, yield a prediction about C, of course. The simulator also needs an assumption that C will think the thing that is the thing to think. That is a defeasible assumption in any given case. But it may enjoy a default status, nevertheless, since unexplained departures from these normative requirements of reasoning call in question our attributions to C of thoughts with such contents as that snow is white or that butter is white.[17] This route to prediction goes via a norma-tive judgement (this is the thing to think in such-and-such a situation) and an assumption about interpretation (C will think the thing that is the thing to think). It is to be contrasted with a route that goes via an empirical judgement (this is what I think when placed experimentally in such-and-such a situation) and an assumption of similarity (C is relevantly like me).

II Prediction Failure

We have distinguished between simulation in reality and simulation in imagination as methods of prediction. Simulation in reality can certainly be an effective way of generating predictions without relying on empirical know-ledge. But the prospects for prediction by simulation in imagination depend on the possibility that imagining being in a situation should engage the same psychological or mental processes as would be operative if one were really in that situation. We considered a range of examples and

---

[17] The general idea here is familiar from discussions of the principles involved in radical interpretation. Some advocates of mental simulation contrast the simulation approach with the rationality approach, and so would not adopt the account of the epistemology of psychological prediction that is sketched here. See, for example, Goldman, 'Interpretation Psychologized'. On the other hand, R. M. Gordon, 'Simulation Without Introspection or Inference from Me to You', in *Mental Simulation,* ed. Davies and Stone, can be seen as resisting the idea that the epistemology of prediction by simulation is the same as that of prediction by way of empirical theory.

concluded that predicting the results of another person's reasoning is a good case for simulation in imagination while predicting how someone will feel after drinking a pint of whisky is not. But while it might be agreed that predicting the conclusions of reasoning could be achieved by mental simulation, this does not settle the question whether prediction is in fact achieved in that way. Perhaps, despite the availability of simulation, we ordinarily make such predictions by relying on an empirical theory about how people reason.

The basis question with which we began is an empirical question about our three-stranded folk psychological practice, and we have been focusing on the question as it applies to the prediction strand. But we have so far said nothing about the kinds of empirical evidence that would count in favour of one or another answer to the basis question. In a series of important papers, Stich and Nichols have urged that the phenomenon of *prediction failure* is strong evidence in support of a theory theory answer to the question about the basis of our prediction practice.[18]

In our everyday folk psychological practice, we sometimes make wrong predictions. Stich and Nichols argue that this happens because our prediction method is *cognitively penetrable* – that is, our psychological predictions are

---

[18] 'Folk Psychology: Simulation or Tacit Theory?', 'Second Thoughts on Simulation', and 'Varieties of Off-Line Simulation'. We note again that Stich and Nichols use the term 'theory' in an extremely inclusive sense.

influenced by our antecedent knowledge or beliefs about the psychological domain. This kind of explanation of prediction failure is available to the theory theorist but unavailable, Stich and Nichols say, to the friend of mental simulation. So the existence of prediction failure is a crucial test of the empirical adequacy of the two competing accounts of the causal basis of our prediction practice, and favours the theory theory account. Thus, on the one hand:

> One virtue of using a simulation to predict the behavior of a system is that you need have no serious idea about the principles governing the target system. You just run the simulation and watch what happens ... In predictions based on simulation, what you don't know won't hurt you ... If there is some quirk of the human decision-making system, something quite unknown to most people that leads the system to behave in an unexpected way in certain circumstances, the accuracy of prediction based on simulations should not be adversely affected. If you provide the simulation with the right pretend input, it should simulate (and thus predict) the unexpected output.[19]

But, on the other hand:

> Just the opposite is true for predictions that rely on a theory. If we are making predictions on the basis of a set of laws or principles, and if there are some unexpected aspects of the system's behavior that are not captured by our principles, then our predictions about those aspects

---

[19] 'Folk Psychology: Simulation or Tacit Theory?' p. 150.

of the system's behavior should be less accurate. Theory based predictions are sensitive to what we know and don't know about the laws that govern the system; they are cognitively penetrable.[20]

The dialectical situation that Stich and Nichols sketch is especially clear when we contrast theory-based prediction and prediction by simulation in reality. Thus, consider again our prediction of the pressure in gas cylinder A. If someone has a false theory about the behaviour of gases, then a theory-based prediction about cylinder A is liable to be false. But, if the predictor uses the behaviour of cylinder B as a simulation of the behaviour of cylinder A, then the prediction arrived at should be correct. Because the prediction method does not draw on any antecedently believed empirical theory about the behaviour of gases, the prediction can, in principle, be insulated from any false theoretical beliefs that are antecedently held by the predictor.[21] If someone makes an incorrect prediction about the pressure of the gas in cylinder A after it has been heated then either the predictor is not using simulation as the prediction method or else the simulation is flawed in one of two ways. It may be that cylinder B is not relevantly similar to cylinder A or it

---

[20] Ibid.

[21] In section I, we noted the similarity between gas cylinder simulation in reality and the use of experiments to establish generalizations about how gas cylinders in a certain class generally behave. The present point, that simulation in reality yields predictions that are insulated from antecedently held theory, is analogous to the point that experiments are apt to yield results that conflict with antecedently held theory.

may be that the gas in cylinder B was not heated to the correct temperature.[22]

In the psychological case, just the same points can be made. If, in order to arrive at a prediction about C, I use D (or myself) for a simulation in reality, then the prediction should be correct. If it is incorrect then either D is not relevantly similar to C (or I am not similar to C), or else D (or I) was not placed into the correct situation (that is, the simulation was not provided with the correct inputs). But the central case of mental simulation is simulation in imagination. Is the dialectical situation the same here? There is some reason to allow that it is. Someone who claims that mental simulation provides even a possible account of folk psychological prediction relies on the idea that imagining being in a situation may engage the same psychological or mental processes as would be operative if one were really in that situation. For some examples, such as the situation in which one drinks a pint of whisky, the idea has no plausibility. But the advocate of mental simulation has to maintain that there are other cases where the idea is plausible, and we have suggested that these would include cases of theoretical and practical reasoning. So, it appears that prediction failure relating to reasoning would present a problem for anyone offering a mental simulation answer to the basis question about folk psychological prediction. Certainly, this is what

[22] Someone using simulation in reality as a prediction method may, of course, refuse to accept the result of a simulation if it conflicts with an antecedently held theory, and may judge that the simulation must be flawed in some way. The same goes for experimentation.

Stich and Nichols have argued; and they have gone on to present examples of this kind of prediction failure.

Examples of prediction failure

There is no shortage of surprising experimental psychological data about conclusions that people draw and decisions that they take. The very fact that we find the data surprising indicates, of course, that we ourselves would have made incorrect predictions about what the subjects in the experiments would conclude or what they would decide. We shall describe two of these examples.[23]

Position effects: right bias in selecting goods

Shoppers are presented with a display of what are, in fact, identical samples of some product. They are asked to assess the quality of these samples and then – by way of payment for participating in the survey – to select one sample to keep. The result is that the shoppers' selections show a bias

---

[23] These two examples are discussed by Stich and Nichols, 'Folk Psychology: Simulation or Tacit Theory?' p. 151, along with the example of belief perseverance; see R. Nisbet and L. Ross, *Human Inference* (Englewood Cliffs, NJ: Prentice Hall, 1980), pp. 175–9. In 'Second Thoughts on Simulation', pp. 101–2, they introduce the further example of failure to predict how subjects will behave in Milgram's obedience experiment. S. Nichols, S. Stich and A. Leslie, 'Choice Effects and the Ineffectiveness of Simulation', *Mind and Language,* 10 (1995), pp. 442–4, also discuss an example of subjects' failure to predict how they themselves will behave when asked to put a price on an article that they own.

towards samples near the right-hand end of the display over samples near the left-hand end.[24]

Most people are surprised to hear the result of this experiment; they would predict that shoppers' selections would be random. If these predictions are arrived at by mental simulation, then simulation is generating incorrect predictions. Yet it is reasonable to assume that the people who are asked to predict the outcome of the experiment are relevantly similar to the subjects in the experiment (the shoppers).

The Langer effect

Two groups of subjects are sold lottery tickets for $1 each. Subjects in one group are allowed to choose their lottery ticket (choice condition); subjects in the other group are simply given a ticket (nochoice condition). Subjects are then (under some pretext or other) asked to be ready to sell their ticket back to the experimenter, and are asked to set a sell-back price. The result is that subjects in the choice condition set very much higher prices on average than subjects in the no-choice condition (over $8 versus just under $2).[25]

Most people are surprised to hear the result of this experiment. For example, Stich and Nichols report anecdotal evidence of presenting undergraduate students with a description of the experiment and asking them to predict

[24] Nisbet and Ross, *Human Inference*, p. 207.
[25] E. Langer, 'The Illusion of Control', *Journal of Personality and Social Psychology*, 32 (1975), pp. 311–28. The example is discussed at length in Nichols et al., 'Varieties of Off-Line Simulation'.

what the subjects would do. The students failed to predict the difference between the sell-back prices set by subjects in the choice condition and subjects in the no-choice condition. If these predictions are arrived at by mental simulation – the students simulating first being in one condition and then in the other – then simulation is generating incorrect predictions. Yet it is reasonable to assume that the students who are asked to predict the outcome of the experiment are relevantly similar to the original subjects.

Response on behalf of the simulation theory

Given the way that the argument about prediction failure has been set up, it will appear that the defender of mental simulation is bound to make a move analogous to saying that gas cylinder B was not heated to the correct temperature. That is, the defender of simulation must say that, in these cases of prediction failure, the (pretended) inputs to the predictor's simulation in imagination are in crucial respects different from the inputs that engaged the psychological processes of the subjects in the real experiments. This is, indeed, the way in which advocates of mental simulation have responded.

Thus, for example, Robert Gordon comments on the example of right bias in selecting goods that, 'unlike the subjects in the original experiment, the subject in the imagination experiment [the person trying to predict how shoppers will behave] must be told that the items on display are identical (and thus of equal quality)'.[26] In a similar vein,

[26] Gordon, 'Reply to Stich and Nichols', p. 176.

Paul Harris notes that a person trying to predict the outcome of the Langer experiment using simulation:

> needs to simulate the vacillation and eventual commitment of the free-choice subjects. Moreover, in making that simulation they must also set aside the tacit reminder embedded in a narrative that juxtaposes the two groups of subjects, namely that any lottery ticket whether selected or allocated, has the same likelihood of winning. Subjects in the experiment who were offered a free choice had no knowledge of the other group, and by implication, no such tacit reminder.[27]

This is a good initial move to make on behalf of the simulation theory. Someone who is aiming to make a prediction by simulation in imagination must imagine being in the very situation that the subjects in the original experiment were in. And this must be done in such a way as to offer the simulator's psychological processes inputs that are equivalent to the inputs that engaged the original subjects' psychological processes. In a case of simulation of reasoning, the simulator must take on in imagination the very same premises that were available to the original subject. But, as Gordon and Harris point out, the way in which the experimental situation is described may prevent this condition from being met.

There is a quite general point here; namely, that the way in which the situation to be imagined is described can make a huge difference to the prospects for successful

---

[27] P. L. Harris, 'From Simulation to Folk Psychology: The Case for Development', in *Folk Psychology*, ed. Davies and Stone, p. 218.

simulation. Consider the case of a lexical decision experiment. Letter strings are flashed up on a computer screen – some strings form real words, and some form (pronounceable) non-words. The subject has to decide whether each letter string is a word or a non-word and press one or another button to indicate this decision. Suppose that I am asked to predict what decisions subjects will make. Simulation in reality is no problem here: I can just sit in front of the screen myself. But if I have to simulate this experimental regime in imagination, then some ways of describing the input make my task nearly impossible. I might, for example, be given a description of the screen display in terms of the pattern of light and dark pixels that form the image of the letter string. If, on the other hand, the screen display is described by the letters being named in order, then I may very well be successful in simulating the performance of subjects in the experiment and thus predicting their responses. This successful prediction would not seem to depend on antecedent knowledge about how normal subjects respond to this or that letter string in a lexical decision experiment. Rather, I would just make what I take to be the correct decision about each imagined letter string, and then assume that other subjects would make the correct decision too. In doing this, I would make use of stored information; but it would be information about lexical items, not information about normal subjects' lexical decisions.

In our view, this line of response (in terms of *wrong inputs*) enables the simulation theorist to fend off the initial versions of the objection from prediction failure. But it does not resolve the debate in favour of either side because the response simply invites the theory theorist to improve the design of the prediction experiment so as to rule out the wrong inputs response. Thus, for example, Nichols, Stich, Leslie and Klein report a prediction experiment in which subjects in one group watch a videotape of a subject in the choice condition of a Langer-style experiment and are asked to predict the subject's sell-back price, while subjects in another group similarly watch a videotape of a subject in the no-choice condition.[28] As in the original Langer experiment, subjects in the choice condition set significantly higher sell-back prices than subjects in the no-choice condition. But there was no significant difference between the prices predicted by subjects shown the choice condition videotape and the prices predicted by subjects shown the video of the no-choice condition. Thus, even with a videotape to help them imagine the experimental situation, subjects are not reliably able to reach correct predictions.

There is no doubt that discussion of these examples can be continued, with the defender of prediction by mental simulation in imagination deploying variations on the wrong inputs theme.[29] But there is a slightly different kind of response to these examples that is suggested by our earlier

---

[28] Nichols et al., 'Varieties of Off-Line Simulation', pp. 49–52.

[29] See for example, A. Kühberger, J. Perner, M. Schulte and R. Leingruber, 'Choice or No Choice: Is the Langer Effect Evidence Against Simulation?', *Mind and Language*, 10 (1995), p. 433: '[I]t is difficult to ensure that simulator participants are provided with sufficient information about exactly the right combination of factors that produces the Langer effect.' Kühberger et al. refer to the requirement that 'the imagined situation captures the relevant features of the

reflections on the prospects for psychological prediction by simulation in imagination (pp. 57–62 above).

The circumscribed domain of prediction by mental simulation

There are all kinds of factors that may affect a person's theoretical or practical reasoning, such as whether the person believes that butter is white, or whether the person has just drunk a pint of whisky. Some of these factors can readily be taken into account by someone attempting a prediction by mental simulation in imagination, while others cannot. Showing me a videotape of a subject drinking

---

simulated person's actual situation' as the requirement of *imaginative adequacy* (p. 424).

A theory theorist may object that the use of the wrong inputs response by the friend of mental simulation is ad hoc and that the defender of the simulation theory in the face of examples of prediction failure should be willing to state in advance under what conditions the requirement of imaginative adequacy would be met. (See Stich and Nichols, 'Second Thoughts on Simulation', p. 102.) But it is not clear that the theory theorist's own approach to examples of prediction failure is any more principled. The theory theorist's explanation of prediction failure is in terms of the predictor's use of an incomplete or false theory about psychological matters, or the predictor's use of incorrect initial conditions to instantiate correct generalizations. But no independently motivated account of the exact nature of the predictor's failure is provided. (This point is made in an unpublished paper by Ian Ravenscroft, and also by Stich and Nichols, 'Cognitive Penetrability, Rationality and Restricted Simulation', p. 323, who credit it to Meredith and Michael Williams.)

a pint of whisky before engaging in some reasoning will not enable me to predict the outcome of the subject's reasoning, however accurately I may imagine the subject's situation. As we noted on p. 59 above, what I need is empirical information about the effects of whisky drinking.[30] (Recall, too, that the use of this empirical information need not wholly supplant engagement in mental simulation.)

The fact that prediction by mental simulation in imagination requires an intrusion of theory in such cases of 'non-rational' influences has been recognised from the beginning of the contemporary debate.[31] Furthermore, it seems quite likely that some of the factors at work in producing the Langer effect or the right bias in selecting goods may be more like whisky than like reasons. For example, most people who are told about the position effects experiment find it surprising that the shoppers' selections show a bias towards samples near the right-hand end of the display. They would predict a random distribution of selections.

---

[30] Alternatively, I could drink a pint of whisky myself, combining simulation of the subject's beliefs in imagination with simulation of the subject's whisky drinking in reality. This might enable me to make a correct prediction, if whisky has the same effect on my reasoning from hypothesised contents as on the subject's reasoning from believed contents. However, it is important to note that the effects of my drinking the whisky will not be restricted to my simulation of the subject; my reasoning in my own person will be perturbed as well. This might be a disadvantage if I need to think carefully and accurately about how best to act towards the subject.

[31] J. Heal, 'Replication and Functionalism', in *Folk Psychology,* ed. Davies and Stone, p. 48; Harris, 'From Simulation to Folk Psychology: The Case for Development', p. 219.

A plausible explanation for this prediction is that there is no evident reason to make one selection rather than another; the fact that a sample is towards the right-hand end of the display scarcely constitutes a justification for selecting that sample rather than any of the others.[32] It is not *ad hoc*, then, to maintain that these examples of prediction failure fall outside the proper domain of prediction by mental simulation unaided by empirical theory.

A narrow circumscription of this domain is explicit in Heal's work:

> The kind of simulationism I would like to defend says that the only cases that the simulationist should confidently claim are those where (a) the starting point is an item or collection of items with content, (b) the outcome is a further item with content, and (c) the latter

---

[32] So-called non-rational influences may have their effects in a very direct way – by-passing reasoning altogether – as, perhaps, in the case of the shoppers. But they may also work by making something that is not in fact a reason for acting in a certain way nevertheless appear to be a reason. We are not committing ourselves to any specific account of the various examples of prediction failure. Indeed, we are not even committed to the idea that the examples of prediction failure all involve non-rational influences. Perhaps subjects in the Langer-style experiment have good reasons for setting their sell-back prices, but those reasons are somehow obscured from subjects in the prediction experiment. In that case, a defender of simulation will, in the end, be right to use some version of the wrong inputs response. What we are pointing out is just that there is a different kind of response – in terms of non-rational influences – that is, in principle, available to the simulation theorist. See J. Heal, 'Simulation and Cognitive Penetrability', *Mind and Language*, 11 (1996), pp. 60–6.

content is rationally or intelligibly linked to that of the earlier item(s).[33]

But her proposal faces an objection. In many cases of prediction failure, the subjects about whom the predictions are made seem to depart in some way from right reasoning. But, in some other cases of equally flawed reasoning, correct prediction seems to be quite straightforward. In these latter cases, why do not the non-rational influences put the reasoning beyond the range of prediction by mental simulation?

Consider an example discussed by Daniel Kahnemann and Amos Tversky.[34] At a flying school, instructors adopt a policy of responding positively to good performance (such as successful execution of complex manoeuvres) and negatively to bad performance. When reviewing this policy, they note that pilots who do particularly well and are praised are likely to perform less well next time, while pilots who perform particularly badly and are criticized are likely to do better at their next attempt. The instructors conclude that, contrary to what psychologists tell

---

[33] Heal, 'Simulation and Cognitive Penetrability', p. 56.

[34] D. Kahnemann and A. Tversky, 'On the Psychology of Prediction', in *Judgment Under Uncertainty: Heuristics and Biases,* ed. D. Kahnemann, P. Slovic and A. Tversky (Cambridge: Cambridge University Press, 1982), pp. 67–8. The example was used by Ned Block (in conversation) to make the objection under discussion here. Essentially the same objection against Heal's circumscribed version of simulation theory is pressed by Stich and Nichols, 'Cognitive Penetrability, Rationality and Restricted Simulation'.

us about positive reinforcement, rewarding good performance is not an effective training method.

Most people find the flight instructors' conclusion
to be quite unsurprising; it is just as they would predict. Yet
the instructors' reasoning is flawed; it overlooks the phenomenon of regression towards the mean. (A pilot who has
reached a certain level of competence and performs out-
standingly well on one trial is likely to perform less well on
the next trial, independently of the reaction of the
instructor.) Is this not a problem, the objector asks, for the
idea that the proper domain of prediction by mental simulation is the domain of rational linkages?

It is clearly relevant to note, here, that the reasoning
of the people who successfully predict the instructors' conclusion is flawed in just the same way as the reasoning of
those instructors. But that point is liable to suggest, again,
that there is something wrong with the proposal to circum-
scribe the proper domain of prediction by mental simulation
in terms of the contrast between right reasoning and non-
rational influences. What matters for mental simulation, the
objector may say, is not rationality but similarity.[35]
Prediction by mental simulation will be successful just where
a process that operates in imagination in the predictor is
relevantly similar to the process operating in reality in the
subject about whom the prediction is being made. By that
account, probabilistic reasoning that overlooks regression
towards the mean falls squarely within the proper domain

[35] Dan Sperber (in conversation) pressed the objection in this form.

of prediction by mental simulation, since the error is one that virtually everyone is disposed to make.

Our view is that it is possible to defend Heal's circumscription of the proper domain of mental simulation by drawing on two ideas from section I: the idea of a normative theory and the idea of a distinctive epistemology of psychological prediction. First, as critical reasoners, we are each in possession of a normative theory of right reasoning (p. 61 above). We are also subject to non-rational influences and so we are all liable, on occasion, to reason in ways that are out of line with our normative principles. However, some departures from right reasoning may actually be sanctioned by our normative principles; that is, our normative theory may itself be flawed. Second, in virtue of our possession of a normative theory, we can arrive at judgements about what is the thing to think in a certain situation; and we can use those judgements, coupled with an assumption that the subject will think the thing that is the thing to think, in order to arrive at predictions. This predictive strategy can bestow a distinctive kind of epistemic warrant (p. 63 above). When a subject departs from right reasoning in a way that is out of line with our normative theory, this strategy will yield a wrong prediction, and will need to be augmented by empirical information about the non-rational influences at work on the subject. When the subject departs from right reasoning in a way that is sanctioned by our normative theory, in contrast, this strategy will yield a correct prediction. But it will be a prediction that does not constitute knowledge, since it is based on two false claims – that this is the thing to think, and that the subject will think the thing that is the thing to think – where the error in the second claim compensates for the error in the first.

On this account, if the predictor and the subject share an incorrect normative theory then the predictions arrived at will be fortuitously, rather than knowledgeably, correct. The narrowly circumscribed domain of mental simulation is the domain of knowledgeable predictions that are arrived at by that epistemologically distinctive route.

However, we should also consider what happens if the predictor learns about the importance of not ignoring regression towards the mean. For now the predictor will, provided that he or she is properly attentive, arrive at a correct judgment about what is the thing for the flight instructors, for example, to think. But the predictor may also recognize that, in this kind of case, most people are apt not to think the thing that is the thing to think. So, the predictor will take this empirical information into account when arriving at a prediction about the flight instructors. It may be that the informed predictor characterizes the way in which most people depart from right reasoning simply as the way in which he or she used to reason before learning about regression towards the mean. Perhaps, indeed, the predictor still finds it all too easy to slip back into that flawed pattern of reasoning. In that case, the predictor may suspend his or her recently acquired normative knowledge, and engage in a piece of not wholly critical reasoning, so as to arrive at a correct – and knowledgeably correct – prediction about the flight instructors.

This is quite properly regarded as a piece of prediction by mental simulation. But the route that it takes is via an empirical judgement (this is what I used to think – how I used to reason) and an assumption of similarity (the flight instructors are relevantly like me as I used to be). So, while the distinctive epistemology of prediction that goes with the idea of a normative theory of right reasoning is of some importance, it would be wrong for us to suppose that all knowledgeable prediction by mental simulation exhibits that distinctive epistemology.

III   Simulation, Explanation and Understanding

We began with the three strands of folk psychological practice – description, explanation, and prediction – but we have been almost exclusively concerned with folk psychological prediction, and with the basis question concerning that strand of our practice. In this final section, we turn briefly to folk psychological explanation.

Explanation and generalizations

Suppose that we want to explain the increase of pressure in our gas cylinder that results from an increase in temperature. The theory theory account of prediction (pp. 55–6 above) can readily be converted into an account of explanation by subsumption.[36] The conjunction of an increase in

---

[36] C. Hempel, *Aspects of Scientific Explanation* (New York: The Free Press, 1965), who provides the seminal account of the deductive-nomological model of explanation, regards the distinction between prediction and explanation as being merely pragmatic.

temperature and an increase in pressure is subsumed under the temperature-pressure law. The truth of this generalization is not, however, something brute. The relatively superficial temperature-pressure law belongs, not only with a more general principle relating temperature, pressure and volume, but also with a body of empirical theory about the movement and energy of gas molecules, and about forces exerted on the walls of the cylinder. In terms of this theory, it is possible to give a mechanistic account of how it is that the relatively superficial law is true – of how the temperature-pressure connection is implemented. In short, according to the theory theory account, prediction and explanation go naturally together, and a predictor who knows not only the superficial generalization but also the broader body of theory is able to achieve an explanatory understanding of the predicted increase in pressure.

In the folk psychological case, too, the theory theory account of prediction goes along with an account of explanation. Knowledge of a body of psychological theory provides the resources for explanations that work by subsuming events under causal generalizations. There may be variations on this theme. Some theory theorists will regard knowledge of relatively superficial psychological generalizations as the visible tip of an iceberg of more elaborated tacit knowledge, while others will commit themselves only to knowledge in the ordinary sense of the term. Some theory theorists will regard cognitive scientific theories about subpersonal level information processing machinery as offering deeper explanations of psychological matters, while others will hold hard to the personal level. But the general picture is clear.

Given that familiar picture of explanation by subsumption, it may seem obvious that the basis question about the explanation strand of folk psychological practice has a ready answer in terms of the theory theory, but cannot be answered in terms of the simulation alternative. Explanation requires generalizations; but mental simulation is supposed not to depend on antecedent knowledge of psychological generalizations. However, what seems obvious is not quite correct.

Consider again the case of the gas cylinders. We have noted already (p. 62 above) the similarity between prediction by simulation in reality and the use of experiments to license generalizations. So, gas cylinder simulation, carried out without antecedent knowledge about the behaviour of gases, could yield knowledge of generalizations that could, in turn, be used in subsumptive explanations. Gas cylinder simulation in reality would naturally be called *black box simulation*; we simply give the simulation device (gas cylinder B) a temperature as input and receive back from it a pressure as output. Consistently with that description, the experimentally licensed generalizations would be superficial and, because of the lack of explanatory depth, the simulation would scarcely provide any explanatory understanding of the predicted increase in pressure. But still, the basic point remains. Simulation, conceived as experiment, may yield knowledge of generalizations under which events can be subsumed. We could call this *simulation-driven theory*.

So also, in the folk psychological case, simulation can be regarded as experiment and may yield knowledge of empirical generalizations. This is particularly clear in the case of simulation in reality. By drinking pints of whisky, looking at pairs of lines, dangling on ropes and drawing inferences, I may not only arrive at predictions about another person C (pp. 57–62 above). I may also, by induction from these bouts of simulation considered as experiments, arrive at empirical generalizations under which events in the mental life of C may be subsumed. This is also true – though over a circumscribed domain – for mental simulation in imagination. When I simulate C's reasoning in imagination, I draw on a normative, rather than an empirical, theory about reasoning. But I may arrive at empirical generalizations by induction on the results of simulation in imagination; and, to the extent that mental simulation may yield correct predictions, it may also yield correct generalizations.[37]

Simulation and understanding

If explanation is conceived as subsumption under generalizations, then the debate initiated by the basis question about the explanation strand of folk psychological practice will take a course that is essentially parallel to the debate over the prediction strand. But in fact, many advocates of the simulation alternative would defend the idea that there is a distinctive – not straightforwardly subsumptive – kind of

---

[37] We are committed to the possibility that there may be both normative and empirical principles cast in very similar terms. Both kinds of principle would make use of *ceteris paribus* clauses; but those clauses would be interpreted differently in the two cases.

explanation involved in folk psychological understanding. Thus, for example, Heal says:

> The difference between psychological explanation and explanation in the natural sciences is that in giving a psychological explanation we render the thought or behaviour of the other intelligible, we exhibit them as having some point, some reason to be cited in their defence.[38]

This kind of normative explanation reveals what someone thought or did as having been the rational thing to think or do, or the thing that it made sense to think or do, given the circumstances and the agent's beliefs and preferences. Clearly, explanation in this style fits together with our account of prediction by mental simulation (in a circumscribed domain) in somewhat the way that explanation by subsumption is the natural companion of prediction that draws on empirical generalizations.

But we do not get an adequate view of the distinctive kind of psychological understanding that might be provided by mental simulation if we focus only on the normative aspect. For, as we have noted (p. 61 above), it is possible to

---

[38] Heal, 'Replication and Functionalism', p. 52. See also, J. McDowell, 'Functionalism and Anomalous Monism', in *Actions and Events: Perspectives on the Philosophy of Donald Davidson,* ed. E. LePore and B. McLaughlin (Oxford: Basil Blackwell, 1985), p. 389: '[T]he concepts of the propositional attitudes have their proper home in explanations of a special sort: explanations in which things are made intelligible by being revealed to be, or to approximate to being, as they rationally ought to be.'

deploy a normative theory about an activity in which one does not, oneself, engage. What mental simulation promises is a kind of understanding that is not only normative but also *first personal*.[39] We see the combination of these two aspects most vividly in the simulation of reasoning in imagination; and the idea that mental simulation can provide a distinctive kind of understanding of another person's reasoning is strikingly similar to R. G. Collingwood's claim that historical understanding is to be achieved by the re-enactment of the historical character's thought:

> But how does the historian discern the thoughts which he is trying to discover? There is only one way in which it can be done: by rethinking them in his own mind. The historian of philosophy, reading Plato, is trying to know what Plato thought, when he expressed himself in certain words. The only way in which he can do this is by thinking it for himself. This, in fact, is what we mean when we speak of 'understanding' the words. So the historian of politics or warfare, presented with an account of certain actions done by Julius Caesar, tries to understand these actions, that is, to discover what thoughts in Caesar's mind determined him to do them.

[39] Thus, for example, Gordon, 'Simulation Without Introspection or Inference from Me to You', p. 56 quotes Kant *(Critique of Pure Reason,* A353) approvingly: 'It is obvious that, if I wish to represent to myself a thinking being, I must put myself in his place, and thus substitute, as it were, my own subject for the object I am seeking to consider (which does not occur in any other kind of investigation).' For an illuminating discussion of issues not far removed from those of the present section, see Moran, 'Interpretation Theory and the First Person'.

> This implies envisaging for himself the situation in which
> Caesar stood, and thinking for himself what Caesar
> thought about the situation and the possible ways of
> dealing with it. The history of thought ... is the re-
> enactment of past thought in the historian's own mind.[40]

Indeed, just as the domain of prediction – and correlatively
of understanding – by mental simulation may be narrowly
circumscribed (pp. 71–2 above), so also understanding by re-
enactment may seem to be restricted to right thinking. This
would be a severe limitation on historical understanding.

Patrick Gardiner considers this objection to
Collingwood in a recent paper:

> [I]t may ... be objected that the re-enactment conception
> of understanding remains unrealistically restrictive in the
> amount it seems to exclude from the historian's proper
> scope. However scrupulous the care taken to judge an
> action from the agent's own standpoint, there can be no *a
> priori* guarantee that the reasoning ascribable to him will
> turn out to have been cogent or sound; as Francis Bacon
> once remarked, 'it is a great mistake to suppose men too
> rational'. It is always conceivable in principle, and it is
> surely often the case in practice, that there is a lack of

---

[40] R. G. Collingwood, 'Human Nature and Human History', in *The Idea
of History* (Oxford: Oxford University Press, Revised Edition 1992),
p. 215. As is quite widely remarked, the simulation approach to
psychological understanding has marked affinities with the
hermeneutic tradition of Vico, Herder, Dilthey, Weber and Croce, as
well as Collingwood. See *Verstehen and Humane Understanding: Royal
Institute of Philosophy Supplement 41,* ed. A. O'Hear (Cambridge:
Cambridge University Press, 1997).

coincidence between the conclusions people actually draw on the basis of their beliefs and purposes and the conclusions that rationally they should have drawn. Thus in history as elsewhere people may engage in faulty practical thinking, whether because of such things as haste or unimaginativeness or as a result of underlying emotional factors that sway or distort their judgement. But when that happens – the objection may continue – it does not follow that their behaviour is unintelligible in terms of reasons, only that the reasons are liable to be poor or inadequate ones.[41]

Gardiner's response to this objection is to note that 'Collingwood would be less vulnerable to some of the criticisms brought against him on the present score if his conception [of re-thinking] were interpreted in a more flexible manner.' On such an interpretation, re-enactment of thought would cover not only right reasoning but also, for example, 'empathetically appreciating how an agent could have been tempted or misled into accepting a particular practical conclusion without recognising the faultiness of the reasoning involved'.[42] Is it possible for a friend of mental simulation to expand the domain of understanding by simulation in a similar way?

In the case of prediction by simulation (p. 62 above), we saw that there could be an intrusion of empirical theory without the prediction strategy coming to owe everything to

[41] P. Gardiner, 'Collingwood and Historical Understanding', in *Verstehen and Humane Understanding*, ed. O'Hear, pp. 117–18.

[42] Ibid., p. 118.

theory and nothing to mental simulation. The possibility that we mentioned there was that the empirical information drawn on might be information about how particular influences (such as drinking a pint of whisky) lead to departures from right reasoning. However, there is no guarantee that, if we modulate the re-enactment of thought in the light of empirical information, then the resulting first person narrative (in imagination) will be one that we find intelligible. Thus, for example, Simon Blackburn considers the case of deliberating about what is the thing to do if one is a subject in Milgram's obedience experiment, and then taking account of the empirical evidence about what subjects actually tend to do. The simulator can modify his or her narrative in the light of the empirical information. But, 'this need have no tendency to make the behaviour of Milgram's subjects intelligible. I might still feel quite baffled, both by them, and if I am like them, by me.'[43]

An intrusion of empirical theory may, then, bring with it a loss of intelligibility. But it would not be right to conclude that there is no prospect of a more flexible conception of the domain of understanding by simulation. Consider, for example, the predictor who now knows about regression towards the mean but who still finds it all too easy to slip back into flawed reasoning (p. 74 above). This predictor will surely not be baffled by the reasoning of the flight instructors. Their reasoning does not measure up to the informed predictor's normative theory; but their first person

---

[43] Blackburn, 'Theory, Observation and Drama', p. 283.

narrative is nevertheless one that the predictor will find intelligible.

There are other cases, too, in which it may be possible, without simply being driven by an empirical theory, to re-enact thinking that departs from right reasoning. Let us return to one of our earlier examples. I want to predict how C will feel and what he will decide to do if he is suspended over a cliff on a rope and he cannot find a foothold and his hands are starting to slip (example (iii) on p. 57 above). Seized by fear or panic, C may not think or do the best thing, the most rational thing. Yet, by simulating C's situation in imagination, I might reach a correct prediction about C without drawing on any empirical theory about how people dangling over cliffs on ropes tend to think. For imagining the situation might be enough to produce in me physiological and emotional responses that perturb my reasoning in imagination in just the way that C's reasoning in reality is perturbed.[44] I might arrive at a correct prediction about C; and if I regard the simulation exercise as an experiment I might arrive by induction at some generalizations about how people think and act in dangerous situations.[45] But there is something more. By re-enacting C's

---

[44] These responses may have consequences, not only for my reasoning within the scope of my simulation of C, but also for my reasoning in my own person. Cf. footnote 30 above.

[45] If my prediction about C's thoughts and actions is to count as knowledge then it should not depend on the flawed normative judgement that this is the thing to think, or to do, in these circumstances. In this case, knowledgeable prediction seems to require

desperate thinking, struggling to maintain a grip, deciding to make another attempt to find a foothold – all in imagination, of course – I surely gain some kind of empathetic understanding of the thoughts, feelings and decisions that I predict. This is not a case of theory-driven simulation; and it is not black box simulation either. It is simulation that, in Gordon's phrase, 'essentially engages [my] own practical and emotional responses'.[46]

There is an alternative way in which I can gain a measure of first personal understanding of C's thoughts, feelings and decisions – a way that does not require actual physiological and emotional responses in me at the moment of understanding. I may take into account my own remembered similar experiences.[47] In this case, I draw on stored information – about how I felt, physically and emotionally, and about how this affected my thinking and decision taking – and I use this information to help me imagine what it is like to be C. (I may also draw on memories of imaginings in which I was fully physiologically and emotionally engaged.)

---

some recognition of the fact that one's reasoning is indeed being perturbed.

[46] R. M. Gordon, 'The Simulation Theory: Objections and Misconceptions', in *Folk Psychology*, ed. Davies and Stone, p. 103. Since understanding is a kind of knowledge, there will once again be a need for me not to be wholly in the grip of the re-enactment (cf. footnote 45 above).

[47] Nichols et al., 'Varieties of Off-Line Simulation', pp. 59–67, discuss empathy and in particular the role of memory in empathetic emotion. What we are concerned with here, however, is remembered emotion, not emotion aroused by memory.

Producing a correct narrative about another person is not always sufficient for finding what that person thinks and does to be intelligible. But it is plausible that in some cases we can make sense of what someone thinks and does by drawing on memory to help us imagine being in the other person's situation – indeed, to help us imagine being that person. This is an intrusion of empirical theory, given the inclusive way in which the term 'theory' has been used. But it does not obstruct first personal understanding, and it does not move us back towards explanation by subsumption.

Conclusion

In the first two sections of this paper we were concerned with the prediction strand of folk psychological practice. The theory theory and the simulation alternative agree about what folk psychological prediction is; but they disagree about its basis. According to the theory theory, the predictor draws on a body of information about psychological matters. According to the simulation alternative, prediction is sometimes possible by simulation in imagination without the aid of empirical psychological theory. However, the domain of prediction by mental simulation – particularly if the epistemology is to be different from the epistemology of empirical theory – is rather closely circumscribed: it is the domain of reason.

When we turn to the explanation strand of folk psychological practice, we find that the contours of the debate are very different. For there is a disagreement about what folk psychological explanation is. According to the theory theory, it is explanation by subsumption under causal generalizations. So, if the basis of the explanation strand of folk psychological practice is to be knowledge of a psychological theory, then that theory must contain generalizations of the right kind – objective, counterfactual supporting – to figure in subsumptive explanations. It is a theory in a more restricted sense. According to the simulation alternative, folk psychological explanation is normative and first personal; it is a matter of finding the other person's life intelligible 'from the inside'.[48] This is an imaginative project; and understanding involves not only reasoning in imagination but also emotion and memory. What is remembered is, of course, information about psychological matters. So, if psychological understanding is to range beyond the domain of reason then, even by the lights of the simulation account, it must draw on psychological theory. But this does not constitute a victory for the theory theory, because the psychological theory on which simulation and understanding draw is theory in the inclusive sense, but not in the restricted sense that is relevant to the theory theory's account of psychological explanation.

If we do not distinguish the inclusive sense of 'theory' which is relevant to the debate about prediction from the restricted sense of 'theory' which is relevant to the debate about explanation, then we may obscure from ourselves the role of empathy and emotion in commonsense psychological understanding.

---

[48] See Jane Heal's paper in this volume.

Understanding Other Minds from the Inside

JANE HEAL

C an we understand other minds 'from the inside'? What would this mean? There is an attraction which many have felt in the idea that creatures with minds, people (and perhaps animals), invite a kind of understanding which inanimate objects such as rocks, plants and machines, do not invite and that it is appropriate to seek to understand them 'from the inside'. What I hope to do in this paper is to introduce and defend one version of the so-called 'simulation' approach to our grasp and use of psychological concepts, a version which gives central importance to the idea of shared rationality, and in so doing to tease out and defend one strand in the complex of ideas which finds expression in this mysterious phrase.[1]

Let us here recap the salient ideas of the simulation approach.[2] Simulationism is to be contrasted with another

---

[1] Talk of persons 'having a point of view' and of there being such a thing as 'what it is like to be that person' are also parts of the same set of ideas. But I would like to stress that the whole issue of the existence of 'qualia' is not touched on at all in what follows.

[2] For more on this see M. Davies, in this volume and also the two collections *Folk Psychology and Mental Simulation*, ed. M. Davies and T. Stone (Oxford: Blackwell, 1995) and *Theories of Theories of Mind*, ed.

approach to philosophy of mind which has, at least among Anglo-American analytic philosophers, been the dominant one of the last decades and which has also been an important influence on psychologists and cognitive scientists. We may call this familiar alternative the theory theory. The version best known to philosophers is functionalism in philosophy of mind. This says that to grasp psychological notions is to grasp that there are certain inner states of persons which are typically caused by such and such external events, which interact among themselves to cause further inner states and events, and which finally combine to cause behaviour.[3] To possess the concept of some particular mental state is to grasp the particular causal-explanatory role associated with that state. When we use our understanding of psychological notions, for example in predicting what another will think or do, we deploy this theoretical knowledge.

There are many ways of spelling out this general idea, depending on what view we take of how we acquire and represent this supposed theoretical knowledge – whether it is innate or learnt, whether explicitly or tacitly known etc. But let us leave all these issues on one side, just noting however that the theory theory does not seem at all hospitable to the 'from the inside' idea. Indeed part of its

P. Carruthers and P. K. Smith (Cambridge: Cambridge University Press, 1996).

[3] For a collection which includes many of the classic papers arguing for this view see *Readings in the Philosophy of Psychology*, vol. 1, ed. N. Block (Cambridge, MA. Harvard University Press, 1980).

motivation is to find an account of the psychological which is naturalistic, i.e. which does away with certain deeply suspect forms of dualism and sees human beings as part of the natural order. Theory theory does this precisely by claiming the similarity of psychological concepts to non-psychological concepts such as those of natural science, presenting the former merely as particular complex and interesting cases of the general style of thought invoked in the latter.

So much for theory theory. Now for a thumbnail sketch of its rival, the simulation approach. This is by no means an entirely new idea. A version of it goes back to Vico in the early eighteenth century; it gets a passing mention in Kant; it is associated with Dilthey and is forcefully defended by Collingwood.[4] And under the name 'Verstehen' one broadly simulation-style approach is familiar, and has been extensively debated, in the philosophy of history and social science. But in the last ten years the idea has been revived in the context of psychology and philosophy of mind. And here it provides a new perspective on a great number of familiar topics – for example the nature of imagination, the differences between practical and theoretical reasoning, the nature of emotion – as well as initiating an interesting body of

---

[4] I. Berlin, *Vico and Herder* (London: Hogarth Press, 1976); I. Kant, *Critique of Pure Reason*, trans. Norman Kemp Smith (London: Macmillan, 1953), p. 336; W. Dilthey, *Selected Writings*, H. P. Rickman (ed.) (Cambridge: Cambridge University Press, 1976), R. G. Collingwood, *The Idea of History*, (Oxford: Oxford University Press, 1946), esp. pp. 282–302.

empirical work in psychology and a suggesting new models in cognitive science.[5] I shall touch on only a very small part of this.

A way of putting the central idea of the simulation approach is this. When we think about another's thoughts or actions we somehow ingeniously exploit the fact that we ourselves are or have minds. What we do is to make our own mind in some way like the mind of the one we seek to predict or understand. We simulate his or her thoughts, we recreate in ourselves some parallel to his or her thought processes. Many simulationists further articulate this by talking of my having 'pretend beliefs' or 'pretend desires' and of my 'inference mechanisms' being run 'off-line'. But others (and here I include myself) would prefer to use more everyday vocabulary and to talk of my using my imagination and of my thereby entertaining the same thoughts and making the same inferences as the other. We shall come to the significant differences here in due course.

I shall not here consider in detail the reasons for preferring a simulation approach to a theory theory one. Let me just indicate one central and immediately apparent advantage of simulationism. It is this. Others' thoughts are very varied and numerous and interact with each other in countless different ways. The remarkable thing is how successfully we deal with this, correctly adjusting our expectations of others' thoughts, feelings and actions in an immense variety of circumstances. Clearly any theory

[5] These themes are all illustrated in the collections mentioned above in footnote 2.

adequate to systematize our competence here would itself be immensely complex. But simulation can explain our competence without crediting us with knowledge of any such vast, and very probably unwieldy, body of information. Rather in thinking about other's thoughts, in order for example to predict their intentions, we harness our own cognitive apparatus and make it work in parallel with that of the other and then use the result we arrive at to ground our prediction. And for this to occur all that is required is, first, that we have cognitive apparatus which is sufficiently similar to that of the other to produce usefully similar results and, secondly, that we can make it work in a parallel way. It is *not* required that we have some representation of the apparatus itself or its workings. We do not need to possess a 'know that' about the processes of thinking, what thoughts lead to what others and so forth, provided that we can harness relevantly our own 'know how' of doing the thinking itself and can thus follow through in ourselves the same train of thought as the other has pursued. The economy of the proposal is striking.

The phrase 'thinking about others' thoughts' covers a great variety of importantly different kinds of reflection which we now need to distinguish. There is something very importantly right in the overall picture painted by functionalism, namely the facts which it highlights that psychological states may be caused by events in the world, that such states interact with each other to give rise to further states and that they may give rise to bodily behaviour. This gives us a useful framework for considering the different sorts of issue which may arise for me concerning another's thoughts.

1. I may wonder what effect the circumstances around her will have on the psychological states of another person. (E.g. She is being whirled round in a fairground ride: will she feel sick? There is a disturbance going on in the corner; will she notice it?) Let us call the connections I focus on here 'world–mind links'.

2. I may wonder what further thoughts she will have, given some thoughts about which I already know. (E.g. She believes thus and so about the cash flow of our firm: will that lead her to think that we are about to go bankrupt? She endorses these and those principles: what decision will she reach in this particular case?) Let us call these 'mind–mind' or 'intrapsychic links'.

3. Thirdly, I may wonder what behaviour, i.e. what actual bodily movements, she will exhibit, given her thoughts. (E.g. She will hear a balloon popped behind her: will she jump? She intends to smash her opponent's ball away to the side line: will she succeed in jumping high enough to get the needed angle?) Let us call these 'mind–world' links.

    But let us also note that there is a fourth thing I may be doing under the general heading 'thinking about others' thoughts'.

4. I may try to work back from the behaviour she has produced to a view about the psychological states from which the behaviour arose. (E.g. She pulled a funny face: was she really amused? She said such and such: was she annoyed?)

These are four extremely different contexts in which psychological concepts are used: and competence at each may call upon different aspects of the skill which is grasp of these concepts. We should beware of lumping them all together and supposing that a philosophical account of our competence with such concepts, whether simulationist or otherwise, should say the same about each. And the claim I want to make about simulationism is that it is particularly at home, its strengths and plausibility particularly apparent, in the second of the listed circumstances, i.e. in an account of our grip of mind–mind or intrapsychic links. And this will be mainly what I shall discuss below. I do not think that simulationism has anything distinctive to say about our ability to answer the third sort of question. It does have distinctive ideas to contribute on the first and fourth, but I shall not discuss them in detail here. However, a few remarks about the fourth may help to ward off some misunderstandings.

It is important to note how, on any view, the fourth context – that of interpreting and explaining behaviour – must be a very different matter from the others. All philosophers, whatever their theory of mind, acknowledge that many alternative explanations of the same behaviour are possible. For example, even if we can identify something with fair confidence as an intentional raising of the arm, when we move to identify the purposes behind the raising, and to the feelings, goals, beliefs which in turn lie behind that purpose, it is clear that many accounts could be given. Even on a functionalist or theory theory view there is no such thing as just 'applying the theory' in some fixed and algorithmic way to derive an interpretation. In the other cases (those falling under 1–3 above), as conceived by functionalism, there is such a fixed and algorithmic procedure; if one has sufficient information about prior conditions then one just has to identify the bits of the theory which deal with those conditions and apply them. One's prediction may be hedged because one knows that further information may reveal the case as more complex than it at first appears or as requiring adjustments in the light of subsidiary theoretical principles. But (these kinds of complications aside) forward-moving theory-invoking prediction is quite a different matter from backward-looking theory-invoking explanation. An account of how we do the latter cannot just call on 'our knowledge of the theory' but must also tell some story about how we generate a range of possible explanations compatible with the theory and how we assess them.

The same general kind of point needs to be made in connection with simulationism. Even if we accept a simulationist account of how prediction about others' thoughts or behaviour are arrived at (e.g. in cases of type 2 above), this does not of itself tell us how backward-looking interpretations and explanations are arrived at. So we should beware of the idea that simulationism is the proposal that mere awareness of another person – of his or her circumstances and behaviour – automatically produces in the observer, via some natural sensitivity, a simulation of the other's mental state. Simulationism ought not to be the claim that we have some kind of quick route to knowledge of other minds, or that we can empathetically 'tune in' to others, or anything of this kind. Perhaps such a thing exists in a few basic cases. But patently other people are often difficult to understand; often we know that we are ignorant of their thoughts and feelings or we have little confidence in our conjectures about what they may be. Simulationism is not the promise of some easy answer to these difficulties.[6]

Let us now turn to a consideration of the distinctively simulationist story about mind–mind links, i.e. about how I might come to some prediction or further belief about another's thought on the basis of knowledge of some subset of her thoughts. To take a very schematic case, suppose the other believes pl–pn and is interested in whether or not q. How might I work out her likely opinion on whether or not q? Theory theory of course says that I, so to speak, look up what the theory tells me about what is the likely upshot of the combination of believing pl–pn with an interest in whether q; I look up the relevant axioms about beliefs and interests of that kind and apply them to this particular case; so it is by applying my knowledge about thoughts and their effects that I work out what to expect.

Simulationism will say something different. But there are two contrasted ways in which the simulationist story can be told. One story starts with a picture of the mind

---

[6] Some simulation theories do postulate a natural tendency to 'catch' others' mental states. For example in normal infants we find very early a disposition to attend to what others attend to, to be frightened if adults in their company are frightened and the like. It is extremely plausible that we do have some such basic pattern of response and that this is central to our ability to understand other minds. The point I am emphasizing, however, is that this does not take us very far. How we build on it to arrive at interpretations in the more complex cases is something about which simulationists have some proposals but not fully worked out ideas. See the papers by Gordon, Goldman and Heal in the Davies and Stone collections.

which is very congenial to the theory theorist and derived to a considerable extent from cognitive science. The mind, on this picture, consists of a number of subsystems which perform various functions. For example there are two stores in which beliefs and desires are kept; there are various processors which produce beliefs and put them in the belief store; these include a sensory analysing system, which takes sensory inputs and transforms them into beliefs; they include also some inference mechanisms, which take beliefs and derive other beliefs from them; there is also a practical reasoning system which takes beliefs and desires as input and produces intentions as output; and so forth. Each processing system is designed to accept certain kinds of input; receiving input of the appropriate kind causes it to go through its distinctive evolutions and to produce output of distinctive kinds. These inputs and outputs – sensory states, beliefs, desires, intentions and so forth – are realized or coded in vehicles which are, in fact, brain states, for examples neuronal patterns described at some suitable level of abstraction. And, on this picture, what really drives the evolution of the inference mechanisms, practical reasoning system and the like are the intrinsic properties of the vehicles, the brain states or neuronal patterns, which are the beliefs, desires etc.

Given this view of what goes on in the mind, simulationism is now spelt out in the following way. Suppose, as in the schematic example above, that I wish to work out what O, the other, is likely to think about whether or not q, given that she believes p1–pn, when I myself do not share her beliefs. What I do first is construct some 'pretend' beliefs that pl–pn. These are items which do not, in my mental architecture, play the role of beliefs; they do not come from my belief store. Nevertheless they are like beliefs in the nature of the vehicle in which they are coded. I now take my inference mechanisms 'off-line' – that is I detach them from their usual links with my belief store. I feed in the pretend beliefs I have constructed, at the same time making some adjustment to the mechanisms to make them search for q-relevant consequences; I then wait to see what the mechanisms produce as output. If they output a pretend belief that q then I attribute to O the belief that q. Of course I do not do all this consciously. Nevertheless this is what is going on at the level of the operations of my subpersonal cognitive machinery.

Simulation theory presented in these terms is conceived of as an empirical hypothesis. Those who articulate it like this suppose that it has empirical consequences different from those of the theory theory, that we can already see what these consequences are and that we can set about testing them.

But I would like to suggest that there are considerable problems with this conceptualization of the issue. Consider first the fact that we do not have any well-backed-up and detailed view about what kind of functional 'systems' are to be found in the brain or of how the various kinds of mental state and process recognized in common-sense are in fact implemented at the sort of level envisaged. Many kinds of architecture are imaginable other than the one sketched above. For example, is it necessary to distinguish between theoretical and practical reasoning, in the way proposed? To insist that we should is to make substantive and controversial philosophical assumptions about the relation of belief, desire and value. Another, and for our purposes more important, question is whether we have to take it that 'inference mechanisms' operate on beliefs, i.e. the whole complex state including both content and the attitude to it. A different articulation would take it that 'inference mechanisms' operated on mental representations minus their attitude determiners – on, so to speak, 'thought radicals'. There is surely some case for thinking that we can reason with representations which we do not believe. How do we explain what we are doing in arguing by *reductio ad absurdum* or reasoning hypothetically if every piece of reasoning needs a belief as starting point? But if we thus reconceptualize the 'inference mechanisms' as operating on thought radicals, then simulationism, formulated in terms which presuppose the existence of inference mechanisms operating on beliefs, turns out to involve a false picture of the mind and so to be worthless.

Consider also the fact that (even supposing that the original sketch of the architecture of our cognitive machinery is the right one) we have very little idea of what would be involved, neurophysiologically or functionally, in taking a system 'off-line'? We do not know what features of operation would remain the same and what would be different. It may be that we are seduced by the image of a machine made of cogs, levers and pistons, where we can make sense of things like disengaging the gears, detaching the drive belt and so forth. But is the brain in any sense like that? Who knows?

I am not here seeking to make difficulties for whole project of seeking to understand the mind by breaking up its overall operation into various different functions and looking for the biological structures and processes which subserve those functions. Good luck to the cognitive scientists, psychologists, neuroanatomists and so forth who grapple with these fascinating and difficult tasks. The issue is rather that we do not yet have enough grip on how that project might actually work out in detail to have any confidence that we are working in terms of the right architecture when we talk of 'pretend beliefs' and 'off-line running'. Nor do we have enough understanding of how that proposal could be implemented, to see what the talk of 'off-line running' would actually amount to. The latter point means that we do not really know how to test simulationism, regarded as this empirical hypothesis. The former means that simulationism, if it is articulated in terms of this particular architecture, is made hostage to future discoveries in brain science and might, given unfavourable developments there, turn out to be a total mistake.

But it seems that the simulation hypothesis has considerable plausibility quite independent of any empirical developments in brain science, a plausibility noted by Kant, Dilthey, Collingwood and others, who were not at all in the business of speculative cognitive science or high-level neuroanatomy. This suggests that there ought to be a reading of the simulation proposal in which it is articulated in quite different terms, terms which place it much nearer the *a priori* end of the spectrum and on which it is effectively insulated from how things turn out in neuroanatomy and the like.

Let us also note at this point that the idea of 'off-line' use of inference mechanisms and the like does not offer any particularly congenial setting for the idea of 'understanding from the inside'. The attraction of the idiom is not at all illuminated by the simulationist story as spelled out above. If I wish to predict how another person will react to some new supposed cholesterol-lowering medication I may try to find out its effects on her by taking a dose myself and observing the results. Or (indulging in some science fiction) I might be able to unhook a part of my circulatory system and run an experiment on that. In either case I would 'simulate' in myself the operation of the drug on her. But the fact that it is a bit of my own bodily apparatus which is being run in experimental fashion gives no special insight 'from the inside' into the workings of the drug. And we have been told nothing which entitles us to think the case of the mind – i.e. the brain – to be any different. But the idea of simulation did seem to have some resonance with the idea of 'understanding from the inside'. So again, we are led to the idea that there may be an alternative way of conceptualizing the idea.

So now let me sketch such an alternative. Consider a normal person who is capable of having beliefs about a certain subject matter, i.e. of forming them appropriately and reasoning from them appropriately, among other things. Let us take Charles as an example; he is an investment expert and can form the belief that the base rate will rise on seeing evidence that it will and can make sensible inferences from this, for example to a fall in the value of shares. Now we take it entirely for granted that if Charles is capable of doing these things then he is also capable of reasoning hypothetically about what would happen if base rate were to rise. It is difficult to make any sense of the opposite supposition. Remember that Charles is a normal human being, so that in dealing with most subject matters, cups of tea, rain, buying a house and so forth, Charles can cope with both actual and hypothetical. Suppose that we now try to graft on the supposition that, for example, when faced with sentences beginning 'Suppose that base rate were to rise...' Charles goes deaf or berserk or in some other way just fails to cope, although he does respond normally to the straight assertion 'Base rate has risen'. Or suppose we try to add on the idea that Charles can appreciate the need for contingency planning in connection with most kinds of events but never seems to indulge in any kind of contingency planning about base rate rises, although, remember, he copes with great competence when they actually occur.

Can we really fill in the details of such a story in a coherent way? I do not say that it is provably impossible that we should do so. We are familiar with the extremely bizarre and disconcerting way in which what are normally treated as unitary abilities can unravel in cases of brain damage and disease (agnosias, aphasias and the like). But the interesting point is that such cases are extremely rare and that our ordinary psychological concepts do not allow for them. Our ordinary concepts are, quite properly I suggest, tailored to the outward, behavioural contours of the normal case, to the kind of successful performances and achievements one can regularly expect of persons. They are not tailored to respect or record the structure of the machinery which realizes these abilities.

In our thinking about other people one fundamental question we can and often do ask is what subject matters they are familiar with, i.e. roughly what concepts they possess and in what kind of detail. Do they understand about tables and chairs? About royalty? About snow? About car engines? About income tax? And how well do they understand about each? If a person is familiar with a subject matter and understands it to some roughly indicated level then we take it for granted that this ability to think about the subject matter will manifest itself just as much in coming to counterfactual beliefs, in considering possibilities and their upshots, as it does in forming and reasoning from categorical beliefs. The ability will show itself also in desires, intentions, emotions, dreams and fantasies. Competence in thinking about a subject matter is a multifaceted ability. It is an error, a distortion, of our central psychological notions, to think of concept possession as something which shows up only or centrally in the formation of categorical beliefs. Rather, belief formation is just one facet of an ability which naturally manifests itself also in other kinds of thinking.

Note here a further important point, implicit in what has been said already but needing emphasis. A parallelism between certain psychological processes is already presupposed in the everyday conception we have been spelling out, namely a parallelism between, on the one hand, the inferences a person makes with categorical beliefs in virtue of his or her grasp of a subject matter and, on the other, the counterfactual conditional beliefs he or she would form as a result of making suppositions and the like. So Charles infers from 'Base rate will rise' to 'Share prices will fall.' But it is also the case that if he wonders 'What if base rate were to rise?' then he will come to the conditional belief 'If base rate were to rise then share prices would fall.' This parallelism must stay more or less in place on pain of our losing our right to describe the content of Charles' wondering as 'What if base rate were to rise?' It cannot be base rate and its possible rise that he is wondering about if he does not at this point come up with the same idea, to figure in the consequent of his conditional belief, as he would come up with in straight belief to belief inference. The fact that this parallelism exists is what makes viable the whole conceptual structure we use in talking of others' thoughts, plans, desires, reasonings etc. It is the idea of the multifaceted ability which is, in effect, the idea that the same content can be identified as playing a role embedded within other contents and as the object of various different attitudes.

Someone might here offer a hypothesis about how it is that we have such a multifaceted ability, i.e. about the nature of the systems or devices in which the ability is realised. Perhaps what goes on when I wonder 'What if p?' is that I take some inference mechanisms 'off-line' and feed in a pretend belief that p?[7] But to pursue the line of thought I am proposing we do not need to get embroiled in issues like this at all. The parallelism between thinking about what is taken to be actual (having a belief) and thinking about what

---

[7] See, e.g. the paper by Nichols et al. in *Theories of Theories of Mind*, ed. Carruthers and Smith.

is taken to be merely possible (wondering, hypothesizing, imagining and the like) exists, whatever its underpinnings turn out to be. And we are entitled to invoke it in our account of thought about other minds.

So now back again to simulation and other minds. We can now present the simulation hypothesis like this; ability to think about another's thoughts, e.g. to reason from the existence of those thoughts to conclusions about the existence of further thoughts, is an extension or redeployment of ability to think about the subject matter of the other's thoughts.

How does this work? Let us take the following way of spelling things out. Let us revert to our schematic example in which the other believes that pl–pn and is interested in whether or not q. I know this and I am interested in whether or not she comes to believe that q. What she will do is wonder 'In the light of pl–pn is it the case that q?' i.e. she will direct her thought to answering the question whether q, having in mind the evidence that pl–pn. If the propositions that pl–pn imply that q, and she comes to be aware of them as so doing, then she will come to believe that q, taking this to be a belief to which she is entitled, in the light of the facts (as she sees them) that pl–pn. What will I do? If I share her beliefs I may, in effect, pose myself just the same question, viz. 'In the light of the facts that pl–pn is it the case that q?' But if I do not share her beliefs then the question I should address is, rather, 'If it were that pl–pn, would it be that q?' But in either case the other person and I share a central aim, namely trying to get a sense of the relations of implication or otherwise between pl–pn and q. And we carry out this aim by exercising our ability to think about the subject matter of pl–pn and q. And if it comes to me to seem that if it were that pl–pn then it would be that q then I attribute to the other belief that q.

Let us reflect now on the concepts implicit in the story I have just sketched. I have spoken of us as having 'a sense of' some thoughts as implying or being implied by others. Much recent philosophy, influenced perhaps by cognitive science models, tacitly operates with a picture of the progress of thoughts through time, as when a person is reasoning and reflecting, as a matter of there being one thought (perhaps quite a complex one) occupying the conscious mind at one instant and of its being entirely replaced by another thought at the succeeding moment. So, for a schematic example, at first I think 'p, p → q, q?' and then this complex thought is swept away and replaced by 'q'. But this is surely a distortion of our experience as thinkers. A slightly more accurate narrative is one in which I first think 'p, p → q, q?' and then next think 'Well, clearly q, since p and p → q'. That is, I judge that q in the light of a sense of it as following from p and p → q. Relatedly I take this latter belief of mine to be justified by my beliefs that p and that p → q.

So far only beliefs have been considered. But the above is a structure which we find in numerous intrapsychic connections, for example between desires, intentions and emotions (or at least some important aspects of them) and other contentful states. So my fear of something consists, at least in part and in central cases, of my taking it to be dangerous or threatening. But when I so take it, it is in the light of my belief that it may explode, or may bite. So my fear, insofar as it is to be identified with taking the feared thing to be dangerous, is experienced by me as justified or appropriate in the light of other thoughts. Similarly I may take a resolution to perform an action in the light of that action seeming to me to be advantageous and to have no drawbacks. Again it is not just that first I think about the advantages and lack of drawbacks and then next instant those considerations are entirely swept from my conscious mind and replaced by the thought 'I'll do it!' Rather, the ensuing thought is more like 'I'll do it (since it is advantageous and has no drawbacks).'

And what goes for me goes for others, on the account of the use of psychological concepts which I am sketching. We do not think of others primarily or solely as extremely complex biological machines, with many physical structures inside interacting in elegant ways; in thinking of a person as a person, these aspects of human existence are not to the fore. Of course there is complexity in others' psychological states and this complexity is implicated in temporal development which it is quite proper to think of as causal, in some sense of 'causal'. This is what makes the 'biological machine with complex innards' story, and the related functionalist view in philosophy of mind, seem plausible at all. But when we think of persons the complexity we are aware of is unified in a particular way. It is not unified just as 'the states of the bits of stuff inside that skull' but rather as 'the elements of the coherent world view constructed by the person whose body that is'. And the person is unified inasmuch as her mind is unified, i.e. inasmuch as the elements of it are seen as cohering and are brought to bear on one another, to suggest new conjectures, to correct misconceptions, to provide mutual support through their rational connection and so forth.

A person becomes aware of her world and builds up a picture of it, through perception, memory and reasoning. And that view must be unified in the way sketched. But let us note also that her view will necessarily include, woven in among the rest, many indexical thoughts, defining her beliefs about herself, her placement, role, capacities and so forth. For example they will include beliefs of the form 'I am in such and such a location'. 'I am capable of these or those actions.' 'I occupy such and such a role.' 'These and those achievements, dangers, disappointments or pleasures are possible for me' and so forth. These elements may be said to define a 'point of view' on the world, in both a literal and a metaphorical sense. So when I attempt in simulationist style to recreate another's thoughts, insofar as such indexical thoughts are included, then I have, to some greater or lesser extent, attempted to recreate her point of view.

The suggestion I would like to pursue now is that it is this complex of ideas which makes the adoption of the idiom of 'understanding from the inside' so natural and attractive. There are a variety of strands in this metaphor. The mind of the other is 'inside' in the sense that (sometimes at least) it is not immediately apparent in behaviour what a person thinks and so we need to reflect on what her thoughts are. It is also 'inside' in that mental events and states are capable of moving the body to spontaneous (i.e. not immediately externally caused) movement. But there is also the fact that, on the view sketched, when I consider the nature of what is 'inside' another person, in the senses suggested by these two points, what I find myself postulating is a set of thoughts which represent the world from a point of view. So the 'inside' which I find is not mere mechanical or biological complexity. If the inside were of that kind there would not be any question of anything being 'from' it. But things can be 'from the inside' with a person because what is 'inside' is itself outwardly directed. It is an interlocking complex of items with indexical representational content concerning the world around that person. The existence of this kind of outward-directed content is bound up with the person's ability to respond to changing perceptions and reasoning by modifying and enlarging the world view in rationally intelligible ways. We think of the content as having been built up by exercise of the person's cognitive capacities, her perceptual awareness and her abilities to remember and reason. The idea of reason then provides a further strand which enriches the 'from the inside' metaphor, inasmuch as in deploying it I represent other people as beings capable of recognizing and responding to norms, whose thoughts and behaviour therefore have sense and can be justified, in ways which have no analogue in the explanations provided for the behaviour of inanimate items.

What is the status of all this, you might ask. I have just outlined very roughly a picture which we have of ourselves and others – each of us a rational subject with a point of view having multifaceted abilities to think effectively about many subject matters and so forth. And this picture is, I have suggested, the one presupposed by the form of simulationism which I have tried to outline and defend. I would also like to suggest the converse, namely that this kind of simulationism is the natural theory of the understanding of other minds for someone who conceives of persons as unified rational subjects. It is clear, then, that a presupposition of rationality, ability to appreciate what follows from what, to respond to reasons by grasping their force, is central to this whole complex of views. But could it be that this presupposition might turn out to be recognizably false? If so either we must say that, contrary to what I have urged, there is no conceptual link between the mental and rationality or we shall have to reconfigure our idea of the mental so as to extrude the rationality assumption. Or might it turn out that mental notions are inextricably bound up with the illusory idea of rationality and so need eliminating altogether? This is too big a topic to address here. But I would like to conclude by offering a few reflections.

The idea that we are rational has received some excellent probing and clarification from philosophers; and psychologists have also undertaken fascinating empirical investigations bearing on the actual workings of our inferential processes. The joint upshot of this philosophical and empirical work is that it is quite clear that there are a number of grand and demanding senses of 'rational' in which we cannot properly claim to be rational. Such ability as we have is imperfect, limited by the finitude of our memories and by the amount of complexity we can take in. We do not have the time, energy or attention even to do all of the comparatively simple thinking and inferring which would be useful to us, let alone many elaborate reasonings, and letting even further along the grandiose projects of achieving total consistency or coming to recognize all the logical consequences of what we accept. And, worse, we seem to be prone to systematic errors in elementary reasoning; there seem to be inferential versions of perceptual illusions such as the Müller–Lyer case, where we are gripped by the conviction that something follows from something else when it does not.[8]

So our rationality, if it exists, does not amount to anything very grand. But then we do not need anything very grand to defend the picture sketched above, any more than we need to credit ourselves with illusion-resistant eyesight of eagle-like acuity in order to defend the claim that in vision we have a sense which enables us to become aware of the placement and properties of things about us. Sight is reliable enough for us to be able to become aware, when we reflect, of when it is prone to illusion. So we can use in it increasingly subtle and well–focused ways (involving cross-checking, self-critical awareness of possible sources of error, helpfully devised instruments and the like) to progressively improve our grasp on the layout and properties of objects. The central claim we need about rationality is closely analogous. We need to be entitled to the assumption that thinking about a question, deploying all that we know which bears on it, will generally tend to improve our grasp on that issue

---

[8] Two excellent books, the second of which also provides references to much other recent work, are C. Cherniak, *Minimal Rationality* (Cambridge, MA: MIT Press, 1986) and E. Stein, *Without Good Reason* (Oxford: Oxford University Press, 1996).

rather than the contrary. And as in the case of vision, what makes this central idea defensible is that we are capable of such things as reflecting on our reasoning practices, of recognizing mistakes through cross-checking and of turning, where need be, to various aids. And thus we are capable of progressively improving our sense of what follows from what. No empirical evidence currently to hand shows that we are not entitled to the assumption that our basic thinking capacity is not fundamentally pointed in the right direction, i.e. in the direction of leading us, when we employ it, to a better grip on things. Indeed the empirical studies which identify our inferential shortcomings are precisely evidence to support the assumption. And how would anyone who did not make it proceed with his or her thinking? What is the practical alternative to making it? There is none.

Consider finally something about our relations with other people. It is often taken for granted in the discussions of philosophers and psychologists that the central role of psychological concepts is to enable us to predict inner states in others so that we can, in turn, predict and sometimes influence the behaviour those states bring about. But this is a serious distortion. Our relations to other people do not have the same structure as our relations with inanimate objects, plants or machines. We do not deal with our family members, friends, colleagues or fellow citizens as we do with volcanoes, fields of wheat or kitchen mixers, namely by trying to figure out the nature and layout of their innards so that we can predict and perhaps control them.

Prediction and control may (sometimes rightly and sometimes wrongly) be the name of the game for psychiatrists, prison governors or dictators, in some of their dealings with some people. But it is not the name of the game for most distinctively human interactions. A much more central pattern occurs where one person offers to another some articulation of how things strike him or her – a remark, gesture, action or expression – in the course of pursuing some more or less well-defined joint project. Certainly this will be offered in the expectation (or at least the hope) that it will be identified for what it is. Thus far a prediction will probably be made. And also a prediction will be made that a response of a certain very broad class will be forthcoming. So in a philosophical debate one will expect to get back a philosophical question or observation, in a chess game one will get a chess move, in a game of mud pies one will get an elaboration of the mud pie world, in a courtship one will get a move to deepen the intimacy and so forth. But the specific nature of the response is not predicted. Social life would be utterly boring, completely different from the com-municative reality we experience, if it were. What we hope of another with whom we interact is not that he or she will go through some gyrations which we have already planned in detail, but that he or she will make some contributions to moving forward the joint and co-operative enterprise on which we both are, more or less explicitly, engaged.

There will be in any particular case many moves which would fit the general bill; which move an individual makes depends upon his or her individual appreciation of the situation, to which he or she brings not only differences in temperament, inventiveness and the like but also, nearly always, differences in awareness both of empirical facts and of what follows from what. In a philosophical discussion the parties will probably share a good deal of common ground; but they will not be, psychologically speaking, identical twins. That is why there is a point in discussion; we engage in it so that we can pool our knowledge, insights, inventiveness and so forth. This is one way of combating our finitude, namely by having different of us pursue different lines of thought, since there is typically more labour in discovery than in appreciation of the discovery once made. Division of intellectual labour is not something which comes on the scene merely with a large accumulations of knowledge and specialization in the sciences. It is built right in to the idea of conversation and co-operation in the most everyday activities and plans.

And the way in which we carry on such activities shows that we presuppose the rationality of others, presuppose that we share standards of what follows from what and what is relevant to what. Our first move, on finding another's response not immediately intelligible and helpful, is to search round for an interpretation which makes it so. And if others disagree with us about what constitutes good reasoning, making moves which show that at some level they do not share standards of what follows from what, then we seek to put them right in the expectation that they will acknowledge the mistake (or perhaps they will show that it is we who have made the mistake). Let us further note that when a mistake is agreed to have been made we will often look for, and find, a reason why it was made, not just in the sense of a cause or regularity in its making but in the sense of some excuse which reconciles the mistake with the idea that, even in making it, the perpetrator was exercising his or her rationality. This may be done by pointing to the false presuppositions which were accepted, the misleading analogy which was unduly prominent or some similar factor. Few mistakes, whether factual errors or mistakes in reasoning, are just opaquely and blankly completely unintelligible when reflected on. Some shred of justification can nearly always be found.

And how well this general orientation to others serves us, how well things work out, on the whole. And how completely lacking we are of any conception of how things could be differently conducted. Empirical studies of our limitations and proneness to error (together with such things as awareness of the differences of our own outlook from those of other cultures and times or Freudian insights into the deeper workings of our motivations and self-conceptions) may all enrich the mixture and make us aware that the intelligibility we seek is not always to be found easily or on the surface. But such things do not prevent us looking for reason and intelligibility or stand in the way of our thinking, in most cases, that we have found it. So I conclude that rationality, in the schematic but still powerful sense sketched, is a very deeply entrenched assumption in our picture of human beings, ourselves and others, and hence that the understanding of other minds which calls upon the simulationist framework is not to be easily dislodged or replaced.

Self-knowledge: the Wittgensteinian Legacy

CRISPIN WRIGHT

It is only in fairly recent philosophy that psychological self-knowledge has come to be seen as problematical; once upon a time the hardest philosophical difficulties all seemed to attend our knowledge of others. But as philosophers have canvassed various models of the mental that would make knowledge of other minds less intractable, so it has become unobvious how to accommodate what once seemed evident and straightforward – the wide and seemingly immediate cognitive dominion of minds over themselves.

In this paper[1] I'll begin by trying to characterize this dominion with some care. We need to have it as clear as possible why one traditional way of thinking about the matter has seemed so attractive – even unavoidable – and what a satisfactory account of the issues in this region has to accomplish. However my overarching concern will be with the bearing of later Wittgensteinian materials on the question. Ultimately I think we can get an insight into the intended force of something which I do not think has so far been sufficiently well understood: the *anti-explanatory*

---

[1] This is an edited version of my contribution to *Knowing Our Own Minds*, ed. C. Macdonald, B. Smith and C. Wright (Oxford: Oxford University Press 1998).

motif that runs through the pronouncements on philosophical method occurring in the *Philosophical Investigations*.

I

People can be variously deluded about themselves, self-deceived about their motives, for instance, or overly sanguine, or pessimistic, about their strengths of character and frailties. But it is nonetheless a truism that for the most part we know ourselves best – better than we know others and better than they know us.

In one kind of case, the explanation of this would seem straightforward. It is (merely) that our own presence is, for each of us, a constant factor in the kind of situation, usually but not always social, in which the evidence emerges which bears on various of our psychological characteristics. No-one else is so constantly around us. So no-one else observes as much of us or is as much observed by us. Selves have the best evidence about themselves.

Evidently, however, this form of explanation of the truth in the truism can run only in cases where one's own and another's knowledge of oneself must draw on the same kind of evidence. So it is restricted, it would seem, to broadly dispositional characteristics like honesty, patience, courage and conceit – cases where there is no essential self/other asymmetry in the means of knowledge. And this is not, of course, the most salient type of case. In the most salient type of case, we not merely know ourselves best but also *differently* from the way in which we know others and they know us. The distinction is complicated, admittedly, by the fact

that many apparently dispositional psychological characteristics are distinctively manifested not by raw behaviour, as it
were, but by psychological performance in respects that may
themselves exhibit self/other epistemological asymmetries.
Conceit, for instance, will be, *inter alia*, a disposition to form
certain kinds of belief. It remains that the type of case that
sets our problem is that which gives rise to the phenomenon
of *avowal* – the phenomenon of authoritative, non-inferential
self-ascription. The basic philosophical problem of self-
knowledge is to explain this phenomenon – to locate, characterize and account for the advantage which selves seemingly
possess in the making of such claims about themselves.

The project will be conditioned by whatever more
precise characterization we offer of the target phenomenon.
It seems safe to suppose that we must begin by distinguishing two broad classes of avowal. The first group – what I will
call *phenomenal avowals* – comprises examples like 'I have a
headache', 'My feet are sore', 'I'm tired', 'I feel elated', 'My
vision is blurred', 'My ears are ringing', 'I feel sick' and so on.
Such examples exhibit each of the following three marks:

First, they are *groundless*. The demand that somebody produces reasons or corroborating evidence for such a
claim about themselves – 'How can you tell?' – is always
inappropriate. There is nothing they might reasonably be
expected to be able to say. In that sense, there is nothing
upon which such claims are based.

Second, they are *strongly authoritative*. If somebody
understands such a claim, and is disposed sincerely to make
it about themselves, that is a guarantee of the truth of what
they say. A doubt about such a claim has to be a doubt about

the sincerity or the understanding of its author. Since we standardly credit any interlocutor, absent evidence to the contrary, with sincerity and understanding, it follows that a subject's actually making such a claim about themselves is a criterion for the correctness of the corresponding third-personal claim made by someone else: my avowal that I'm in pain must be accepted by others, on pain of incompetence, as a ground for the belief that I am.

Finally, phenomenal avowals exhibit a kind of *transparency*. Where P is an avowal of the type concerned, there is typically something absurd about a profession of the form, 'I don't know whether P' – don't know whether I have a headache, for instance, or whether my feet are sore. Not always: there are contexts in which I might be uncertain of a precondition (for instance, whether I have feet). But in the normal run of cases, the subject's ignorance of the truth or falsity of an avowal of this kind is not, it seems, an option.

None of the examples listed is an avowal of a *content-bearing* state. It is the hallmark of the second main group of avowals – what I shall call *attitudinal avowals* – that the psychological characteristics, processes and states which they concern are partially individuated by the propositional content, or intentional direction, which they contain – for instance, 'I believe that term ends on the 27th', 'I hope that noise stops soon', 'I think that professional philosophers are some of the most fortunate people on earth', 'I am frightened of that dog', 'I am thinking of my mother.' In order to see what is distinctive about an author's relation to avowals of this kind, we need first to take account of the fact that such claims can also be made as part of a

process of *self-interpretation* – in the kind of context when we
say that we have *learned* about our attitudes by finding that
certain events cause us pleasure, for instance, or discomfort.
Consider the following passage from Jane Austen's *Emma*:

> Emma's eyes were instantly withdrawn; and she sat
> silently meditating in a fixed attitude, for a few minutes.
> A few minutes were sufficient for making her acquainted
> with her own heart. A mind like hers, once opening to
> suspicion, made rapid progress. She touched – she
> admitted – she acknowledged the whole truth. Why was
> it so much the worse that Harriet should be in love with
> Mr Knightley than with Mr Churchill? Why was the evil
> so dreadfully increased by Harriet's having some hope of
> return? It darted through her, with the speed of an arrow,
> that Mr Knightley must marry no-one but herself.[2]

Here Emma has just been told of the love of her protégée,
Harriet, for her – Emma's – bachelor brother-in-law, a
decade older than Emma, a frequent guest of her father's,
and hitherto a dependable, somewhat avuncular part of the
background to her life of whom she has entertained no
romantic notions. But now she realizes that she strongly
desires that he marry no-one but her, and she arrives at this
discovery by way of surprise at the strength and colour of
her reaction to Harriet's declaration, and by way of a few
minutes' reflection on that reaction. She is, precisely, not

---

[2] Jane Austen, *Emma* (London: Penguin Books, 1987), p. 398. This nice
passage was drawn to my attention by Julia Tanney, who uses it for her
own purposes in her 'A Constructivist Picture of Self-Knowledge',
Philosophy 71 (1996), 405–22.

moved to the realization immediately; it dawns on her first as something she suspects and *then* recognizes as true. It *explains* her reaction to Harriet.

In such self-interpretative cases, none of the three features we noted of phenomenal avowals is present. There is no groundlessness: the subject's view is one for which it *is* perfectly in order to request an account of the justifying grounds. There is no strong authority: mere sincerity and understanding will be no guarantee whatever of truth – it is for Jane Austen to stipulate, as it were, that Emma's self-discovery is the genuine article, but in any real context such a conclusion could be seriously mistaken. Finally, there is no transparency: within a context of self-interpretation, it is no way incongruous if the subject professes ignorance of particular aspects of her intentional psychology. However, what it is vital to note for our present purpose is that such self-interpretative cases, although common, cannot be the *basic* case. For the body of data on which self-interpretation may draw is not restricted to recollected behaviour and items falling within the subject matter of phenomenal avowals. When Emma interprets her reaction to Harriet's declaration as evidence that she herself loves Knightley, there is an avowable ground – something like 'I am disconcerted by her love for that man and (more so) by the thought that it might be returned' – which is a *datum for*, rather than a product of self-interpretation. Self-interpretation, that is to say, will typically draw on non-inferential knowledge of a basic range of attitudes and intentionally characterized responses. These will not be distinguished, I think, from non-basic, interpretative cases by any generic features of their content; rather they will reflect matters which, for the particular subject in the particular context, happen to require no interpretation to be known about – matters which are precisely *avowable*. It is these basic examples which comprise the attitudinal avowals.

Such avowals will have the same immediacy as phenomenal avowals and will exhibit both groundlessness and transparency – groundlessness rather trivially in so far as, any interpretational basis having been excluded, there will naturally be nothing a subject can say to justify such a self-ascription; transparency in the sense that, except where the matter is one of interpretation, we think a subject ought to know without further ado what she believes, or desires, etc., so that any profession of ignorance or uncertainty, unless coupled with a readiness to allow the matter is not basic but calls for (self-)interpretation, will seem perplexing. However, attitudinal avowals do not exhibit the strong authority of phenomenal avowals: to the extent that there is space for relevant forms of self-deception or confusion, sincerity-cum-understanding is no longer a guarantee of the truth of even basic self-ascriptions of intentional states. Any avowal may be discounted if accepting it would get in the way of making best sense of the subject's behaviour. But with attitudinal avowals it is admissible to look for other explanations of a subject's willingness to assert a bogus avowal than those provided by misunderstanding, insincerity or misinterpretation. This is indeed the space occupied by the ordinary notion of self-deception; but the more general idea is just that we can be caused to hold mistaken higher-order beliefs in ways – wishful thinking, for instance – which do not go through misguided self-interpretative inference.

It is striking that attitudinal avowals would appear to exhibit a form of weak authority nevertheless: that is, at least in basic, nonself-interpretative cases they provide empirically assumptionless justification for the corresponding third-person claims.[3] Other things being equal, I *ought to know* what my beliefs, desires and hopes, etc., are, even if

---

[3] Since it cannot be attributed, as with phenomenal avowals, to the fact of sincerity-cum-understanding guaranteeing truth, it is an interesting question what this weak authority should be taken to consist in. It might be suggested that it is nothing other than the presumptive acceptability of testimony generally. And certainly that proposal would be enough to set our problem: for the presumptive acceptability of *original* testimony – testimony for which the source is not itself testimony – extends no further than to subject matters which an informant is deemed competent to know about. So the question would recur: how is it possible for subjects to know about their intentional states in ways that involve no consideration of the evidence on which a third-party must rely? Actually, however, I think the suggestion is wrong. What distinguishes the presumptive acceptability of attitudinal avowals from anything characteristic of testimony generally, is that the authority which attaches to them is, in a certain sense, *inalienable*. There is no such thing as showing oneself chronically unreliable in relation to the distinctive subject matter of attitudinal avowals. I may have such poor colour vision that you rightly come to distrust my testimony on matters of colour. I may, unwittingly, have a very bad memory and, learning of this, you may rightly come to a state of wholesale suspicion about my testimony on matters of personal recall. But no corresponding wholesale suspicion concerning my attitudinal avowals is possible. You may not suppose me sincere and comprehending and yet chronically unreliable about what I hope, believe, fear and intend. Wholesale suspicion about my attitudinal avowals – where it is not a doubt about sincerity or understanding – jars with conceiving of me as an intentional subject at all.

sincerity and understanding alone do not guarantee the truth of what I say about them.

II

We now have a sufficient focus for our central question. The cardinal problem of self-knowledge is that of explaining *why* avowals display the marks they do – what is it about their subject matter, and the subject's relationship to it, which explains and justifies our accrediting her sincere pronouncements about it with each of groundlessness, transparency and strong authority in the case of phenomenal avowals, and with groundlessness, transparency and weak authority in the case of attitudinal avowals? How is it possible for subjects to know these matters non-inferentially? How is it (often) impossible for them *not* to know such matters? And what is the source of the special authority carried by their verdicts?

There is a line of response to these questions that comes so naturally as to seem almost irresistible – indeed, it may even seem to ordinary thought to amount merely to a characterization of the essence of mind. According to it, the explanation of the special marks of avowals is that they are the product of the subject's exploitation of what is generally recognized to be a position of (something like) *observational privilege.* As an analogy, imagine somebody looking into a kaleidoscope and reporting on what he sees. No-one else can look in, of course – at least while he is taking his turn. If we assume our Hero perceptually competent, and appropriately attentive, his claims about the patterns of shape and colour within will exhibit analogues of each of the marks of phenomenal avowals:

1. The demand that he produces reasons or corroborating evidence for his claims will be misplaced – the most he will be able to say is that he is the only one in a position to see, and that is how things strike him;
2. granted his proper perceptual functioning, it will be sufficient for the truth of his claims that he understands them and is sincere in making them; so that for anyone who understands the situation, our Hero's merely making such a claim will constitute a sufficient, though defeasible reason for accepting its truth; and
3. where P is any claim about the patterns of shape and colour visible within, there will be no provision – bearing in mind Hero's assumed perceptual competence and attentiveness – for his intelligibly professing ignorance whether or not P.

This analogy isn't perfect by any means. In order to construct it, we have had to assume normal perceptual functioning and full attentiveness on the part of our observer. And no such assumption conditions our reception of others' avowals. But once into one's stride with this type of thinking, this difference will not seem bothersome. The line will be that in the *inner* observational realm, in contrast to the outer, there is simply no room for analogues of misperception or of oversight or occlusion – for the objects and features there are necessarily salient to the observing subject. Or at least they are so in the case where they are objects and features recordable by phenomenal avowals. In the case of the subject matter of attitudinal avowals, by contrast, space for an analogue of misperception can and should be found – that will be what explains the failure of strong authority in those cases. In brief: this – Cartesian – response to the problem of avowals has it that the truth values of such utterances are non-inferentially known to the utterer via her immediate awareness of events and states in a special theatre, the theatre of her consciousness, of which others can have at best only indirect inferential knowledge. In the case of phenomenal avowals, this immediate awareness is in addition, infallible and all-seeing; in the case of basic attitudinal avowals, it is merely very, very reliable.

So presented, the Cartesian picture, of the transparency of one's own mind and, by inevitable contrast, the opacity of others', emerges as the product of a self-conscious attempt at philosophical explanation. That may seem congenial to John McDowell's claim that 'We need to be seduced into philosophy before it can seem natural to suppose that another person's mind is hidden from us.'[4] McDowell recoils against the idea that anything like the Cartesian picture might be part of ordinary unphilosophical thought. But I think he is wrong about this, the theoretical setting I have given to the picture notwithstanding. To be sure, it is unclear what should count as a 'seduction into philosophy'. But if every manifestation of the Cartesian picture is to rate as the product of such a seduction, then

---

[4] From p. 149 of John McDowell, 'Intentionality and Interiority in Wittgenstein', in *Meaning Scepticism*, ed. K. Puhl (Berlin: de Gruyter, 1991), pp. 148–69.

the seductive reach of philosophy is flatteringly wide. I do not imagine, of course, that people typically self-consciously follow through the train of thought I outlined. But we ought not to balk at the notion that no intellectual routine characteristically pursued by those in its grip should capture exactly the best reconstruction of why an idea appeals. The privacy of the inner world is a recurrent idea in literature.[5] It is arguably a presupposition of the whole idea of the continuation of one's consciousness after death. The thought of the undetectable inverted colour spectrum is something which can engage quite young children without too much difficulty. And in each of these cases what comes naturally is essentially nothing other than the notion of a kind of privileged observation of one's own mind which works, in the ways we have reviewed, to explain the first-third-person asymmetries in ordinary psychological discourse.

The privileged-observation explanation is unquestionably a neat one. What it *does* need philosophy to teach is its utter hopelessness. One very important realization to that end is that nothing short of full-blown Cartesianism can explain the asymmetries in *anything like the same way* – there can be no scaled-down observational model of self-knowledge which preserves the advantages of the Cartesian account while avoiding its unaffordable costs. The problem,

---

[5] To take another nineteenth-century example, it is, in a sense, the entire subject matter of George Eliot's novella, *The Lifted Veil.* The Cartesian character of that writer's notions about the mental is explored in depth in Catherine Wright's 'The Unseen Window: Middlemarch, Mind and Morality' (Ph.D. dissertation, University of St Andrews, 1991).

very simply, is that the kind of authority I have over the avowable aspects of my mental life is not transferable to others: there is no contingency (anyway, none of which we have any remotely satisfactory concept[6]) whose suspension would put other ordinary people in position to avow away on my behalf, as it were – would transfer, or extend my advantage to them. So the conception of avowals as reports of inner observation is saddled with the idea that the observations in question are ones which *necessarily* only the subject can carry out. And once that conception is in place, others' means of access to the states of affairs which their subject (putatively) observes is bound to seem essentially second-rate by comparison and to be open to just the kinds of sceptical harassment which generate the traditional problem of other minds – the unaffordable cost referred to.

III

If this is right, then a deconstruction of the privileged-observation solution to the problem of self-knowledge is an indispensable prerequisite of an overall satisfactory philosophy of mind. It seems to me that the accomplishment of

---

[6] In particular, I do not think that we have any satisfactory concept of what it would be to be in touch with others' mental states *telepathically*. I do not mean, of course, to rule it out that someone might prove, by dint of *his own* occurrent suspicions and afflictions, to be a reliable guide to the states of mind of another. But that possibility falls conspicuously short of the idea that a subject might share direct witness of another's mental states.

such a deconstruction was one major achievement of Wittgenstein's later philosophy – though it would take another paper, or series of papers, properly to fill out how it goes.[7] In essentials, what he does is to mount a two-pronged attack on the Cartesian picture, with the prongs corresponding to the distinction between the two main kinds of avowals. The idea that phenomenal avowals serve as inner observation reports is challenged by the so-called 'private language argument' – the battery of considerations that surface in §§243 to the early 300s in the *Investigations*. The attack is multi-faceted but the famous central strand is that the Cartesian picture implicitly surrenders the resources needed for a distinction which is essential if such 'reports' are to have anything of the objectivity implicit in the very idea of an observational report: the objectivity implicit in the idea of successful representation of some self-standing aspect of reality, which demands a potential contrast between how matters seem to an observer and how they really stand. The corresponding conception of attitudinal avowals, by contrast, is challenged by the various phenomenological and other considerations which Wittgenstein marshals in the, as we may call them, 'not a mental process' passages recurrent throughout the text.[8] A central problem

---

[7] For further indications, see my 'Wittgenstein's Later Philosophy of Mind: Sensation, Privacy and Intention', in *Meaning Scepticism*, ed. Puhl, pp. 126–47.

[8] See e.g. *Philosophical Investigations* §§34, 146, 152, 154, 205, 303, 330–2, 427, 577, 673; also part II §vi p. 181, and §xi pp. 217–18. The distinction is prominent in the *Remarks on the Philosophy of Psychology* as well,

with the idea that attitudinal avowals describe introspectable mental occurrences concerns the answerability of ascriptions of intentional states like expectation, hope and belief to aspects of a subject's outward performance that may simply *not be available* at the time of avowal. If an expectation, say, were a determinate, dated occurrence before the mind's eye, then in any particular case it would either have taken place or not, irrespective of how I subsequently went on to behave. So we ought to be guilty of a kind of conceptual solecism if we hold claims about expectation to be answerable to subsequent sayings and doings in a fashion broadly akin to the way in which the ascription of dispositional states is so answerable. Yet that is exactly what we actually do. The conception of attitudinal avowals as reports of inner observation thus stands at odds with another, fundamental feature of their grammar – their essential answerability, in broadly the fashion of dispositions, to matters which may be unobservable at the time they are asserted.[9]

The pursuit of these ideas of Wittgenstein leads one to recognize deep incoherences in the Cartesian response to our problem – incoherences that are prior to its inordinate sceptical costs. Note, moreover, that if what I said earlier is right – viz. that there is no alternative for one disposed to

---

where Wittgenstein uses the terminology of *dispositions* versus *states of consciousness*; see, for instance, vol. II, §§45, 48, 57 and 178.

[9] This idea is elaborated a little at pp. 237ff. of my 'Wittgenstein's Rule-Following Considerations and the Central Project of Theoretical Linguistics', in *Reflections on Chomsky*, ed. Alexander George (Oxford: Basil Blackwell, 1989), pp. 233–64.

pursue the privileged-observation route than to see the privilege as *necessarily* the exclusive property of the observing subject – then the incoherence of the Cartesian response is the incoherence of *any* broadly observational model of a subject's relation to her ordinary psychological states. That's a crucial lesson.

IV

But if not an observational model, then what? There is a proposal about our problem that for a time was widely accepted as Wittgenstein's own. At *Investigations* §308 he writes

> How does the philosophical problem about mental processes and states and about behaviourism arise? – The first step is the one that altogether escapes notice. We talk of processes and states and leave their nature undecided. Sometime perhaps we shall know more about them – we think. But that is just what commits us to a particular way of looking at the matter.

And a little earlier (§304) he urged that we need to

> make a radical break with the idea that language always functions in one way, always serves the same purpose: to convey thoughts – which may be about houses, pains, good and evil, or anything else you please.

These sections advance the diagnosis that our difficulties in this neighbourhood are generated by 'the grammar which tries to force itself on us here' (§304). They go, Wittgenstein suggests, with a conception of avowals as *reports* and the associated conception of a self-standing subject matter which they serve to report. We take it that there are mental states and processes going on anyway, as it were – the 'first step' that escapes notice – and that each person's avowals serve to report on such states and processes as pertain to her. The immediate effect is to set up a dilemma. How, in the most general terms, should we think of the states of affairs which confer truth on these 'reports'? There is the Cartesian – events-in-an-arena-accessible-only-to-the-subject – option; this does a neat job of explaining the distinctive marks of avowals, at least at a casual muster, but it relies on an 'analogy which... falls to pieces' (§308) – the analogy between avowals and observation reports made from a privileged position. But the only other option seems to be to 'go public': to opt for a view which identifies the truth-conferring states of affairs with items which are somehow wholly manifest and available to public view – an option which Wittgenstein expects, writing when he did, will naturally take a behaviourist shape so that 'Now it looks as if we had denied mental processes.' Of course, a philosopher who takes this option – whether in behaviourist or other form – will want to resist the suggestion that she is *denying* anything, according to *her* recommended understanding of 'mental process', just as Berkeley resisted the suggestion that he was denying the existence of matter. But the manifest problem is to reconcile any such conception of the truth conditions of avowals with their distinctive marks: for as soon as you go public, it becomes obscure what advantage selves can enjoy over others.

This line of difficulty may seem to point to an obvious conclusion. Conceiving of avowals as reports of states and processes which are going on anyway appears to enforce a disjunction: *either* accept the Cartesian view, which cannot accommodate ordinary knowledge of others, *or* accept some form of externalization – perhaps behaviourist, nowadays more likely physicalist – which cannot sustain the special place of self-knowledge. So we should reject the parent assumption. And one tradition of commentary, encouraged especially by *Investigations* §244,[10] interprets Wittgenstein as doing this in a very radical way: as denying that avowals are so much as *assertions* (that they make statements, true or false), proposing to view them rather as *expressions* of the relevant aspects of the subject's psychology.[11]

'Expression'? To give expression to an aspect of one's psychology just means, presumably, to give it display, in the way in which wincing and a sharp intake of breath may display a stab of pain, or a smile may display that one is pleased, or a clenching of the teeth that one is angry. Propositional attitudes too can be open to natural expression of this kind: a prisoner's rattling the bars of his cell is a natural expression of a desire to get out. (It is not a way of acting on that desire, of course – it is not rationalized by it.) Wittgenstein's famous suggestion in §244 is that we should see the avowal of pain as an acquired form of pain behaviour: something one learns to use to supplant or augment the natural expression of pain and which

[10] But see also *Remarks on the Philosophy of Psychology*, vol. I, §§450, 501, 593, 599 and 832.

[11] The sometime popularity of this interpretation is traceable to its being advanced by several of the first reviewers: P. F. Strawson, for instance, in his critical study of the *Investigations* in *Mind* 63 (1954), 70–99; and Norman Malcolm in his 'Wittgenstein's *Philosophical Investigations*' in *The Philosophical Review* 63 (1954), 530–59.

(the *expressivist* tradition of commentary suggests) is no more a *statement* – something with a truth-evaluable content – than are such natural forms of expression.

The immediate question is how well an expressivist treatment of avowals can handle their distinctive marks. And the answer appears to be: not badly at all. For instance, if the avowal 'I am in pain' is not a statement, true or false, then naturally it is inappropriate to ask its author for grounds for it (groundlessness) and naturally there is no question of her ignorance of its truth value (transparency). And if, when uttered with proper comprehension, it is to be compared to an episode of pain behaviour, then only its being a piece of dissimulation – not sincere – can stand in the way of a conclusion that the subject really is in pain (strong authority). (And of course it will provide a criterion for the subject's being in pain in just the way that ordinary pain behaviour does.)

Nevertheless the expressivist proposal has come to be more or less universally viewed as a non-starter, for reasons preponderantly to do with the perceived impossibility of making coherent philosophy of language out of it. The claim that the avowal 'I am in pain' serves to make no statement, true or false, has to be reconciled with a whole host of linguistic phenomena whose natural explanation would exploit the opposed idea that it is, just as it seems, the affirmation of a truth-evaluable content. Here are four of the snags:

1. What has the expressivist proposal to say about transformations of tense – 'I was in pain' and 'I will be in pain'? If either is a genuine assertion, doesn't there have to be such a thing as an author's making the same assertion at a

time when doing so would demand its present-tense transform? If on the other hand they are regarded likewise merely as expressions, *what* do they serve to express? (Doesn't an expression accompany – hence have to take place at the same time as – what it expresses?)

2. How is the proposal to construe a locution like 'He knows that I am in pain'? If there is a use of the words 'I am in pain' so embedded, which I can use to express the content of someone else's possible knowledge, why may I not *assert* that very same content by the use of the same words?

3. There are genuine – for instance quantified – statements which stand in logical relations to 'I am in pain.' It entails, for instance, 'Someone is in pain.' How can a genuine statement be entailed by a mere expression?

4. 'I am in pain' embeds like any normal assertoric content in logical constructions such as negation and the conditional. 'It's not the case that I am in pain' and 'If I am in pain, I'd better take an aspirin' are syntactically perfectly acceptable constructions. But how can a mere expression, in contrast to an assertion, be *denied*? And doesn't the antecedent of a conditional have to be understood as the hypothesis that *something is the case?*

This kind of point – I shall dub the whole gamut 'the Geach point'[12] – has often been used as a counter to various forms of expressivism, notably in ethics, and much

---

[12] After P. T. Geach's emphasis of such difficulties for moral expressivism, Austin's performatory account of knowledge, etc. See Geach's 'Assertion' in *The Philosophical Review* 74 (1965), 449–65.

ingenuity has been expended (squandered?) by philosophers of expressivist inclination in the attempt to meet it. But in the present case I don't think it ought to have been influential at all. In the ethical case, the expressivist thesis is, crudely, that there are *no* real moral states of affairs; so the occurrence of what are apparently truth-evaluable contents couched in distinctively moral vocabulary has to be some kind of illusion. In that case the Geach point represents a very serious challenge, since it seems to show that everyday moral thought, in exploiting perfectly standard syntactic resources like those afforded by ordinary sentential logic, requires to the contrary that truth-evaluable moral contents exist. By contrast, it is no part of the present, allegedly Wittgensteinian expressivist proposal that there is no such thing as a statement of ordinary psychological fact. No-one is questioning that '*He* is in pain' is an assertion. The expressivist thesis distinctively concerns *avowals*.

How does that difference help? Well, it is clear that we have to draw a distinction in any case between the question whether an indicative sentence is associated with a truth-evaluable content and the question whether its characteristic use is actually *assertoric*. For the two notions routinely come apart in the case of standard performatives like 'I promise to be on time', 'With this ring, I thee wed', 'I name this ship. . .', and so on. Each of these locutions embeds in all the ways the generalized Geach point focuses on; and none of them is standardly used, in the atomic case, as an assertion. We should conclude that what the Geach point signals is merely the presence of truth-evaluable content. It is powerless to determine that the standard use of a locution is to *assert* such a content. And how the expressivist thesis about avowals can be merely that the typical use of such sentences is as expressions rather than assertions. There need be no suggestion that one *cannot* make assertions about one's own psychology. But the suggestion – now initially rather exciting – will be that the appearance of the *epistemic* superiority of the self which avowals convey is an illusion created by attempting to find a home for features of such utterances which they carry *qua* expressions in the context of the mistaken assumption that they are ordinary assertions. When selves *do* make strict assertions about their own psychology, the story should continue, any epistemic advantages they enjoy are confined to those of superiority of evidence which I briefly noted at the beginning.

That, it seems to me, is, in outline, how the best expressivist proposal should go. Now to its real problems. Perhaps the most immediate awkwardness, if a general account of avowals is to be based upon the §244 idea, is that, even in the case of sensations, the range of cases where there are indeed *natural,* non-linguistic forms of expression – cases like pains, itches and tickles – is very restricted: contrast for instance the sensation of coolness in one foot, or the smell of vanilla. In the latter kind of case, the suggested model of the acquisition of competence in the avowal simply won't grip, and the theorist will have to try to live with the idea of a range of sensations whose *only* expression consists in their avowal. The same is evidently true in spades of psychological items other than sensations. This threatens a worrying dilution of the key notion of *expression*.

That's a worry that might, I suppose, be worked on. But the next one seems decisive. Suppose a highly trained secret agent under torture resolutely gives no ordinary behavioural sign of pain. However, his torturers are men of discernment, with subtle instruments, who know full well of his agony nonetheless: they know the characteristic signs – patterns on the electro-encephalograph, raised heart rate, activation of reflexes in the eye, changes in surface skin chemistry, etc., etc. If the suggestion really is to be that the superiority of the first-person viewpoint is *wholly* an artefact of a grammatical misunderstanding – the misconstrual of expressions as assertions – then any *knowledge*, strictly so conceived, which the victim has of his own pain has to originate in the same way as that of his tormentors. But by hypothesis he isn't expressing pain behaviourally. And the signs that leave them in no doubt are things which, in his agony, he may not be attending to, or which, like the print-out on the electro-encephalograph, he may not be able to see or interpret if he could see. So in such a case, when it comes down to knowledge, it looks as though the expressivist account must represent the victim as actually *at a disadvantage*. That's evident nonsense.

In general, merely to conceive of avowals as expressive does not, when it goes in tandem with an acceptance of the reality of the states of affairs which they express, provide any way of deflecting the question: how, broadly speaking, should we conceive of the kind of state of affairs which is apt to confer truth on psychological ascriptions, and in what sort of epistemological relationship do their subjects themselves in general stand to such states of affairs? If this relationship is in any way more than evidentially privileged, we have our original problem back. If it isn't, we seem to get absurdities like that just illustrated.

A different way of seeing the ultimate unplayability of the expressivist position is to reflect that the content of an avowal is always available to figure just in a subject's *thoughts*, without public expression. You may sit reading and think to yourself, 'My headache has gone', without giving any outward sign at all. And anyone versed in ordinary psychology will accept that *if* you have that thought, not by way of merely entertaining it but as something you endorse, then you will be right (authority); that there is no way that your headache could have passed unless you are willing to endorse such a thought (transparency); and that your willingness to endorse it will not be the product of inference or independently formulable grounds (groundlessness). Thus analogues of each of the marks of avowals that pose our problem engage the corresponding unarticulated thoughts. It must follow that the correct explanation of the possession of them by avowals cannot have anything to do with illocutionary distinctions.

We should conclude that while the expressivist proposal flies rather further than is usually thought, it is a dead duck all the same.

V

For sure, the textural evidence for attributing the expressivist view to Wittgenstein was always pretty exiguous. *Investigations* §244 in particular should be contrasted with the much more cautionary and nuanced remarks else-where.[13] Such apparent equivocations, of course, are fuel for the common complaint that while Wittgenstein has suggestive criticisms to offer of certain tendencies in the philosophy of mind, he left any intended positive contribu-tion shrouded in fog. What exactly – or even roughly – is Wittgenstein saying about avowals, if he is not advancing the expressivist view? How exactly does he propose we should liberate our thinking from Cartesian tendencies? What did he think we should put in their place?

Well actually, I don't think it is all that difficult to glean what his positive recommendation is, at least in gen-eral outline. The difficulty is, rather, to settle for it. The first essential in interpreting him here is to give due prominence to the *Investigations*' explicit conception of the genesis of philosophical problems and of proper philosophical method. Wittgenstein wrote, recall, that

> we may not advance any kind of theory. There must not
> be anything hypothetical in our considerations. We must
> do away with all *explanation*, and description alone must
> take its place... [Philosophical problems] are solved,
> rather, by looking into the workings of our language, and
> that in such a way as to make us recognise those

---

[13] For instance *Investigations* part II, section ix: 'a cry, which cannot be called a description, which is more primitive than any description, for all that it serves as a description of the inner life. A cry is not a description. But there are transitions. And the words, "I am afraid", may approximate more, or less, to being a cry. They may come quite close to this and also *be far* removed from it.'

> workings: *in despite of* an urge to misunderstand them. . .
> Philosophy is a battle against the bewitchment of our
> intelligence by means of language.[14]

And, very famously,

> Our mistake is to look for an explanation where we ought
> to look at what happens as a 'proto-phenomenon'. That
> is, where we ought to have said: *this language game is
> played.*[15]

The bearing of these strategic remarks is immediate if we
reflect that our whole problem is constituted by a demand
for explanation. We are asking: what is the *explanation* of
the characteristic marks of avowals? And we easily accept a
refinement of the question along such lines as: what is it
about the subject matter of avowals, and about their authors'
relation to it, which explains the possession by these utterances of their characteristically effortless, non-inferential
authority? Cartesianism takes the question head on, giving
the obvious, but impossible, answer. And the expressivist
proposal, radical though it is in its questioning of the
assumption that the authority of an avowal is the authority
of a claim to truth, is not so radical as to raise a question
about the validity of the *entire explanatory project.* But
Wittgenstein, seemingly, means to do just that. Against the
craving for explanation, he seemingly wants to set a

---

[14] *Philosophical Investigations* §109.

[15] *Philosophical Investigations* §654. It doesn't matter that this is said in
the context of discussion of a different issue (recollection of the content
of a prior intention).

conception of the 'autonomy of grammar'.[16] The features of avowals which set our problem – the features which seem to betray something remarkable about self-knowledge – do so only if we suppose that they are in some way *consequential* upon something deeper, for instance the nature of their subject matter and of their author's relationship to it. But what imposes that way of looking at the matter? Why shouldn't psychological discourse's exhibition of these features be regarded as primitively constitutive of its being *psychological,* so that the first-/third-person asymmetries that pose our question belong primitively to the 'grammar' of the language game of ordinary psychology, in Wittgenstein's special sense – 'grammar' which 'is not accountable to any reality' and whose rules 'cannot be justified by showing that their application makes a representation agree with reality' ?[17]

What did Wittgenstein suppose entitled him to this? In his later work, as everyone knows, he radically rethought his early conception of the relation between language and reality. It is to this readjustment, I suggest, that we must look if we are to understand the doctrine of the 'autonomy of grammar'. As I read the early 300s, the obstacle which Wittgenstein sees as lying in the way of our philosophical understanding of 'mental processes and states' is not the assumption of the truth-evaluability of avowals, as the expressivist interpretation has it, but rather a general picture

---

[16] As Baker and Hacker style it.

[17] *Philosophische Grammatik,* (Oxford: Blackwell, 1969), section X, §§133 and 134.

of the working of *all* truth-evaluable language. Wittgenstein means to reject a certain picture of what truth-evaluability involves: the picture gestured at in §304, that our statements always serve 'the same purpose: to convey thoughts – which may be about houses, pains, good and evil, or anything else you please'. This picture involves thinking of assertions as expressing propositions which are laid over against reality in the manner of the *Tractatus*, so that there have to be self-standing states of affairs to correspond to avowals, when they are true, and it has therefore to be possible to raise general questions about the nature of these self-standing states of affairs, and the nature of the subject's knowledge of them. And then, when we are mindful of the distinctive marks of avowals, it appears that the states, and the mode of knowledge, must be something rather out of the ordinary – the relevant states of affairs have to be conceived as somehow especially transparent to the subject, or, at the least, as working on her by some form of curiously reliable 'blindsight' (whose curious reliability, moreover, would have to be common knowledge if the authority credited to avowals is to be explained). Wittgenstein's diagnosis is that the 'philosophical problem about mental processes and states and about behaviourism' arises because we insist on interpreting the truth-evaluability of avowals – the source of the linguistic features on which the Geach point fastens – as imposing a conception of their being true, when they are, in terms which have to raise these consti-tutive questions about nature and access. But these are the very questions – Wittgenstein is saying – which we must free ourselves of the temptation to raise; they are the questions which lead to the fast-track into the fly-bottle.

Of course, the conception of truth and truth-makers which, in Wittgenstein's diagnosis, is here at the root of our difficulty is the core of the outlook which Hilary Putnam has called metaphysical realism. Perhaps his single most significant departure from the metaphysics of the *Tractatus* was Wittgenstein's coming to believe that we have to stop thinking about the relationship between language and reality, and about truth, in that kind of way.

VI

What is involved in this re-orientation deserves a more refined depiction that I can attempt here. If we abstract from the globally anti-explanatory background mantra, the cash-value of the proposal, just for the issue of self-knowledge, involves a generalization to all avowable subject matter, phenomenal and attitudinal, of a view which might be characterized like this:

> the authority standardly granted to a subject's own
> beliefs, or expressed avowals, about his intentional states
> is a *constitutive principle*: something which is not a
> consequence of the nature of those states, and an
> associated epistemologically privileged relation in which
> the subject stands to them, but enters primitively into the
> conditions of identification of what a subject believes,
> hopes and intends.[18]

I'll call this general viewpoint the Default View. According to the Default View, it is just primitively constitutive of the

---

[18] From p. 142 of my 'Wittgenstein's Later Philosophy of Mind: Sensation, Privacy and Intention', in *Meaning Scepticism.*, ed. Puhl.

acceptability of psychological claims that, save in cases whose justification would involve active self-interpretation, a subject's opinions about herself are default-authoritative and default-limitative: unless you can show how to make better sense of her by overriding or going beyond it, her active self-conception, as manifest in what she is willing to avow, must be deferred to. The truth conditions of psychological ascriptions are primitively conditioned by this constraint. In particular, it is simply basic to the competent ascription of the attitudes that, absent good reason to the contrary, one must accord correctness to what a subject is willing to avow; and limit one's ascriptions to her to those she is willing to avow.

It would be a great achievement of Wittgenstein's discussion if it made it possible to understand how the Default View might be the last word on the issue. But it is anything but clear, actually, how a repudiation of the metaphysical realist picture of truth could just by itself directly enjoin this conception. Moreover it is difficult to rest easy with the general anti-explanatory mantra, which is seemingly in tension with a diagnostic thought which is very important to Wittgenstein himself: that philosophical problems characteristically arise because we are encouraged by surface-grammatical analogies to form expectations about an area of discourse which are appropriate only for a particularly salient surface-grammatical analogue of it. That is *exactly* Wittgenstein's diagnosis in the present case: the target analogy is that between the use of avowals and ordinary reports of observation. So then that diagnosis itself requires that the explanatory questions which we are required *not* to press in the case of avowals are, by contrast, perfectly properly raised, and unanswerable, in the case of ordinary reports of observation. There cannot, accordingly, just be a blanket prohibition against explanatory questions of that kind. Put that thought alongside the plausible claim that there are perfectly legitimate modes of *conceptual* explanation – informal mathematics, in particular, is full of them – and it appears that it cannot in general be merely a confusion to seek to explain features of the practice of a discourse *a priori* by reference to our concepts of the kind of subject matter it has and of the epistemic capacities of speakers. Thus the insistence that these questions are misplaced in the target case of psychological self-ascriptions begins to seem merely dogmatic.

Is there any way this impression of dogmatism might be dispelled? In the analogy of the kaleidoscope, our conception is that of a range of independent features and events: evolving patterns of shape and colour to which the privileged observer is sensitive – responsive – by dint of his situation and his possession of certain germane cognitive capacities, notably vision. There is a story to be told about the kind of things on display and how things of that kind can elicit a response from someone with a suitable cognitive endowment. Now, one way to try to exculpate the Default View from the charge of dogmatism, it seems to me, is to seek a framework which places controls on the relevant idea of *responsiveness*.[19] One form of control might be elicited from pursuing recently prominent issues to do with

[19] I suppose this is a programme of what McDowell has disparagingly called 'constructive philosophy'.

judgement-dependence and the *Euthyphro contrast*: we may pursue the details of the relations, in different regions of thought, between best opinion and truth, attempting thereby to arrive at a conception of what it is for them to relate too closely, so to speak, for their congruence to count as a *success in tracking*. Another control might emerge from consideration of the question how wide the potential *explanatory range* has to be of a certain type of states of affairs if we are to think of our judgements about them as genuinely responsive to their subject matter at all (*Width of Cosmological Role*).[20] We can seek a general framework of such controls and try to show that first-person psychological discourse emerges on the wrong side of the tracks, so to speak, under their application. Then, if its apparent urgency does indeed derive from a tacit assumption of the *responsiveness* of selves to their own psychological states, the general explanatory question about self-knowledge, which official Wittgensteinian philosophical method would have us ignore, might emerge as something which we can understand *why* we ought not to ask.

By contrast, if that kind of project is dismissed, it is hard to see how the Default View can come to much more than a take-it-or-leave-it recommendation: a mere invitation to *choose* to treat as primitive something which we have run into trouble trying to explain, and to do so just on that account. Wittgenstein notoriously came to view philosophical problems as akin to a kind of self-inflicted intellectual

---

[20] Both these ideas are explored in my *Truth and Objectivity* (Cambridge, MA: Harvard University Press, 1994).

disease; they would thus contrast starkly with *mathematical* problems as traditionally viewed (not by Wittgenstein, of course) – a kind of sublime, objective puzzle whose force can be felt by any rational intellect. If philosophical problems are justly deflated in Wittgenstein's way, then a kind of 'Here: think of matters this way, and you'll feel better' remedy might be the best we can do. But the remedy seems enormously disappointing, intellectually. For most of us, after all, the attraction of philosophy is all about gaining understanding. Except in cases where one can *explain* a priori why the quest is inappropriate, it is apt to seem a mere abrogation of the subject to be told there is nothing to understand.

VII

Let me try to draw some strands together. We owe to Wittgenstein the insight that we are making an assumption in regarding it as a deficiency of understanding to lack a satisfactory explanation of the distinctive marks of avowals. The assumption is, roughly, that those distinctive marks must be *consequential*: that either they must derive from the nature of the subject matter – something which therefore drives our discourse about it into the relevant characteristic turns – or else they must derive from some unobvious feature of the semantics of first-person psychological discourse (its being, for instance, expressive rather than assertoric). So, according to the assumption, there must *be* an explanation – which we have yet to assemble and get into focus.

There is a frontal collision between this way of thinking and the conception of the nature of legitimate philosophical enquiry seemingly quite explicit in Wittgenstein's later official methodological pronouncements. According to Wittgenstein, the limit of our philosophical ambition should be to recognize the assumptions we are making in falling into philosophical difficulty and to see our way clear to accepting, by whatever means, that nothing forces us to make them. It is, for Wittgenstein, with the very craving for *legitimizing explanations* of features of our talk about mind, or rules, or mathematics, that we are led into hopeless puzzles about the status – the epistemology and ontology – of those discourses. Philosophical treatment is wanted, not to solve these puzzles but to undermine them – to assuage the original craving that leads to the construction of the bogus models and interpretations by which we attempt to make sense of what we do, but which are the source of all our difficulties, and yet whose want is felt as a lack of understanding. The problem of self-knowledge is a signal example. It can have – I believe Wittgenstein thought – no solution of the kind we seek; for that very conception of a solution implicitly presupposes that there must be a something-in-virtue-of-which the distinctive marks of avowals are sustained. But those marks are part of 'grammar' and grammar is not sustained by anything. We should just say 'this language game is played'.

The generalization of this position – the 'estoppel' of all philosophical explanation – seems to me vulnerable to a version of what one might call the Paradox of Postmodernism. The paradox is that while, like all deflationists, Wittgenstein needs to impress us of the illegitimacy of more traditional aspirations, *argument* for that is hard to foresee if it is not of the very coin which he is declaring to be counterfeit. For what is needed here is precisely a *philosophical explanation*. To be sure, what belongs to 'grammar', in Wittgenstein's special sense of that term, requires no explanation. *Of course;* that's a matter of definition. But even a sympathetic reading of him will find a frustrating inattention to the question when something may legitimately be taken to be part of 'grammar'. It may be a crucial first step to recognize that the problem of self-knowledge is occasioned by an assumption of explicability – an assumption that may be discarded with a clear conscience if the special position of subjects in determining what is true of their psychology is indeed 'grammatical'. But, one wants to say, what shows that? Once one recognizes the Default View as a possibility, the immediate instinct is to ask: what might *justify* the idea that it is the whole truth? That is the instinct to attempt to understand when and why it is a good move to dismiss the attempt to understand. To succumb is to reenter the space of explanatory philosophy. To resist is to have no reason for the Default View.

To feel this dissatisfaction is not to have a reason to deny the insight that in a wide class of cases philosophical perplexity does indeed take the form of a casting about for what strike us as satisfying explanations of features of our language and of failing to find any that do not generate singularities, of one sort or another. (Just briefly to mention a second prominently Wittgensteinian example: how are we to make sense of the intelligibility of the distinction between whether a statement is really true and whether anybody ever takes it to be true unless the rule incorporated in its truth condition may be thought of as issuing its verdict autonomously and independently of any human judgement? So isn't the very idea of unratified truth an implicit commitment to 'rules-as-rails' platonism?!) But to accept Wittgenstein's insight, that some of the hardest-seeming philosophical problems take this form, is not a commitment to an explanation-proscribing view of philosophy. Even if it is misguided to persist in assuming that there must be *something* satisfactorily to take up the explanatory slack left by the demise of platonism, or Cartesianism, it may yet be possible to explain why such an assumption needn't be true in particular cases. It does not seem merely confused to seek, in particular, to characterize with some care the conception we have of the kinds of ways the marks of avowals might in principle be explained. It is even foreseeable that such a characterization might lead to a clear-headed realization that nothing could fulfil it. *That* would be – at least in this area – the discovery 'that gives philosophy peace'.[21]

---

[21] The phrase, of course, is from *Philosophical Investigations* §133.

Joint Attention and the First Person

JOHN CAMPBELL

I   Models of Joint Attention

It is sometimes said that ordinary linguistic exchange, in ordinary conversation, is a matter of securing and sustaining joint attention. The minimal condition for the success of the conversation is that the participants should be attending to the same things. So the psychologist Michael Tomasello writes, 'I take it as axiomatic that when humans use language to communicate referentially they are attempting to manipulate the attention of another person or persons.'[1] I think that this is an extremely fertile approach to philosophical problems about meaning and reference, and in this paper I want to apply it to the case of the first person. So I want to look at the case in which you tell me something about yourself, using the first person, and we achieve joint attention to the same object. But I begin with some remarks about how this approach applies to proper names and to perceptual demonstratives.

---

[1] Michael Tomasello, 'Joint Attention as Social Cognition', *Joint Attention: Its Origins and Role in Development*, ed. Chris Moore and Philip J. Dunham (Hillsdale, NJ: Erlbaum, 1995).

Suppose, for example, that you are explaining to me the role that a particular person plays on a particular committee. You may be presupposing an enormous amount of knowledge on my part about the other people on the committee and the work that it does. You are focusing on the history of the committee, how it was set up and who the founding members were, as well as the idiosyncrasies of the current members. We are achieving joint attention here, as you manage to highlight the way this individual fits into the structure. There is nothing particularly perceptual about this exercise of joint attention, beyond what is required to hear each other's speech; the operation of attention here has to do with the way in which background knowledge we have is being mobilized and put to work.

It is a familiar idea that understanding a proper name involves having some dossier of information, which may or may not be correct information, about the bearer of the name. Using the name of the person we are talking about, in the above example, is a way of activating the right dossier, so that we each have the relevant dossier in play for the purposes of the conversation.

Joint attention is not just a matter of us both, coincidentally, attending to the same object. Rather, we know we are attending to the same thing, and aim to make it so. So we can use proper names and brief descriptions to make sure we are activating the relevant dossier, as when I say, 'John Wayne, the actor from all those Westerns'. For mutual understanding it is not essential that we have exactly the same information about John Wayne; it is enough if our dossiers derive from the same source and we know that they do.

Contrast the case of perceptual demonstratives. If you say to me, 'Isn't that man over there an actor?', you have to point or look in marked kind of way, or otherwise give me some perceptual cue as to who you are talking about. The most common kind of cue we use is spatial: pointing is the most basic kind of perceptual demonstration. So achieving joint attention in this kind of case is a matter of spatial co-ordination. I may direct my gaze so that its line intersects with the direction in which you are pointing or the direction in which you are looking. Of course, spatial cues are not the only ones we ever use. If you say, 'What is that noise?', we may manage to achieve joint focus on the noise though neither of us can tell where it is coming from; it has other features which make it salient for both of us. Even in these demonstrative cases, though, where one component of shared attention is perceptual, the sharing of attention is not exhausted by the perceptual. There is more to joint attention than spatial co-ordination of gaze, for example: we have to be mobilizing common background knowledge and some attunement to one another's interests to be attending to the same thing.

I turn now to my main topic, the case of joint attention achieved by the use of the first person. Suppose, for example, that you are telling me some story about yourself, about something that happened to you; or perhaps you are telling me about your current emotional instability, or perhaps about whether you would like tea or coffee. In these cases, you use the first person, and if the communication is effective, we achieve, however briefly, joint attentional focus on the same thing. My question is what we are doing when we do this; what it comes to, that we have achieved attentional focus on the same object.

I am not questioning whether we actually do manage the thing; it seems to be a datum that we do, and it seems so easy and effortless, in the short term at any rate, that it can seem completely unproblematic. What is there to ask about joint attention achieved through the use of the first person?

Suppose we consider the two models that we have so far for joint attention: proper names and perceptual demonstratives. Can we apply either of them to the case of the first person? Suppose we look at the model of proper names. Here joint attention is a matter of our both having activated the relevant dossiers. Suppose that you tell me, 'I have been hurt.' Is the joint focus here a matter of our having activated the relevant dossiers? For me to interpret your remark, I do have to know who it was that spoke. But I may never have met you before, so I may not have anything in the way of a previous dossier on you. There may be no dossier for me to activate; this looks much more like the case of a perceptual demonstrative. Certainly my identification of you may be perceptual-demonstrative identification. There is, indeed, the case in which I read some first-person remarks made by Bill Clinton, and to interpret them I have to bring my Clinton dossier to bear; but that is not the general case. And what about your own understanding of your statement, 'I have been hurt'? Is this a matter of you activating the relevant dossier? Of course, typically you will have some background knowledge about yourself. Typically you will have some kind of 'self' dossier. But it is hard to believe that your understanding of your own remark can consist in your activation of the right dossier, as if 'I' were a kind of proper name that you reserved for application to the person whose dossier this was. One reason is that although the case is unusual, you might be unable to activate any relevant dossier, yet still make comprehending use of the first person. If you are coming round after an accident, for example, you might say, 'Where am I?', or 'I have been hurt', without having any relevant dossier active at all. You still understand your own use of the first person, and you and your interlocutor may be achieving joint attention to the same person.

This may make it seem that the model of the perceptual demonstrative is more to the point here. Does the joint attention consist in something like spatial co-ordination of gaze, as when you and I focus on the same place? It certainly is true that I have to know who is speaking to interpret your remark, and that may involve my focusing on the person at the right place; and even if we are talking on the telephone, I will be using some perceptually salient cue, like the fact of your speaking on the line, to direct my attention. But your attention to yourself is not of this type. You do not have to direct attention to any particular place in interpreting your own uses of the first person, and you do not have to be using any perceptually salient cue, like the pitch of your voice, to direct your attention to one person rather than another. So the model of perceptual demonstratives also seems to fail us. Joint attention in the case of the first person is not achieved by spatial co-ordination, nor is it a matter of the joint use of any other perceptually salient cue.

At this point, far from seeming unproblematic, the securing of joint attention in the use of the first person may seem quite impossible. Your attention to yourself seems to be a kind of 'inner pointing', whereas my attention to you is either perceptually based, in the case in which we are talking, or draws on my knowledge of a proper name, as in the case in which I read Clinton's remarks. How could two such different types of attention be co-ordinated? So perhaps we do not in fact ever achieve joint attention through the use of the first person. But something has gone wrong here; joint attention achieved using the first person is commonplace.

II   Reference, Input and Output

Let us draw back, and ask how we do understand the first person. Part of understanding is an ability to use the term. There is an enormous variety of inputs to and outputs from first-person judgements. We use the first person in judgements about our current location, current psychological states and objectives, memories, physical condition, and so on, which are made on a wide variety of different bases. And accepting a first-person proposition, like 'I've been swindled', or whatever, may have any of a wide range of implications for action or further thought.

There ought to be more to our grasp of the first person than merely knowing how to use it, in grasping the inputs and outputs. There should be knowledge of the semantic value of the term, which would rationalize our use of those input and output procedures, which would explain why those are the correct input and output procedures to be using.

The first person is a singular term, so a specification of its semantic value will be a matter of specifying the reference of the term. The truth or falsity of a judgement using the first person will be determined, in part, by the reference of the term.

On the face of it, we have a very straightforward and absolutely reliable way of specifying the reference of the first person. The reference of the first person is given by the token-reflexive rule:

> The Token-Reflexive Rule: Any token of 'I' refers to whoever produced it.

The problem now is to explain how the token-reflexive rule relates to the inputs and outputs of first-person judgements, the bases on which they are made and the consequences we draw from them. Straight off, it seems too much to ask that inputs and outputs to first-person judgements should in general be truth-preserving. We accept that we are fallible in many of the first-person judgements we make, in that even if we were right about the data on which we base our judgement, the judgement itself may be wrong. Similarly, even if the judgement is correct, the consequences we draw from it may be mistaken. But surely we could ask that the inputs to a first-person judgement should be capable of yielding knowledge of the truth of the judgement, given that its truth-value is determined in the way suggested by the account of semantic value. This suggests what I will call the principle of concord:

> Concord: The bases on which judgements using a singular term are made must yield knowledge of the object assigned as reference.

We might expect there also to be a complementary principle of effective action:

> Effective Action: The consequences of judgements using a singular term must be actions effectively directed to the object assigned as reference.

And then the problem is to understand how the use of the first person can be rationalized in the sense explained by these two principles; how we can show that the assignment of semantic value made by the token-reflexive rule explains the correctness of the inputs and outputs we actually use in making first-person judgements.

This problem is not just a problem for the theorist. Someone who understands the term 'I' also grasps the semantic value of the term and finds the input–output procedures intelligible because he grasps the semantic value of the term. So an ordinary understanding of the first person does not just include an ability to make first-person judgements in appropriate circumstances, and to act on them appropriately. On the face of it, you might do all that without having the slightest glimmering of the point of all these procedures; you might have no sense whatever of the reason why these procedures were correct. An ordinary understanding of the first person includes knowledge of the semantic value of the term, and knowledge of how that rationalizes the ordinary procedures of verification and consequence-drawing. It is when you have that understanding of the term that you can be said to be self-conscious; that is what self-consciousness is.

So how are we to describe our ordinary knowledge of the semantic value of the first person? It is just at this point that it can seem so compelling to appeal to 'inner attention', which provides you with conscious awareness of the self as an object. Inner attention, so conceived, would let you know what you were about in making first-person judgements, it would let you know which thing it was that you were making judgements about. Once you had that knowledge, you would be able to see why the procedures you used actually conformed to these principles of Concord and Effective Action. And as I said, this idea of inner attention seems to make the possibility of joint attention to the self quite problematic.

III   Attention and Knowledge of Semantic Value

It is a basic point of contrast between the first person and perceptual demonstratives that there is that single reference rule, the token-reflexive rule, which fixes the reference of the term over time, so that whenever the term is used the rule operates, and across speakers, so that whoever uses the term, the rule operates.

Moreover, the input and output procedures that we use for first-person judgements are constant across time and across speakers. So when we ask how the reference rule can rationalize the input and output procedures we use, we are not talking about a rationalization that has to be available at a single moment or for a single speaker; we can be talking about a rationalization that is essentially available only across time in a situation in which there are many speakers using the first person.

To find an alternative to the 'inner attention' approach, we have to find an alternative way in which the subject could find intelligible the particular input and output procedures we use for first-person judgements. It is easiest to explain the alternative I have in mind if we have before us a concrete example of the kind of input and output procedures I have in mind. So I will first state a particularly simple and central case: the inputs and outputs from judgements about one's own location, and then consider how knowledge of the reference of the first person can rationalize the use of these procedures.

There is a basic distinction that we have to draw between what I shall call relational and what I shall call monadic egocentric spatial notions. Relational egocentric notions are those that we use when we say, for example, 'he is sitting on my left', 'the chasm yawned before him', 'look behind you', and so on. These notions specify the person whose right or left, up or down is in question. They are two-place notions: 'x is to y's left', 'x is below y' and so on. Now in stating the spatial content of vision, we do not seem to need these relational notions. We do not need the general conception of something's being to the right or left of an arbitrary subject. Rather, we need the much more primitive monadic egocentric terms. These are notions such as 'x is to the right', 'x is below', and so on. An animal could quite well have spatial vision even though it did not have the relational egocentric notions; it could not represent anyone else's left or right, only its own. But it is not even as if its vision makes explicit the spatial relations that things bear to it; it is not always itself an object in its own visual field. Its vision represents things as 'to the right' or 'above'; it does not seem correct to say it represents things as 'to my right' using the relational notion, because of the lack of generality in whose right or left can be represented. And the same seems to be true of ordinary human vision. It represents things as 'to the right' or 'above' using the monadic egocentric notions, rather than the relational terms.

When we learn the first person, we learn a procedural rule: that if vision represents an object as to the right, we are then in a position to say, 'The object is to my right.' We learn how to make relational judgements involving the first person on the basis of monadic spatial input.

We also learn how to act on the basis of relational judgements involving the first person. This at some point will involve the production of a 'motor image' detailing the spatial organization of the planned movement; and we may use relational judgements involving the first person in constructing such an image. For example, if I have formed the judgement that x is to the left of me, and I want to pick up x, then I have to form a motor image which directs reaching to the left.

In effect, then, we have an introduction and an elimination rule for the use of the first person. The introduction rule takes us from the monadic egocentric representation we have in vision, to the relational judgement involving use of the first person:

$$\frac{\text{VISION} : x \text{ is to the left}}{\text{hence}, x \text{ is to the left of me}}.$$

The elimination rule takes us from a relational judgement involving use of the first person, to the construction of a motor image using only monadic egocentric notions:

$$\frac{x \text{ is to the left of me}}{\text{MOTOR IMAGE : hence, to pick up } x, \text{ move to the left}}$$

The question now is whether we can find a semantic justification for these rules. If we say that the first person is subject to the token-reflexive rule, can we use that point to rationalize our use of these procedures for making first-person judgements and drawing implications for action from them? In the terms I just used, we have to show that the principles of concord and effective action are observed here.

Suppose someone has, in vision, a monadic spatial representation of an object as being to the left. If he consequently forms a judgement, 'the object is to my left', does the token-reflexive rule give any reason to think that his judgement may constitute knowledge? If someone has, in vision, a monadic spatial representation of an object as being to the left, does that in any way confirm the idea that the person who has the visual representation, if he forms a judgement, 'the object is to my left', will be forming a true judgement? By the token-reflexive rule, what this requires is that the person who forms the judgement, the person who produces the token of 'I', should have the object on his left.

Evidently the critical point here is that the person who has the visual representation should be the same as the person who makes the first-person judgement, and that visual-monadic right and left should in general be good guides to what is to the right or left of the person who has the visual representation.

How can you achieve an understanding of why this is in general true? In your own case, you can determine what is monadically right or left, but you have no better check on what is relationally to your right or your left than by the use of the rule. So there does not seem to be any understanding here of why monadic right and left are good guides to relational right and left. And in the case of other people, you can check what is relationally to their right or left by using visual-attentional skills to set up a frame of reference centred on the other object, but how can you check which monadic spatial representations the other person has? The whole point about a monadic spatial representation is that it is available only to the person who has that particular perceptual system.

Suppose you are trying to grasp the egocentric positions of things from someone else's point of view. One way to proceed is to use relational egocentric notions. That is what we are doing when we say, 'it's behind you!', and so on. But there is another possibility. You might form an image of the scene from the other person's position. The spatial content of the image is given in monadic spatial terms; that the image is from the other person's position is not itself part of the content of the image. You are forming the image as part of the project of grasping the indexical facts from another viewpoint, but that this is the project is not itself part of the content of the image you form. To say that, you have to step back from the formation of the image, and use some other method of representation. So here there is a two-level construction: at one level there is the imagistic representation of the monadic egocentric facts, and at the other level there is the statement of which person it is that has the image.

Why should we bother with this kind of two-level construction? It has to do with our need to use ways of representing the world, such as monadic egocentric spatial notions, that involve a viewpoint only implicitly, where the viewpoint from which the world is being described cannot be made part of the description. These ways of representing the world include perceptual or imagistic representations, where which person is having the image is not itself part of the content of the image. So if you are to use these ways of representing the world to indicate how things stand from viewpoints other than your current viewpoint, you will need a two-stage construction. At the first stage you describe which viewpoint is going to be represented, and at the second stage you use the implicitly viewpointed system to describe how the world is from that viewpoint. The two stages cannot be collapsed together, because the implicitly viewpointed system will resist any attempt to make it incorporate an identification of which viewpoint is being described.

We are all part of a community capable of this kind of imaginative construction, and that is what we use to explain and understand the correctness of the transitions back and forth between monadic and relational egocentric spatial notions, the introduction and elimination rules for the use of the first person. We can use this procedure to achieve an understanding of why it is that the introduction and elimination rules being used by another person do yield knowledge and facilitate action, in the way demanded by the principles of concord and effective action, with respect to the object assigned as reference by the token-reflexive rule.

Each of us can use this imaginative procedure to understand why in general the pattern of use of the first person is correct, given that it is governed by the token-reflexive rule. And this understanding does not need to appeal to any conception of the reference of the first person other than that given by the token-reflexive rule. In particular, there is no need to appeal to 'inner attention'; it does no work in rationalizing the input–output procedures we use for the first person. In fact, it does no work at all.

IV   Inner Attention

When we make perceptual-demonstrative reference to an object, we do so on the basis of attention to it. If I want to refer to an object we can both see, I have to draw your attention to it, and my own reference to the object depends on my attending to it. When we think about self-consciousness and self-reference, it is easy to think of this in terms of attention too. Self-reference, on this view, depends on attention to the self. Views of self-consciousness then divide. Is reference to the self a matter of attending to a physical object, or is it a matter of attending to the psychological? As I have said, I think that we should resist the assimilation of the first person to the perceptual demonstratives, and in particular, to resist the idea that the use of the first person should be thought to depend on attention to the self, whether understood as attention to the physical or attention to the mental. This seems to me to be the deep divide between perceptual demonstratives, where there is no systematic rule determining the reference of the term, only one's attention to the object, and token-reflexive terms, such as the first person, which are governed by systematic rules, such as 'Any token of the first person refers to whoever produced it.'

What is wrong with the idea that reference to yourself is a kind of 'inner pointing'? One possibility, which a Cartesian would favour, is that attention to oneself is attention to a purely psychological object. This would be a non-spatial, non-physical object which bears only psychological properties. But it is not easy to see how you yourself could ever attend selectively to such an object. How could you know that you were singling out one rather than any other such object? How do you know you always single out the same such object in an act of inner attention? And how do you know there is only one such object to be the bearer of all the psychological properties you take yourself to have? It seems impossible that we could find any account of the principles by which such inner attention might work.

There is a certain suspension of disbelief when we are considering this kind of picture of self-reference, anyhow, because as Hume remarked, we do not ordinarily take ourselves to be encountering any such exotic object; hence his comment that when he entered into himself, he encountered only particular perceptions. This might suggest an alternative picture of inner attention, on which it is not a matter of attending to a purely psychological substance, but a matter of attending to what Hume called particular perceptions. Since Hume thinks of the self as whatever it is that is the object of our attention in introspection, he concludes that the self is nothing but a bundle of perceptions.

Wittgenstein's radical contribution to the subject was to remark that attention to one's own perceptions is not a matter of attention to a particular kind of thing. Rather, it is a matter of attending to the ordinary physical objects around you; what turns your report into a report of your own psychological state is a particular twist that you give it. If you look at the sky and say 'How blue the sky is!', it is quite clear that your attention is directed to the common sky; and if you give that report the twist that turns it into a report of your perception, by saying, for example, 'I see the sky as blue', this is not a matter of you finding some new, inner object of attention. Rather, you have continued to attend to the sky, but in your report you have made use only of your current vision, giving the report you would have made without the benefit of any other information you might have. Prefacing your report with 'I see...' is just the way in which you signal that the following judgement was made on a purely visual basis. The problems of privacy, according to Wittgenstein, all arise because we mistake this kind of twist in the report for the discovery of a new, inner object of attention, rather than the external sky. Once we recognize that the only object of attention to be found is the external scene, the problem of the inverted spectrum, for example, vanishes; for the colour of the sky can be seen by all.

A similar point can be made about belief: if I am trying to find out whether I believe that p, I do not do it by attending to a special kind of inner object, which somehow indirectly bears on how things are in the world around me. Rather, to determine whether I believe that p, I use the following procedure. First, without stirring, I ask whether p is so. If the answer is that p is so, I make the report: 'I believe that p.' This only involves attention to whether p. At no point do I have to exercise some inner attention on a purely psychological realm.

Any account of self-reference is going to have to give a central place to this ability to twist our reports of what is around us into reports of psychological state. For the moment, though, the point is that self-reference cannot be thought to be a matter of introspective attention to a particular kind of psychological object, the self.

You might object that we can continue to think of the first person as like a perceptual demonstrative, so long as we abandon the idea of psychological-introspective attention, and view it instead as a matter of inner attention to your own physical states – to the way your body is. There certainly is such a thing as somatosensory attention, and it certainly is linked to our sense of ownership of our bodies. One way to bring this out is to remark that there are some neuropsychological conditions in which the patient does not recognize that he or she is the owner of various body parts – the left arm, for instance, may seem alien. What makes the difference between the case in which you do experience the limb as yours and the case in which you do not experience the limb as yours? It has been suggested what makes the difference is the possibility of somastosensory attention to the limb.[2] This link between somatosensory attention and the sense of ownership may

[2] Marcel Kinsbourne, 'Awareness of One's Body', in *The Body and the Self*, ed. Anthony Marcel and Naomi Eilan (Cambridge, MA: MIT Press, 1995).

seem to support the idea that grasp of the first person depends on somatosensory attention.

In fact, though, the relation of dependence seems to be round the other way. We can make a distinction between non-conceptual and conceptual somatosensory attention. Non-conceptual somatosensory attention is available to an animal or child, when pain directs its attention to an injured body part, for example. This need not involve thinking about the body part at all, and it may involve no exercise of self-consciousness; it is just that the animal is now poised to protect the body part. This kind of non-conceptual attention is evidently not enough for first-person thought. In contrast, it can happen that someone capable of thought has somatosensory attention directed to a body part, and thinks about that body part. But this kind of somatosensory attention does not make available new ways of thinking about body parts, as 'that hand', for example. (In contrast, seeing a hand really does make it possible to identify the thing in a new way, as 'that hand'.) Somatosensory attention to one's hand, if it involves thought about the thing at all, involves thought of it not as 'that hand', but as thought about, e.g., 'my right hand'. Somatosensory attention uses a system for identification of the body parts which is available prior to the individual acts of attention, and which presupposes, and so cannot explain, our use of the first person.

If we suppose that the reference of the first person is fixed by somatosensory attention, we would have to think of 'I' as meaning something like 'whoever's hand this is', 'whoever's foot this is', and so on. But that would mean that the notion of ownership could be explained prior to an understanding of the first person; that in advance of an understanding of the first person, you could know that it means to say that this or that body part belongs to one or another person. And this does not seem to be correct: the only conception of ownership we have that the owner of the hand is the one who is entitled to speak of it as 'my hand', and so on.

V   Joint Attention and the Token-Reflexive Rule

I began with the problem of describing what it consists in, that joint attention can be secured in an ordinary conversation by the use of the first person. We saw that the models of co-ordination of background knowledge and perception do not seem to work in this case, and turned to look in detail at how self-reference and attention to oneself might be related. I have argued that we cannot view self-reference as depending on inner attention, whether that is thought of as psychological or as somatosensory attention. Rather, there is only the use of the first person, subject to the token-reflexive rule, and our imaginative understanding of each other to rationalize the input and output procedures we use.

The question I have been addressing has to do with how deep the token-reflexive rule goes in describing our understanding of the first person. According to the view I have been opposing, there is nothing deep about the token-reflexive rule. It is true that our use of the first person is governed by this rule, but, on this view, it tells us nothing about what joint attention achieved through the use of the first person consists in.

On this view, the use of the token-reflexive rule is only instrumental to achieving an understanding of particular uses of the first person. When you hear someone else using the first person, you know that the person is using a term subject to the token-reflexive rule, but that tells you nothing until you know who it is that is speaking; until you have some other way of identifying the speaker. Then you can use that identification to interpret the first-person statement. Suppose you hear someone saying, 'I have been hurt'. You find that the speaker was Gustav Lauben. Lauben said, 'I have been hurt', so to interpret the use of 'I', you strike out the 'I' and write in 'Lauben'. Similarly, to understand your own use of the first person, it is not enough that you should be using a term subject to the token-reflexive rule, and employing the right input–output procedures. You need to have some further identification of yourself, so that you can interpret your own uses of 'I', using some 'inner demonstrative' like 'this person'. It is when you are following this line of thought that the appeal to inner attention seems absolutely inescapable. It is also this line of thought that makes the phenomenon of joint attention achieved through the use of the first person seem quite impossible.

The alternative I have been recommending is that the speaker using the first person does not need any other kind of self-identification than is provided by the use of the first person, subject to the token-reflexive rule, and grasp of the ordinary grounds on which we make first-person judgements and their consequences for action.

The puzzle this raises is how we can use knowledge of the reference of the first person to explain the correctness of the input and output procedures we ordinarily use. The desire to understand this is, I think, at the heart of the appeal to 'inner attention'. But I have tried to show that we can explain the correctness of the input and output procedures we actually use by employing our capacity for an imaginative understanding of each other, and our knowledge that we are ourselves targets of imaginative understanding.

On this view, an understanding of someone else's use of 'I' does depend on knowledge of who it was that spoke; you need some such further identification if you are to attend to the right person. But an understanding of your own use of 'I' does not depend on any further identification at all, and in particular, not on an identification that appeals to inner attention. Rather, your attending to yourself just consists in your use of 'I', subject to the token-reflexive rule, and in accordance with our ordinary input–output procedures. So the phenomenon of joint attention achieved through the use of the first person is straightforward. All that is required is a use of the first person in a context in which it is manifest to the audience who the speaker is; a context which immediately makes available some further identification of the speaker. It is by finding this further identification that the audience manages its side of the joint attention. But the speaker has no further identification to find; the speaker discharges his side of the joint attention simply by continuing to use the first person.

Consciousness as Existence

TED HONDERICH

I   Leaving Consciousness Out, or Trying to

The difference for present purposes between ourselves and stones, chairs and our computers is that we are conscious. The difference is fundamental. Being conscious is sufficient for having a mind in one sense of the word 'mind', and being conscious is necessary and fundamental to having a mind in any decent sense. *What* is this difference between ourselves and stones, chairs and our computers? The question is not meant to imply that there is a conceptual or a nomic barrier in the way of non-biological things being conscious. It may happen one decade that the other minds problem will shoot up the philosophical agenda and get a lot of attention as a result of a wonderful computer attached to perceptual and behavioural mechanisms, and that the thing will in the end be taken as conscious, rightly. Our question is not what things can be conscious, but what the property or nature of consciousness is.

Conscious or mental events, as we know them now, are in some kind of necessary connection with neural events. This fact of psychoneural intimacy, which is consistent with what has just been said of the possibility of non-biological things being conscious, provides the best argument for *strict or true identity theories of consciousness.* These take the property of consciousness to be a neural property, or, as we can say instead, take conscious events to have only neural properties. The objection to these theories seems to me not that they make conscious events physical. I take it that in a good sense of 'physical', definitely not the indeterminate one relativized to the science of the moment or to future unknown science, conscious events are indeed physical. That is, they are either in the category of things that are spatio-temporal and perceived or the category of things that are spatio-temporal and are nomically connected with spatio-temporal things that are perceived. Stones and the like are in the first category, particles and the like in the second.[1]

This paragraph should be a footnote (can be asterisk acknowledgement attached to chapter title)

What disposes very many people against strict identity theories is of course that our experience of conscious events, the having of them, leaves us thinking that they have a property or nature other than the properties or nature had by wholly neural events – transmitter-substance properties and so on. Strict identity theories leave something out. They seem to me to leave out not something elusive, or something diaphanous, or something peripheral, but the reality of our mental lives. They leave out the most immediate of all the facts we know. Hence many of us feel that psychoneural

[1] For an exposition of this fundamental conception of physicality, see Anthony Quinton, *The Nature of Things* (London: Routledge & Kegan Paul, 1973) pp. 46–53.

215

intimacy must be accommodated by a means other than asserting that conscious events have only neural properties. All other identity theories, the lenient or arguable ones such as Donald Davidson's Anomalous Monism and also the Union Theory on which I am keen,[2] all of which bear the slight burden of being called property-dualisms, raise the very question we are considering. They allow that consciousness brings in something non-neural. What is it?

Conscious or mental events as we know them also have causal roles. That is, they stand in many kinds of necessary connections with input and output. Some desires stand in necessary connection with things that have been perceived and with subsequent acquisition-behaviour. Some pain stands in necessary connection with certain sensory stimuli and avoidance-behaviour. There are also distinctive connections in the case of thinking, perception and so on. Here is a respectable and daunting subject-matter in itself, worth the diligence invested in it by cognitive scientists.

But the basic fact, conscious events being many kinds of effects and causes, is also used to provide the argument for what can be called *strict or philosophical cognitive science and functionalism*. These doctrines are distinguished by taking conscious events in general to be nothing more than the many kinds of effects and causes. It is

[2] Donald Davidson, 'Mental Events', in *Essays on Actions and Events* (Oxford: Clarendon Press, 1988); Ted Honderich, *A Theory of Determinism: The Mind, Neuroscience and Life Hopes* (Oxford: Clarendon Press, 1988), chapters 2–3, or *Mind and Brain* (Oxford: Clarendon Press, 1990), chapters 2–3.

fundamental to these doctrines, so long as they remain philosophically distinctive, that there is nothing further to be said of the nature of these events, anything else they have in common. Stated in this summary way, deprived of obscuring elaboration, strict cognitive science and functionalism are open not only to the objection that they leave out the reality in or of our conscious lives, but to another objection that seems insuperable.

Stones, chairs and our computers, considered in themselves, also involve events which are kinds of effects and causes. There is also the event of, say, my own unnoticed little gain in weight, which never comes to my mind. To put the objection in one way, how did strict cognitive science and functionalism then find, or discriminate from other things, their general subject-matter, the large but of course limited range of kinds of effects and causes with which they are concerned? How did these doctrines separate off irrelevant events, in particular irrelevant events in us? Nothing is more essential to the doctrines. We need to know what they are talking about. Put differently, what is their general conception of consciousness? Evidently to speak only of kinds of effects and causes will not work. There are very many kinds, of which I have just mentioned a few, that do not and must not get into the story.

It therefore seems these doctrines were covertly from the beginning, or must now collapse into, the view that conscious events are events in only *some* causal sequences – not any old causal sequences, Which ones then? The only possible answer seems to be the sequences involving consciousness in another sense. What is necessary is a characterization of conscious events in addition to the insufficient one which almost all of us accept, that they are certain effects and causes. This raises exactly the question we are considering. On reflection, this same objection of incoherence can be made to strict identity theories. *Which* wholly neural events are the conscious ones?[3]

You may be made uneasy by all this, on account of what it could lead to. Your uneasiness will not be reduced if the property of conscious events missed out by the theories we have glanced at is named in advance the property of real subjectivity. The picture in the offing, given my physicalism avowed at the start, seems to be of our heads having two kinds of properties or events in them, the first being neural and the second non-neural although physical, Properties of the second kind are perhaps not rightly to be abused as ghostly stuff, but they are bad enough. The idea is that there exist properties or events which, although physical and in the causal and nomic web, are not at all akin to kinds now accepted, but properties or events whose actual discovery would transform or overturn neuroscience as it is. If this idea is perhaps not an awful one, it is alarming enough.[4]

---

[3] For more of the incoherence objection to functionalism, see 'Functionalism, Identity Theories, The Union Theory,' in *The Mind–Body Problem: The Current State of the Debate*, ed. T. Szubka and R. Warner (Oxford: Blackwell, 1994).

[4] I was driven, alas, to tolerate or anyway contemplate this sort of thing in 'Consciousness, Neural Functionalism, Real Subjectivity', *American Philosophical Quarterly* 32/4 (October 1995), 379. It is to be confessed, too, despite pp. 64-5 of 'Seeing Things,' *Synthese*, 98 (1994), that in that paper there is a great deal that seems, as you might say, in another

I hope in the end to be able to reassure you. That is, I hope it will be possible to maintain what is unquestionable, that conscious events have more than neural properties and particular causal relations, without adding to the kinds of properties or events we already know to be in our heads. Those are the kinds allowed in contemporary neuroscience. Further, since conscious events will be taken to involve more than what goes on inside heads, I hope the view will not add to the kinds of properties and events we already know to be outside our heads. Those are roughly the kinds allowed by ordinary experience and contemporary science.

What is needed is not more things, but a different way of looking at or categorizing the ones we have.

II   The Existence of a World

The difference between me now and a chair in this room, it can be said, is that for me a world exists, and for the chair a world does not exist. Or rather, as I prefer to say, *my consciousness now consists in the existence of a world.* The rest of this paper will have to do with understandings of this seemingly metaphorical sentence. It is owed to contemplating consciousness directly, despite its obscurity. This policy of mental realism may unsettle some philosophers in the current philosophy of mind, since they are averse not only to

world from the view that follows here. But it wasn't all wrong. Some of 'Seeing Things' would have echoes in a further development of the present view.

dualisms which no one should contemplate,[5] but also to the mystery which is the fundamental question of the nature of consciousness. But you, if you are in a way stronger-minded, may share the hope that the sentence points in the right direction, does indicate the nature of consciousness. That is, the sentence may express more than one proposition, and the hope is that one of them, a literal one, will really shed light on the nature of consciousness. It seems to me that trying to dissipate this mystery is better than recoiling from it.

The sentence can naturally be taken for another one. It is that *all* of my consciousness now, including any thoughts unprompted by this room, maybe some day-dreaming, consists in the existence of a world. Perhaps we can on some other occasion get to an account of consciousness generally, or all of the consciousness of one person, which is pointed to by that sentence. But on this occasion let me limit myself to something else, my *perceptual* consciousness now – my consciousness in so far as it consists in my seeing, hearing and so on. So what we have is that *my perceptual consciousness now consists in the existence of a world.* Let us think about only this, and trust, as seems reasonable, and in accord with several philosophical traditions, that perceptual experience is the base of all

---

[5] The most numbing of these dualisms, perhaps, well beyond ghostly stuff, is to be found in K. R. Popper and J. C. Eccles, *The Self and Its Brain* (Berlin: Springer, 1977), where to conscious and neural events a Self is added.

consciousness, and that on some other day an understanding of it will be used to explain the rest.

Thinking of my perceptual experience now as consisting in the existence of a world needs to be distinguished from and may be more promising than another piece of mental realism, a well-known one. Here, my perceptual consciousness is characterized as part or most of *what it is like to be something,* or *what it feels like to be something.*[6] What strikes me as wrong with these locutions, if they are intended seriously, as being on the way to a general understanding of consciousness, and of course not just about differences between conscious things or states, is that the *analysandum* is right there in each *analysans.* The locutions surely presuppose and depend for their understanding on what some supporters of them assert, that there is not something which is what it is like to be a stone, chair or computer, and of course not something which is what it feels like to be one.[7] Does the familiar piece of mental realism not come to this, then, that my perceptual consciousness is characterized as part or most of what it is like *to be conscious,* or *to feel conscious*? This is of no use to us, no analytic help.

---

[6] Thomas Nagel, 'What Is It Like To Be A Bat,?' *The Philosophical Review* 83 (1974), reprinted in his *Mortal Questions* (Cambridge: Cambridge University Press, 1979). See also Timothy Sprigge, 'Final Causes.' *Supplementary Proceedings of the Aristotelian Society* 45, (1971).

[7] John Searle, *The Rediscovery of the Mind* (London and Cambridge, MA: MIT Press, 1992), p. 132.

But does the sentence I am promoting, 'My perceptual consciousness now consists in the existence of a world',
share a different disability with talk of what it is like or feels
like to be something? (I postpone for a little while the very
large question of whether it shares the first disability, being
no analytic help.) You may grant that conceiving of my
perceptual consciousness as amounting to the existence of
a world points at something, indicates the nature of something. But, you may say, that thing, as in the case of talk of
what it is or feels like to be something, is only the *phenomenology* of consciousness. It is only consciousness as it seems
or appears to be, not the reality of it. This objection may
amount to one of several things.

It may simply be insistence on strict identity theory
or strict functionalism and cognitive science as the truth
about consciousness. Or perhaps insistence on those doctrines lightly amended by something about *qualia*. The latter
over-worked items, I take it, are elusive differences between
kinds of perceptual consciousness.[8] They are 'feels' rather
than contents, or more of the nature of 'feels' than of
contents, and very evidently not the character of all of
consciousness. These amended doctrines, as you will anticipate, have not been sufficiently amended to satisfy me. They
too leave out an explicit and general account of what is
fundamental about consciousness. As you will gather, my
sentence about the existence of a world is not an assertion of

[8] Thomas Nagel, 'Qualia', *The Oxford Companion to Philosophy* (Oxford:
Oxford University Press, 1995).

the existence of qualia. No doubt they exist, but they are not the general nature of perceptual consciousness.

If the phenomenology objection fails when taken in this way, is there a better way? Is there a better reason than the given doctrines for dismissing my sentence as only talk of the appearance of consciousness? Well, the dismissal may be misleadingly expressed, but be intended as conveying that there is some other fact about consciousness more important than anything conveyed by the sentence – say the relation of conscious to neural events, or the causation of consciousness, or the role of consciousness in the explanation of behaviour. There is also the truth already indicated, which strict functionalism and cognitive science wonderfully exceeded, that kinds of conscious events, say desire, pain and thinking, and subkinds of them, are differentiated by their causal connections, and could not be characterized adequately without reference to those connections. But surely none of this, although it involves disagreements about what is important, amounts to the proposition that the general conception of consciousness we are contemplating is of only the appearance of it, not its reality.

In fact this proposition, if taken literally and not as a misleading expression of other things, seems to presuppose a falsehood. It is that we can attach sense to talk of a reality-behind with respect to consciousness itself. Things, say stones, chairs and computers, may of course be otherwise than they seem, but that is not a distinction within consciousness. The distinction presupposes consciousness, our having different views of things, but what it has to do with or is about is the chairs, stones and computers.

If we stick to consciousness, is it not the case that *all* there is, in so far as it itself is concerned, is what is being misdescribed as an appearance? Is it not the case that all there is, in so far as consciousness itself is concerned, is what is pointed to by my sentence and perhaps related ones, and also, despite its disability, by talk of what it it is or feels like to be something? Consciousness, after all, is what we *have*. And what we don't have in this sense isn't consciousness. Also, we don't have *it* in two ways. Certainly we can't get behind or beyond consciousness itself by introspection or recollection and bring back a hidden part of *it*. There isn't any other experiential access to it than the single one we've all got.

The only conceivable other access, so to speak, would be a theory about *it*. But, so far as I know, we haven't had any philosophically successful theory about *it*, the reality of *it*, as distinct from about its causation, explanatory role, other relations, kinds of it and their differentiation, secondary features of it, and so on.[9] The theories that do seem to be about consciousness itself, having to do with aboutness or intentionality, cannot be regarded as successful. None has come to the fore.

It is worth adding, finally, something implied by what has just been said, that if there are ways or techniques of bringing things into consciousness, perhaps dispositions

---

[9] It is the burden of my 'Consciousness, Neural Functionalism, Real Subjectivity' that Searle's admirable attempt to characterize consciousness in *The Rediscovery of the Mind* does not come to grips with the fundamental reality of it.

of ours of which we have been unaware, these are not a different access to consciousness itself. As for those very dispositions, often called the subconscious or the unconscious, evidently they are not *in* or part of consciousness. No doubt they are neural. To repeat, what we don't *have* isn't consciousness, and we don't have it in more ways than one.

So much for the objection that my sentence points at only the phenomenology of consciousness. Let me now make a start on the inevitable objection that it is of no analytic help.

Saying that my perceptual consciousness now consists in the existence of a world, if this is understood in certain ways, will indeed be of no help. For a start, it cannot usefully come to just this, that my perceptual consciousness consists in my seeing, hearing and otherwise sensing what exists around me spatio-temporally. If the sentence is taken this way, it will be useless, a really overt instance of the *analysandum* turning up as the *analysans,* the *analysans* being no advance on the *analysandum.* We already understand perceptual consciousness to be seeing, hearing and otherwise sensing spatio-temporal things. That is the ordinary content of talk about perceptual consciousness. That is what we are trying to improve on.

This objection of uselessness, of course, is likely to come up for a particular reason. Perceptual consciousness, according to the sentence, is *the existence of a* world. Furthermore, it was first said above that the difference between me and a chair is that *for me* a chair exists. Both those sentences can indeed be taken to suggest that the idea is that perceptual consciousness is more than a world – it is the world's *existing*. And, the thought continues, all that *that* can mean is that the consciousness consists in a world's being seen, heard, etc. Well, that is not the hope. There is some heuristic advantage in saying, as I shall sometimes persist in saying, the perceptual consciousness is the existence of a world – that might just wake us up to something we have been missing or mislaying – but no more is being suggested than is also suggested by saying, simply, that *perceptual consciousness consists in a world*.

There is something else to be put aside. We would not get anything useful by interpreting my sentence as taking perceptual consciousness to consist in awareness of subjective things – representations, sense-data or the like. This would amount to giving the particular account of perceptual consciousness which is the representative theory of perception or phenomenalism. My reason for saying that giving this account would not help is not that to do so would be to impose on the sentence a theory supported only by doubtful arguments, although this is surely true, and my thinking so will inform some later comments. The reason we would get nowhere is that in this interpretation of the sentence, what we would have is that perceptual consciousness is *awareness,* if in an obscure sense, but it is indeed awareness that we are trying to understand. 'Awareness' in the obscure sense is not synonymous with 'perceptual consciousness', but it is too close for comfort. We would get no understanding of perceptual consciousness itself by being directed away from certain objects of it, objective ones, and towards other supposed objects of it, subjective ones.

This reason for not imposing the representative theory on our sentence is equally a reason for not imposing on it direct or naive realism, the theory which grows out of what was mentioned a moment ago, the ordinary content of talk about perceptual consciousness. It is to the effect that perceptual consciousness consists not in the awareness of subjective but rather of objective things. Let us say that such things, unlike representations and sense-data, are public, which is to say perceivable by more than one person, and are perceivable by more than one sense, and also exist unperceived.[10] Plainly this different theory, first of all in speaking of awareness, also contains the problem. We need to approach the problem on our own.

III   A Mental World?

It happens near the start of our lives that each of us does what each continues to do afterwards, distinguish herself or himself in a particular way from all else, all other things and persons. Each of us comes into possession of the fact of something unique and persistent in a life, certainly not a body, or all of a body. Each of us comes to have some kind of sense of subject, self or person – a sense of oneself, as we can say. This claim can be true, of course, without our having a respectable theory of consciousness or relying on daring philosophical theories of the self. We do not have to swallow Descartes in order to have senses of ourselves. More will be

---

[10]   The distinction is taken from A. J. Ayer, *The Central Questions of Philosophy* (London: Weidenfeld & Nicholson, 1973).

said about a subject later but let us for the moment rely on what we all have in order to state the first of five considerations bearing on what has been said so far and seeming to point in a particular direction.

1. The particular subject each of us senses enters into the existence of a world, a person's perceptual consciousness as I understand it, in a certain way. The essential thing for now is that this state of affairs could not exist in the absence of the subject. The particular subject is a necessary condition of the state of affairs. It is so because it is in some manner a part of it. But that is not all. In the absence of the subject, there would not exist anything of the world whose existence is what perceptual consciousness consists in.

Such a dependency on a particular subject is not true of three larger worlds, the first being the one that is *physical* in the sense mentioned earlier.[11] This is the world, of which much will be said, that is spatio-temporal and has perceived properties or is in nomic connection with things with perceived properties. This world does not have the mentioned dependency. The part that is perceived is not dependent on any particular subject. And the part that isn't perceived is also not dependent on any particular subject – it doesn't enter into perceptual consciousness at all. There is the same want of dependency on a particular subject with a second world, with which we shall also be concerned. This is one lately in view, the *objective* world. It has in it things perceivable by more than one person, and perceivable by

---

[11] See above, p. 137

more than one sense, and such as also to exist unperceived. Evidently it shares a feature or two with the physical world as defined. Finally, there is the same want of dependency on a particular subject with a third world, also in view earlier. This is the world of *things in current or anticipated science,* an indeterminate world to say the least. Let us call these three worlds mind-independent worlds.

I trust it will be clear, incidentally, that speaking of these various worlds, of which we now have four, is not to be taken as indulgence in any sort of ontological extravagance. In the primary and most ordinary sense of the word, there is but one world. Of it or of some of it, we have different conceptions. What falls under a conception is, in my secondary sense of the word, a world. My endeavour in this paper, as will become plain, is to see relations between several conceptions and worlds, and to recommend one conception and world in connection with consciousness.

2. There is also another dependency that needs to be attended to. If I take my perceptual consciousness now to consist in the existence of a world, this necessarily is a world which also has a second dependency seemingly different in kind from the one on a particular subject. It is hard for me to resist the conclusion that the correct understanding of the fact of psychoneural intimacy mentioned at the start is not the strict identity theory but the theory that consciousness is in nomic or lawlike connection with neural events, events with only neural properties. Although the story of the Union Theory gets complicated, part of it is that my perceptual consciousness has a dependency on, has a kind of

nomically necessary condition in, my simultaneous neural events.[12] So the world that is my perceptual consciousness, for this second reason, cannot be the physical world as understood, or the objective world, or the world indicated by science.

3. There is something else, another part of the story of lawlike connection between consciousness and simultaneous neural events. A neural event is not only a kind of necessary condition but also a nomic correlate of a conscious event. That is, although the conscious event is not an effect of the neural event, it is true that given the occurrence of the simultaneous neural event, the conscious event necessarily happened. In a traditional terminology, the neural event was not only a kind of necessary condition for the conscious event, but also a kind of sufficient condition. We can say the neural event was a guarantee of the conscious one.

Of course these considerations having to do with the brain, together with what should be added about dependencies in the other direction, of brain on consciousness, go against some engrossing and influential doctrine which includes a denial of the existence of psychoneural laws.[13] But allow me to take psychoneural lawlike connection for granted on this occasion. If it does not exist, by the way, that will certainly be bad news for neuroscience, since standard neuroscience certainly presupposes it. Shouldn't that fact

---

[12] *A Theory of Determinism or Mind and Brain*, chapters 1, 2.
[13] Donald Davidson, 'Mental Events' and other papers in his *Essays on Actions and Events*.

give pause to any philosopher of mind who wants to keep an eye on science? And on the most relevant part of science, which certainly is not physics? To stick to my subject, however, we have in the neural guarantee a third reason for supposing the world which is my perceptual consciousness cannot be identical with the physical world as understood, or the objective world, or the world indicated by science.

What you will now suppose is that the world in which my perceptual consciousness is being said to consist must be a mental world, an interior world, a mind-world. It is what the dictionary calls the totality of my thoughts and feelings, or all of a class of them. Certainly you need a particular subject for one of these. Maybe such a world *is* a subject. It is such a world, too, that has a person's neural events as a kind of necessary and sufficient condition. And you will say, very truly, that if this is what the speculation about perceptual consciousness comes to, we are back in the débâcle of having the *analysandum* in the *analysons*. To say that my perceptual consciousness consists in a mental world would be no help at all. In addition to the three dependencies, another reason or two are likely to occur to you for your disappointment, or maybe *Schadenfreude*.

4. Is it not implicit in what has been said of my world of perceptual consciousness, most notably about dependence on a subject, that this is a *private* world? Is it not the case that what is being postulated, despite the rhetoric, is no more than a multitude of worlds each private to their owner? Well, part of the answer is yes, in a way. You do

not have access to my perceptual world. That seems to me no deep proposition, incidentally, nor one that necessarily will be true of those who come after us. There seems no conceptual impossibility or incoherence in the speculation that in some future decade one member of our species will have replicated in her head the neural events of someone else, and so by guarantee have access to what otherwise would have been only the other person's experiences. Still, the point remains that a world of consciousness is in this way private. This, at least in an ordinary understanding of them, is not true of any of the three mind-independent worlds. The objective world is explicitly said to be perceivable by more than one person.

5. Finally, although it may seem that no more needs to be said in support of the supposition that a world of perceptual consciousness is a mental world, there is the idea that a world of perceptual consciousness, because of the three dependencies, does not exist unperceived. The point, is worth separating out from (1) the necessity of a subject to a world. But unperceived existence is an explicit feature of the objective world, and of one part of the physical world, and it is fundamental although implicit in what was said of the world indicated by science.

One burden of five considerations, then, is that the worlds I am promoting, the worlds of perceptual consciousness, are not identical with any of three other worlds. Is there another burden – that the worlds being promoted are no more than mental worlds? And hence that we get no useful understanding, certainly no analysis, of perceptual consciousness? Just talk?

IV   My World of Perceptual Consciousness and the Physical World

I wonder. There is a troublesome fact. The world in which my present perceptual consciousness seems to consist is surely spatial. That chair over there is bigger than that other one, and to the left of it, and I can measure the distance between them. It's not a *representation* of the first chair that is bigger than a representation of the second, and it's not representations that are relatively positioned in that way or the given distance apart. So with time. In this world of my perceptual consciousness, one thing happens before, simultaneous with or after another, and things come out of the future into the present and then go into the past. It's not thoughts of them that do this. Nor, does this world have in it only sense-data or ideas or whatever of other properties of things. It has in it the solidity and brownness of the chair.

In short, despite all that has been said, it seems this world at least *resembles* something else we have noticed regularly on our way. It seems to resemble the physical world in one of its two parts: spatio-temporal things that are perceived as against spatio-temporal things in nomic connection with the perceived things. Having arrived at this proposition about resemblance, fundamental to this paper, it is my aim in what follows to clarify and defend it, and, above all, to draw a proposal from it. As you will gather, the proposition about resemblance is not the weak one that the world of perceptual consciousness has in it representations of what is in the given part of the physical world. The point, strongly put, is that both worlds have chairs in them.

Let me pass by what I hope is the battered idea that the troublesome fact and the proposition of resemblance are just a matter of the phenomenology of perceptual consciousness, not the real fact of it, and also put aside for a while (1) the dependency of my world on a subject, and attend to something else. It is the second consideration going against the resemblance, the fact that my world is dependent on my neural events. However much it may seem to have chairs in it, not representations of chairs, must this neural dependency not destroy any talk of real resemblance between my world of perceptual consciousness and the perceived physical world? And must any lingering hope not be finished off by the third consideration, that this world of consciousness is no less than guaranteed by my neural events?

Several things need to be recalled or taken on board at this stage, and in particular in connection with the second consideration. One is that it is no part of what has been suggested that only the worlds of perceptual consciousness exist. There is the unperceived part of the physical world, and the objective world, and the world indicated by science. It has certainly not been doubted that these conceptions are true of what there is, or anyway of some of what there is. Something of their sort is undeniable.

Also, these conceptions evidently overlap to certain extents, and will overlap with other mind-independent conceptions of what there is. Let us now focus on one fundamental overlap. It is asserted or implied in at least two of these conceptions that part of what exists is not perceived, not in perceptual consciousness. It will be convenient to have a name for this. Let us have one last world, the *world-in-itself* or noumenal world, but leave out any implications from the past, notably the doctrines of Kant and Plato. Think of the world-in-itself, if you like, in scientific terms, perhaps as a world of particles in fields of force, or, of course as spatio-temporal events in nomic connection with spatio-temporal events that are perceived.

The principal role of the unperceived part of the physical world as we have understood it is to do some explaining with respect to the perceived part. That is also the principal role of the world indicated by science. We carry over this idea, of course, to our world-in-itself. What we then get is that my world of perceptual consciousness, while having a dependency on my neural events, also has a dependency on the world-in-itself,

How this works is clear enough. My neural events do not come out of nowhere, If they are in a way the necessary conditions of my conscious events, they are also effects of something else. Each neural event is the upshot of a causal sequence, every stage of which is a causal circumstance or kind of causally sufficient condition for what follows. Of what initial causal circumstance is my neural event at some time an effect? Well, some will simply say the world-in-itself. I have in mind particularly those who take the world-in-itself to be a world of science, and in particular of physics, But, to be more cautious, it must surely be that there is a causal circumstance for my neural event in which the world-in-itself plays at least a large part.

These propositions are of importance to us. We are considering the argument that since my world of perceptual consciousness is dependent on my neural events, has a kind of necessary condition in them, it must be merely a mental world, and not something that importantly resembles the perceived part of the physical world. Is that a good argument if my world is *also* dependent in the way outlined on the world-in-itself? It seems not to be.

I say so because the perceived part of the physical world, as we ordinarily understand it, has the same dependency. We do not subtract the chair from the physical world, and, so to speak, put it *in the mind,* on account of our undoubted personal contribution to it. This contribution has to do with our perceptual apparatus and our conceptualizing and so on, and in particular the physical chair's neural dependency. The relationship between the physical chair and the chair-in-itself gets in the way of putting the physical chair in the mind. This consideration against identifying my perceptual world with a mental world does seem persuasive. Why should the neural dependency of my perceptual world degrade it into being 'mental' if the same fact does not degrade part of the physical world? In both cases the second dependency, on the world-in-itself, makes for an independence that is lacked by what we have been calling a mental world.

What of the third consideration, that my perceptual world has not only a kind of necessary condition in my neural events but also what was called a guarantee? My neural events are a kind of sufficient condition for my world. Is that not a disaster? If my neural events stand in this relation to that chair over there, how can it be other than in my mind?

I certainly grant that our conception of the perceived part of the physical world does not include the proposition of psychoneural correlates, of a neural guarantee for what is in this part of the physical world. But, as it seems to me, this is not essential to my line of argument. It *is* part of our conception of the given part of the physical world, as just noticed, that the world-in-itself is in some way necessary to it. There is, as we also know, this same dependency with respect to my perceptual world. The world-in-itself is a necessary condition for my neural events, the correlates of my conscious events. Evidently this provides a response to the argument that if my world of perceptual consciousness is guaranteed by my neural events, it must be merely a mental world and not something that substantially resembles the perceived part of the physical world. The world-in-itself is necessary to the guarantee.

What of the fourth consideration, about privacy? Does what has been admitted as to the privacy of my perceptual world stand in the way of claiming that it substantially resembles the part of the physical world? Well, what has been admitted is that in a sense you do not have access to my perceptual world. Such a thing could happen in the future, but it is not a possibility now. That does make a difference between the two worlds. What size is the difference?

One thing that wouldn't help my claim of substantial resemblance would be something about my perceptual world now and yours: their having numerically different things in them. Do they? As you may anticipate from my earlier scepticism about the representative theory of perception or phenomenalism, the answer seems to be no. To revert to our ordinary talk about perception, it does not follow from the fact that you and I have different accesses to a chair that we are aware of two things. More particularly, it does not follow from our perceiving a chair differently that we are not perceiving just one thing. What is a chair? What is one of these things? It is something that looks different from different points of view or angles. If something *didn't* look different from different points of view, it wouldn't be a chair. It would be something like a number or a concept or a proposition, or maybe the Eternal Idea of Chair, but not a chair. So, as it seems to me, we two are aware of the very same thing.[14]

There is something else in this neighbourhood that would do more damage to my claim of substantial resemblance between my perceptual world and the perceived part of the physical world. That would be *these* two worlds' having numerically different things in them. Do they? There seems no good reason for saying so. Why should the chair in my perceptual world not be the very same thing as the chair in the physical world? What is relevant about my perceptual chair, so to speak, is unique access to it. What is relevant about the physical chair is that it is perceived. But cannot these two descriptions be true of just one thing?

The fifth consideration was that because of the three dependencies my perceptual world is something that does not exist unperceived, but that unperceived existence is an explicit feature of the objective world, and fundamental if implicit in what is said of the world indicated by science.

---

[14] For, further arguments against a revised phenomenalism, see 'Seeing Qualia and Positing the World', in *A. J. Ayer: Memorial Essays*, ed. A. Phillips Griffiths (Cambridge: Cambridge University Press, 1991).

And, most relevantly, as I remarked,[15] it is an explicit feature of the physical world – that part that is spatio-temporal but only in lawlike connection with what is spatio-temporal and perceived. My remark, since we were then reflecting on differences rather than resemblances, left something out, maybe a little heuristically or even deceptively – the part of the physical world we are now interested in above everything else, the perceived part. It is *there* that we need to look for likeness or the lack of it to my perceptual world. Does *this* stuff, the perceived part of the physical world, exist unperceived?

What does it mean to ask if anything exists unperceived? It is the question, presumably, of whether any properties can be assigned to a thing when it is unperceived. What property is assigned to the perceived part of the physical world if it is said that it also exists unperceived? That is not very clear to me, but perhaps the answer is that it is capable of being perceived. Can any properties be assigned to the items in my perceptual world when they are not in it? That is, taking my perceptual world to be a large temporally discontinuous particular, can any properties be assigned to an item in it in the times when this world is not in existence?

Well, there seems to be a good deal to say. This item too has a capability – of being in my world when my world reappears. Also, it may now be in *your* perceptual world. Both of these facts are tied up with another, the item's relation to the thing-in-itself. Further, since we have lately identified the chair in my perceptual world with the one in the perceived part of the physical world, my chair when unperceived by me still has whatever properties give it membership of the perceived part of the physical world. Finally, if this is a different fact, my chair when unperceived by me remains spatio-temporal.

One final remark here. My perceptual world was casually described a moment ago as a discontinuous particular. Like a club, it pops in and out of existence over time. That idea, it might seem, itself stands in the way of asserting any important resemblance between my world and the perceived part of the physical world, Still, something can be said. The latter thing is, as we can say, 'a world as perceived' or 'a world as experienced'. In that case, it too is a discontinuous particular. It is not dependent on any particular subject, but it is not there when we are all asleep, and parts of it are not there when they are in nobody's experience.

This fifth consideration about unperceived existence gets us into deep or anyway troubled waters. Let us emerge from them with only the proposition that the consideration does not easily defeat my claim about resemblance, and turn back to what was passed by, the first consideration, about my perceptual world and a subject, self or person.

Here too, as elsewhere, there certainly is a difference between my perceptual world and the perceived part of the physical world. It is perhaps the main difference. The perceived part of the physical world has no dependency on a particular subject. But the extent of the difference between the two worlds will depend on how we try to understand the subject, the fact of real subjectivity with respect to my world.

I have no full and satisfactory understanding of the fact, needless to say. But, since the matter of a subject is bound up with the matter of perceptual consciousness, there is the consolation of being able to say something, and of the idea that it is possible to come to a tentative conclusion about perceptual consciousness without being able to say more.

One thing that can be said is that the view of perceptual consciousness being contemplated allows for a literal understanding of some common philosophical talk about a subject: that it is or involves a point of view, a view from somewhere rather than nowhere, a perspective. There is one of those, literally, in the world of my perceptual consciousness. It is the point of view from where my head is, This is a little blessing – an escape from metaphor, the besetting problem of the Philosophy of Mind when it does not abandon its mission.

Furthermore, it is possible on the view we are contemplating to start to explain what was remarked on earlier, that a subject not only is a necessary condition of perceptual consciousness in the sense of somehow being a part of it, but is such that the state of affairs would not exist at all in its absence. The explanation is that a point of view, literally speaking, is constitutive of the state of affairs. There could be no understanding of it which left out a real point of view. It is all a matter of the way things are from here, where my head is.

It would be rash to suppose that all that there is to the fact of subjectivity is a real point of view. I have left out what is true, that my world is a matter of my particular conceptualizations. This fact enters into subjectivity, as does the fact of privacy, and no doubt a person's feelings and desires. I shall not take these reflections further, but merely remark that the view we are contemplating of perceptual consciousness gives some promise of a satisfactorily naturalistic conception of a subject. In so far, as it does that, we get some *consonancy* between my perceptual world and the perceptual part of the physical world. I also pass by the role not of a particular subject but of subjects in the perceived part of the physical world. *Some* subject is necessary to it. And the role of conceptualization. These help too.

V   Consciousness as Existence

Let me sum up the comparison now completed between my world of perceptual consciousness and the perceived part, of the physical world. My world has dependencies on (1) a subject, myself, and (2, 3) on my neural events. It is (4) in a way private and (5) is said not to exist unperceived. This is enough, certainly, to make a difference from the mind-independent worlds and in particular the perceived part of the physical world. However, and to be brief, my world has chairs in it. Also, there is more to be said about the perceived part of the physical world. This (2′, 3′) shares a good deal of the neural and thing-in-itself dependencies with my world, and (4′) it has in it, among other things, the very same things that are in my world. (5′) In the matter of unperceived existence, it is not all that far from my world, and (1′) it can be said to be consonant with my world's dependency on a subject.

These propositions, in my submission, amount to an important resemblance between the two worlds. That is to say that my world cannot be regarded as just what was called a mental world – a totality of thoughts and feelings of mine. More particularly, my world is not being conceived in a useless, pre-analytic way. On the contrary, what we have, by way of the resemblance with part of the physical world, is an articulated and relatively rich conception. My perceptual consciousness, my world of perceptual consciousness, is an articulated state of affairs.

I own up to doubts about the details of all this, and a residual worry that some inconsistency has gone unnoticed. But not enough doubts and worry to stand in the way of my main proposal in this paper. It is in part that in thinking about the mind and what exists, we have been stuck with two categories. These are, in the most general terms, the mind-independent worlds and mental worlds. It is not only philosophers of the mentally realist kind[16] who have been stuck with not only mind-independent but also mental worlds. Philosophers sceptical about mental worlds, indeed with some reason disdainful of them, have nevertheless not escaped them, but write more and more books trying to accommodate them.

To come to the very nub, what we need, in order to deal first with perceptual consciousness and thereafter with all of consciousness, is a new category: worlds of perceptual consciousness. They take a good deal from both mind-independent and mental worlds. We do not need new kinds of properties or events. We need this different way of looking at what we have got. Or, to remember my doubts

[16] See above, p. 140, and *A Theory of Determinism*, pp. 77–83.

and worry, and to be properly hesitant, we need some new way like this, something along these lines, We need *some* view of perceptual consciousness *as existence*, or, if you like, existence as perceptual consciousness. We need an idea to the effect that for something to be conscious is for a world to exist, although certainly not a world wholly dependent on it. This, in my submission, is what we have missed out in being anchored in the two categories of mind-independent and mental worlds.

Is there not much to be said for this different category? Four more things come to mind.

The category is not factitious. Our worlds of perceptual consciousness, in fact, are the *only* worlds that are not worlds of theory. They are not got by inference or speculation, however well-founded or even coercive the inference or theory. They are epistemically and perhaps conceptually prior to all other worlds, notably the objective and scientific ones. It is not clear, since the idea of ontological priority is more difficult than sometimes supposed, that they are not ontologically prior to the rest.[17]

Does the category of worlds of perceptual consciousness offend against a commitment to physicalism, taking the latter to be a commitment to the physical world and the world indicated by science, and perhaps the objective world, and at least a scepticism about mental worlds? The answer is that what has been proposed *is* a kind of physicalism. One reason

---

[17] 'Dependence,' in *Cambridge Dictionary of Philosophy*, ed. Robert Audi (Cambridge: Cambridge University Press, 1995).

is that our worlds of consciousness are approximate to the perceived part of the physical world.[18]

Nothing has been said until now of what seems to be a fact about consciousness and in particular perceptual consciousness. It is that it itself has a role in the explanation of behaviour. Conscious events are ineliminable parts of full explanations of our actions. Accounts of the mind must fail or be incomplete, it seems, if they entail or allow for epiphenomenalism. My world of perceptual consciousness has no such shortcoming. Far from it. It has in it the very things that can most naturally be said to motivate us, chairs for a start.

Finally, one more word about the crux of all of the philosophy of mind that deserves the name. That is the fact of our real subjectivity. Something was said earlier[19] of how the proposed view of perceptual consciousness contributes to understanding here. It seems to me that consciousness as existence gives us more than other views of what we want, and more than has been mentioned. For one thing, subjectivity has to do with reality and immediacy. My world of perceptual consciousness is very real and very immediate.

---

[18] Cf., alas, 'Seeing Things', p. 52.   [19] See above, pp. 152–3.

Setting Things before the Mind

M. G. F. MARTIN

L istening to someone from some distance in a crowded room you may experience the following phenomenon: when looking at them speak, you may both hear and see where the source of the sounds is; but when your eyes are turned elsewhere, you may no longer be able to detect exactly where the voice must be coming from. With your eyes again fixed on the speaker, and the movement of her lips a clear sense of the source of the sound will return. This 'ventriloquist' effect reflects the ways in which visual cognition can dominate auditory perception. And this phenomenological observation is one that you can verify or disconfirm in your own case just by the slightest reflection on what it is like for you to listen to someone with or without visual contact with them.

Talks from which this paper was drawn were given at a conference in Miskolc Tapolca, University College Dublin and the Institut für Philosophie Universität München; I am grateful to those audiences and the one at the Royal Institute for their questions and comments. I would also like to thank Paul Boghossian, Tim Crane, Naomi Eilan, Norbert Niclauss and Scott Sturgeon for detailed comments and discussions of these matters. Work for this paper was carried out while on research leave sponsored by the British Academy.

A common assumption in most philosophical discussions of appearances and experience is that, when one does engage in just such reflection, the character of how things appear to one is just obvious to me. Just this assumption seems to lie behind Ned Block's comment

> what is it that philosophers have called qualitative states? As Louis Armstrong said when asked what jazz is, 'If you got to ask, you ain't never going to get to know.'

It is implicit in much of the recent debate about the problems of explaining consciousness, in particular what has come to be called phenomenal consciousness, in purely naturalistic terms: although we may not be able to explain how such consciousness can arise without a physical world, we have a clear sense of what the problematic subject matter is just by focusing on one's own case.

Now while the assumption is widespread, and in many ways seems sensible, it does raise a deep puzzle concerning the ways in which philosophers debate the nature of perception and perceptual appearances. For it is clear in such debate that philosophers disagree, and that they disagree about the nature of appearances. Some philosophers claim that it is just obvious that there are aspects of your experience, say of your currently looking at this page, which are entirely independent of any aspect that you may perceive the mind-independent world to have. Others, however, are insistent that it is just obvious to us that our perceptual experiences of the world are purely representational or intentional, and that what it is like to be in such states is a matter of no more than how things are represented as being by those states. It is difficult to interpret these disagreements as other than being disagreements about the nature of appearances, how things look, or feel, or taste to us when we explore the world around us. Yet, if the nature of appearances really is just open to simple reflection, how can there be room for any serious disagreement? Surely one can confirm or disconfirm any theory of appearances straight off. The persistence of disagreement would suggest that either the inner lives of philosophers are much more varied than we previously had reason to suspect, or that at least one party to the debate must be deeply confused.

Instead, I suggest that the fact that such disagreement does occur indicates that even if the character of experience is obvious to us, it is not obvious how obvious it is. To make sense of these different theories, we must interpret them as able to draw a contrast between the real nature of appearances and how their opponents may be misled in describing how such appearances seem. And this thought raises the question whether we can find an appropriate common ground among parties to the dispute: some description of what experience is like which neutrally expresses how appearance seem to us. We could then see the competing parties as attempting to give competing explanations of this common ground.

It is this interpretative task that I attempt to undertake in this paper. I shall not be offering any final or definitive account of the nature of perceptual experience or the relation between experience and perception in this talk. On the other hand, the reader is sure to be able to find many such accounts in other discussions of perception. It is more difficult, however, to discern the common root or the starting point for these incompatible accounts of the supposedly obvious, and that is why I trust there is sufficient interest in trying to find a suitable overview of the disagreements here.

I

In recent discussion, the notion of *qualia* has dominated debate about the nature of sensory consciousness. This has occurred particularly in the context of debate about the viability of a purely physicalist understanding of the mind. A common view is that the intentional or representational properties of mind, those in virtue of which our thoughts are about objects or properties in the world around us, present no insuperable problem to a physicalist account of the mind. In contrast, it has been suggested that the fact that we are conscious, and more specifically that we have sensory phenomenal consciousness, has been thought inexplicable given the state of neurosciences and cognitive psychology. Associated with posing the problem in this way is the thought that if we do have phenomenal consciousness, then such consciousness is not to be understood in representational terms.

I want first to focus critically on the notion of qualia since it stands in the way of our getting a proper over-view of the disagreements concerning the nature of perceptual experience. Although many philosophers write as if it is

249

simply obvious to us that there are qualia, and that we know what they are, I shall argue instead that this is all chimerical. For the most common usage of the term 'qualia' is equivocal, and the most familiar means of elucidating the term, by a kind of inner ostension of one's conscious states, simply fails to pick out a unique target. Furthermore, lying behind this confusion is a long-standing dispute about the nature of experience and our knowledge of it which needs to be made explicit before we can advance in our task of setting up a common framework for understanding the debate about perception.

The term has been used in a number of different ways, but we would do well to start with the usage found in this passage from David Chalmers:

> a mental state is conscious if there is something it is like to be in that mental state. To put it another way, we can say that a mental state is conscious if it has a *qualitative feel* – an associated quality of experience. These phenomenal feels are also known as phenomenal qualities, or *qualia* for short.[1]

So used, the term is intended to pick out in the most general and neutral way the various aspects of conscious episodes. In taking conscious experience to be suitably evident to a reflective audience, philosophers often avoid any explicit or informative definition of the term 'qualia'. Indeed, it is sometimes suggested that no informative definition could

---

[1] D. Chalmers, *The Conscious Mind* (Oxford: Oxford University Press, 1996), p. 4.

be given. Instead, we are often offered a verbal equivalent of an inwardly directed gesture, which in the context of the discussion is intended to direct one's attention on the appropriate subject matter. While it is generally assumed that it is simply obvious to us then what qualia are to be taken to be, I shall argue that in fact the term is generally used equivocally, and that independent of some further clarification, we cannot determine how people are using the term.

We can trace the equivocation to the way in which we are introduced to the term. A notable such example is provided by Daniel Dennett, in a discussion which more generally is hostile to the notion of qualia. Despite Dennett's hostility to the notion, his opponents have been happy to accept his initial elucidation of the notion right at the outset of his paper. It is worth looking at in some detail:

> 'Qualia' is an unfamiliar term for something that could not be more familiar to each of us: the *ways things seem to us* ... Look at a glass of milk at sunset; *the way it looks to you* – the particular, personal, subjective visual quality of the glass of milk is the *quale* of your visual experience at the moment. The *way the milk tastes to you then* is another, gustatory *quale,* and *how it sounds to you* as you swallow is an auditory *quale.* These various 'properties of conscious experience' are prime examples of *qualia.*[2]

Now this gloss on what Dennett complains is 'frustratingly elusive' contains a central, and, I shall argue, significant

---

[2] D. Dennett, 'Quining Qualia', in *Consciousness and Contemporary Science*, ed. A. Marcel and E. Bisiach (Oxford: Clarendon Press, 1988), p. 42.

problem: Dennett equivocates on the term 'qualia' even as he introduces it. As the last sentence of the passage makes clear, and as the course of the paper it comes from also indicates, Dennett assumes, with many other authors, that we should use the term 'qualia' to pick out 'properties of experience'. We may think of seeing a glass, or more neutrally having a visual experience as of a glass, as being a state of mind, the having of an experience. Someone who has such an experience thereby has the property of having an experience of a glass. Qualia are then to be seen either as properties of properties – that is, what it is like to have an experience of a glass is a property of having the property of having an experience of the glass. Alternatively, we can think of the ways in which things seem to one as further determinations or specifications of the determinable, having an experience. Each of the specific experiences that you might have – the feeling of the hardness of the chair beneath you, hearing the rustle of frustration around you – are different ways of having an experience. Qualia are then just these different ways of having experience. However, Dennett does not stick with this usage, for the moment he gives us any concrete examples of qualia we seem to shift to something of an entirely different order to that of a property of an experience: for Dennett's examples are themselves not properties of experiences, but properties of the objects we come to perceive. He writes first of the way the glass of milk looks to one, where the object which has the property is itself part of the world around us and not part of the mind, namely a glass. Likewise, it is the particular quantity of milk which tastes some way to one, and the milk, one's throat (and lack of manners), all together which are responsible for the sound which Dennett picks out as an auditory quale. But surely nothing can be both the property of an object independent of the mind and at the same time a way of having an experience. So Dennett seems to have introduced just the wrong examples to indicate as 'properties of experience'.

It is not difficult to see where the problematic ambiguity is introduced in the discussion. For the phrase 'the way things seem to us' is itself ambiguous. Dennett, and others, seek to introduce the term 'qualia' by reference to such English locutions for how things look, feel, sound or more generally appear. But appearance talk is itself complex and hence allows for abstraction of terms in more than one way. The different instructions for fixing on an example of a quale result from abstracting now in one way, and now in another.

For example, when I tell you:

> It looks to Dan as if there is a rosy-hued glass of milk before him

I may intend to emphasize how things are with Dan, and to contrast the fact that Dan has a certain kind of experience with the fact that Mary is asleep, or that Ben has an altogether different kind of experience. So we can imagine that the following underlined aspect of the sentence would be up for substitution in contrasting the way Dan is, with how else he might have been:

> 1'. *It looks to* Dan *as if there is a rosy-hued glass of milk before him*

On the other hand, given that this is in fact a case in which Dan is perceiving the glass of milk, we might rather be interested in what aspects of the milk are evident to Dan. In this case we may be interested that it is the specific shade that the milk has that is manifest to him, in contrast to the maker's mark on the glass. In that case, the following underlined aspect of the sentence would be open to substitution to contrast ways in which the situation might have differed:

> 1″. It looks to Dan as if there is a *rosy-hued* glass of milk before him

So in moving from talk of something appearing F to someone, to talk of appearances, qualities of experience or qualia, the loss in complexity of the semantic structure leaves one open to equivocation between properties of what appears and properties of what is appeared to. Just such slippage occurs in the passage quoted from Dennett: within one paragraph we move from properties of experience to properties of the object of experience, the glass of milk, back to properties of experience again.

Dennett is not an isolated example of this shift, but perhaps we can make do with just one other more recent example. Fred Dretske, like Dennett, is hostile to a tradition of thought which sees qualia as presenting an insuperable problem for a naturalistic account of the mind. In his monograph *Naturalizing the Mind,* Dretske puts forward 'the Representational Thesis' as his account of how the mind can be part of the natural order. The thesis itself consists of two claims: '(1) *All mental facts are representational facts,* and (2) *All representational facts are facts about informational functions.*'[3] When Dretske turns to the issues raised by conscious experience in the third lecture, he makes the following claim:

> The Representational Thesis identifies the qualities of experience – qualia – with the properties objects as representeds as having.[4]

Whatever one thinks of the Representational Thesis itself, one ought to hesitate before accepting this identity claim as a consequence of it. As the first half of the identity claim makes clear, qualia are assumed to be properties of experiences, properties of properties of one's mind, or ways in which one may come to have an experience. But Dretske, like most philosophers who ascribe a representational content to experience, supposes that our experiences represent how objects independent of the mind are. Such mind-independent objects cannot have properties which are properties of states of mind. So it is implausible to suppose that our experiences should represent mind-independent objects as having properties of states of mind. Yet this manifest absurdity is what Dretske claims in this passage.

Well, if we try to reconstruct what Dretske might be trying to say here, we can see the same equivocation in play as in the Dennett paper. Although Dretske starts the

---

[3] F. Dretske, *Naturalizing the Mind* (Cambridge, MA: MIT Press, 1995), p. xiii.

[4] Ibid., p. 65: 'represents' is Dretske's term for sensory or phenomenal representation as opposed to conceptual representation – the details of the distinction he draws has no import for the point made in the text.

sentence by talking about qualities of experience, the only intelligible claim he could be making is one which identifies qualia understood as the properties *objects* appear to have with the properties our experiences represent those objects as having. This thesis is perfectly intelligible, even if some people might find it mildly controversial.

On the other hand, one might think that this identity claim alone falls short of telling us much about what experiences are like, and how Dretske's position differs from those who insist that there are qualia but who reject the Representational Thesis. But the need for Dretske to link up claims about how objects may come to appear to have properties with claims about what our experience can be like is obscured for him by use of the equivocal term 'qualia'. Since he can now use it in one sense, now in another, it may seem as if he covers all angles at once.

This example not only increases our sample of equivocal uses, but directs us towards the significance of this slip of the pen. For it would be mistaken to respond to this problem by claiming that we can easily re-interpret both authors so as to avoid any such equivocation and ambiguity. A charitable response to these problems would no doubt be one which understood both authors as intending strictly just to talk about the properties of what experiences are like when they talk of qualia, and hence to re-interpret any passages where they slip into talking instead of the properties that objects appear to have. But one could undertake this interpretative task only if we could reconstruct the theses put forward solely in terms of properties of experience on the one hand, and properties that objects appear to have on the other. Once we make the distinction we can see that the theories do not offer us any explicit account of how the two sets of properties are related, even though the equivocation between the two suggests that in interpreting the notion of qualia we are to understand that there should be some important relation between them.

Indeed, the need to do so can be made even more explicit by setting this issue in an historical context with which it is not normally associated, that between sense-datum theories of perception and so-called adverbial approaches. Consider first this notorious passage from H. H. Price:

> When I see a tomato there is much that I can doubt. I can doubt whether it is a tomato that I am seeing, and not a cleverly painted piece of wax. I can doubt whether there is a material thing there at all ... One thing however I cannot doubt: that there exists a red patch of a round and somewhat bulgy shape, standing out from a background of other colour-patches, and having a certain visual depth, and that this whole field of colour is presented to my consciousness ... that something is red and round then and there I cannot doubt ... that it now *exists,* and that *I* am conscious of it – by me at least who am conscious of it this cannot possibly be doubted... This peculiar and ultimate manner of being present to consciousness is called *being given,* and that which is thus present is called a *datum.*[5]

---

[5] H. H. Price, *Perception* (London: Methuen, 1932), p. 3.

Perhaps the most salient aspect of this picture of perception and experience are those aspects of it which used to be called 'the act-object' model of experience. According to Price the occurrence of an experience involves a subject, a relation of being given which relates that subject to various objects, and the data, which are presented or given to her. Furthermore, Price is insistent that such objects will be present even in cases of illusion or hallucination, so at least some of these data are non-physical.

However, the passage is of most concern to us for the kind of view of knowledge of experience that it expresses. For Price seems to be of the view that one knows about the character of one's experience, that some red bulgy thing is present to one's mind, through attending to the object which is given in the experience, the red bulgy thing itself. Indeed, like Moore before him, Price thinks that consciousness is entirely diaphanous, and hence that all differences between conscious states of mind are differences in the objects which those states can have.[6] So, when one comes to know what one's experience is like, and how it may differ from other conscious states one could have come to have, one does so through attending to the objects of awareness given to one through having such states.

In the middle of the twentieth century, sense-datum theories, as 'act-object' accounts of experience, provoked an alternative kind of account normally known as 'adverbial'

---

[6] Moore's opinion can be found in G. Moore, 'The Refutation of Idealism', in *Philosophical Studies* (London: Routledge & Kegan Paul, 1922); Price commits himself to the view in *Perception*, p. 5.

theories of perception. The epithet comes from a suggestion first made by C. J. Ducasse, in response to Moore that

> 'blue', 'bitter', 'sweet', etc., are names of objects of experience nor of species of objects of experience but of *species of experience itself.* What this means is perhaps made clearest by saying that to sense blue is then to sense *bluely,* just as to dance the waltz is to dance 'waltzily' (i.e., the manner called 'to waltz') to jump a leap is to jump 'leapily' (i.e., in the manner called to leap) etc.[7]

The primary motivation for such adverbialism is to avoid any commitment to the existence of non-physical objects of the sort that Price is happy to accept. The assumption of such discussions is that a commitment to *ways* in which one experiences, as opposed to *objects* which one senses, cannot be thought objectionable since we will be committed to the existence of such states of mind, as long as we are not eliminativist about the mind or sensory consciousness.

But the adverbialism which Ducasse favours goes beyond the purely negative thesis that we should not commit ourselves to the existence of non-physical objects of sense, to a contrasting picture both of the role that experience plays in our perception of the world, and of how it can be that we come to be aware of our own experiences. The key idea is that we should principally think of our experiences as effects upon us by the environment; effects which have a distinctive qualitative character, and which are such

[7] C. Ducasse, 'Moore's "Refutation of Idealism"', *The Philosophy of G. E. Moore,* ed. P. A. Schilpp (La Salle, IL: Open Court, 1942), pp. 232–3.

that they bring about beliefs about the environment. Such states have sufficient dimensions of variation that there can be a reliable connection between environmental conditions which bring them about. In turn such states will act as the causes of beliefs about the presence of such environmental conditions which reliably correlate with the states of affairs they are about. We can think of our descriptions of experience as being of red, or of green triangles, or of musk, all as indicating the kind of cause which brings them about and correlatively the belief which they could reliably fix. On this view, awareness of the objects of perception and how they appear to be is one thing – the mind is directed out at the world – and attention to one's own experience another thing. The experience is a merely a causal intermediary between world and our knowledge of it: our awareness of experience requires directing attention not at the objects of sense, but rather within the mind.[8]

---

[8] Ducasse's main concern, it must be said, is with Moore's contention that the object of consciousness in sensing is independent of the mind – and the dispute between Moore and Ducasse involves much talking past each other. For a further development of adverbialism which takes on the elements described in the text, see R. Chisholm, *Theory of Knowledge* (Englewood Cliffs, NJ: Prentice Hall, 1966), pp. 91–8 and M. Tye, 'The Adverbial Approach to Visual Experience', *Philosophical Review* 93 (April 1984), 195–225. This approach has its roots in Thomas Reid, see T. Reid; 'Essays on the Intellectual Powers of Man', in *Inquiry and Essays,* ed. R. Beanblossom and K. Lehrer (Indianapolis: Hackett Publishing Co., 1983). Note that not all philosophers whose views on sensation have been classified as adverbialist have made the assumption about our knowledge of experience mentioned in the text. The most notable exception is Wilfrid Sellars: see 'Empiricism and the Philosophy

Now if we bracket for the moment a concern with the metaphysical status of the objects of sense, whether they can be non-physical or not, the contrasting attitudes towards knowledge of experience on Price's view and on the adverbialism opposed to it offer us contrasting interpretations of the connection between the properties of what experiences are like, which we can come to be aware of, and the properties which objects appear to us to have. For Price, there is nothing more to learn about the nature of one's experience than to learn what objects, and what qualities of objects, are given to one. To learn about the properties of one's experience just is to learn what properties objects are presented as having. We might put this in terms of qualia by saying that on this view, qualia is the sense of the what-it-is-like properties of experience, $qualia_1$ as one might say, are partly constituted by the properties which objects appear to have or are presented as having, $qualia_2$. And one comes to know what the $qualia_1$ of one's experience are, through knowing what the $qualia_2$ of one's experience are. In contrast, for the adverbialist, properties of one's experience need to be sharply distinguished from properties that objects appear to have: the properties objects appear to have, on the whole, are those which our experiences are liable to cause us to believe that they have. The properties our experiences have, $qualia_1$, are the properties which are responsible for our coming to acquire these beliefs, but they are distinct and

of Mind', in *Science, Perception and Reality* (London: Routledge & Kegan Paul, 1963), and *Science and Metaphysics* (London: Routledge & Kegan Paul, 1968).

our awareness of them is distinct from our awareness of the properties that objects appear to have, qualia$_2$.

If we look back to Dretske and Dennett, then we can see this controversy mirrored in what they have to say. In Dretske's case it is clear that the conception of knowledge of experience is closest to the sense-datum approach, although he is surely keen to avoid the metaphysical extravagances of that view: why the identity of qualia$_2$ for him with the properties objects are represented as having may be relevant to the Representational Thesis is simply that if one accepts with Price that qualia$_2$ determine qualia$_1$, and that we have knowledge of qualia$_1$ through knowledge of qualia$_2$, he can claim that our knowledge of what experience is like is simply knowledge of how it represents things to be, and hence knowledge of its representational properties.

With Dennett, on the other hand, it is clear what we could interpret the passage in either way. For if one sides with the adverbialist then, given the close correlations between properties objects can be perceived to have and the experiences to which those objects give rise, one might imagine that thought of the one would be liable to bring to mind the other. Dennett can be seen as employing a form of metonymy: in mentioning the properties the glass of milk may be perceived to have, he enables his audience to latch on instead to the distinct set of properties which one's experiences would have, were one perceiving the milk. Furthermore, since there is no obvious vocabulary for the qualities of experience so conceived, one might think that this is the most natural and obvious way to introduce such ineffable aspects of the mind into conversation.

It is clear that there is a substantive disagreement here over the nature of qualia, even when we restrict that term simply to mean the what-it-is-like properties of experience. The instructions provided for simply directing one's attention to these elusive properties are inadequate to the task of settling which account is the right one; yet the terms in which philosophers discuss these matters tend to equivocate between talk of properties of experience and talk of properties of objects; and the ways in which they talk slip between supporting now one account of the relation of these properties and now the other.[9] I suggest it is no accident that these two things come together. As long we simply equivocate over the use of the term 'qualia' we can hide from ourselves the need for answering the difficult question how

[9] Paul Boghossian suggested to me that one could define a perfectly good notion of qualia without this threat of equivocation: qualia just are the non-representational properties of the mind which make a difference to what it is like to be one. We can determine whether there are any qualia, simply by asking whether two individuals could differ with respect to what it is like to be them without differing in their representational properties. However, the problem with this suggestion concerns how we are to apply the test: for in order to use the test within a thought experiment we need to determine when two individuals are to be considered as sharing all the same representational properties. This we cannot do without attending to the properties which things appear to them to have. This, somewhat indirect, test for the existence of qualia implicitly exploits the kind of direct test discussed in the text: we are either meant to recognize those aspects of consciousness which are purely representational or those which are not. So the problem of what one is to direct a subject's attention to, when their attention is directed to the qualitative aspects of sensory experience remains.

the properties of experience relates to the properties which things appear to have.

II

The issue here is substantive, but how are we to settle it? Well, the idea that our conception of what our experience is like and our conception of what properties objects appear to us to have might be separate is attractive only as long as we look at the simplest of descriptions of experience: for example a visual experience of a red bulgy thing; an experience of a bitter or tangy thing. There seems to be nothing about these descriptions that should make us prefer one account over another. But when we look to more complex cases, we see that the description of what is apparent to us is not independent of our appreciation of what experience is like, and that for some aspects of experience it is difficult to conceive of how they could be independent of how things appear to us. Proper attention to experience, I suggest, shows that the adverbialist conception of our knowledge of experience is in the end unintelligible.

To focus on a concrete example, consider the following passage from a discussion of the nature of shadows by the art theorist Michael Baxandall:

> I am writing this at a table with a wall each side of it, on a day of mixed sun and cloud. The wall on the right is modern, made of brick, and painted white with a matte but even emulsion paint. At the base of the wall the paint is blistering from damp. The wall on the left is much older, rough-cast rendering over undressed sandstone

masonry, and there have been various attempts to patch gaps in the rendering with cement of various consistencies. It too is painted white, but with a rougher sand-textured stuff. This is flaking off in places due to an impermeable white flint element in the rough-cast; and in some but not all of these places desultory touching up has been done with a different, slick and clinging white paint, some of it applied by a roller and some boldly by a brush. The conspectus of the walls to left and right is almost as monochrome white, nevertheless...

As the sun comes and goes the various kinds of radiation change level by a large factor, certainly to the point of discomfort – there are windows on three sides – and yet the walls remain white: brightness constancy, of course. But, partly because of these shifts between direct strong light and diffused weak light on the monochrome walls, partly because of a special interest, I am very aware of being in an indescribably intricate ambience of microshadow. It may usually be called texture, a word that somehow invokes the sense of touch, but it consists visually of almost pure shadow – very small self-shadows, derived shadows, and slant/tilt shadings ... It is almost purely from shadow that my visual access to the microstructure of the two plane surfaces of the walls derives. I do not think stereopsy is helping much.

What I do not do, or would not be doing but for a special interest, is to attend to the individual microshadows as shadows or as objects of perception in their own right. If I attend to part of a wall I get a sense of its surface quality and that seems enough. Even with a special interest, it takes an effort of will, a decree of the mind, to attend to the same area of wall, to categorize its shadow types, and read the bearing of their lighting. It is

> not an optical problem of acuity, in this strong light;
> rather, it seems to go against the grain of the perceptual
> process. . .[10]

Baxandall is concerned with the question whether 'we can [attend to individual shadows] and at the same time preserve the pattern of our more usual utilization of the same shadow in the course of normal variously directed perception'.[11] His concern is with the ways in which we can attend to shadows, the difficulty in doing so, and the ways in which our perception of our environment may subtly change as we do so. In the description of his study, we are given familiar types of description of his surroundings, intermingled with observations about the existence and nature of certain types of shadow and visual phenomena, together with some technical commentary on the physical nature of the light array. These three elements mingled together may give one a greater or lesser sense of what it must have been like for Baxandall glancing over his study and staring out at the countryside beyond. The more one knows the kind of room discussed, the more one can link it with one's own knowledge of what it must have been like; the more one follows Baxandall in attempting to attend to elements of the visual array, and discern the structure of shadows, the more one has the sense of what he has done, and how one can do it well or badly. However, the passage is also a bravura display of how one might try to describe a visual scene combining

---

[10] M. Baxandall, *Shadows and Enlightenment* (London: Yale University Press, 1995), pp. 125–6.

[11] Ibid., p. 128.

266

such elements: Baxandall draws our attention at least as much to what he is reporting himself as doing and how he is reporting it, as to what he discerns; we have the sense of what it is like keenly to attend to the visual world, so as to discern various of its elements, and the difficulty and effort involved in drawing out the role of shadow in our visual perception of the world.

One might react to this passage by wondering what its bearing is on the question we are interested in, namely the nature of experience and our first person access to it. One might think that while it tells us much, more than we wished to know, about what its author perceived that afternoon in the environment around him, it does not tell us about his experience. But such a response, I suggest, would be wrong: what Baxandall does here, and reports himself as doing, is to attend to what it is like for him to look out at the world around him, and attend now to the objects he recognizes, now to the shadows by which they come to be visually defined for him.

When we follow the passage and see some surface now as textured and now as covered in a skein of shadows, we learn not only something about the object we are attending to but also how we learn things visually about that object. The relation between the shadows and the texture seem to be ones which are forged within one's experience. It is this type of phenomenological fact which Baxandall focuses on. For this reason, if we are to find anything which deserves the epithet of description of what it is like for one to see, then Baxandall's account deserves such a title. It is, of course, a fragmentary such account, offering only a limited such description, partial in what it highlights and what it omits, and undoubtedly in much of its description highly theory-laden. None of that, I suggest, can take away from the clear sense a reader has that what Baxandall does in the passage, and can be taken as intending to do, is describe his visual experience of the world, and not merely the objects of perception. But if it is a description of his experience it also has to be a description of the objects he perceives, or takes himself to perceive. For what else could this feature be, if not an aspect of how the wall appears to one to be when one focuses on it now one way, now another?

What does this tell us about how we know what our experiences are like, and what we thereby know? First, the passage articulates much of what the experience is like, while at the same time leaving much unsaid, and perhaps unsayable. So it would be a mistake to suppose that the character of experience is entirely ineffable. Second, Baxandall indicates that he learns things about what it is like for him to view his study by paying careful attention in the way that he does to various features, and we the readers can certainly learn things not only about his inner life, but about our own, through reading the passage, and by following similar procedures. Even if there is a sense in which the character of our own experience is somehow obvious to us, that should not be taken to preclude the possibility that we can make discoveries about what experience is like. Third, and related to the above, learning about one's experience can involve active exploration, primarily of the experienced world around one, but in doing so of one's experience as well. Finally, correlative with the last, attending to what one's experience is like cannot be separated from exploring and attending to features of the world as perceived.

This suggests that the way in which we learn what our experiences are like is by attending first to the objects and features which are presented to us in perception. But there is an obvious problem with this suggestion: we can have perceptual experiences even when we are not perceiving anything in the physical world at all. One might have induced a perfect visual hallucination of a red tomato, rather than simply having the pleasure of seeing one all by itself. Furthermore, one might know full well that that is the position one is in. In such a case, one would not be in a position to scan the elements of the physical scene before one, nor would one take oneself to be in that position. Even in cases of hallucination, there is a way that one's experience is for one, and one can come to know what one's experience is like, yet there are no objects of perception for one to attend to.

Nevertheless, the basic model can still be applied even to this kind of case. For, in as much as an hallucination may be indistinguishable for one from a genuine perception, it will still seem to one as if there is an array of objects there for one to scan and explore. This will not necessarily be banished simply by the knowledge that one is suffering an hallucination, any more than the knowledge one is staring at a Müller–Lyer illusion is liable to make one see the lines as entirely equal in length. So in such a situation, one can still be interested in aspects of one's experience, and proceed to explore it by attending to the putative objects of awareness.

Note that the way we attend to our experiences when we reflect on them involves two distinct ways of attending. One can attend to something simply in thinking about it, as when I attend to the average rainfall in August in thinking that it is less than ½ inch. When one reflects on one's own state of mind, one attends to it much as one attends to any object of thought. In addition, we can attend to objects that we perceive in ways not present when merely thinking about them. As you read along this line, you may note that there are words ahead of the one your eye rests on at the moment, and that there are lines above, and below this one. Your eyes and your attention shift in turn from one word to the next. Now, as a whim, you might be inclined simply to turn your head away from the page to see what is going on in the world behind you. In that case, you shift your attention to a feature of your environment of which you are not currently aware. But, if you do not turn your head, but simply keep reading along the line, it may seem to you as if your attention is guided from the words that you now focus on, to the next set of words, by shifting among the features of which you are already aware. To the extent that you shift your attention, as a matter of voluntary control, rather than having your attention shifted, as when some distraction occurs at the periphery of vision, you seem to have the choice of moving your attention among the range of things of which you are already aware. So in perception, focal attention seems to range over objects which are already objects of awareness, and a motive for directing your attention to something is to find out more.

Now in the case of reflecting on one's own experience, one attends to one's state of mind through directing one's attention over the actual or putative objects of awareness. Whether one is perceiving or merely hallucinating, there is an apparent array of objects for one to direct one's attention across. How things are as presented to one is surely one aspect of one's current state of mind: indeed, in a case of hallucination, directing one's attention to what is present will tell one nothing about what is present in one's environment in a case of hallucination. So, for this reason at least, exploiting perceptual attention is a way of coming to know about and attending to one's own experience. When one does so, one can't conceive of what one directs one's attention at as merely a property of one's experience, the way one is affected. For in directing one's attention across a visual scene, one may chose to direct one's attention to the feature on the left, rather than the one to the right. What one selects among are the putative objects presented at various apparent locations. But we do not think of our own experiences or their properties as spatially arrayed in this way. So the only sense that we can make of what one intends to do in attending to one's experience is that one does so through attending to things not taken to be merely properties of the experience.

As the Baxandall passage indicates, just such perceptual attention is exploited in coming to know about one's visual experience. So one cannot in so attending take what one attends to simply to be a way of being modified, as the adverbialist conception of experience claims. In as much as one exploits selective attention in learning about experience, such attention must range over the actual or putative objects of perception, and so attention to experience is not entirely distinct from attending to the objects of sense. To this extent at least, we should side with Price and the sense-datum theorists and not their adverbialist opponents. Of course, to attend to one's own state of mind is not the same thing as attending to some aspect of the world one is interested in, but given that one's state of mind has a certain subject-matter, one can attend to the state of mind only by attending to that subject-matter. In the case of sensory experience, that requires that one direct one's attention at what is presented to one.

This point is revealed most clearly in the case of visual experience and other experiences where the subject-matter is presented as spatially arrayed. For we clearly do not take entities arrayed spatially to be merely the properties of mind. But it also holds more generally. We have here two contrasting conceptions of experience. On the adverbialist conception, we are to think of experience as simply being a state of the subject, a way of being modified. We are not to think of this event as intrinsically involving the presentation of anything to the subject, for that would be to import an 'act-object' conception of experience. Instead, experience is to be a modification in the way that being 13 stone is a way of being modified. What marks the former out from the latter is just that this way of being is a way of being conscious. The alternative conception of experience places much more weight on the subject of experience, and the subject's viewpoint. On that conception, to have an experience is to have a viewpoint on something: experiences intrinsically possess some subject-matter which is presented to that viewpoint. To understand such experience and what it is like, one has to understand the viewpoint on that subject-matter, and hence also to attend to the subject-matter as presented to the viewpoint.[12]

So, if we could really just think of our experiences as ways of being affected, where the awareness of a subject-matter was not intrinsic to being in such a state, then we would have no reason to reject an adverbialist conception of such states of mind. However, when we think about sensory states such as visual experience, and more generally experiences of audition, smell, taste, even most bodily sensation, we cannot separate our knowledge of what it is like to be in that state from knowledge of the subject-matter presented to one in being in such a state of mind. But that suggests for all such experience that our awareness of what the experience is like is inextricably bound up with knowledge of what is presented to one in having such experience. To know what such experience is like is in part to know how things are presented to one as being.

Indeed, I would suggest, all of this can seem so obvious, once one thinks about it, that it should raise a

---

[12] One can see Nagel's famous discussion of consciousness and physicalism, T. Nagel, 'What is it like to be a bat?' in *Mortal Questions,* (Cambridge: Cambridge University Press, 1979), as principally employing the second conception of experience – it is the role of a subject's point of view within experience which explains why one must adopt a subject's point of view to understand what his experience is like; cf. pp. 166, 172, 173–4. In contrast, much of the discussion of the so-called 'Knowledge Argument' against physicalism tends to focus on the adverbialist conception of experience, where the focus on a subject's own perspective comes in only at the level of thinking about one's experience, and not in having the experience itself.

problem of interpretation: how could anyone have plausibly put forward the adverbialist conception of experience as a serious option, given what we know of our experience? There are, I suggest, two aspects to the explanation of this: on the one hand, adverbialists were driven by a desire to reject the metaphysical commitments of sense-datum theories of perception; if taking seriously what we introspect of our experience would commit one to the existence of non-physical objects, then they were prepared to reject the apparently obvious. More insidious than this, though, the equivocation inherent in talk of 'qualia', which collapses the distinction between properties of being appeared to and properties apparent to one, simply obscures the inadequacy of the account.

III

We are now in a position to return to our initial task of laying out a common framework for the debate about the nature of experience and perceptual appearances. To know what one's experience is like is to know what properties, aspects or features are presented to one in having the experience. There seems to be no way to pick out the what-it-is-like properties of the experiences without also picking out corresponding properties which objects may appear to have. It is no surprise, then, to find that the term 'qualia' is happy to migrate between the two. Our first step should then be to replace such ambiguous terminology with an explicitly defined terminology which allows of no such slippage.

We need to keep track of two distinct things and pose the question how they are to be related. On the one hand, we are concerned with states of mind, experiences, and how they can be the same or different from each other, in particular how they can be the same or different for the subject of such states: how it is for a perceiver when they are in one of these states rather than another. When talking about this aspect of perceptual situations, we might talk of the *phenomenal character,* or *phenomenal properties* of the experience. We shall use these terms strictly to apply only to experiences and their properties and not to the objects of experience and the properties they appear to possess. When we need to talk of the latter, as the above discussion indicates we need to in understanding the phenomenal properties of experience, we shall instead talk about the *presented elements* or *presented aspects* of an experience.

With these terms in hand we can then state the conclusions of the last section as the keystone for our framework to the debate: reflection on sensory experience should lead one to accept that there are at least some phenomenal properties of experience which have corresponding presented elements, and our understanding of the phenomenal properties is dependent on our understanding of their presented elements. On this view, difference in presented elements between two experiences will be sufficient for difference in their phenomenal properties. Note, incidentally, that Price commits himself to something much stronger in insisting on the diaphanous nature of experience: namely that sameness and difference of phenomenal properties just are sameness and difference is presented elements. It is doubtful that this claim is true: why cannot the *ways* in which things are presented in experience make a difference to what the experience is like, in addition to what is presented?

We should at this point address the principal worry which motivates an adverbialist conception of experience: when we introduce talk of the presented elements of experience, and make differences between phenomenal properties of experience turn on them, are we not simply re-introducing sense-data into our account of experience? In seeing why not, we shall see how we are in a position to gain an overview of the whole debate. If we are to do justice to a subject's own point of view in having such experience, we need to fix on such presented elements; otherwise our account of experience will not be an account of what it is like for the subject of such experience to be so. From the subject's point of view, in both cases of perception and in cases of illusion and hallucination it certainly is as if there is something presented to her. So we can't do justice to that perspective without mentioning such a presented element in saying what the phenomenal character of her experience is. If we fail to mention such things then, as we saw, we end up with a view of experience on which it is not intrinsically a way of being aware of things.

But in doing this we need not take ourselves necessarily to be committed to the actual existence of these elements. For one might take a relaxed view of what the mention of a presented element in expressing the subject's point of view in having experience should commit one to. After all, we might think, in order to fix on young James's state of mind we have to mention Santa Claus, saying that

James has asked his aunt for a Buzz Lightyear doll, but Santa Claus for a playhouse. At the very same time, we might simply add that James is more likely to be satisfied by his aunt than Santa Claus, since at least the former but not the latter exists.

So too we might think that in occupying the point of view in having an experience, we must act as if the elements presented or given are there. If we are to attend to what our experience is like, we need to attend to the various aspects of the presented array, and to do so is to treat them as if they really do exist. But in taking a certain distance from someone's experience, or even in a moment of disbelief from our own, we may not suppose that there really is anything answerable to what is presented to that point of view.

The key here is to realize that the thesis endorsed concerning the relation between phenomenal properties and presented elements is principally a claim about how we are to understand what experience is like for a subject, from the subject's point of view. To fix on what we are attempting to explain, what it is for one to have experience, we need to take seriously the first person point of view both in and on experience. It is then a further move to explain the metaphysical commitments of such experience, and to ask what it takes for there both to be points of view and to be things, presented elements, on which such points of view are points of view. We can understand the fundamental debate about the nature of experience as a debate about these metaphysical commitments and the relation between phenomenal properties and presented elements.

Consider first the kind of intentional approach to perception which Dretske clearly favours. One will think that it is clear that the kind of experiences we have are intrinsically states of awareness of mind-independent objects and properties. So, one will identify the presented elements of such experiences with things that can exist independently of whether one has such experience.[13] At the same time, in insisting on the representational nature of experience, Dretske allows for the possibility that such experiences may be illusory or hallucinatory. On this approach, one's experience may have the relevant phenomenal property without its corresponding presented element actually being there. We have here a two-way independence of presented elements and phenomenal properties.

On the other hand, we can interpret those philosophers who insist that there is a subjective aspect to perceptual experience as claiming that there are presented aspects of experience which could not exist independent of one's awareness of them, but which at the same time are guaranteed to be instantiated just in case one does have an experience with the appropriate phenomenal properties. Here we have the mutual dependence of presented elements and phenomenal properties.

We can see these different views, then, as disputing two questions. On the one hand, they are concerned with what can be present to the mind: can the presented elements

---

[13] And in doing so, the theorist may claim to show how physical objects can be the direct objects of perception.

in experience exist independently of our awareness of them? On the other hand, they are concerned with the manner or mode in which objects are presented to one in having experience: can the presented elements of experience be so presented as not to require their actual existence for one's experience to be so? Indeed, we can think of these two questions as defining for us a complete set of options for the kinds of phenomenal property in question, depending on the mutual dependence of presented elements on phenomenal properties:

Is it possible to have: Presented Aspect & Not Phenomenal Property?

	Yes	No
Yes	Intentional	Naïve
No	Dependent	Subjective

Note that this generates *four* possible kinds of phenomenal property. For, one might agree with a defender of the intentional theory of perception that the presented elements of experience include the very mind-independent objects in the world around us which we take ourselves to perceive, and in that case that such presented elements can exist without one having the relevant experience. On the other hand, one might suppose, consonant with a sense-datum theory, that such experience really can only occur if its object really does exist, and hence that one can have an instance of the relevant phenomenal property only if its presented element exists. This possibility is marked in the matrix by the top right hand box: naïve phenomenal properties, as might call them.[14] Likewise, one might think that while the subject-matter of experience could not exist independent of one's experience, and so its presented elements could not be instantiated without corresponding phenomenal properties, nevertheless the experience itself would not be sufficient to guarantee the existence of that subject-matter. This possibility is reflected in the bottom left box, labelled Dependent Phenomenal Properties.

The debate about experience has tended to focus simply on the intentionality and subjectivity of experience, and hence on only two of these four properties, intentional phenomenal properties and subjective phenomenal properties in the terms of our matrix.[15] Furthermore, those who insist on the intentionality or representational nature of experience have tended to emphasize its world-directedness: that the presented elements of our experiences are trees, tables

---

[14] Of course, one might think that the existence of illusions and hallucinations are enough to show that there cannot actually be any experiences with such phenomenal properties. Whether such arguments from illusion really establish that conclusion turns in part on how one assesses so-called disjunctive theories of perception as presented in P. F. Snowdon, 'Perception, Vision and Causation', *Proceedings of the Aristotelian Society* (1980–81), J. McDowell, 'Criteria, Defeasibility and Knowledge', *Proceedings of the British Academy* (1982), H. Putnam, 'The Dewey Lectures', *Journal of Philosophy* (1994).

[15] Cf. C. Peacocke, *Sense and Content* (Oxford: Clarendon Press, 1983), chapter 1, particularly the definition of sensational properties on p. 5; G. Harman, 'The Intrinsic Quality of Experience', in *Philosophical Perspectives* 4, ed. J. Tomberlin (Arascadero: Ridgeview Publishing Co., 1990); S. Shoemaker, 'Self-Knowledge and "Inner Sense"', *Philosophy and Phenomenological Research* 64, (1994), 249–314.

and chairs which are there whether we experience them or not. But that aspect of experience is not sufficient to show that experience has intentional phenomenal properties rather than naive ones. Likewise, arguments for the existence of subjective phenomenal properties which attempt to show that there is more to what experience is like than how the external world is presented to be cannot show by that that there are subjective phenomenal properties rather than that there are either subjective or dependent ones. One moral to draw from this discussion is that the debate in the literature has been drawn in terms which are too narrow.[16] This gives us yet further evidence that the supposed obviousness of the terms of debate about subjective experience and qualia is nothing of the sort. We cannot hope to make proper progress on the debates about consciousness and the metaphysics of the mind until we have a better understanding of the issues surrounding perceptual experience and appearances.

The problem with which we started was that of finding some common ground between parties disputing what is supposedly just obvious to us. When that debate is

---

[16] Note that the possession of any one phenomenal property does not exclude the possibility of having any of the others: so this generates fifteen possible accounts of perception. The discussion in the literature tends to focus solely on two or three of these: those which appeal purely to intentional phenomenal properties, cf. Harman, 'The Intrinsic Quality of Experience', and those who think that there must be a mixture of phenomenal and subjective properties, cf. Peacocke, *Sense and Content,* chapters 1 and 2; there are a few defenders of purely subjective accounts of experience, for example, F. Jackson, *Perception: A Representative Theory* (Cambridge: Cambridge University Press, 1977).

framed simply in terms of the existence of qualia, or purely subjective qualities of experience, the problem is liable to seem intractable. But, I argued, such difficulties arise from the confusion inherent in the debate about qualia, with its almost unavoidable equivocation in the term. This we traced back to the adverbialist response to sense-data. The idea of experience merely as a mode of being affected by the world arises from the desire to avoid the metaphysical extravagances of sense-data, but it achieves metaphysical austerity only at the cost of leaving out of its conception of experience what seems to be essential to any account of what experience is like, that experience has a subject-matter. Once we reject this misconception, we are then better placed to find the common ground between different views: they all do wish to hold onto a common conception that what experience is like is a matter of what is present to the mind. The differences between sense-datum theories of experience and intentional accounts of perception are disagreements about what can be set before the mind, and how it can be so set. These matters take us well beyond that which is simply obvious to one from reflection on one's own visual or auditory experiences. The question that remains is how we are to settle these disputes.

Perceptual Intentionality, Attention and Consciousness

NAOMI EILAN

A representative expression of current thinking on the 'problem of consciousness' runs as follows. There is one, impenetrably hard problem; and a host of soluble, and in this sense easy problems. The hard problem is: how could a physical system yield subjective states? How could there be something it is like to be a physical system? This problem corresponds to a concept of consciousness invariably labelled 'phenomenal consciousness'. It is here, with respect to phenomenal consciousness, that we encounter an 'explanatory gap', where it is this gap that makes the problem so hard. Nothing we can say about the workings of a physical system could begin to explain the existence and nature of subjective, phenomenal feel.

But, the story goes, we also have another cluster of concepts of consciousness, the explanation of which give rise to easy, that is, soluble problems. One such easily explicable

I have been greatly helped by discussions with Bill Brewer, John Campbell, Mike Martin, Tony Marcel and Mark Price of issues raised in this paper, and by Mike Martin's and Colin Sparrow's criticisms of an earlier draft. I am also grateful to the audience at the Royal Institute of Philosophy, and to audiences at Stirling, Edinburgh and St Andrews, who heard a distant ancestor of the paper.

concept is that of 'consciousness of', an account of which is exhausted by a theory of mental representation, or intentionality. The other easy concepts all bring in the idea that conscious states are accessible, in some sense, to the subject. Accounting for 'access-consciousness' is a matter of distinguishing in functionalist terms among different kinds of access-conferring relations among mental representations. These problems are all easy in the sense that we have a relatively clear picture of what it would be for a physical system to have states that represent the world and stand in such functional relations to each other.[1]

While this bifurcation between easy and hard problems of consciousness is of some polemical value, it is fundamentally misguided, in my view, if it is treated as a resting place. Neither intentionality ('consciousness of') nor access-consciousness are easy concepts in the sense suggested, and phenomenal consciousness is not impenetrably hard in the sense suggested. In what follows I will be focusing exclusively on the so-called easy problems of access-consciousness and 'consciousness of' in the case of perception. A fundamental assumption in treating them as easy is that we can give an account of intentionality and accessibility wholly independently of an account of phenomenal

---

[1] The labels 'easy' and 'hard' are David Chalmers' in D. Chalmers, *The Conscious Mind* (Oxford: Oxford University Press, 1996). See, for example, p. xiii. They reflect a generally accepted bifurcation among problems of consciousness, a bifurcation very clearly described by Martin Davies in the introduction to *Consciousness*, ed. M. Davies and G. Humphreys (Oxford: Basil Blackwell, 1993).

aspects of experience. In the first section I will be suggesting that insisting on such independence prevents us from formulating properly, let alone addressing, the problem of perceptual intentionality. The rest of the paper will be devoted to spelling out some basic ingredients that have to go into an account of how phenomenal aspects of experience and intentionality are interwoven with each other in perceptual intentionality. I will be suggesting that addressing such problems generates a problem of consciousness which is, if anything, harder than the so called hard problem of phenomenal consciousness, though in a different sense.

I

The distinction between phenomenal and access-consciousness that I want to have before us is Ned Block's.[2] I begin with a brief summary of the distinction as he presents it, and then go on to raise questions about whether it can account for the way in which conscious perceptions make the world available to the subject.

On Block's account, phenomenal consciousness (P-consciousness) is experiential consciousness; it is consciousness of the kind that yields a 'something it is like' to be in the state that has such consciousness. It is the kind of consciousness we ascribe primarily though not exclusively to perceptual experiences. Access-consciousness (A-consciousness), in contrast, is the kind of consciousness a state has in virtue

---

[2] N. Block, 'On a Confusion about a Function of Consciousness', *Behavioural and Brain Sciences* (1995), 18, 227–87.

of being (1) 'inferentially promiscuous', that is, poised for use as a premise in reasoning, (2) poised for rational control of action and (3) poised for the rational control of speech. On Block's account access-consciousness is a 'cluster' concept in which (3) bears the least weight though it is often the practical guide to the existence of access-consciousness. Natural candidates for such consciousness are beliefs such as the belief that two and two is four, or that it might rain today.

Block's example of P-consciousness without A-consciousness, which will not be our central concern in what follows, is this. You may be engaged in deep conversation and suddenly at noon realize that right outside your window there is and has been a deafening pneumatic drill digging up the street. There is a way you were aware or conscious of it all along, and a way that you now become conscious of it which was previously lacking. According to Block 'you were P-conscious of the noise all along, but at noon you were both P-conscious and A-conscious of it'.[3]

Block's example of A-consciousness without P-consciousness, which will be our chief concern in what follows, is a counterfactual development of blindsight. Blind sighted patients report more or less complete absence of experience in the functionally blind area of their visual field. But when induced to guess what is there they can do so for quite a wide range of properties. Superblindseers are subjects who suffer from blindsight but learn how to induce

[3] Ibid., 234.

themselves to issue guesses unprompted, so that they find themselves issuing perceptual judgements somewhat in the manner in which a solution to a problem may suddenly spring to mind. The judgements are described by them as not being based on any experience, in contrast to their normal perceptual judgements.

The first question I want to raise is this. Do we have here a description of a case of access-consciousness without phenomenal consciousness, on Block's own account of access-consciousness? Access-consciousness is a relational property, and the relation, on Block's own account of it, is essentially rational. So a state is access-conscious if it provides reasons for judgements, actions, speech etc. Blindsighted subjects' perceptual inputs do not provide reasons for actions or judgement (they have to issue guesses) so they are not access-conscious. The case of superblindsight should be one in which the subject's perceptual states *do* provide reasons for the judgement. But as described by Block himself they do not. The superblindseer finds himself accosted with thoughts out of the blue, in the way a solution may suddenly spring to mind. The perception on which the judgement is in some sense based is not *his* reason for issuing the judgement. That is, unlike the normal case, the superblindseer does not appeal to the fact of perception or to the content of his perception as his *justification* for the content of his judgement. The perception is not therefore accessible to the subject, on Block's own account of access-consciousness.

One way out of the problem would be to drop the emphasis on rationality when explaining the consciousness-conferring access relation, a route followed for example by

Chalmers, who requires only a non-rational causal link between the perceptual state and the judgement.[4] But this is to miss the point. As we have just seen, when the perceptual state cannot be cited as the subject's own reason for her judgement, the perceptual state is not, intuitively, accessible to the subject in a consciousness-conferring way. If the state is not a reason for the subject, from her perspective, it is not conscious. Block got this right in his definition of access-consciousness, but in his example he probably reverted to thinking of the access-conferring link in non-rational causal terms. For what the superblindseer manages is the establishment of some kind of non-rational causal connection between the occurrence of perceptual input and the issuing of a judgement.

In the normal case perceptions present the world to the subject as being such and such and it is this presentation of the world to the subject, or its appearance as such and such to the subject, which gives the perception its evidential status.[5] More specifically: in the normal case, the way our perceptions make us conscious of the environment (by making it present to us, or by yielding appearances of it) suffices for giving the perception its evidential status. This is

---

[4] On this difference between his own account of 'awareness' and Block's account of access-consciousness see Chalmers, *The Conscious Mind*, p. 228.

[5] B. Brewer, 'Experience and Reason in Perception' in this volume. My approach to the relation between experience and knowledge owes much to Brewer's work in this area.

what is lacking in both blindsight and superblindsight. Explaining how perceptual directedness onto the world has this dual property is the problem of explaining perceptual intentionality. The question now is: can we explain the requisite notion of presence, appearance or 'consciousness of' on a theory that draws a sharp distinction between phenomenal and access-consciousness?

A central assumption in the way Block and others have drawn the distinction is this. Phenomenal consciousness is a function of *non*-representational properties of the experience; and, correlatively, representational properties which yield 'consciousness of' can be explained in complete independence of appeal to phenomenal feel. Now the notion of presence or appearance to the subject is a phenomenological notion, so on the kind of theory we are considering representational properties could not account for it. We must turn, then, to an account of the non-representational properties to do the job of infusing the perception with this phenomenological property of presence of the world to the subject. Recall, a central constraint is that the notion of presence we come up with will be such that its possession by a perception suffices for explaining what gives the perception its evidential status relative to judgements based on it. So we must appeal to the non-representational properties of an experience to provide the perception with phenomenology and, simultaneously, with evidential status. There are two ways they might be said to do so. Either by means of giving rise to the judgement: such and such sensations are in the normal course of events accompanied or caused by a perceptual state with such and such representational properties, so I must have perceptions with such contents and they are my reason for judging that such and such is the case in the world. Or, more directly and familiarly: such and such sensations are normally caused by such and such a state of the world and that is my reason for judging such and such to be the case. As Bill Brewer argues in his paper in this volume, it is dubious whether such indirect reflective judgements could actually provide an alternative justification to the kind of direct, non-reflective justification our perceptions normally provide us with.[6] For our immediate purposes the central point is that, intuitively, neither of these reflective routes makes the perceptual representation *accessible* to the subject in the way in which we think conscious states are accessible. Intuitively, the subject could issue such judgements while the representational properties of the perceptual state remain wholly non-conscious.

So the requisite notion of presence cannot be explained by appeal to the notion of non-representational properties of experience. And this is not surprising. What we need in accounting for perceptual intentionality is an explanation of how the representational properties of an experience make the world phenomenally present to the subject. This in turn requires an account of how representational and phenomenal aspects of experience are interwoven with each other in such a way as to yield such presence of the world to the subject. What is preventing us from giving such an account is the requirement that we explain the way

---

[6] Ibid.

perceptions represent the environment wholly independently of any appeal to the phenomenal aspects of experience. So we must drop the leading assumption underpinning the distinction between phenomenal and access-consciousness if we are to so much as formulate the problem of perceptual intentionality properly, let alone make progress with addressing it. And, if this is how we should see the problem of explaining the nature of perceptual intentionality, then neither 'consciousness of' nor access-consciousness is an easy concept, in the case of perception at least, if what makes a concept easy is the possibility of accounting for it independently of appealing to phenomenal aspects of perceptual consciousness. The rest of the paper will be concerned with two suggestions about how the problem of accounting for perceptual intentionality should be addressed, and with raising one kind of hard problem generated by the attempt to get this right.

II

In very broad terms the suggestion I want to pursue, which is hardly original, is that getting perceptual intentionality right is a matter of getting right the peculiar mixture of activity and passivity distinctive of perceptual experience. I begin with a very brief summary of a widely held philosophical approach to the issue, and use some problems in this approach to introduce the issues I will be concerned with.

It is common practice in both philosophy and psychology to castigate the empiricist picture of perception, on which pure perception delivers uninterpreted sensations, on the grounds that it conceives of perception as wholly passive. The philosophical corrective to this picture normally involves some kind of endorsement of Kant's dictum that 'intuitions without concepts are blind'. Experiences are, in Strawson's terms, permeated with concepts,[7] where conceptual content is the mark of representations governed by rationality constraints. The insistence on this infusion of experiences with concepts is supposed simultaneously to solve for the phenomenology (it is in virtue of the concepts that one is presented in perception with a world, rather than sensations) and for the epistemology. It is in virtue of possessing conceptual content that experiences 'occupy the space of reasons', in Sellars' phrase, and, hence, can be a source of rationally constrained knowledge about the world.[8]

But, as McDowell, for one, notes, leaving matters at that raises epistemological and phenomenological problems which the sense-data theory was expressly designed to deal with. First, sense-data were supposed to mark the impact of the external, mind-independent world upon the subject; mere insistence on the essential infusion of experience by reason leaves us with the threat of a purely coherentist account of the way in which experiences serve as a source

---

[7] P. F. Strawson, 'Perception and Its Objects', in *Perception and Identity: Essays in Honour of A. J. Ayer*, ed. G. Macdonald (London: Macmillan, 1979), p. 45.

[8] On this, see J. McDowell, *Mind and World* (Cambridge, MA: Harvard University Press, 1994), Lecture 1, and Brewer, 'Experience and Reason'.

of knowledge about the external world. Secondly, insisting on the possession of conceptual content seems to leave with us without any means of distinguishing the phenomenology of experiences from that of thought. Some way of meeting both the phenomenological and the epistemological points must be found, which simultaneously holds on to the requirements met by insisting on the conceptual content of experience. McDowell's own solution is to say that we should do this by allowing a passive ingredient in perception, where the way to do justice to it is by noting that in experience 'conceptual capacities are drawn on *in* receptivity'.[9] The mark of this way of using concepts is that it involves an essential passivity in one's relation to the content of the representation. 'In experience one finds oneself saddled with content.'[10]

A noteworthy feature of this way of approaching the problem of the mixture of passivity and activity in perception is that it has nothing at all to say about the psychological process whereby rationality or concepts get involved in perception. It has nothing to say about *how* in perception one finds oneself saddled with rationally constrained content. One position here is that the appeal to rational activity in characterizing the phenomenology and epistemology of perception has no bearings on, and is wholly independent of, whatever the correct theory of the mechanisms of perception is. On the personal level there is no mechanism story to be told. In appealing to activity we are making purely

[9] McDowell, *Mind and World*, p. 9.   [10] Ibid., p. 10.

phenomenological and epistemological points, accurately summarized in the claim that experiences have conceptual contents. When we speculate about mechanisms we are bound to get led into the kinds of traps the sense-data theorists, and Kant himself, in a more subtle way, were led into. Any accounts of the mechanisms of perception should restrict themselves to a description of subpersonal computations.

I want to suggest that this cannot work. We cannot get right the mixture of activity and passivity distinctive of perceptual intentionality without addressing the question of how concepts become integrated into the process of perception. The correct account of such integration is one essential ingredient in the account we should give of the mixture of activity and passivity to be found in perceptual experience. I will first illustrate what I mean by considering some everyday examples of remembering about which it is also appropriate to say that the subject, in remembering, is 'saddled with content'. In the next section I return to perception.

Consider the following kinds of questions one might ask oneself in the course of a normal working hour. Where did I put my keys? What did Mary ask me to get from the shop? What is that student's name? What was I about to say? Why did I come into this room anyway? And so forth. Sometimes the answer comes, as we say, immediately, sometimes with irritating delay and sometimes not at all. Much of what passes for mental activity consists in asking oneself such questions and waiting for longer or shorter periods for the answer.

Now, in all such cases we may speak of the answer 'coming' to us, though this is especially vivid when there is some delay. And in all cases of the answer coming to us it is appropriate to speak of the thinker being 'saddled with content'. A first stab at describing the mixture of activity and passivity in these cases is to say that the answer coming is the passive bit, and the asking of the question the active bit. But this cannot be right. On the one hand, answering the question is something we do (certainly this is so when someone else asks the question). And, on the other hand, when we ponder how it can be that asking oneself a question yields a response we are bound to conceive of the asking bit involving some non-conscious ingredient which is from our perspective passive and which is responsible in some way for getting the answering going.

I recently heard a six-year-old complain that she kept on asking her brain where her crayons were, and he wouldn't answer so she went out to play and then while she was on the swing he suddenly told her they were under her bed. This was said partly in exasperation that he should be so slow, but also in appreciation and some wonder that, as she put it, he should go on thinking about it when she herself had stopped. This story of communication with a reluctant but ultimately quite helpful brain contains within it a metaphorical rendering of the mixture of passivity and activity in our pre-theoretical concept of remembering that any philosophical and psychological theory must aim to do justice to. And many do not. One way of failing is to give an account of remembering exclusively in terms of relations between subpersonal information-processing systems. The subject, active and passive, drops out altogether. Another, more subtle way is to insist that our everyday 'personal level'

concept is wholly independent of any reference to the mechanisms that make remembering possible. But this kind of
claim, unlike the child's story, fails to do justice to the
passivity involved in asking oneself questions, for the passivity here is partly a function of the fact that in doing what
one is doing (asking and answering the question) there is
something going on that makes this possible, that one does
not have access to.

The way to do non-metaphorical justice to this
passivity while holding on to the active subject is to treat
information-processing theories of the mechanisms
involved in remembering as descriptions of non-conscious
ingredients in what the subject actively does when asking
and answering her own questions. The fact that there is this
non-conscious cognitive ingredient just is what introduces
the passivity. So reference to such mechanisms is not an
optional extra relative to our everyday conception of
remembering, but, rather, an extension of them.

My first suggestion is that this last point applies
equally to the mixture of activity and passivity in perception.
Or, more precisely, I suggest that one important strand in
getting right the mixture of activity and passivity in perception will involve moves exactly analogous to those made
above about remembering. In the next section I will be
concerned to draw out these analogies, focusing especially
on the epistemology of perceptual intentionality. In the last
section, I will focus mainly on phenomenology and introduce one important disanalogy between perceiving and
propositional memory, and, relative to that, an extra level
of activity and passivity distinctive specifically of perceptual

experience. Finally, I will suggest that trying to combine these two layers of activity and passivity generates a problem of consciousness which is in some sense harder than the 'hard' problem of phenomenal consciousness.

III

Let us return to one of the examples of a memory question: where did I leave my keys? I might ask this simply because I like to keep a check on where everything is, but more probably, at least in my case, because I need them, immediately, as I am already late for something. Suppose I am lucky and the answer comes, that they are on the kitchen table. Guided by this memory I will take myself off to the table. If I am lucky I will find them there; and here too, there might be delays, which I will afterwards describe as the keys staring me in the face all the while I was looking for them, until something clicked. On this happening I will pick them up and rush out to the car.

As described, such a sequence involves one kind of mixture of activity and passivity which I think any theory would hold is necessary if perception is to count as a source of knowledge, and to which I will not, therefore, devote much space. In very general terms: for perceptions to serve as a basis for knowledge it must be possible for the subject to use her perceptions to answer questions about the environment and to incorporate the deliverances of her perceptions into further rational deliberation and action. Reason is in there from the start in that the subject who can use her perceptions in this way is rationally involved in the acquisition of information from the environment. And the correct account of the kind of active reasoning required for perception to be used in this way of itself introduces a level of passivity, if one likes, of a kind lacking in memory. For, as the above example demonstrates, in using my perceptions to answer a question I have to exploit my grip on what Gareth Evans has called a 'primitive theory of perception'.[11] I exploit my grip on the idea that if I am to perceive what I want to perceive various causal conditions must be met, including being in the right location. I only get the answer to my question if I put myself in the right position to acquire it. This in turn gives me (the beginning of) a grip on the idea of an objective world out there which is such that getting information about it requires that these further conditions are met. The role of the theory in perceptual answering of questions, as distinct from memory, introduces one extra level (of several) of passivity in perception. In memory, as we say, one asks oneself what is or was the case. In perception one asks the world. For such interrogation of the environment[12] to occur one has to put oneself in a position

[11] G. Evans, 'Things Without the Mind', in *Collected Papers* (Oxford: Oxford University Press, 1985), pp. 249–90. On the role of such a theory in providing for our grip on the idea of an objective world see John Campbell, 'The Role of Physical Objects in Spatial Thinking', in *Spatial Representation: Problems in Philosophy and Psychology* ed. N. Eilan, R. McCarthy and B. Brewer (Oxford: Blackwell, 1993), pp. 88–93.

[12] I borrow the phrase 'interrogation of the environment' from unpublished work by Rowland Stout, in which he employs it to describe the relation between attention and perception. The link with attention will be taken up shortly.

to receive information from the world, be receptive to the world as it is at the time of questioning. It is true that in order to think of an autobiographical memory as such I must think of myself as having been in the past in a position to acquire information from the world. But I don't depend on the world as it is at the time of questioning; all that is needed is me and my memories. In perception I need the world.

Now, put in these very general terms there is nothing the sense-data theorist, for example, need object to. True, such theorists tended to emphasize the role of reason in the interpretation of data already acquired, rather than in the actual acquisition of it; but there is nothing here, yet, that their conception of perception cannot accommodate. So, if perception is only active in this sense, appeal to such activity cannot ground rejection of the idea that all that perceptions deliver is a bundle of uninterpreted sensations. What we need is a sense in which perception is active which does have this result, in particular which yields an account of the deliverances of perception which is such that concepts and thoughts are integral to them. And we need a corresponding sense in which perceptions are passive which is such that concepts and thought are not integral to the deliverances of perception thus conceived.

What is important here is the account we give of what it is that the subject does when, as we say, she scans or searches the environment, looking for an answer to her question. For a very wide range of theories what the subject does is physically manipulate her sense organs in such a way as to make them receptive to information. The subject's active contribution ends here. Thereafter the process of perception takes over. The process is passive in that sense; the subject's rational activity has no part to play in the process of perception itself. This is certainly true for theories that hold that perceptions deliver sensations. But it is equally true, for example, for most of the Gestaltists. They rejected atomism: perception delivers organized wholes, but it does so without the subject's intervention, without the intervention of thought. And it is true for all theories that say that the process of perception is to be explained exhaustively in terms of subpersonal information-processing mechanisms.

It is the passivity of the perceptual process in this sense that Gibson, for example, rejected. In its stead he proposed a picture on which perception is an activity of picking up information, by looking, smelling, touching etc., where these in turn are conceived of as modes of attending to the environment.[13] What has made this aspect of his account attractive to many is, I think, a sense that there is no other way of solving a problem inherent in all theories that treat perception as passive in the sense just outlined. This is the problem of giving an epistemologically, phenomenologically and psychologically plausible account of how concepts and rational thought get linked to experience. The sense-dataist's account is familiarly off-key. The same problem besets many Gestalt theories, which held that the immediate objects of thought and attention, once perception has

---

[13] See, for example, J. J. Gibson, 'The Perceptual Systems', in *The Senses Considered as Perceptual Systems* (London: George Allen and Unwin Ltd., 1968), pp. 47–58.

done its job, are not entities in the physical world but the phenomenal wholes delivered by perception.[14] And in the case of wholly subpersonal information-processing accounts of the process of perception, we seem to be faced with the options of either installing various systems of communication between the subject and its subpersonal mechanisms, or giving a wholly reductive account, purely in subpersonal terms, both of the subject's activities and of her perceptions.

Suppose it is this kind of background reason which makes the Gibsonian conception of perception as an activity of attending to the environment attractive. Leaving aside, for a moment, the question of how exactly such activity is conceived of, one immediate problem, highlighted by McDowell, is that it seems to miss out on an essentially passive ingredient in our concept of perceptual experience. This is McDowell's stated motivation for introducing the claim that in perception, as opposed to thought, concepts are 'drawn on in a mode of receptivity', and the accompanying metaphor of 'being saddled with content' in perception.

Now, McDowell does not say what it is about the Gibsonian story that is responsible for the absence of passivity, or what is needed to correct it. I want to suggest that part of what is wrong with the Gibsonian account is the insistence that perception is to be exhaustively explained by appeal to the metaphor of 'direct pickup' of information and

[14] This is made explicit in Koffka's *Principles of Gestalt Psychology* (New York: Harcourt Brace and World, 1935). See also G. Kanizsa, *Organization in Vision* (New York: Praeger Publishers, 1979), 'Seeing and Thinking', pp. 14–24.

the accompanying refusal to allow the need for any information-processing accounts of what goes on when we
actively engage via perception with the environment.
Correlatively, I suggest that one thing needed for getting
the mix of activity and passivity right here is getting right the
relation between what the subject does when extracting
answers to her questions from the environment, and the
information-processing involved in her so doing. More specifically: the correction to the picture of perception as passive that is needed is one on which rational activity is said to
have an influence on the processing of information in perception; it is this which all accounts of perception as a purely
passive process disallow.

According to the psychologists Daniel Kahneman
and Avishai Henik the 'enduring fascination with the problem of attention can perhaps be traced to the Jamesian
account of the nature of selective attention as a pure act of
will which controls experience.'[15] The concept of attention
they employ, which has its origins in William James, and is
in widespread use in current information-processing
approaches to attention, is one on which attention is the
selection of information for further processing. John
Campbell has recently suggested that we should treat the
various information-processing accounts of the mechanisms
involved in such selection and further processing as the non-
conscious cognitive components of what the subject does

[15] D. Kahneman and A. Henik, 'Perceptual Organization and Attention'
in *Perceptual Organisation* ed. M. Kobovy and J. Pomerantz (Hillsdale,
NJ: Lawrence Erlbaum Associates, 1981), p. 201.

when attending;[16] or, in the terms of the above quotation, non-conscious ingredients in attention conceived of as a possible expression of will. This seems to me to be the correct general line to take about one very central way attention and perception are related. From our perspective, its importance is that it captures one essential ingredient in the mixture of passivity and activity that we find in perception.

Let us return to scanning the table for one's keys. It is simply not true that all the subject does here is manipulate her head and eyes. Such manipulation is neither necessary nor sufficient, as shown by experiments on so called 'covert attention'. Subjects are asked to fixate some point ahead of them and then told they will be asked questions about an area distinct from the area of fixation, say to its left. Their task is to answer the questions about that area on the left of fixation without moving their eyes. Subjects can do this (so moving the eyes is not necessary); and, when they do this, by switching their attention to the left of fixation, they become correspondingly bad at answering questions about the area they are fixating (fixating an area is not sufficient). So we need a different account of what it is that subjects do when they answer the question. What they do is attend to a portion of the world. So we need an account of what attention is. Attention is what we use to answer the question. But how do we do it? What do we do? Part of the bafflement here is analogous to the one we find in memory. What we

---

[16] John Campbell, 'Wittgenstein on Attention', submitted.

are doing is making something happen, such that the answer will come to us through perception. The child's metaphor of communicating in a more or less successful way with the brain who does the work for her is as natural here as it is in memory. And the way to do non-metaphorical justice to it here too is by introducing a passive cognitive loop in the process of asking and answering questions.

Campbell's proposal captures exactly what is needed in accounting for the kinds of cases we have been considering. In all these cases the correct account of what we do when we attend, the correct response to the kind of bafflement noted earlier, is, precisely, to say that what is happening is that the subject is actively selecting information to be processed. Most of the steps in the processing are the passive, because non-conscious, cognitive component in the activity of asking and answering questions about the environment.

IV

The suggestion I have been pursuing is that getting perceptual intentionality right is a matter of getting right the mixture of activity and passivity distinctive of perceptual experience. To generalize from the specific cases I have been considering, the drift of the remarks so far made can be sharpened up somewhat by means of the following three claims:

1. Perceptual experiences have conceptual content only when there has been rational influence on the process of

perception. More specifically, experiences are imbued with conceptual content only when it is correct to think of them as answers to theoretical questions that the subject directs at the environment.

2. Attention is, among other things, the means by which we answer such questions about the environment. The conceptualized contents of experiences are those that are the deliverances of attention used in this way.

3. When attention is used in this way it should be conceived of as the selection by the subject of information for further processing.

I realise that these claims, in particular (1), raise a host of immediate, largely phenomenological objections. First, there are specific cases for which it doesn't seem right to say that the experience is an answer to a question. For example, when the pneumatic drill surfaces, as we say, in conceptualized consciousness, it does not seem right to describe this surfacing as a response to a question one has asked. Then, there is the general objection that it does not seem right to say that one is incessantly interrogating the environment, and only has experiences as a consequence of such non-stop interrogation. Surely one just soaks up what is going on in a more relaxed way.

I cannot hope to deal adequately with all such objections; and it may well be that a comprehensive treatment of them would lead to some modifications of the three claims I have made. Nonetheless, I think the claims are along the right lines, and perhaps a quick response to the two objections I mentioned will do something to make them less immediately counterintuitive. First, the pneumatic drill: the interesting question here is not why and how it becomes accessible to reason, but, given that it is described as deafening, why it remained inaccessible for the period it did. Some kind of suppression mechanism must have been working (on one account of attention, one of its roles is to suppress processing, rather than to encourage it). But once this is recognized, it seems, I think, natural to say that what has been suppressed are various questions that come flooding back, once the operation of the suppressing mechanisms has been suspended, for whatever reason. I suspect something along these lines is true for a wide range of cases we want to describe in terms of something suddenly surfacing, unbidden, in consciousness.

As to the idea that in general one isn't constantly throwing questions at the world: one point worth making is that I am talking, here, only about the conceptualized contents of experience, the contents that can serve as inputs to theoretical knowledge. In a moment I will be touching on the problem of how we should account for the ongoing non-theoretical awareness we have of the environment. Suppose, then, we do focus only on conceptual contents. Consider cases we describe as 'throwing a well-practised eye' over a social gathering, say, or as 'casing the joint'. One of Gibson's central contentions was that perceiving is something we learn to do. I suggest that much of what this involves is the acquisition of routines of specific questions which become automatic or habitual extensions of the general question: what is going on here? (somewhat in the manner in which components of a physical skill become automatic). And, once this is recognized, one can allow experiences to be the outcome of what from the subject's conscious perspective are very loose, general questions. The claim that experiences have conceptual content in virtue of being answers to theoretical questions the subject directs at the environment need not and should not be understood as implying the constant firing of batteries of conscious detailed questions at the world.

I hope I have done something to make the three claims seem phenomenologically more acceptable, though I realize there is more work to be done here. I now turn to their implications for the account we should give of what is wrong with the blindseer's and superblindseer's perceptual input. With respect to blindsight: the three claims, as they stand, would suffice to rule out the blindseer's perceptions from having the kind of content our experiences have. The subject does not and apparently cannot direct questions at the area in his visual field in which he is functionally blind; and whatever perceptual input he has cannot therefore be conceived of as answers to such questions. It does not have conceptual content.

But nothing so far said would appear to engage with the problem of explaining what is wrong with the superblindseer's perceptual input. The argument pressed in the first section of the paper was that the superblindseer's perceptions are not, contra Block, accessible in the way required for consciousness because they do not provide the subject with his reason for judgement. The claim then was that they do not do so because they do not present a world to the subject; and that any account of perceptual intentionality must show how phenomenal and conceptual aspects of experience are interwoven with each other in such a way as to yield such presence. The problem for the account of perceptual intentionality so far given is that it does not seem to account for such presence; and it is for this reason that nothing has been said to rule out the superblindseer's perception from having the kind of intentionality distinctive of conscious experiences.

Imagine the superblindseer prompting himself to issue guesses about the functionally blind area in his visual field. Such issuing of guesses can be represented as the answering of questions about objects and their properties in that area. Compare such asking of questions and answering them by means of guesses with the asking and answering of questions about areas of the visual field represented by means of conscious experiences. Intuitively, the main difference is that in conscious experience the questions he directs at the environment are guided and constrained by a presence of the environment, of some kind, to the subject. It is such presence which is lacking in the functionally blind field, and intuitively, it is because of its lack that the answers that he gets strike him as bolts from the blue.

I want to suggest that an additional element in getting right the mixture of activity and passivity in perceptual experience, additional to the one so far discussed, is a matter of getting right the relation between such 'guiding presence of the environment' and attention. At the end of the paper I will come back to the question of how these two mixtures of activity and passivity are related to each other.

I begin with illustrations of two distinct ways in which the environment might be said to be present to us in a way that guides and constrains attention.

1. Consider, first, Heidegger's famous example of engaged or wholly immersed intentionality, using a hammer to perform some task. This is contrasted by him with theoretical (thematic) intentionality. Dreyfus explains the distinction by the following appeal to attention. In the case of immersed intentionality, as in the hammer example, one is not attending to the hammer but, rather, one's attention is absorbed by the task at hand. Such absorption in the task can of course be suspended, and one's attention might be diverted, voluntarily or otherwise, to the hammer itself, for example when the head feels loose. It is when one's attention is diverted to the hammer itself that we have a thought about it, an instance of theoretical intentionality.[17] A visual example of such switches of attention from task to perceived objects might be the switch of attention onto some feature of one's surroundings that may occur when one is wholly absorbed in driving and suddenly wonders where on earth one is, or someone suddenly darts across the road.

There are three features of these kinds of switches that are worth emphasizing. First, intuitively, there is no thought about the hammer or my surroundings in driving until I have switched attention to them. Secondly, the hammer and various objects and features in my surroundings are nonetheless present to me prior to such thought; they are articulated for me, for the purposes of action (it is for this reason that Heidegger is right to speak of a kind of

[17] H. Dreyfus, *Being in the World* (Cambridge, MA: MIT Press, 1991), chapter 4, 'Availableness and Occurrentness', pp. 60–87.

intentionality here). Thirdly, when I direct my attention to the hammer or various objects in my surroundings it is, in the first instance, to the hammer and objects thus articulated and present.

I suggest that much of what we mean by attention-guiding presence in everyday perception is on the level of Heidegger's notion of absorbed intentionality. A lot of what he says about it and theoretical or thematic intentionality is captured in John Campbell's distinction between causally indexical and non-indexical content. The causally indexical contents of perceptions are contents the causal and spatial significance of which is exhausted in terms of their implications for the subject's actions. The non-indexical contents are contents the grasp of which requires grasp of a primitive theory of perception, and the attendant conception of oneself as one object among others. Such a conception is, in turn, described by Campbell as being essential for theoretical as opposed to purely practical knowledge.[18] Getting right the account of the relation between phenomenal and conceptual ingredients in perceptual intentionality is, then, partly, a matter of getting right the way in which such causally indexical immersed articulations of the environment inform and guide attention-mediated conceptual thought about it.

2. In the paper quoted earlier by Kahneman and Henik, Gestalt groupings and figure ground segregations are said to 'define the frustrating boundaries of what we can will ourselves to do' (in selectively attending to the

---

[18] Campbell, 'The Role of Physical Objects', pp. 82–8.

environment).[19] And, although not always put in exactly these terms, many of the extensive studies on the workings of selective and divided attention are in fact just studies of the constraints imposed by various organizational phenomena on the possibilities of divided and selective attention. Some quick examples will give a flavour of the kind of connection being talked about. The term 'selective attention' refers to subjects' capacity to isolate an object or property from others presented to them. An example of such failure is this. Suppose you are looking at a picture of a Rubin vase, which can appear either as a vase or as two profiles facing each other, depending on what is taken as figure and what is taken as ground. Suppose you see it as two profiles. Your task is to attend selectively to the contours of one of the profiles. You will not succeed. You will not recognize it if presented on its own, and certainly not if it represented as enclosing some other figure, say a vase. This is seen as showing that Gestaltists' claims about contours being treated as essentially belonging to the objects they enclose reveal constraints on what we can selectively attend to in perception.[20] (There is no comparable difficulty in thought of the contour on its own.) A famous example of the effects of

---

[19] Kahneman and Henik, 'Perceptual Organization', p. 201.

[20] E. Rubin, 'Figure and Ground', in *Readings in Perception*, ed. and trans: D. C. Beardslee and M. Wertheimer (New York: Van Nostrand, 1958), pp. 194–203. For an excellent account of Rubin's own work, and reports on experiments designed to update his findings and to give them computational underpinnings, see Jon Driver and Gordon Baylis, 'Edge– Assignment and Figure-Ground Segmentation in Short Term Visual Matching', *Cognitive Psychology* 31 (1996), 248–306.

Gestalt organizational phenomena is the Stroop test. If your task is to name the colour in which a word is printed, say red, but the word printed is, say, 'green', there will be interference: you will say 'green' instead of 'red'. But if the word 'green' appears very near the target word, there is no interference. This is taken to show the effects of Gestalt organization into objects on the working of selective attention. If properties are perceived as belonging to a single object they are hard to attend to selectively.[21] A simplified example of Gestalt-imposed constraints on divided attention is this. Suppose your task is to report the colour of two dots. If they are seen as contained within a single object, as defined by Gestalt laws, you will be as good at that as in reporting the colour of one. But you will be significantly slowed down if the two dots are presented as being in two separate objects, as defined by Gestalt laws, even though the spatial separation is exactly the same as when they are presented as being within one object.[22]

The examples of immersed intentionality and the effects of Gestalt organization give us two distinct ways in

---

[21] See Kahneman and Henik, 'Perceptual Organization', and also for a wide range of other examples, including auditory ones. Also A. W. Garner, 'The Analysis of Unanalysed Perceptions', in *Perceptual Organization,* ed. Kubovy and Pomerantz, pp. 141–80.

[22] See e.g. John Duncan, 'Selective Attention and the Organisation of Visual Information', *Journal of Experimental Psychology: General* (1984), 113, 501–17; G. Baylis and J. Driver, 'Visual Attention and Objects: Evidence for Hierarchical Coding of Location', *Journal of Experimental Psychology: Human Perception and Performance* 21 (1995), 1323–42.

which there is in perceptual experience a presence of the world to the subject, in contrast to thought and propositional memory. In the immersed case, what we have is an articulation of a world for the purposes of action which yields a presence of the world which is prior to attention and to which we may attend when we attend. But as we attend to it, the way it was present to us prior to attention disappears from view: we switch to a theoretical conception of the object. The kind of presence brought to light by examining the effects of Gestalt phenomena is quite different. Here what we are shown are non-conceptual aspects of perceptual experience that are present *as* we attend to objects and which are partly determinant of the distinctive phenomenology of attention-mediated, perception-based thought in contrast to that of pure thought.

There are many other ways in which extra-conceptual ingredients come into an account of perceptual presence, but these two will suffice for raising the final set of problems I will be discussing. The claim has been that the problem of getting perceptual intentionality right is the problem of showing how conceptual and phenomenal aspects are interwoven in perceptual intentionality. This in turn was said to lie in getting right the mixture of activity and passivity in perceptual experience. The mixture of activity and passivity we have now been discussing can be put as follows. Both immersed articulation of the environment and the Gestalt organizations in some way constrain the operation of attention. This constraint introduces a kind of passivity, lacking in pure thought. The problem of getting perceptual intentionality right is, in part, the problem of how we should explain and fill out this constraining relation between such non-conceptual, presence-yielding aspects of experience, on the one hand, and attention, conceived of as the vehicle of reason and concepts, on the other.

Neither the immersed articulation of the environment for the purposes of action nor Gestalt organization of the environment into groups and objects provides reasons for attention-mediated thought about it. The relation of constraint is, then, not rational. Nor is it correct to speak of them as merely causing the attention-mediated thought. Constraint is not a purely casual relation. At this point the right thing to do would seem to be to reach for what was earlier said, in describing the first strand of mixture of activity and passivity in perception, namely that we should conceive of attention as active selection of information for further processing. What we might say here is that this account will yield, at the same time, the account we need of the relation of constraint. More specifically: both Gestalt groupings and object segregations, and the articulation of the environment for the purposes of action involve some way of representing the environment and should therefore have some kind of computational underpinning. What is needed for explaining the constraint imposed by them on attention is that we treat them as the information selected for further processing. We should then go on to say that they just are the inputs to the information processing involved once active selection has occurred. The relation of constraint is a computational one.

This seems the right way to go; but I now come to what seems to me to be a difficulty with this picture, however attractive, which is, in turn, a difficulty that I think any account of perceptual intentionally must face, in some form or other. The notion of a 'preattentive' stage in perception (the phrase was coined by Neisser[23]), is used by psychologists to describe information available in perception prior to, and independently of, attentional processing. If we are guided by phenomenological constraints only we will apply this notion both to the articulation of the environment for the purposes of action (in a way that accords with the spirit of how Neisser himself originally used it) and to the Gestalt groupings and object segregations (as Kahneman and many others use it.) Used in this way, the claim would be that an account of the mechanisms of perceptual intentionality just is an account of the way in which such presence-yielding preattentive information serves as input to the rational activity of selecting preattentive information for further processing.

There is, however, a different use of the notion of a preattentive stage in perception which is guided not by phenomenological constraints but, rather, by computational constraints only. Here, preattentive information, for example in vision, is identified with whatever early vision delivers, in parallel, bottom-up. This is then conceived of as input to top-down operations, for example the kind of visual routines proposed by Shimon Ullman for the representation of spatial relations and shape properties.[24]

[23] Ulric Neisser, *Cognitive Psychology* (New York: Appleton-Century Crofts, 1967).

[24] Shimon Ullman, 'Visual Routines', in *Visual Cognition*, ed. S. Pinker (Cambridge, MA: MIT Press, 1985), pp. 97–160.

A problem in the way I have set out the relation between phenomenally determined preattentive information and attention is that there is no guarantee that the two ways of describing the preattentive level will coincide. In fact, there are numerous examples of them not coinciding as things currently stand. One example is this: if we use 'preattentive' to describe the articulation of the environment for the purposes of action then, according to Ullman's account of visual routines, we will have to say that such visual routines go into this kind of articulation.[25] So what is preattentive phenomenologically speaking is not what is preattentive computationally speaking. More generally: on the going account, preattentive vision delivers features (rather than object representations) which are then combined in top-down processes to yield representations of objects. But as we have appealed both to Gestalt organizations and to the articulation of the environment for the purposes of action, this was in order to describe a kind of preattentive presence of whole objects to the subject, rather than disconnected features.

This (more than merely) possible divergence might appear to present us with a dilemma, neither horn of which is obviously attractive. One option is simply to abandon the link with the phenomenally motivated account of the preattentive level. But if the arguments presented in the first section of this paper are right, we cannot do that while simultaneously holding onto the idea that attention is the means by which rational activity and thought get into

[25] The need for the use of such routines for the purposes of action is made explicit by Ullman, in ibid., p. 98.

perceptual experience. Recall, the argument was: neither the blindseers' nor the superblindseers' perceptions provide them with reasons for judgement because of the absence of whatever is needed to explain phenomenal presence. Rationality here is a function of the link with such phenomenal presence. Drop the commitment to getting presence right and you forfeit your right to be treating attention as the vehicle by means of which rationality gets into experience in such a way as to provide experience with its epistemic role.

The other option is to hold onto the link with phenomenology and to drop the attempt to link up with information processing stories. There are two reasons why this is not attractive, both connected with getting right the mixture of activity and passivity distinctive of perceptual experience. First, it leaves us with no way of giving a plausible, non-metaphorical articulation of what we mean by preattentive presence constraining the operation of attention. Secondly, the appeal to information-processing was, I argued, the only way to do non-metaphorical justice to the kind of mixture of activity and passivity common to both remembering and perceiving.

The hardness of the problem of consciousness is usually said to stem from a clash between a general thesis to the effect that everything should, ultimately, have a scientific, objective explanation, and arguments to the effect that phenomenal aspects of experience necessarily resist capture in the objective net. It might be tempting to view the above dilemma as presenting us with a new version of this problem, incorporated here into accounts of 'consciousness of' and access-consciousness in the case of perception. But this would be a mistake, for two reasons. First, to say there is no guarantee that phenomenally driven and computationally driven descriptions of the preattentive level will coincide, is not to say anything about whether we can give an account of what phenomenal presence is in purely information-processing terms. That latter is what concerns those preoccupied with the 'hard' problem of phenomenal consciousness, an issue which I noted at the outset I would not be addressing in this paper. The claim has been only that if the need to account for phenomenal aspects of consciousness is what makes a concept hard then 'consciousness of' and access-consciousness are hard concepts, at least in the case of perception.

Secondly, and more importantly, to say there is no guarantee of coincidence is no resting place; and it is the fact that it is no resting place which introduces a different kind of hardness here. There are various moves yet to be explored and it is, to my mind, an open question whether and how they might work. For example: it might be possible to motivate a distinction between attention as it is used in the articulation of the environment for the purposes of action and attention as it is used in the articulation of the environment for the purposes of theoretical thought about it; and, relative to that, to motivate a distinction between two kinds of preattentive level such that what is preattentive for thought is not so for action. More generally, it may be possible to motivate a distinction between the use of attention pre and post the level of object representations, and, again, relative to that to introduce a distinction between two kinds of preattentive level. Moreover our phenomenological intuitions are hardly sacrosanct here: it is not as if we know in advance what should go into an account of presence. What is needed here is detailed open-ended investigation of the relation between psychologically and philosophically guided formulations of the nature of attention and its relation to consciousness and thought. The hardness here consists precisely in this open-endedness, in the fact that *a priori* arguments about the relation between science and phenomenology offer us no guidance as to how to proceed.

Experience and Reason
in Perception

BILL BREWER

The question I am interested in is this. What exactly is the role of conscious experience in the acquisition of knowledge on the basis of perception? The problem here, as I see it, is to solve simultaneously for the nature of this experience, and its role in acquiring and sustaining the relevant beliefs, in such a way as to vindicate what I regard as an undeniable datum, that perception is a basic source of knowledge about the mind-independent world, in a sense of 'basic' which is also to be elucidated. I shall sketch the way in which I think that this should be done. In section I, I argue that perceptual experiences must provide *reasons* for empirical beliefs. In section II, I explain how they do so. My thesis is that a correct account of the sense in which perceptual experiences are experiences *of mind-independent things* is itself an account of the way in which they provide

Many thanks to John Campbell, David Charles, Bill Child, Naomi Eilan, Marcus Giaquinto, Peter Milne, Adrian Moore, Christopher Peacocke, Carolyn Price, Johannes Roessler, Tom Stoneham, Peter Sullivan, Rowland Stout, Charles Travis, Ralph Walker and Tim Williamson, for their helpful comments on previous versions of this material. My views on these issues have also been greatly influenced by as yet unpublished written work by John Campbell and Naomi Eilan. Work for this paper was supported by Research Leave funded by the British Academy.

peculiarly basic reasons for beliefs about the world around the perceiver.

I

Why must perceptual experiences provide reasons for empirical beliefs? I shall argue that their doing so is crucial to the determination of specific contents for such beliefs. In other words, I shall argue that unless perceptual experiences provide reasons for empirical beliefs, there can be no genuine beliefs *about* the mind-independent spatial world.[1]

This obviously needs clarification. Which experiences are claimed to provide reasons for which empirical beliefs; what exactly are reasons in this sense; and in what way do perceptual experiences provide them? Roughly, the relevant empirical beliefs are those with contents which it is

---

[1] This claim is a crucial component of J. McDowell's position in his *Mind and World* (Cambridge, MA: Harvard University Press, 1994). Indeed, the argument I offer in support of it is my own extended development of his very suggestive comments on the matter (see especially Lecture I). Both mind-independence and spatiality are crucial to the claim. Arithmetical thought, for example, even though its subject matter may correctly be conceived as mind-independent, is clearly a different issue. Conversely, I am concerned with our knowledge of the empirical world in a sense in which this is incompatible with any attempted idealist understanding of spatial particulars as, ultimately, mind-dependent. See J. Foster, *The Case for Idealism* (London: Routledge, 1982), chapter 5, for a development of this idealist alternative. To avoid undue repetition in what follows, though, I shall often use just one of the two adjectives as shorthand for the pair.

possible to come to know directly on the basis of perception; and the corresponding perceptual experiences are those which would be involved in the acquisition of such knowledge. Equally roughly, reasons for beliefs are features of the overall set of circumstances a person finds himself in – by which I mean to include both his mental condition and its wider context, perhaps over a significant amount of time – which make it reasonable *from his point of view* to come to have or retain the beliefs in question in those circumstances. Furthermore, as reasons *from his point of view,* they figure as such in the subject's reflective thinking about his situation. In some way or another, he recognizes these features of his circumstances as the reasons which they are. Only so can they actually succeed in moving him in such a way that it is appropriate to cite their status as reasons in an explanation of his having the beliefs. Finally, perceptual experiences provide such reasons in the sense that they are essential to his entertaining certain demonstrative contents, simply grasping which constitutes a prima facie reason for endorsing them in belief.

In outline, my argument is this. It is only in virtue of their relations with his perceptual experiences – that is, the immediate impact of mind-independent reality upon his conscious mental life – that a person's beliefs acquire genuine empirical content. These relations contribute essentially to fixing a given belief as a belief *about* a particular mind-independent thing *to the effect that* it is determinately thus and so. Yet if his experiences give him no more reason to believe that things out there are one specific way rather than any other, then they cannot possibly fulfil this role.

His beliefs therefore fail to *be* beliefs about the mind-independent spatial world at all. So, unless perceptual experiences provide reasons for empirical beliefs, there can be no such beliefs.

Two premises can be distinguished here. The first insists that beliefs concern mind-independent spatial reality only in virtue of standing in certain relations with perceptual experiences; the second claims that only *reason-giving* relations between experiences and beliefs will do here. I shall consider each of these in turn.

Belief and Experience

Perceptual experience is the world's direct impact upon a person's mind. It is the only immediate difference which is made to his mental life by his being the particular person which he is, tracing the particular spatio-temporal route which he does through the world. So, unless his beliefs about the world are systematically related in some way to this experience, they are utterly insensitive to his actual environment. Even if his world-view somehow survives this 'confinement' as a series of quasi-rational manipulations – the most abstract imaginable algebra perhaps – mind-independent reality drops out as quite irrelevant to whatever residual norms may govern it. It therefore fails to be a world-view, or set of beliefs *about* that reality, at all.[2] Thus, beliefs concern mind-independent reality only in virtue of standing in certain relations with perceptual experiences.

[2] McDowell, *Mind and World*, pp. 15ff.

I should stress that this requirement is weaker than the quite general empiricist claim that every concept either has its source in experience, or is composed exclusively from simple concepts which do. It is certainly weaker than the extreme verificationist idea that the significance of any empirical belief whatsoever is exhausted by its association with a set of experiences which conclusively verify it. Rather, it simply insists that without some anchoring to his particular worldly environment through some relations or other which they bear to his actual or possible perceptual experiences, certain of a person's purported beliefs about the way things are in the world around him collapse into an empty game. All that this premise really amounts to is a denial of the extreme rationalist suggestion that such beliefs simply sit there in a person's mind, with their determinate, *empirical,* contents engraved upon them, quite independently of any relations which they may or may not have with the actual things around him through the impact of worldly affairs upon his conscious experiential life.

This first premise appears to face a dilemma. Either experiences themselves have empirical content or they do not. If they do, then there is some explanation of how this is so; and what is to prevent this same explanation being applied directly as an account of how beliefs acquire their empirical content without any relations to conscious experiences at all? If, on the other hand, experiences do not have empirical content, then it is at best unclear how they might be supposed to endow the beliefs with which they bear certain relations with any either, whatever these relations may be. The appearance of a dilemma here is illusory. For I shall argue that the correct account of the empirical content of experiences is such that its application to contents of a given kind is sufficient for these to be *experiential* contents themselves. Thus, although the second horn of the proposed dilemma is indeed unacceptable, its first horn is perfectly compatible with my premise that the empirical contents of beliefs depend upon their relations with experiences. The explanation of how it is that experiences themselves have empirical content is inapplicable directly to anything else. So the crucial role of experiences cannot be finessed by attempting to apply the same account in the domain of non-experiential beliefs.

This reply to the dilemma objection would be completely vindicated by the following claim. A correct account of the content of perceptual experiences, in particular, of their reference to mind-independent spatial particulars, is both necessary and sufficient for explaining their status *as conscious experiences*.[3] Although I am confident that this claim is true, I settle here for a slightly less ambitious justification for my response to the proposed dilemma. I shall argue that perceptual reference to particular mind-independent things is essentially experiential. So, again, nothing non-experiential could have its empirical content in just the way in which perceptual-experiential contents do.[4]

---

[3] See N. Eilan, 'Self-Consciousness and Experience' (D.Phil, Thesis, Oxford University, 1988), for a sustained discussion of this kind of claim.

[4] The argument which I am about to give is my development of P. F. Strawson's famous discussion of these matters in his *Individuals*

I assume that perceptual reference to determinate spatial particulars is possible; and that a person often knows that he is referring in his belief to a particular mind-independent thing when he is. Indeed, he is normally at least in a position to know this. For, suppose that he believes on the basis of perception that a is F. That is to say, asking himself how things stand in the world around him, he arrives at the judgement that a is F. Then, given the concept of belief, he can simply prefix this judgement with the operator 'I believe that', to arrive at the *knowledge* that he believes that a is F.[5] From here, he can knowledgeably infer that he is referring to a.

So, consider a person, S, with a perceptually-based belief about a particular mind-independent thing, a; and suppose that S actually knows that he is referring to a. Given what has just been said, stipulating this situation is legitimate. Now, assume, for reductio, that S's Idea of a is purely descriptive.[6] That is, his conception of which thing a

(London: Methuen, 1959), chapter 1, part I. I draw heavily upon N. Eilan, 'Self-Consciousness', chapter 5, in which she also acknowledges the importance of conversations with Adrian Moore.

[5] See G. Evans, *The Varieties of Reference* (Oxford: Clarendon Press, 1982), chapter 7; R. Gordon, 'Simulation Without Introspection or Inference from Me to You', in *Mental Simulation,* ed. M. Davies and T. Stone (Oxford: Blackwell, 1995), p. 60; and J. Roessler, 'Self-Knowledge and Belief' (D.Phil. Thesis, Oxford University, 1996), chapter 2, for discussion of this so-called 'ascent routine', and its status as a source of knowledge.

[6] See Evans, *The Varieties*, pp. 104ff., and P. Geach, *Mental Acts* (Bristol: Thoemmes Press, 1992), pp. 53ff., for introduction and elucidation of this notion of a person's *Idea* of an object.

is is exhausted by a wholly general description, 'The F' which purports to identify a by reference to its own properties and its spatial and other relations with other things which are also identified purely descriptively. Thus, his entertaining the Idea is quite independent of any experience of the object in question. Now, however detailed and extensive this description of a may be, it is bound to be an epistemic possibility for S that 'F' is multiply satisfied, in the following sense. It is logically consistent with all that S knows that 'F' is satisfied by more than one thing. For he cannot knowledgeably rule out the possibility of a massive qualitative reduplication elsewhere in the universe of the relevant sector of his environment.[7] So there is a possible world in which 'F' is multiply satisfied and everything which S actually knows is true. Thus, there is a possible world in which 'F' is multiply satisfied and S refers as he does to a; for that he does so is something which he knows. This is a contradiction. For in that case, 'The F' *fails* to refer. Hence S's Idea of a cannot be purely descriptive after all.[8] It must involve some kind of

[7] The underlying equivalence here can be demonstrated as follows. Suppose that S is a person, p a proposition, and K_s the conjunction of every proposition which S knows. It is epistemically possible for S^1 that $p \Leftrightarrow$ it is logically possible that $[K_s \& p] \Leftrightarrow \{K_s, p\}$ is consistent $\Leftrightarrow$ 'K_s, therefore not-p' is invalid $\Leftrightarrow S$ cannot argue validly from what he actually knows to not-$p \Leftrightarrow S$ is not in a position knowledgeably to rule out that p.

[8] It may be objected at this point that the epistemic possibility of multiple satisfaction can be ruled out if S's descriptive Idea is of the following form: 'The unique G'. This is correct; but, in that case, reference failure due to the emptiness of this description is an epistemic possibility. For,

demonstrative component, with respect to which his experience is *essential* to his grasp of which object is in question.[9]

again, S cannot knowledgeably rule out the possibility of massive
reduplication with respect to G. So an appropriately adjusted version of
my argument goes through. Note, also, that the argument does nothing
to undermine the possibility of thought about spatial particulars by
what might be called *impure description*, in which reference is secured,
in part, by an embedded demonstrative, as in, for example, 'The red
ball under that table'.

[9] This step in the argument requires further defence too. For it might be
thought that either names or certain descriptions embedding
indexicals provide an equally acceptable alternative to pure
descriptions, in a way which finesses my appeal to essentially
experiential perceptual demonstratives. What is wrong, for example,
with the following Ideas: 'Frege'; and 'The ball in front of me'? I cannot
respond in detail to these points here. My claim in each case, though, is
that, insofar as the Ideas in question are immune to my objection from
the possibility of massive reduplication, a complete account of what is
involved in understanding them cannot avoid reference to perceptual
experience. In the case of names, this is either a result of the
connection between the subject's understanding of the name and his
possession of a recognitional capacity for its bearer (if he is a Producer,
in Evans' sense), or of the connection between his understanding of the
name and the various experiences involved in his being informed
about its bearer in testimony of some kind (if he is a Consumer). See
Evans, *The Varieties,* chapter 11, for this distinction between Producers
and Consumers in a name-using practice, and an outline of the
account of proper names upon which my reply here draws. In the
second case, experience comes in in the crucial role of demonstrative
reference to physical things other than himself both in the subject's
grasp of the spatial concepts figuring in such descriptive-indexical
Ideas, and in his grasp of the first person pronoun itself. These issues
require extended discussion though. A further source of objection
might be the claim that experience is essential to *demonstrative*

Perceptual reference is therefore essentially experiential. Nothing non-experiential can refer to spatial particulars in the way in which experiences do; and, indeed, beliefs about spatial particulars of any kind have their contents only in virtue of their relations with essentially experiential demonstrative contents.

My reply to the dilemma objection is therefore correct; and the first premise of my argument for the thesis that perceptual experiences must provide reasons for empirical beliefs is established. Certain beliefs about the spatial world have the contents which they do – that a particular mind-independent thing is determinately thus and so – only in virtue of their standing in certain relations with various perceptual experiences.

Experience and Reason

The second premise of my argument is that these crucial relations must be *reason-giving* relations, in the sense I outlined earlier: reason-giving from the subject's point of view, rather than from the perspective of some external theorist. Why do I claim that the content-determining role

reference. After all, a blindsighted patient apparently refers to a particular object in his blind field when encouraged to point to it. Yet he has no experience of it. Here I simply insist that he does not *understand* any demonstrative thought he may appear to others to be having. For he does not know which object is in question. See L. Weiskrantz, *Blind Sight: A Case Study and Implications* (Oxford: Clarendon Press, 1986) for a comprehensive study of such cases.

of perceptual experiences necessarily involves their providing reasons in this sense for empirical beliefs?

Well, suppose that the relevant content-determining relations between experiences and beliefs are not reason-giving relations; and consider a person, S, who believes that p, where this is supposed to be an empirical belief, about how things are in the mind-independent world around him. Since their relations with certain perceptual experiences play an *essential* role in the determination of the contents of empirical beliefs, there is a range of alternative such beliefs – beliefs which he might have had instead – whose difference in content with his actual belief that p would have been due *entirely* to their standing in the relevant relations with different perceptual experiences. Suppose that the belief that q is one of these.

So, the situation is this. S actually believes that p, because his actual perceptual experiences determine this, as opposed to q, as the empirical content of his belief. He does not believe that q. Had his perceptual experiences been appropriately different, though, his position would have been precisely the reverse: he would have believed that q, and not believed that p. Yet the relevant content-determining relations between experiences and beliefs are not reason-giving relations. So S's actual perceptual experiences give him no more reason to believe that p than to believe that q. Thus, he has, and could have, no reason whatsoever to believe that p rather than that q, or vice versa. For, recall, nothing other than their relations with experiences decides between the two contents – this is how q was introduced. Which belief he actually has is due entirely to the course of his perceptual experience. Any supposed difference between believing that *p* and believing that *q* is therefore nothing to him; for there *could be* no reason *for him* to decide between them. So he does not really *understand* them *as alternatives.* Believing that *p* and believing that *q* are identical for him. Hence the supposedly content-determining role of S's perceptual experiences is empty. For there is nothing more, or less, to the content of a belief than the way the subject takes the world to be. Thus, if the relevant relations between experiences and beliefs are not reason-giving relations, then they contribute *nothing* to the determination of specific worldly truth-conditions for empirical beliefs.

This all sounds a little abstract; but the crucial point is really quite simple. It can be brought home by the failure of a putative counterexample. Of course, it might be admitted, empirical beliefs draw essentially for their contents upon certain relations with perceptual experiences; but these need not be reason-giving relations, in the relevant sense. Perhaps experiences indicate worldly phenomena in virtue of various systematic causal relations in which they stand with them; and this empirical significance is transmitted in turn to the beliefs to which these experiences themselves give rise. Thus, empirical contents are secured for beliefs by their *non-*reason-giving relations with experiences. For, although these experiences stand in various relations with the worldly phenomena which they are thereby supposed to indicate, they do nothing to make beliefs about just those phenomena any more appropriate *from the subject's point of view,* than beliefs about any alternative such phenomena, which might reliably have caused the relevant experiences instead.

A familiar, although in my view mistaken, account of our experiences of, and beliefs about, secondary qualities provides an illustrative example of the proposal. On this view, certain immediately recognizable sensations constitute our experiences of the secondary qualities of things around us, in virtue of the systematic causal relations between the two. The sensations in question are specific modifications of consciousness, the subject's recognition of which on any particular occasion, as tokens of the relevant types, is supposed to be unproblematic: subjectively evident, or 'given'. The corresponding secondary qualities of objects in the world are those microphysical properties, or massive disjunctions of such, which causally explain the occurrence of sensations of the type in question in normal observers under normal circumstances. Peacocke's introduction of 'primed predicates' helps to clarify the position.[10] Red' experiences are those which are normally produced by red objects. Correlatively, red objects are those which normally produce red' experiences. Although the former claim serves to introduce the notion of observational predicate priming, it is the latter which captures the correct order of explanation. For token red' experiences are unproblematically identifiable as experiences of the same subjective type by their subject. Red objects are those which have the (perhaps massively disjunctive) microphysical property which normally produces red' experiences: this defines what redness in the world actually is. Red' experiences *indicate* the presence of red

[10] C. Peacocke, *Sense and Content* (Oxford: Clarendon Press, 1983), pp. 20ff.

objects in virtue of the reliable relations between them. Beliefs that things are red acquire their content, in turn, as beliefs that things have just that colour – that microphysical property – on the basis of their relations with red' experiences. They are precisely the beliefs which are normally formed in response to such experiences. This is what makes them beliefs that the things in question are red.

On this account, the crucial content-determining relations between experiences and beliefs are *not* reason-giving relations. For having a red' experience in itself gives the subject no more reason to believe that there is something in front of him with the micro-physical structure constitutive of something's *being red* than to believe that there is something there with any other such structure. It is simply the occurrence of a sensation of a particular identifiable type, which is intrinsically no more appropriately associated with *that* structure than with any other. Nevertheless, it is supposed to indicate the presence of just that microphysical property, as opposed to any other, because that is the property which happens to be its normal cause. Hence it is that property which he believes is instantiated when he believes that there is something red in front of him. His beliefs about redness therefore acquire their empirical significance in virtue of the relations they bear to red'-type experiences, even though these experiences give him no reason to take the world to contain just that property rather than any other. Indeed, had it been a quite different property in the world which happened to be the normal cause of red' sensations, then his beliefs about redness would, on this account, have been beliefs to the effect that that is instantiated instead, regardless of the fact that what is supposed to provide such beliefs with their determinate content – namely their relations with red´ experiences – is exactly the same in both cases.

The consequence of this proposal, then, is that the putative source of the empirical content of beliefs about redness in the world is, *as far as the subject himself is concerned,* entirely neutral on which property of things their redness actually turns out to be. In believing that there is something red in front of him, a person is bound to be believing that there is something which is some way or other which things can be, and sometimes are, out there. Furthermore, given that redness is defined as the *normal* cause of red´ sensations, he will normally be right that there is something that way in front of him. Yet he has not the slightest idea *which* way this is. Hence it must be wrong to claim that he nevertheless believes that the thing in question is just that way rather than any other. So the account under consideration fails after all to provide a satisfactory explanation of the contents of a person's beliefs about the colours of things around him.

Two strategies are possible in reply to this *switching argument.*[11] First, it might be argued that the non-reason-giving account is not committed to a person's ignorance of the semantic values of certain of the concepts figuring in the contents of his empirical beliefs in the way I suggest. Second, it might be argued that, insofar as a non-reason-giving account is committed to this ignorance, it is nevertheless

---

[11] See C. Peacocke, 'The Limits of Intelligibility: A Post-Verificationist Proposal', *Philosophical Review* 97, (1988), for characterization and discussion of such arguments.

perfectly compatible with the relevant beliefs having just those contents all the same. I cannot possibly respond to everything which might be said here. I content myself with a few remarks about each of two possible versions of the first strategy, and a fairly obvious version of the second.

Knowledge by Description. A first response to the switching argument is to deny that the present account necessarily consigns a person who believes that there is something red in front of him to ignorance of which property he thereby believes the thing to have on the following grounds. He may know perfectly well what it is for something to be red, say, by thinking of redness in the world (correctly according to the account in question) as, something like, 'the microphysical property which is causally explanatory of this type of sensation in normal observers under normal circumstances'. There are at least the following three difficulties with this line of response, though.

First, there is an obvious danger of circularity in the proposed identification of redness as the cause of red' sensations in normal observers under normal circumstances. For the following two supplementary clauses have to be added in order to make sense of the descriptive identification as it stands: (i) normal observers are, *inter alia,* those in whom red things cause red' sensations in normal circumstances; (ii) normal circumstances are those in which red things cause red' sensations in normal observers. Yet without an independent constraint upon normality, the resultant identification as a whole is clearly useless.

Second, it is implausible to suggest that a person's beliefs about the perceived colours of things around him essentially require this conceptual sophistication. For example, it is surely possible for a person without any explicit understanding of the idea of a normal observer under normal circumstances to believe that a certain item in his environment is red, and know perfectly well how he takes the thing to be.

Third, even if the red things in the world are all and only those which produce red' experiences in normal observers under normal circumstances (or are disposed to do so), this is not the only, and certainly not the most basic, way in which a person thinks of their colour when he does so on the basis of such experiences. It is inappropriate to assign to all of a person's beliefs about the colours of things in the world around him the structural complexity which is currently being proposed. The most simple perceptually based beliefs about such matters are more naturally articulated by way of a demonstrative, 'that colour', than any causal description. Indeed, the inappropriateness of the present suggestion can be brought out by the fact that a person who knows precisely what colour he believes something is when he sees it in front of him in ordinary viewing conditions can perfectly rationally doubt whether the object in question has the microphysical property causally explanatory of certain specific appearances in normal observers under normal circumstances. In other words, any such description fails to capture *his conception* of which colour property is in question. So the way in which relations with colour experiences provide empirical significance for a person's beliefs about colours in the world is not by furnishing sensational effects by reference to which these colours can be identified as their normal causes.

Conceptual Redeployment. A second version of the first strategy, of denying ignorance of semantic value on the non-reason-giving account, is to insist that a person's knowledge of which property he believes that the relevant object has, when he believes that there is something red in front of him, has already been provided for on the familiar account of secondary qualities under consideration, independently of any descriptive knowledge which the subject may have about the relation between his red' experiences and red things in the world. Indeed, it may be argued, it has been provided for in a way which has the advantage of *explaining* its notoriously problematic first person authority. For the subject can simply redeploy the concept of redness which figures in his first order belief about the world in the thought 'I am thinking that there is something *red* in front of me.'[12] Then, whichever property it is that his first order belief ascribes, which depends upon which microphysical property happens to be the normal cause of red' sensations and thereby constitute mind-independent redness, his second order belief will successfully self-ascribe a belief to the effect that the object in question has just that property. So he does, after all, know exactly how he believes the object to be, or at least he can authoritatively come to do so if only he turns his mind to the matter. This routine, then, provides an authoritative source of knowledge of the semantic values of his

---

[12] T. Burge, 'Our Entitlement to Self-Knowledge', *Proceedings of the Aristotelian Society* 96 (1996); and C. Peacocke, 'Entitlement, Self-Knowledge and Conceptual Redeployment', *Proceedings of the Aristotelian Society* 96 (1996).

secondary quality concepts, which is consistent with the current account, on which these are determined by the non-reason-giving relations between secondary quality experiences and the beliefs in whose contents such concepts occur. So the switching argument is invalid.

I find this response quite unconvincing. Unless he already knows what redness is, a person cannot inform himself simply by reusing the word in an attempt to tell himself what it is. I am absolutely not insisting here that concept possession is in every case a matter of having some explicit, reductive definition of the concept in question in terms of more basic concepts. That would obviously be viciously regressive. It is just that a person does not grasp a concept unless he knows its semantic value, that is, the contribution it makes to determining the truth-conditions of beliefs in whose contents it occurs. Only then is he in a position genuinely to understand such beliefs; for only then can he appreciate what their truth-conditions must be. If he does not grasp this semantic value, then he cannot hope to help matters simply by taking on further beliefs, this time about his own beliefs, which invoke the very same concept, and which he therefore equally fails to understand. Although this charade guarantees that the subject's (pseudo-) self-ascription of a (pseudo-) belief about redness will be (pseudo-) true, it leaves him hopelessly ignorant about which truth this is supposed to be, which belief he has thereby self-ascribed. So the appearance that he thereby knows how he supposedly believes the world to be in the first place is just an illusion. Rather, the fatal ignorance at that first-order level is simply recycled at the level of the self-ascription itself. Once again, it is clear that we do not really have an account of genuine belief here at all, that is, belief with understanding, about the mind-independent world, about the subject's own beliefs, or about anything else.

Natural Kinds. The second strategy in response to my switching argument is to accept that it does follow from the proposed account that a person is in a sense ignorant of certain of the details of the semantic values of the secondary quality concepts which he applies to the things around him; but to argue that this is perfectly compatible with these concepts figuring in the contents of his empirical beliefs all the same, which have precisely these contents in virtue of their non-reason-giving relations with his perceptual experiences according to just this account. Indeed, it might be insisted that ignorance of semantic value in this sense is a familiar phenomenon, perfectly compatible with grasp of a determinate empirical content. Consider, for example, beliefs about natural kinds. My beliefs about gold, say, are about just that chemical stuff, regardless of whether I know which stuff this is, and regardless of whether I can distinguish it in any way from the stuff which presents the same superficial appearance on twin-earth, or from fool's gold around here.

This is a large and complex area, about which I cannot say anything entirely comprehensive or conclusive here. The first thing to do, though, is to distinguish this response to my criticism of the familiar secondary quality model from the first reply I considered above, on which knowledge of semantic value is supposed to be provided by description in these cases. The present suggestion is not that natural kind beliefs involve implicit descriptions of the form 'the microphysical structure of S_1, S_2,... S_n' (where the S_i's are various samples of gold, say, with which the subject has had suitable contact – through perception, testimony or whatever) and that all beliefs about particular mind-independent things to the effect that they are determinately thus and so are to be assimilated to these descriptive natural kind beliefs. It is rather that beliefs about natural kinds constitute a ubiquitous example of cases in which a person succeeds in having beliefs to the effect that certain things have a particular microphysical structure in the absence of any detailed knowledge of which structure this is. Indeed, the present respondent will continue, everything involved in the subject's conception of which property is in question might be shared by a twin-earth counterpart, who equally succeeds in referring to a determinate property in the beliefs he expresses using the word 'gold', whilst these are nevertheless beliefs to the effect that the relevant objects have a quite different chemical composition. Thus, a person might believe that certain things are gold – Au – as opposed to believing that they are twin-gold – ABC, say – even though, had it been precisely the reverse, he would himself have been none the wiser. Here there is determinacy in content which outstrips anything in the subject's knowledge of the appropriate semantic value. Yet these are clearly *his beliefs*. Hence this type of ignorance of semantic value is consistent with the understanding required of a person for him to be the subject of the beliefs in question. Similarly, it must be a mistake for me to infer, in the *reductio* argument given above, from a structurally similar position in the envisaged case of the secondary qualities, that the subject has no real understanding of his own beliefs. Genuine understanding is, after all, perfectly compatible with wholly non-reason-giving content-determining relations between experiences and beliefs. So it has not yet been established that perceptual experiences must provide reasons for empirical beliefs.

I have a bold and a cautious reply back to this third line of response to the switching argument. The bold line is to stand by the original argument, and to conclude, therefore, that the account offered above of beliefs about natural kinds must be mistaken for the very same reason: it assigns determinate truth-conditions in a way which goes beyond the subject's own knowledge of the semantic values which purportedly determine them. A person's understanding of his own natural kind beliefs requires that 'gold' has different semantic values on two speaker's lips *only if* they have different conceptions of what gold is, in some sense. There are then a number of ways of developing the position, depending at least upon the answers given to the following two questions. (1) Do these conceptions necessarily supervene upon the physical condition of a person from the skin in? (2) Are differences in conception necessarily something about which the subject is infallible? I cannot possibly go into all the issues which are raised here;[13] but the way in

---

[13] See *Thought and Object*, ed. A. Woodfield, (Oxford: Clarendon Press, 1982); and *Subject, Thought and Context* ed. P. Pettit and J. McDowell (Oxford: Clarendon Press, 1986), for a good orientation.

which I would be inclined to develop this bold reply is as follows.[14]

First, familiar arguments, paradigmatically from the causal-explanatory efficacy of the mental, for an affirmative answer to (1) are unconvincing. Second, familiar arguments, paradigmatically from the transparency of the subjective, for an affirmative answer to (2) are also unconvincing. Third, stories can be told on which Putnam's original insight that 'gold' (in his case 'water') has different semantic values on an earthling's lips and on those of his twin-earth counterpart is compelling, even when the two counterparts are physically identical from the skin in, and neither can infallibly distinguish his position from that of the other.[15] Fourth, they nevertheless have different conceptions of what the stuff is which they call 'gold'; and these conceptions contribute to their respective knowledge of the (different) truth-conditions of the beliefs which they each express using that word. Of course, this knowledge cannot require possession of the concepts of proton, neutron and electron, or any grasp of the way in which they are employed in the systematic construction of the periodic table in which Au has its

[14] I take it that this is one way of filling out the suggestion in section 3 of the introduction to *Subject, Thought and Context*, ed. Pettit and McDowell, of a more radical response than Putnam's own 'composite' account to the original discussion of these matters, in H. Putnam, 'The Meaning of "Meaning"', in *Mind, Language and Reality* (Cambridge: Cambridge University Press, 1975). My sketch of this development owes a great deal to their treatment, and to other work by McDowell too.

[15] Putnam, 'The Meaning of "Meaning".'

characteristic place. For the word 'gold' in English had its current semantic value before these theoretical advances were made by anyone; and presently has it on the lips of competent English speakers without this knowledge of basic chemistry. The conception itself is likely to be essentially demonstrative, *that stuff,* or *that metal,* say: a legitimate conception of which stuff is correctly called 'gold', nevertheless, which differs, as required, between earthlings and their twin-earth counterparts. This is a perfectly consistent position. Its key component is a strongly externalist account of the nature of thinkers' conceptions of semantic values: these features of a person's mental life are themselves essentially world-involving demonstrative-recognitional capacities.[16] So the case of beliefs about natural kinds does not constitute one in which determinacy of belief content is really compatible with ignorance of the semantic values determining the associated truth-conditions. It is not one in which understanding transcends the subject's knowledge of these truth-conditions at all. Thus, it does not constitute a counter-example to the original switching argument.

The cautious reply admits the possibility of cases of beliefs about natural kinds which are as described in this

---

[16] Evans, *The Varieties,* chapter 8. Of course, the precise nature of such capacities is a very difficult matter. Their possession presumably requires some sensitivity to the fact that any putative re-identification of the kind in question is defeasible by scientific investigation; and, relatedly, the ability to keep track of samples over certain changes in appearance, along, perhaps, with a rough idea of what types of change are compatible with continued instantiation of the kind.

third response to the switching argument. A person might have the understanding required for a specific empirical content to be the content of his belief, even if he is ignorant of certain of the details of the semantic values of the component concepts which determine these very truth-conditions, in the sense that he would have been none the wiser had these semantic values been different in some way. The key claim here, though, is that ignorance of semantic value, in this sense, is compatible with determinacy of content in such cases, only if possession of the relevant natural kind-like concepts depends upon possession of more basic *observational concepts,* grasp of which is *in*compatible with such ignorance of their semantic values. Thus, the model of beliefs about natural kinds exploited by this third line of response to the switching argument cannot possibly be universally appropriate. Hence, given the present dialectical situation, a non-reason-giving account of the content-determining role of perceptual experiences with respect to empirical beliefs cannot be correct in all cases either. There must be a basic class of *observational concepts,* for which a reason-giving account of the determination of their semantic values is imperative.

I acknowledge that my discussion of both of the strategies which I distinguished above for responding to the switching argument is incomplete and unsatisfactory as it stands; and there are no doubt further variants of each to consider. Nevertheless, if what I say is at all on the right lines, and other variants can also be blocked, then any content-determining relations between perceptual experiences and the most basic empirical beliefs, at least, are necessarily reason-giving relations. The non-reason-giving alternative which I have been considering is unacceptable in such cases. Conjoining this with my first premise, that these relations are indispensable to genuine beliefs about the mind-independent spatial world, it follows that perceptual experiences must provide reasons for empirical beliefs.

II

My question now is this. How exactly *do* perceptual experiences provide reasons for empirical beliefs? The discussion will have to be fairly brief and, no doubt, disappointingly sketchy; but my answer, in a sentence, is this. Perceptual experiences are essential to a person's grasp of certain demonstrative contents, whose reference to particular mind-independent objects and properties is achieved in such a way that his simply entertaining these contents gives him a prima facie reason to endorse them in belief.

The relevant perceptual demonstrative contents are expressible, in the first instance, only as 'that thing is thus'. Given the relevant facts about the way things are in the world around the perceiver, the direction and focus of his attention, and so on, which contents these are is beyond his control; and his grasp of such contents depends upon his actually standing in certain perceptual-attentional relations with the particular things to which they refer. I want to press further this issue, though, of exactly what is involved in his *understanding,* that is to say, his actually being the subject who is entertaining, these perceptual demonstrative contents. What does his knowledge of their truth-conditions consist in? More specifically, to begin with, what is involved in his grasp of the embedded singular demonstrative Idea of the particular object in question?

I argued above that this Idea cannot be purely descriptive. Reference to spatial particulars is, in the most basic cases, *essentially* experiential. So the questions to ask now is exactly what a person's perceptual experiences contribute to his Idea of a particular object on a given occasion. The answer, at least in certain central cases, and especially where vision is the prominent modality, is that perceptual experience displays the *spatial location* of the object in question. This is what experience contributes to determinate reference to spatial particulars in these cases. For there is a fundamental interdependence between making a numerical distinction between qualitatively identical spatial particulars and assigning them different locations at a given time: for every time t, every mind-independent object which exists at t has a location at t, it has just one such location, and no two numerically distinct things (of the same sort) have the same location at t. So a key to reference to spatial particulars is knowledge of their location, or knowledge of what would make true an identification of the object in question with that at a given location. This constitutes knowledge of *which* object is in question. It provides the subject with a genuine Idea of that particular thing, which is employed in the particular content in question, and in any other content entertaining which involves thinking of the same thing in the same way.

As I have effectively already established, if this location is given only in terms of certain spatial relations to other objects identified purely by description, then the possibility of massive reduplication returns to undermine the purported uniqueness of location and hence of determinate reference to any particular occupant. What is required, therefore, for genuine reference to a particular mind-independent thing, is knowledge of what would make true an identification of that object with one whose location is given *relative to the subject making the reference himself*.

This may be given indirectly, as it would be by appeal to a suitably demonstratively anchored, impure description, such as 'the red ball in the box under that table'. But this possibility obviously rests upon that of a person's more direct identification of a particular location, relative to his own – in this case, that exploited in his demonstrative reference to *that table*. In general, I claim, perceptual demonstrative contents of the appropriate kind are precisely those which display the locations of the relevant objects *directly* in just this way. Perceptual reference and egocentric location come together, at least in the central cases which I am currently considering, in which determinacy of reference is secured by exploiting the interrelation between the numerical identity and location of spatial particulars at a time. This is (at least part of) the essential contribution made by a person's perceptual experiences at a given time to his understanding of certain demonstrative contents making reference to particular mind-independent things around him at that time.[17]

---

[17] There is of course a debate at this point about precisely what the relations of priority are, if any, between identifications, of various kinds, of objects and their locations in this basic case, in which the

Now, if such a perceptual demonstrative content is to refer to a particular *mind-independent* thing, in this way, then the subject's Idea of its location must be an Idea of a location *in a world of places and things which are independent of his actual experiences of them.* For his Idea of its location contributes essentially to his Idea of its identity. He must therefore understand that the very same location might have been spatially related in a quite different way with him: that thing *there* might equally have been perceived from any number of different points of view.[18] Yet how is

things and places in question are displayed in experience. See Strawson, *Individuals,* chapter 1; D. Wiggins, 'The Individuation of Things and Places (I)', *Proceedings of the Aristotelian Society,* Sup. Vol. 37 (1963); M. Woods, 'The Individuation of Things and Places (II)', *Proceedings of the Aristotelian Society,* Sup. Vol. 37 (1963); Evans, *The Varieties,* chapter 6; and J. Campbell, 'The Role of Physical Objects in Spatial Thinking', in *Spatial Representation,* ed. N. Eilan, R. McCarthy and B. Brewer (Oxford: Blackwell, 1993). I am confident, though, that what I have to say here is independent of the detailed differences of view on these matters.

[18] What if the thing in question is a part of the subject's body? Things get very complicated in this case. First, bodily awareness is likely to be involved in a peculiar way. Although I am sympathetic to the idea that perceptual systems are normally both exteroceptive and proprioceptive, as elaborated by J. J. Gibson in his *The Ecological Approach to Visual Perception* (Boston: Houghton Mifflin, 1979), the object of exteroception is not normally itself an object of proprioception, as it is in this case. Second, and relatedly, a person's body-parts are normally experienced as *his own.* See B. Brewer, 'Bodily Awareness and the Self', in *The Body and the Self,* ed. J. Bermudez, A. Marcel, and N. Eilan (Cambridge, MA: MIT Press, 1995), for a discussion of these two points and their interrelations. Nevertheless, if

this condition to be met, since I insist that, in order to avoid reference failure due to the possibility of massive reduplication, the location in question must be given *relative to the subject's own*?

There are two lines of response to this problem. First, it might be denied that a person's recognition that the same thing, at the same place, might have been perceived from a different point of view really is a necessary condition upon perceptual demonstrative reference to mind-independent spatial particulars. Second, it might be argued that the apparent inconsistency between the claim that this condition must indeed be met and my insistence that determinate reference to particular places and things is ultimately subject-relative in some sense is only illusory. I take it for granted that a third possible suggestion, to resist the essentially perspectival nature of spatial reference – to both places and things – is simply ruled out by my discussion of Strawson's argument from massive reduplication earlier (pp. 206–208 above), and its obvious extension to locations above. I consider each of the two genuine responses in turn.

If the singular Ideas involved in perceptual demonstrative contents refer to mind-independent things, then it certainly follows that these are Ideas of things whose

the body-part in question is anaesthetized and experienced only as 'that hand', as opposed to 'my hand', then the condition in the text applies. At least, in cases in which it is the hand's displayed location which informs the subject's perceptual reference to that particular hand, then he must grasp that that location might have been displayed as differently located on some egocentric reference frame.

locations are in fact independent of the subject's experiences of them. It does not follow, though, according to a proponent of the first line of response above, that any person entertaining such an Idea must therefore *recognize* the independence of the location of the relevant mind-independent thing from his actual experiences of it in any way. He need have no understanding whatsoever, then, that that thing there might equally have been perceived from any number of different points of view. The claim that he must, she will continue, can only be sustained by appeal to an absurd principle along the following lines. If a person refers to an object, *o,* which is *F,* on the basis of a perceptual demonstrative Idea, *I,* then in grasping *I* he necessarily recognizes that its object is *F.*

This principle is indeed absurd, not least because it entails a person's omniscience about the objects of such thoughts; but it is *not* required by my argument. The crucial point is rather that it is only on the basis of his grasp of its location – displayed relative to him in experience – that the subject has an Idea of *that object* at all, in the cases under consideration. Unlike its other properties, its location is not something he can go on to wonder about, having already identified the relevant object in thought. For his Idea of its location contributes essentially to his identification of which object is in question. Hence, which object *is* in question – which object his Idea is an Idea of – is determined in part by his Idea of its location. Thus, if he has no understanding whatsoever of the independence of this location from his actual experiential point of view upon it, then it is wrong to claim that he has an Idea of a mind-independent spatial thing at all. This is not the sort of thing which *could* be determined as the object of his Idea in that case. So the condition is quite genuine. A person's Idea of the relevant location must be an Idea of a location which might have been spatially related in a quite different way to him, in the following sense. He must actually grasp that that thing *there* might equally have been perceived from any number of different points of view. The first line of response is therefore untenable.

Can anything really be made of the second suggestion either: to argue that meeting this condition is after all consistent with the requirement that determinate reference to particular locations is ultimately subject-relative in some sense? For if the location of a perceived particular is necessarily given in relation to the perceiver's own, then how can his perceptual demonstrative Idea involve any genuine understanding at all that that thing there, in just that place, might equally have been displayed as quite differently spatially related to him, from another point of view?

To see how this might be done, it is crucial to get clear about a distinction due to John Campbell.[19] There is both a *monadic* and a *relational* use of egocentric spatial terms such as 'to the left'/'to the right', 'above'/'below', 'in front'/'behind' and so on. Whenever a person uses these to give the location of something, its location is thereby specified in relation to something else: the terms are essentially

---

[19] J. Campbell, 'Spatial Decentring and Other Minds', forthcoming. I am also indebted at this point to Naomi Eilan for some very helpful suggestions.

relational. The subject can have more or less understanding of their relational nature, though. Representing sentences in which such terms occur as applications of the relation '*xRy*', to begin with – '*x* is to the right of *y*', as it might be – then the issue is over the appropriate range of the notional variable '*y*'. There is a primitive use of such sentences in which this is effectively fixed to the thinker himself, in his actual location at just that time, in such a way that he has no comprehension of the possibility of that very same 'relation' obtaining to anything else. So he is not really thinking *relationally* at all. His thought is more properly regimented '*R´a*': '*a* is to the right and a little in front', say, as opposed to '*a* is to the right and a little in front *of me*'. For it is a minimal necessary condition upon discerning the genuinely relational structure in this thinking, '*aRi*', where '*i*' is a singular term referring to himself or his own present location, that he has some conception of what it would be for '*aRb*', '*aRc*' and so on to be true, for some appropriate range of alternative singular terms '*b*', '*c*', etc.[20] The primitive use of egocentric terms, in which the subject has no such conception at all, is what Campbell calls '*monadic*'; the associated concepts, or Ideas, of spatial 'relations' and particular locations are monadic spatial concepts, or Ideas.

There are different types of genuinely relational uses of such terms, different types of relational spatial concepts and Ideas, which vary according to the generality introduced

---

[20] This is of course an application to the current case of G. Evans' 'Generality Constraint'. See his *The Varieties*, esp. Chapter 4.3. The requirement is derived from Strawson, *Individuals*, esp. Chapter 3.

by the range of the variable $'y'$: the range of appropriate alternative singular terms to $'i'$ – $'b'$, $'c'$, etc. above – which are such that the subject's grasp of the thought $'aRi'$ commits him to knowledge of what it would be for $'aRb'$, $'aRc'$ and so on to be true. Two significant types of relational egocentric thinking would be, first, that in which $'y'$ ranges over alternative possible points of view of the same thinking subject; and, second, that in which its range explicitly allows for generality across different thinkers. For present purposes, though, the basic distinction between monadic and relational egocentric spatial concepts, or Ideas, is enough.

I have argued that determinate reference to particular locations is ultimately egocentric in some sense. That is to say, the embedded Idea of a particular place in the subject's environment must identify it in some way relative to himself, or his own present location. Our current problem is to explain how this requirement is consistent with his meeting the further condition upon perceptual demonstrative reference to particular *mind-independent things,* in cases where this exploits the subject's grasp of their location, that he should recognize that the very thing in question, just there, might equally have been perceived from any number of different points of view. Now, suppose that his egocentric perceptual identification of the location in question is purely monadic. So his conception of which place is in question is exhausted by its actual present spatial relations with him. It follows that he is incapable of any recognition that the thing in question, *at just that location,* might equally have been displayed as differently located – relative to him. For there is no degree of freedom in his thinking, along which to register the changes in his own position required to make sense of these alternative perspectives. He therefore fails genuinely to refer to any mind-independent spatial particular. His thought is not really thought about *mind-independent* reality at all. Put slightly differently, the difficulty here is that the perceptual demonstrative content in question is bound by a kind of idealism about space, on which there is nothing more to where things are than where they appear to be. Given that his knowledge of their location is supposed to contribute to his knowledge of which particular objects are in question, it follows that he can equally have no conception of these as existing independently of his particular experiences of them. His experience therefore fails altogether to display the way things are in a *mind-independent* world around him.

Thus, if it is to refer to a particular mind-independent thing, a person's perceptual demonstrative, 'that thing – there – is thus', must comprise a singular Idea, 'that thing', which exploits a genuinely relational egocentric identification of the location of the thing in question. How exactly does this help? Well, a person whose perceptual demonstrative content is relational, in this sense, can immerse himself in his present perspective, so to speak, and entertain the corresponding purely monadic spatial content, 'that thing – there$_m$ – is thus'. This captures how things *appear* (spatially) to him – from that perspective, wholly immersed in it, and suspending any reflection upon it or its contribution to his experience. Yet in arriving at the appropriate monadic content *on the basis of his prior understanding of the corresponding relational content*, in this way, he grasps its grounding in the prior relational facts. In other words, this is to appreciate the joint dependence of how things currently appear to him (spatially) upon the way particular mind-independent things are actually distributed in the world around him, *and his present location amongst them* – his current perceptual *point of view* upon them. Equally, he is therefore at least in a position to simulate, to some extent, the monadic contents which would be associated with his taking up different points of view upon the same range of particular things, in the particular places they occupy. That is to say, he has the materials to construct, in imagination, the systematically varying monadic contents which he would arrive at by immersing himself in various alternative, possible but non-actual, perspectives upon the same mind-independent things, just where they are around him.[21]

In this way, I believe, he recognizes that the thing in question, at just that location, might equally have been displayed as differently located relative to him, from various

[21] I do not mean to claim here that the subject must explicitly operate with a *theory* about the way in which spatial appearances vary with changes in his point of view. Rather, he has the potential, at least, to trip to and fro between a fixed relational conception of where a certain thing is relative to him, and both his actual, immersed monadic impression of its location, and various non-actual possible alternatives to it had he perceived that thing from a different point of view, simulated in imagination. Although his skill in this regard need not be at all well developed, this must at least be *possible* for him, in sense that his relational egocentric spatial Ideas are the essential ground for whatever such imaginative routines are actually engaged.

different points of view. He is therefore able to meet this crucial condition upon genuine perceptual demonstrative reference to mind-independent things consistently with the requirement that the location exploited by his Idea of the particular thing in question should be specified egocentrically, in relation to his own. Parallel points apply, I believe, in cases where determinate reference is secured other than by appeal to perception of spatial location, in explanation of how *essentially experiential* reference can nevertheless be reference to *mind-independent* particulars.[22]

---

[22] The common structure here is this. Suppose that the contribution of experience to securing determinate reference to mind-independent particulars in the cases under consideration is its displaying the relevant object's characteristic ϕ. In the central cases I have been discussing, ϕ is spatial location; equally, it might be timbre, for example, in auditory reference to a particular member of an unseen wind quintet. My development of Strawson's argument in section I implies, on the one hand, that this contribution is to make available to the perceiver an *essentially experiential* demonstrative Idea of the object in question, such as 'that ϕ–thing'. The mind-independent reference of this Idea, on the other hand, requires that his grasp of the characteristic ϕ in question should not be exhausted by the way in which it is actually presented in his current experience. The apparent tension between the two is to be resolved by the subject's grasp of the actual experiential appearance of ϕ, from immersed within his present perspective and suspending any reflection upon it or its contribution to his experience, as the joint upshot of the mind-independent ϕ of the object in question and the relevant features of his particular perceptual perspective upon it. As will become clear, it is precisely this understanding which I think constitutes his prima facie reason to endorse the demonstrative content in question in belief.

Something very similar also sustains the mind-independent significance of the predicative component of perceptual demonstrative contents. Experiential demonstratives, like 'that thing is thus', refer to mind-independent particulars – as we have just seen – of which they predicate, not just subjective appearances, but mind-independent properties, which are the categorical grounds of the relevant objects' powers to produce such appearances in appropriately placed perceivers. A given such content presents a particular thing as mind-independently, categorically *thus*. A person whose experience enables him to grasp this content can immerse himself in his own perspective, so to speak, and entertain the corresponding appearance – from there and in those circumstances – that that thing appears thus. In arriving at the appropriate appearance *on the basis of his prior understanding of the corresponding perceptual demonstrative presentation of the way things mind-independently are*, in this way, he grasps its grounding in the prior categorical facts. In other words, this is to appreciate the joint dependence of how things currently appear to him upon the way particular mind–independent things actually are, and his current point of view upon them and other relevant circumstances. Equally, he is therefore at least in a position to simulate the appearances, in this immersed sense parallel to monadic spatial contents, associated with his taking up different points of view on the same things, with the same properties, in different circumstances. That is to say, he has the materials to construct, in imagination, the systematically varying appearances of those things' being just the way they are from various alternative, possible but non-actual, perspectives and in various alternative, possible but non-actual, circumstances. Thus, he recognizes that the thing in question, being just as it is, might equally have appeared differently in different circumstances. This is part of what is involved in its being the case that his initial perceptual demonstrative content predicates a genuinely mind-independent, categorical property of the particular thing in question.

With respect both to the singular and to the predicative components of perceptual demonstrative contents, then, the genuine mind-independence of their reference resides in the subject's recognition of what they present as the categorical ground of the corresponding immersed monadic contents and appearances from his present point of view in the present circumstances, and, equally, of the various alternative monadic contents and appearances associated with possible but non-actual points of view and circumstances, some of which he may be able to grasp in imaginative simulation. Hence, a subject of such contents necessarily recognizes that the way things currently appear to him is the joint upshot of the way things are anyway, in the mind-independent world around him, and his current point of view upon them and other relevant circumstances of perception. It is this, I claim, which provides his prima facie reason to endorse those very contents in belief. For, simply in virtue of entertaining perceptual demonstrative contents of this kind, he recognizes that it is that thing, there in relation to him, and mind-independently thus, which is currently displayed – from where he is and in those circumstances – as apparently thus monadically there. That is to say, he understands that his current apprehension that things are thus and so is in part due to the very fact that they are. He recognizes the relevant content *as* his apprehension of, or epistemic openness to, the facts.

So, a person's experiences contribute essentially to his grasp of certain perceptual demonstrative contents. These contents refer to particular mind-independent things in the world around him, of which they predicate determinate mind-independent properties. In doing so, they give him a prima facie reason to endorse those very contents in belief. Simply in virtue of grasping the content that that thing – there – is thus, he has a prima facie reason to believe that that thing is indeed thus; for he necessarily recognizes that his entertaining that content is a response to that thing's actually being thus, given his location and present circumstances.

I argued in section I that perceptual experiences must provide reasons for empirical beliefs; and in section II I have outlined how they do so. As I put the thesis right at the outset, the correct account of the sense in which perceptual experiences are experiences of mind-independent spatial things – that is to say, the correct account of the reference of perceptual demonstratives to mind-independent particulars and their properties – is itself an account of the way in which such experiences provide prima facie reasons for the perceiver's beliefs about the way things are in the world around him.

Intentionality as the Mark of the Mental

TIM CRANE

I   Brentano's Thesis

'It is of the very nature of consciousness to be intentional'
said Jean-Paul Sartre, 'and a consciousness that ceases to be
a consciousness of something would *ipso facto* cease to
exist.'[1] Sartre here endorses the central doctrine of
Husserl's phenomenology, itself inspired by a famous idea
of Brentano's: that intentionality, the mind's 'direction upon
its objects', is what is distinctive of mental phenomena.
Brentano's originality does not lie in pointing out the existence of intentionality, or in inventing the terminology,
which derives from scholastic discussions of concepts or
intentiones.[2] Rather, his originality consists in his claim that

I am very grateful to Michael Martin and Gregory McCulloch for many
conversations which have greatly influenced my views on this subject. I
am also grateful to the participants in the discussion at the Royal
Institute of Philosophy meeting in February 1997, and to Victor Caston,
Katalin Farkas, Marcus Giaquinto, Paul Horwich, Michael Martin,
Gregory McCulloch, Paul Noordhof and Scott Sturgeon for comments
on earlier versions of the paper.

[1] *The Psychology of the Imagination* (London: Routledge, 1995; originally
published 1940) p. 211.
[2] For the origins of the concept of intentionality, see Christian Knudsen,
'Intentions and Impositions', in *The Cambridge History of Later*

the concept of intentionality marks out the subject matter of psychology: the mental. His view was that intentionality 'is characteristic exclusively of mental phenomena. No physical phenomenon manifests anything like it.'[3] This is *Brentano's thesis* that intentionality is the mark of the mental.

Despite the centrality of the concept of intentionality in contemporary philosophy of mind, and despite the customary homage paid to Brentano as the one who revived the terminology and placed the concept at the centre of philosophy, Brentano's thesis is widely rejected by contemporary philosophers of mind. What is more, its rejection is not something which is thought to require substantial philosophical argument. Rather, the falsity of the thesis is taken as a starting-point in many contemporary discussions of intentionality, something so obvious that it only needs to be stated to be recognized as true. Consider, for instance, these remarks from the opening pages of Searle's *Intentionality*:

> Some, not all, mental states and events have
> Intentionality. Beliefs, fears, hopes and desires are
> Intentional; but there are forms of nervousness, elation
> and undirected anxiety that are not Intentional ... My
> beliefs and desires must always be about something. But

Medieval Philosophy, ed. A. Kenny *et al.* (Cambridge: Cambridge University Press, 1982); Victor Caston, 'Aristotle on the Problem of Intentionality', forthcoming. For a general survey, and further bibliography, see Tim Crane, 'Intentionality', forthcoming in the *Routledge Encyclopedia of Philosophy*, ed. E. J. Craig (London: Routledge, 1998).

[3] F. Brentano, *Psychology from an Empirical Standpoint* (London: Routledge, 1995; originally published 1874), p. 89.

my nervousness and undirected anxiety need not in that way be *about* anything.[4]

Searle takes this as obvious, so obvious that it is not in need of further argument or elucidation. And many others agree with him.[5]

Brentano's thesis is normally rejected for one or both of the following reasons. First, it is supposed to be obvious that there are both intentional and non-intentional mental states: intentionality is not necessary for mentality. Non-intentional mental states can either be of the kind Searle mentions (emotions or moods, like undirected anxiety) or they are the so-called purely 'qualitative' mental phenomena – states which have 'qualia' of which sensations (like pains) are the most commonly cited examples. Both kinds of example are mentioned in an implicit rejection of Brentano's thesis by Louise Antony:

> while mental items like beliefs and desires clearly have objects or contents (an idea is an idea *of* something, and a desire is a desire *for* something), things like pleasures, pains, moods and emotions don't, on the face of it, appear to be *about* anything at all.[6]

---

[4] John R. Searle, *Intentionality* (Cambridge: Cambridge University Press, 1983), p. 1.

[5] A representative example of this position is Colin McGinn, *The Character of Mind* (Oxford: Oxford University Press, 1982), chapter 1.

[6] Louise Antony, 'What It's Like to Smell a Gardenia', *The Times Literary Supplement* 4897 (7 February 1997), p. 25. See also Fred Dretske, *Naturalizing the Mind* (Cambridge, MA: MIT Press, 1995), p. 28.

Antony remarks in passing that the opposing view – in effect, that pains, moods and emotions are intentional – 'seems counter-intuitive'.

The second reason for the rejection of the thesis is that there are *non*-mental phenomena which exhibit intentionality: intentionality is not sufficient for mentality. Examples are more controversial here, but we find phenomena such as the disposition of plants to move towards the source of light offered as primitive non-mental forms of intentionality.[7] Not every philosopher who rejects Brentano's thesis rejects it for both of these reasons, but it is nonetheless fair to say that there is a tacit consensus that the thesis should be rejected.

But this consensus raises a puzzling historical and exegetical question. If it is so obvious that Brentano's thesis is false, why did Brentano propose it? If a moment's reflection on one's states of mind refutes the thesis that all mental states are intentional, then why would anyone (including Brentano, Husserl, Sartre and their followers) think otherwise? Did Brentano have a radically different inner life from the inner lives of contemporary philosophers? Or was the originator of phenomenology spectacularly inattentive to phenomenological facts, rather as Freud is supposed to have been a bad analyst? Or – surely more plausibly – did Brentano mean something different by 'intentionality' than what many contemporary philosophers mean?

---

[7] For examples of this kind of approach, see Fred Dretske, *Knowledge and the Flow of Information* (Cambridge, MA: MIT Press, 1981); B. Enç, 'Intentional States of Mechanical Devices', *Mind* 91 (1982).

The question of what Brentano and his followers meant by 'intentionality' is an important one, both for our understanding of the origin of current debates, and, relatedly, for our conception of these debates themselves.[8] However, my concern in this paper is not with Brentano's theory of intentionality, but with a more general question: what *would* you have to believe about intentionality to believe that it is the mark of the mental? I argue here that if we think of intentionality in the light of this question, a conception of the mental begins to emerge which abandons some of the usual assumptions of contemporary philosophy of mind.

The rest of this paper falls into three parts. In the next two parts I examine the standard counterexamples to Brentano's thesis – certain kinds of sensations and emotions. I argue that they are not genuine counterexamples, and I sketch a conception of intentionality which arises from the discussion of these examples. In the final part, I claim that intentionality, properly understood, should be thought of as exclusive to the mental domain, and I conclude with some more speculative remarks about the significance of the question: why do we need a mark of the mental at all?

II   The Intentionality of Sensation

Since 'intentionality' is a technical term, it is standard practice when introducing it to use some slightly less technical

---

[8] For a helpful attempt to relate Brentano's concerns to current debates, see Dermot Moran, 'Brentano's Thesis', *Proceedings of the Aristotelian Society*, Supplementary Volume 70 (1996).

synonym or gloss. In contemporary philosophy this is often done by saying that intentionality is the *about-ness* or *of-ness* of mental states.[9] Intentional states are those which are *about* or *of* things, normally things other than themselves. So one might demarcate the class of intentional states by considering a mental state and asking 'what is it about?' If the question doesn't make much sense, or if it has the obvious answer 'nothing', then the state is classified as non-intentional. Consider a pain you may have in your ankle; what is it *of* or *about*? Silly question: it isn't *of* or *about* anything. And so, since intentionality is of-ness or about-ness, pain is not intentional. In this way, we find Colin McGinn arguing that 'bodily sensations do not have an intentional object in the way perceptual experiences do' on the grounds that 'we distinguish between a visual experience and what it is an experience of; but we do not make this distinction in respect of pains'.[10] This is one quick way to arrive at a denial of Brentano's thesis.

It certainly sounds awkward to talk of a distinction between a pain and what a pain is 'of' or 'about'. But all this means is that those who follow Brentano in holding intentionality to be the mark of the mental – call them 'intentionalists' – will not gloss the concept of intentionality solely in terms of 'of-ness' or 'about-ness'. Intentionalists must

[9] See (for example) Martin Davies, 'Philosophy of Mind', in *Philosophy: A Guide Through the Subject,* ed. A. C. Grayling (Oxford: Oxford University Press, 1995); Searle, *Intentionality,* p. 1; Jerry Fodor, *Psychosemantics* (Cambridge, MA: MIT Press, 1987), chapter 4.

[10] McGinn, *Character of Mind,* p. 8.

introduce what is involved in the phenomenon of intention-ality in another way. How should they do this?

Brentano's own view was that every mental phe-nomenon exhibits what he called 'intentional inexistence'. The term 'inexistence' has little or nothing to do with the fact that intentional states (or 'acts') can be about objects which do not exist.[11] Rather, the term describes the way in which every intentional act 'includes something as an object within itself'.[12] 'Inexistence' expresses the idea that the object on which the mind is directed exists *in* the mental act itself. For example: in hearing a sound, the sound which one hears – a physical phenomenon – is contained within the act of hearing the sound – a mental phenomenon. So, to general-ize, we can say that 'in the idea something is conceived, in the judgement something is affirmed or denied, in love loved, in hate hated and so on'.[13]

Brentano rejected the claim that sensations of pain and pleasure are not intentional. He argued that although intentional acts can take external phenomena as their objects, sometimes their objects are internal. In the case of

---

[11] For examples of this common misunderstanding of Brentano, see Daniel C. Dennett, *Content and Consciousness* (London: Routledge and Kegan Paul, 1969), p. 21; Michael Tye, *Ten Problems of Consciousness* (Cambridge, MA: MIT Press, 1995) pp. 94–5. A useful account of Brentano's views is contained in chapter 1 of David Bell's *Husserl* (London: Routledge, 1990). For the scholastic views to which Brentano is alluding, see Knudsen, 'Intentions', and John Marenbon, *Later Medieval Philosophy (1150–1350): An Introduction* (London: Routledge 1987), chapter 8.

[12] Brentano, *Psychology*, p. 88.   [13] Ibid.

sensation, for instance, the mind is directed on an internal object – a sensation.[14] Just as 'in the idea something is conceived', we can say that 'in the sensation something is sensed'. So one response an intentionalist can give to McGinn's argument is this. Intentionality is directedness on an object, and in having a sensation, one's mind *is* directed on an object: a sensation. A pain, for instance, is the object of the mental state of being in pain. (This way of thinking of sensation is what used to be called an 'act-object' account.)

The idea that sensations are objects is associated with the sense-datum theory of perception, which is not a popular view in contemporary philosophy. These days it is widely agreed that perception does not involve the mind directing itself upon internal, mental objects – sense-data. But this agreement does not derive from a general rejection of the directedness, or intentionality, of perception. On the contrary, there is a widespread consensus – as illustrated by McGinn's remark just quoted – that perception *is* intentional. It is just that the objects of perception are not inner mental objects or sense-data, but the ordinary outer objects of the external world. So there will be no dispute between intentionalists and many contemporary philosophers over the question of whether perception exhibits intentionality.

---

[14] This is the essence of Brentano's response to Sir William Hamilton's view that in sensation 'there is nothing but what is subjectively subjective; there is no object different from the self'; see Brentano, *Psychology*, p. 90.

If perception were the only mental state under discussion, intentionalism would not be a controversial thesis.[15]

There are philosophers, of course, who think that although perception exhibits intentionality – perceptions are directed on things outside the mind – this does not exhaust their nature. This is the view, defended for instance by Sydney Shoemaker, that in addition to their intentional properties, perceptual states also have non-intentional properties, called 'qualia', which account for the particular conscious or 'phenomenal' character of perceptual states.[16] Qualia are not sensation-objects, but properties of mental states. If there are qualia, then there are aspects or properties of mental states which are not intentional, even if those states also have intentional aspects.

Qualia raise many questions which I want to avoid for the purposes of this paper. Certainly the strongest form of intentionalism will reject qualia outright, as contemporary intentionalists like Michael Tye and Gilbert Harman

---

[15] Here I am taking as 'intentionalist' two kinds of theory of perception: the theory which holds that perception is the direction of the mind upon mental objects, and the theory which treats perception as a kind of propositional attitude, akin to belief. My usage involves a broader sense of 'intentional' than is sometimes adopted in discussions of the intentionality of perception, where it is restricted to theories of the latter kind: see, for instance, the useful discussion in M. G. F. Martin, 'Perceptual Content', in *A Companion to the Philosophy of Mind,* ed. S. Guttenplan (Oxford: Blackwell, 1995).

[16] See, for example, Sydney Shoemaker, 'Qualities and Qualia: What's in the Mind?' in his *The First-Person Perspective and Other Essays* (Cambridge: Cambridge University Press, 1996).

have done.[17] But in this paper, I want to consider only a weaker form of intentionalism, which says that all mental states are intentional, regardless of whether these states also have non-intentional properties. This weaker claim is certainly within the letter of Brentano's thesis that intentionality is the mark of the mental, although it is not so obviously within its spirit. However, there is a good dialectical reason for discussing the weaker thesis first: for if the weaker thesis is false – i.e. there are mental states which are entirely non-intentional – then there is no chance whatsoever of the stronger thesis being true. So from now on, I will mean by 'intentionalism' this weaker thesis.

Let's return now to the first group of apparent counterexamples to intentionalism: bodily sensations like pains, itches and so on. McGinn says that we can distinguish between a visual experience and what it is of, but we do not make this distinction in the case of pains. Pains, on this view, are not *about* anything, they are not *of* anything, they *represent* nothing: they have no intentionality. Rather, pains are purely subjective qualities: their existence consists in the existence of a subjective state that tells us nothing about the external world.

To hold this view is to distinguish pain from other cases of bodily sensation where we are able to distinguish

---

[17] See Gilbert Harman, 'The Intrinsic Character of Experience', in *Philosophical Perspectives 4: Action Theory and Philosophy of Mind*, ed. J. Tomberlin (Ascadero, CA: Ridgeview, 1990); and Michael Tye, 'Visual Qualia and Visual Content', in *The Contents of Experience*, ed. Tim Crane (Cambridge: Cambridge University Press, 1992).

between the sensation and what it is of: sensations of warmth, of cold, of pressure, of tiredness, of hunger can all be described in terms of what they are sensations of, and what they are sensations of are properties of the external world (temperature, pressure etc.) So these are examples of bodily sensations which can be accommodated by intentionalism: the intentionalist can say that these states of mind are intentionally directed at those objective properties of the world in terms of which we characteristically describe them. But what should an intentionalist say about sensations where it does not seem as if this distinction can be made, as seems to be the case with pain?

The answer mentioned above is that there *is* an object presented in a state of pain, but it is an internal or mental object. Now even if we reject mental objects in the case of the perception of the external world, can a case be made for their existence in the case of bodily sensation?

Phenomenologically, the case for mental objects seems somewhat stronger here than in the theory of visual perception. For it could be argued, against McGinn, that a distinction can be made between a pain and the feeling of the pain. Consider, for example, someone being woken up from a dreamless sleep by a pain. For the pain to have woken the person up, and therefore to have caused the person to wake up, it must have existed prior to the awakening. But since the awakening is a matter of becoming conscious of various things, including the pain, it might seem that the pain can exist without the consciousness of it. Less controversially, perhaps, we can distinguish between having a pain and noticing or paying attention to a pain; we might therefore think that we can 'pull apart' the pain itself and our attitude to or awareness of it. These phenomena seem to provide some support for the view that pains are distinct from the consciousness of awareness of pain, and that we can therefore think of pains as the entities on which the mind is directed in states of pain. Further features of the way we think and talk about sensations lend some plausibility to the view. Pains normally seem to have location and extension in space and time, and we effortlessly talk about them using singular terms and we predicate properties of them as we do of objects and events.[18]

While many contemporary philosophers are happy to accept the existence of irreducible mental properties, it is fair to say that most would prefer to reject irreducible mental objects.[19] Mental objects are generally rejected for metaphysical reasons: their criteria of identity are obscure, and it is hard to see how they can be accommodated by a 'naturalistic' world view. However, my concern in this paper

---

[18] Those who approach questions of ontology via questions of logical form might say that just as we can argue for the existence of propositions, the objects of belief, by analysing the logical form of valid inferences involving belief-sentences, so we can argue for the existence of pains, the objects of pain-states, by looking at the valid inferences which are made with statements concerning pain. For example: X has a pain in his foot; therefore there is something X has in his foot. The plausibility of these arguments is, in my view, relatively superficial, for the reasons given in note 21 below.

[19] A notable exception is Frank Jackson, *Perception* (Cambridge: Cambridge University Press, 1977). However, Jackson no longer holds these views.

is not with metaphysics, but with phenomenology: the correct account of how things seem to us. It would be consistent to hold that although phenomenology commits us to mental objects, nonetheless we know on metaphysical grounds that there are no such things. To say this would be to hold an 'error-theory' of the phenomenology of sensation, analogous to J. L. Mackie's error theory of the phenomenology of ethical value.[20]

Although I think that we must be alive to this possibility, it seems to me that – independently of the metaphysical objections to mental objects – phenomenology does not decisively establish their apparent existence. For each of the examples discussed above admit of alternative, equally plausible descriptions which do not require us to posit mental objects. The phenomenon of being woken by pain, for instance, can be redescribed as follows: I might be in pain when I wake up, but it does not follow from this that the pain woke me up. It is equally consistent with the story that I was awoken by some non-conscious event in my brain, which then gave rise to pain when I became conscious. Likewise, the attempt to separate pain from the consciousness of pain by appealing to the distinction between having a pain and attending to it ignores the complexity of the phenomenology of attention and awareness. There are different ways of being aware of an event in consciousness: even when I am not paying attention to it, a

---

[20] See J. L. Mackie, *Ethics* (Harmondsworth: Penguin Books, 1977), chapter 1.

pain can nonetheless be in the background of my consciousness.[21]

But I do not need to dwell on the arguments for mental objects here, since the defence of intentionalism does not need to appeal to them. Intentionalism about bodily sensations can be defended instead by appealing to a perceptual account of bodily sensations, such as that of D. M. Armstrong, or the kind more recently defended by Michael Martin.[22] On this account, bodily sensation is a form of perceptual awareness of one's body. It is by experiencing bodily sensations that we come to be aware of the state of our body, and of events happening within it. The qualities of which we are aware in bodily sensation – the sensory qualities of hurting, feeling cold or warm and so on – are predicated in these experiences of parts of the body. When

---

[21] As Michael Martin says: 'at best [these cases] demonstrate the gap between having a feeling and making a judgement about it'. See M. G. F. Martin, 'Bodily Sensations', forthcoming in the *Routledge Encyclopedia of Philosophy*, ed. Craig. Nor are the inferences involving statements about sensations uncontroversial; for although we might be happy with the inference from 'X has a pain in his foot' to 'There is something which X has in his foot', the inference from 'X has a pain; Y has a pain; therefore there is something which X and Y both have' is clearly invalid if the something is supposed to be a particular object, and irrelevant to the present issue if it is supposed to be a property.

[22] See D. M. Armstrong, *A Materialist Theory of the Mind* (London: Routledge and Kegan Paul, 1968); M. G. F. Martin, 'Bodily Awareness: a Sense of Ownership', in *The Body and the Self*, ed. J. L. Bermudez, N. Eilan and A. Marcel (Cambridge, MA: MIT Press, 1995); and his 'Sense Modalities and Spatial Properties', in *Spatial Representation*, ed. B. Brewer, N. Eilan and R. McCarthy (Oxford: Blackwell, 1993).

one feels a pain, one normally feels it to be in a part of one's body; and even when a pain is felt where there is no body-part in which to feel it – as in the case of phantom limb pains – what subjects feel is that their body extends further than it actually does. They do not feel as if their pain exists in mid-air, a few inches from where they have lost their limb.

The strongest considerations in favour of this view derive from this felt location of bodily sensation. An ache in my hand feels to be in my hand, not in my mind. Rather than being something which is contained within my body, it presents itself as something which my mind can concentrate on, attend to and try to ignore. In fact, this much is common ground between the believer in mental objects and the perceptual theory. But what tells in favour of the perceptual theory is the fact that to concentrate on the ache, I must necessarily concentrate on the part of my body which aches; the mental object theory cannot explain this necessity. Attending to bodily sensations is achieved by attending to a part of the body where these sensations feel to be. This is because bodily sensation is a form of awareness, the awareness of things going on in one's body.[23]

---

[23] Note that an advantage of this view is that it can give a univocal account of both the bodily sensations which are naturally identified in terms of what they are of – warmth, cold, pressure etc. – and those which are not, like pains and so on. This version of the thesis that bodily sensations are intentional should be contrasted with Tye's view that pains give one non-conceptual representations of damage to one's body: see Tye, *Ten Problems*, chapter 4. Tye's view is, however, consistent with the view defended here. Pains may have many levels of representational content; my concern in this paper is with the uncontroversial phenomenological content they appear to have.

Why call this intentionality? What this perceptual theory says is that in bodily sensation, something is given to the mind, namely the body, or a body part. Calling this phenomenon 'intentionality' classifies it together with the case of outer perception, where the perceived portion of the world is 'given' to the mind; and with thought, where some object, property or state of affairs is 'given' to the mind. What is in common between these different states of mind is expressed in Brentano's formulation: 'in the idea something is conceived, in the wish something is wished'. And in the sensation something is sensed: the body.

III   The Intentionality of Emotion

That is the basis of my case for an intentionalist view of bodily sensation. I now want to move on to the second kind of counterexample to Brentano's thesis: Searle's examples of 'nervousness, elation and undirected anxiety'. How should an intentionalist deal with these apparent examples of non-intentional mental phenomena?

First we need to identify the phenomena in question. This is actually harder to do than it might initially seem. Everyone will agree that there is such a thing as being anxious and yet not being able to give an answer to the question 'what are you anxious about?' But this by itself does not show that anxiety can lack intentionality. For one thing, we have just seen that asking 'what is X about?' is not always the most uncontroversial way of deciding whether X is intentional. And more importantly, it should not be a condition of a state's being intentional that the subject of that state must be able to express what the state's content is, or even which kind of state it is. Every theory of intentionality must allow that subjects are not always the best authorities on all the contents of their minds.

A possible intentionalist account of the state of mind in question would be to say that the intentional object of the state of mind is its cause. So on this view, when we describe ourselves as 'just anxious without being anxious about anything in particular', we mean that we do not know the cause of our anxiety. Now in some cases, it is certainly true that to identify the cause of an emotion is to identify its intentional object. But this cannot be true in general. For one thing, the object of the emotion might lie in the future. Or the cause of an emotion might be a past event which is too remote from the present manifestation of the emotion to be properly regarded as its object. (It may be true that the cause of someone's fear of dogs was a childhood encounter with a certain dog – but it would not always be right to say that *that* dog was the object of their current state of fear in the presence of a different dog.) Or the cause of the emotion might be something completely unrelated to its object. (A drug may cause you to hate some person or thing.) So the fact that an emotion has a cause does not by itself entail that it has an intentional object. The intentionalist cannot refute Searle merely by pointing to the fact that emotions have causes of which we are sometimes ignorant.

But, as we have just seen, nor can Searle infer that there are non-intentional emotions merely from the fact that we sometimes say we are anxious without being able to say what we are anxious about. Searle presents the existence of non-intentional emotions as if it were something entirely obvious. An intentionalist, however, will deny that it is obvious. There can be no real debate about this matter if we are restricted to each participant stating what they think is obvious. So how can the debate proceed?

In order to assess what is at issue between Searle and the intentionalist, we need to know more about how they would classify the various emotions into kinds. What is it that makes anxiety, for instance, the state it is? Whatever it is, it must be common to the cases where anxiety clearly does have an intentional object and the cases which Searle is calling 'undirected'. Remember that these are the cases where someone is anxious but it is not clear to them what they are anxious about. The issue between Searle and the intentionalist is whether the existence of these cases establishes that there are mental states which have no intentionality. If we learn more about what the intentionalist and non-intentionalist think emotions are, we can assess their competing claims over whether any of them are 'undirected' in Searle's sense.

Let's start with non-intentionalism, Searle's position. Perhaps non-intentionalism could say that anxiety is distinguished from (say) an undirected state of contentment by the functional roles of the two states. The functional roles must be explicable in common-sense psychological vocabulary, since we are after a phenomenological classification of the emotions. And yet the functional roles must be relatively informative – 'behaving anxiously' will not do, in this context, as a characterization of part of the functional role of anxiety. So perhaps we can say that anxiety is characterized by the anxious person's inability to concentrate, or by an obsessive concern with trivial details of life, or by a jumpy, nervous form of behaviour. Contentment, by contrast, might be characterized by a benign way of behaving towards the world, an enthusiasm for its daily tasks and so on. However, this style of identifying the functional roles of anxiety and contentment does so in terms of forms of behaviour which are manifestly intentional. So while it might suffice for an account of intentional ('directed') anxiety, it will not do for undirected anxiety.

For the non-intentionalist, there must be something directed and undirected anxiety have in common, which licenses them both being called 'anxiety'. And this 'something' must be detectable from the subject's point of view, if Searle's claim is going to have any force – remember that Searle was appealing to what is obvious to us. Yet this something must also be non-intentional: it cannot be directed on anything. So the non-intentionalist must say that an emotion like anxiety (directed or undirected) has properties which are phenomenologically detectable to the subject, but are non-intentional, involving nothing beyond themselves. These properties must therefore be *qualia*: non-intentional, subjective properties. Just as there are (according to many philosophers) pain-qualia and seeing-red-qualia, there are also emotion-qualia which give the emotions the characteristic phenomenal 'feel' which they have.

Let us suppose, then, that anxiety is partly characterized by its distinctive qualia. Now it is a plausible general thesis about qualia that there is no intrinsic connection between any particular quale and being in any particular objectively-identifiable mental state. For instance, there is nothing intrinsic to the qualia involved in seeing red that links these qualia with the state which plays the functional role of seeing red in normal observers. The coherence of inverted qualia thought-experiments depends on there being no such links, and most defenders of qualia, like Shoemaker, believe that qualia inversion is possible.[24] In fact, it seems part of the very idea of qualia that there be this possibility: for qualia 'point to' nothing beyond themselves, which would make them associated with one kind of objectively-identifiable state rather than another.

So on the non-intentionalist view of emotion, it must be true that there is nothing about the qualia associated with anxiety themselves which make them anxiety-qualia: that is, associated with a state with the particular functional role of anxiety. Just as seeing-red-qualia could, in some other possible world, be associated with the state which in the actual world is seeing green, so anxiety-qualia could be associated with some other emotion-state, say contentment. This is because there is nothing in the qualia themselves which connects them with particular kinds of

[24] See Shoemaker, 'Qualities and Qualia', pp. 108–13, where he discusses the inverted qualia speculation.

emotion, objectively identified (for instance, in terms of functional role).

So now it appears that a non-intentionalist has to accept the possibility that there is a world in which contentment feels to someone as anxiety feels to me. And while the inverted qualia story seems plausible when applied to simple colour-qualia – after all, why shouldn't green things look to you the way red things do to me? – the story is very hard to believe when applied to the putative emotion-qualia. For here we are supposing that the same emotion might feel in opposite ways to two subjects in different possible worlds – emotions have their distinctive 'feel' only contingently. But does this possibility really make sense?

One might respond to this: so much for the plausibility of the view that there are emotion-qualia. And I agree: even if there are qualia, to assimilate anxiety to the experience of seeing red is a distortion of ordinary experience. But how else is the non-intentionalist going to describe the characteristic phenomenology of anxiety, undirected and directed? The nature of these states cannot be described in terms of how things seem to the subject, however vaguely stated. For descriptions of how things seem are patently intentional, and so they will not capture the phenomenology of undirected anxiety. Non-intentionalism is committed to emotion-qualia because it is committed to emotions having properties which are non-intentional yet phenomenologically salient – and non-intentional, phenomenologically salient properties of mental states just are qualia, by definition.

But what is the alternative to this non-intentionalist view? How should an intentionalist give an answer to the question about how to distinguish the different emotions? One answer has already been suggested. Someone experiencing anxiety might not be able to put into words what it is they are anxious about; but they may still be able to say how things seem to them in their state of anxiety. And even if they can't express it, there is still nonetheless such a thing as how things seem to them. To begin with, the intentionalist will start by distinguishing being anxious for oneself, and being anxious for another. This is clearly an intentional distinction: in the one case, one's mind is directed on oneself, in the other case, it is directed on another. The cases Searle mentions are not cases where one is anxious for another: otherwise it would be directed anxiety. So the intentionalist will say that these are cases where one is anxious for oneself – so in these cases, one's anxiety is directed upon oneself. Being anxious in this way is a matter of having a certain attitude to oneself and one's position in the world: it is to regard the world, for example, as a potentially disturbing place for oneself. This is one way in which anxiety exhibits directedness. And it is an alternative to seeing Searle's cases as examples of mental states which are directed on nothing, as Searle does.

It might be helpful to contrast, in these very general terms, anxiety with depression. In depression, the world seems to the subject to be a pointless, colourless place: nothing seems worth doing. The change involved in coming out of a depression is partly a change in the subject's apprehension of the world. Things seem to have a significance, a purpose which they previously lacked. And this can be true of a subject even when they cannot say what they are depressed about. In this way, the phenomenon Searle would call 'undirected depression' can be seen as having a certain directedness or intentionality.

These brief remarks suggest that the difference between anxiety and depression resides in the different manners in which the world, and the subject's place in the world, are apprehended in the emotion. This was Sartre's view:

> My melancholy is a method of suppressing the obligation
> to look for. . . new ways [to realize the potentialities of the
> world] by transforming the present structure of the
> world, replacing it with a totally undifferentiated
> structure. . . In other words, lacking both the ability and
> the will to carry out the projects I formerly entertained,
> I behave in such a manner that the universe requires
> nothing more from me. This one can only do by
> acting upon oneself, by 'lowering the flame of life to a
> pin-point' – and the noetic correlate of this attitude is
> what we call *Bleakness*: the universe is bleak; that is, of
> undifferentiated structure.[25]

Sartre's view of emotions, in general, is that they are characterized by their intentionality. 'Emotion is a specific manner of apprehending the world,'[26] he writes, and 'all the emotions have this in common, that they evoke the appearance of a world, cruel, terrible, bleak, joyful etc.'[27] Sartre's view provides one general framework in which to

---

[25] *Sketch for a Theory of the Emotions* (London: Methuen 1971; originally published 1939), pp. 68–9. For an illuminating introduction, see Gregory McCulloch, *Using Sartre* (London: Routledge, 1994), chapter 2.
[26] Sartre, *Sketch,* p. 57.   [27] Ibid., p. 81.

defend the intentionality of all emotions – even those which Searle describes as 'undirected'.

Let me summarize this line of thought. Searle says that there are emotions which have no intentionality. But this does not follow from the fact that people cannot say what it is that their emotions are about. Nor does its denial follow from the fact that the objects of emotions are sometimes their causes, of which we are sometimes ignorant. To decide the issue about whether there are non-intentional emotions, we should first ask what distinguishes, from the phenomeno-logical point of view, the different emotions. The non-intentionalist answer to this question is committed to the existence of emotion-qualia, and the implausible possibility of inverted emotion-qualia. But the intentionalist who accepts (for example) Sartre's view of emotion as a mode of apprehend-ing the world is not committed to this possibility. The differ-ences between the different emotions would not be explained in terms of qualia but in terms of the different ways the emotions present the world and the subject's place in it. This is one way an intentionalist can characterize the emotions Searle is talking about, like anxiety and depression, where the subject is not able to say what they are anxious or depressed about.

The phenomenology of emotion is a very complex area, and I have only touched the surface of the issues. What I have tried to do is to suggest a way in which an intention-alist can argue that these apparent counterexamples to Brentano's thesis are not really counterexamples.[28] But what

---

[28] Of course, this is not the only way for an intentionalist to account for emotion. Compare Tye's views: Tye, *Ten Problems,* chapter 4.

does this treatment of the counterexamples show about the nature of intentionality in general?

My original question was: what would you have to believe about intentionality in order to believe that it is the mark of the mental? The way I have approached this question is to try and specify the sense in which something is 'given' to the mind in sensation and emotion, just as something is given to the mind in thought and experience. The heart of the view is inspired by Brentano's remark that in the idea, something is conceived; I say that in the sensation, something is felt, in the emotion, something is apprehended – and so on.

The issue is in danger of collapsing into an uninteresting question of terminology if the notion I am identifying as intentionality had nothing in common with what others call intentionality. But this is not the case. It is possible to isolate two main elements of the concept of intentionality as discussed by recent philosophers.[29] The first is the apparently relational structure of intentionality, the structure Sartre and other phenomenologists express by saying that consciousness is always the consciousness *of* something.[30] While intentional states *appear* to be relations between

---

[29] For a representative of recent discussions, see Tye, *Ten Problems,* pp. 94–6.

[30] For instance: 'all consciousness, as Husserl has shown, is consciousness of something' *Being and Nothingness* (London: Methuen, 1958; first published 1943, p. xxvii). Compare Searle: 'It is characteristic of Intentional states, as I use the notion, that there is a distinction between the state and what the state is directed at or about or of.' (Searle, *Intentionality,* p. 2); for a different way of formulating the same kind of point, see E. Levinas, 'Beyond Intentionality', in *Philosophy in*

thinkers and the objects of their thoughts, this cannot be true in general, since intentional states can be directed on things which do not exist, and relations entail the existence of their relata.[31] (This point holds independently of the truth

France Today, ed. A. Montefiore (Cambridge: Cambridge University Press, 1983), p. 106.

[31] This fact gives rise to one of the main problems of intentionality. For an excellent presentation of this problem, see Michael Dummett, *Origins of Analytical Philosophy* (London: Duckworth, 1993), pp. 35–6. See also Caston, 'Aristotle'. Brentano came to appreciate the importance of this point when he wrote the appendix to his *Psychology from an Empirical Standpoint*. There he says that 'If someone thinks of something, the one who is thinking must certainly exist, but the object of his thinking need not exist at all.' He goes on to observe that 'we might doubt whether we are dealing with something relational here, and not, rather, with something somewhat similar to something relational in a certain respect, which might therefore better be called "quasi-relational"' (p. 272). Sometimes it is supposed (see Dennett, *Content*, and Tye, *Ten Problems*) that Brentano was concerned with the question of non-existence even before he wrote the Appendix to his *Psychology*. It is true that in a famous passage, Brentano says that the object of thought 'should not be understood as a reality' (p. 88); but by this he is just reminding his readers that he is talking about 'phenomena' or 'appearances', not about the 'underlying reality'. In this sense, the physical phenomena with which he contrasts mental phenomena 'should not be considered a reality' either. Compare, for example, the following passage: 'the phenomena of light, sound, heat, spatial location and locomotion which [the natural scientist] studies are not things which really and truly exist. They are signs of something real, which through its causal activity, produces presentations of them. They are not however, an adequate representation of this reality... We have no experience of that which truly exists, in and of itself, and that which we do experience is not true.' (Brentano, *Psychology*, p. 19).

or falsity of the doctrine of externalism, since even the most extreme externalist must allow that intentional states can concern the non-existent.) The second element is what some call the perspectival or fine-grained nature of intentionality, what Searle calls 'aspectual shape'.[32] This is just the familiar idea that when something is apprehended as the object of an intentional state – whether a particular object, fact or property – it is always apprehended in a certain way.

Both features of intentionality are present in my treatment of the counterexamples to intentionalism. I claimed that instead of seeing bodily sensations as instantiations of purely subjective, monadic properties, we should see these experiences as presenting something – a part of the body – as modified in a certain way. Bodily sensations, then, are primarily states of awareness, and therefore apparently relational states. They are only *apparently* relational since, according to the perceptual theory, phantom limb phenomena (e.g.) are cases of awareness of a felt quality in merely apparent body part. They are therefore analogous – in this respect only – to cases of perceptual hallucination, where one perceives a quality to be instantiated in an object which does not actually exist.[33] If

---

[32] John R. Searle, *The Rediscovery of the Mind* (Cambridge, MA: MIT Press, 1992), p. 155.

[33] Only in this respect, since it is not quite correct to say that a phantom limb pain is an illusory *pain* – the pain certainly exists, one just perceives it as having a location which it does not (indeed, in the circumstances, cannot) have. An analogy would be perhaps with some device which made it seem to you as if sounds were coming from one direction when they were in fact coming from the opposite direction (as when a ventriloquist 'throws' his voice).

Sartre's account of the phenomenology of emotions is right, then there is a similar apparent relationality in emotional experience: there is the experiencing subject, the world experienced (or the thing in the world experienced) and the particular way of apprehending the world.

The second element of intentionality – its fine-grained character – is also contained within my account of sensations and emotions. A pain in one's ankle is a state of awareness of one's ankle, presented *as such*, not as the organic organization of tendons, bone and muscle which one's ankle actually is. Similarly with the so-called 'undirected' emotions. In a particular undirected emotion, the same world appears under one aspect – bleak, terrible, threatening – rather than another. (Of course, there may be debate about whether the world could properly be said to *have* the aspects or properties attributed to it in an emotion – but this does not affect the present point.)

So the core of the concept of intentionality, as discussed in much contemporary philosophy of mind, is present in the theses advanced by intentionalism. The dispute between the intentionalist and the non-intentionalist is substantial and not just terminological. Where this characterization does depart from some recent discussions is in not starting the discussion of intentionality with the notion of a propositional attitude. A propositional attitude is an intentional state whose content – that which characterizes its directedness – is something evaluable as true or false. I do not question the applicability of the notion of a propositional attitude itself, but rather the tendency in some

contemporary philosophers to see the propositional attitudes as the sole home of the concept of intentionality.[34]
Obviously, the form of intentionalism I am defending here
cannot accept such a view, but even putting this to one side,
the thesis that all intentional mental states are propositional
attitudes lacks phenomenological plausibility. To take a nice
example of Victor Caston's: when asked to think of a
number between one and ten, what comes to mind is a
number, not a proposition. And it is a familiar fact that
certain emotions, notably love and hate, can be directed on
objects rather than always on states of affairs. While the
notion of a propositional attitude must play an important
role in any theory of intentionality, it does not exhaust the
application of the concept of intentionality.

IV   Intentionality, the Non-Mental and the Mark of the Mental

I have been defending the claim that all mental phenomena
exhibit intentionality. Now I want to return to the other part
of Brentano's thesis, the claim that intentionality is exclusive

[34] For a clear-headed (but in my view mistaken) statement of this policy,
see Dennett, *Content* pp. 27–9. Even Searle, *Intentionality,* who admits
that much intentionality cannot be expressed in terms of whole
propositions (pp. 6–7), seems to commit himself implicitly to the
opposite in his analysis of intentional states by analogy with his
account of speech acts (p. 26). The tendency is still pervasive: see, for
instance, the definition of 'intentionality' given in William Lyons,
Approaches to Intentionality (Oxford: Oxford University Press, 1995),
pp. 1–2.

to the mental domain. This will give me the opportunity to air some speculations about why we should be interested in the idea of a mark of the mental.

Now, in the way I am suggesting we should think about intentionality, it is a concept which applies to all mental phenomena, including conscious, phenomenally salient mental states such as perception, sensation and conscious emotional episodes, but also unconscious beliefs, desires and other mental dispositions. The binding idea is captured by the Brentanian slogan that in the intentional state something is given. But can we find intentionality in the non-mental?

It is sometimes said that Brentano's thesis is a threat to physicalism because it implies that intentionality can only be found in the mental and never in the physical. Dennett, for instance, says that 'the Intentionalist thesis... proclaims an unbridgeable gulf between the mental and the physical.'[35]

But we must distinguish between the view that intentionality is not present in the *physical*, and the view that intentionality is not present in the *non-mental*. For if physicalism is true, then the physical is not the same as the

---

[35] Dennett, *Content*, p. 21. The point derives from Quine: see *Word and Object* (Cambridge, MA: MIT Press, 1960), p. 221. See also the opening pages of Hartry Field, 'Mental Representation', in *Readings in the Philosophy of Psychology* vol. II, ed. Ned Block (London: Methuen, 1980). Obviously, if one thinks of intentionality as a property of sentences (as Quine and Dennett do), Dennett's quoted remark makes more sense than it would do otherwise. I quote it here because the idea that Brentano's thesis presents a problem for physicalism has survived the waning of the popularity of the linguistic criterion of intentionality.

non-mental. Of course, Brentano himself – to whom the question of physicalism would have been of little interest – says that 'no physical phenomenon manifests anything like' intentionality. But if we want to remain neutral on the question of physicalism, we should prefer a weaker version of Brentano's thesis which only says that intentionality is characteristic of the mental alone. Whether the mental is reducible to the physical is a further question; if it is, then some physical things manifest intentionality. But no non-mental things do.

However, some philosophers take a view of intentionality which makes it unproblematically a feature of many non-mental things. For instance, some follow Chisholm and Quine and take the non-extensionality of certain linguistic contexts as criterial for the intentionality of the phenomena described in those contexts.[36] Chisholm's approach was to 'formulate a working criterion by means of which we can distinguish sentences that are Intentional. . . in a certain language from sentences that are not'.[37] In essence Chisholm's criterion was that a sentence S is intentional iff: S contains a singular term yet does not entail the usual

[36] See Roderick Chisholm, *Perceiving* (Ithaca: Cornell University Press, 1957), chapter 12, and Quine, *Word and Object*, esp. the section on 'The Double Standard'. Note especially the following passage: 'the Scholastic word "intentional"' was revived by Brentano in connection with the verbs of propositional attitude and related verbs. . . e.g. 'hunt', 'want' etc. The division between such idioms and the normally tractable ones is notable. We saw how it divides referential from non-referential occurrences of terms.'

[37] Chisholm, *Perceiving*, p. 170.

existential generalization; or S contains an embedded sentence in a non-truth-functional context; or the principle of the substitutivity of co-referring singular terms does not apply to S. This disjunctive criterion is supposed to establish the intentionality (in Brentano's sense) of the phenomena described by the sentence S. Dennett, for instance, says that 'Chisholm's three criteria come close to reproducing Brentano's distinction.'[38]

I will call this the 'linguistic criterion' of intentionality. Some of those who adopt the linguistic criterion take a deflationary approach to the distinctively mental characteristics of intentionality. They point out that intentionality, in their sense, is common to non-mental linguistic contexts, too – for instance: modal, causal, dispositional, probabilistic or functional contexts – and they draw various conclusions from this fact. They might draw the relatively weak conclusion that intentionality is not the mark of the mental; or they might draw the stronger conclusion that there is no special problem of intentionality, if intentionality is shared by so many different and (in some cases) unproblematic phenomena.[39]

---

[38] Dennett, *Content*, p. 23. Compare Searle, *Intentionality*, pp. 22–5, who takes the correct view of this matter, as I see it. See also William Kneale, 'Intentionality and Intensionality', *Proceedings of the Aristotelian Society*, Supplementary Volume 42 (1968).

[39] A good example of this general approach is Enç, 'Intentional States'; see also C. B. Martin and Karl Pfeifer, 'Intentionality and the Non-Psychological' *Philosophy and Phenomenological Research* 46 (1986), and U. T. Place, 'Intentionality as the Mark of the Dispositional; *Dialectica* 50 (1996).

TIM CRANE

The version of intentionalism defended here cannot accept this. This is not to say that it would have to reject the view that causal, probabilistic and the other contexts are non-extensional. Nor does intentionalism have to deny that the features of intentionality I have just mentioned receive expression in the linguistic structures which we use to describe it. So, for instance, the apparent relationality is evident in ascriptions of intentionality (in the failure of existential generalization in non-extensional contexts) as is the fact that intentionality is perspectival (in the failure of substitutivity of co-referring terms).

What intentionalism must reject is rather the linguistic criterion of intentionality itself. These linguistic phenomena are guides to the presence of intentionality in ascriptions of intentionality, but they do not constitute its essence. And given the way I have been proceeding in this paper, this should not be surprising. Intentionality, like consciousness, is one of the concepts which we use in an elucidation of what it is to have a mind. On this conception of intentionality, to consider the question of whether intentionality is present in some creature is of a piece with considering what it is like for that creature – that is, with a consideration of that creature's mental life as a whole. To say this is not to reject by stipulation the idea that there are primitive forms of intentionality which are only remotely connected with conscious mental life – say, the intentionality of the information-processing which goes on in our brains. It is rather to emphasize the priority of intentionality as a *phenomenological* notion.[40] So intentionalists will reject the linguistic criterion of intentionality precisely *because* the criterion will count phenomena as intentional which are clearly not mental.

This would be a perverse or circular way to proceed if we did not already have a grasp on the concept of a mind. But we do have such a grasp: it is that concept which we try to express when we say that to have a mind is to have a point of view or perspective on the world, or when we say that there is something it is like to be conscious, or when we talk about the world being manifest to a subject of experience, or when we talk about the world being a phenomenon for a subject. Some philosophers associate these ways of talking solely with the *conscious* or *phenomenal* side of the mind, where the conscious or the phenomenal is contrasted explicitly with the intentional.[41] Consider, for instance, how

---

[40] For the idea of intentionality as a phenomenological notion, see Gregory McCulloch, 'The Very Idea of the Phenomenological', *Proceedings of the Aristotelian Society* 93 (1992–93); and 'Intentionality and Interpretation', this volume; J. E. Malpas, in *Donald Davidson and the Mirror of Meaning* (Cambridge: Cambridge University Press, 1992), section 4.2, gives an interesting reading of intentionality as a phenomenological notion, drawing on the Heideggerian notion of a 'horizon'. For a survey of various ways in which the idea of intentionality can be applied beyond the central cases, see Martin Davies, 'Consciousness and the Varieties of Aboutness', in *Philosophy of Psychology: Debates on Psychological Explanation*, ed. Cynthia and Graham Macdonald (Oxford: Blackwell 1995).

[41] For the contrast between the phenomenal and the intentional, see, for example, Sydney Shoemaker, *The First-Person Perspective and Other Essays* (Cambridge: Cambridge University Press, 1996), pp. 112, 138.

TIM CRANE

McGinn formulates his pessimism about our inability to explain consciousness:

> We can, it is felt, explain what makes a mental state have the content it has; at least there is no huge barrier of principle in the way of our doing so. But, it is commonly conceded, we have no remotely plausible account of what makes a mental state have the phenomenological character it has.[42]

Here 'phenomenological character' is explicitly contrasted with 'content', as if the two categories were exclusive. Sometimes composite states are envisaged – as when perceptions are conceived of as having content and qualia. But in general, the picture of the mind which lies behind remarks such as McGinn's is one on which we have two kinds of mental state: intentional states which are not essentially conscious, and conscious states whose consciousness is intrinsically unrelated to any intentionality they may have.

The trouble with this picture of the mind is that the classification of both kinds of phenomena as *mental* seems to lack a rationale. The most we can say is that *mental* is an accidental category, which presupposes no underlying nature to the phenomena it picks out. As Kathleen Wilkes puts it, 'it is improbable that something bunching together pains, and thoughts about mathematics, is going to be a reliable pointer towards a legitimate natural kind'.[43] Wilkes

---

[42] Colin McGinn, 'Consciousness and Content,' in *The Problem of Consciousness and Other Essays* (Oxford: Blackwell, 1991), p. 24. See also his later remark that 'subjective features lie quite outside the proper domain of the theory of content' (p. 33).
[43] Quoted by Davies, 'Consciousness', p. 358.

here echoes Richard Rorty's complaint about the heterogeneity of the concept of mind:

> The attempt to hitch pains and beliefs together seems *ad hoc* – they don't seem to have anything in common except our refusal to call them 'physical'.[44]

There are two possible ways of reacting to these points. One is simply to accept that there is no more than a nominal unity to the concept of mind. The other is to object that there is something wrong with the whole picture – specifically, with the way of distinguishing between intentionality and consciousness that we find expressed, for instance, in the above passage from McGinn. If this is our reaction, then we need to find a way of characterizing mental phenomena which reflects the underlying unity of their classification as mental: that is, we need a mark of the mental.

Some philosophers have argued recently that consciousness is the only true mark of the mental.[45] But this view battles with the widely accepted and uncontroversial view that many mental states are unconscious, so its defence is an uphill struggle. The alternative, which I have been canvassing here, is that it is intentionality, the mind's directedness on the world, which should be thought of as the mark

---

[44] Richard Rorty, *Philosophy and the Mirror of Nature* (Oxford: Blackwell, 1979), p. 22.

[45] See Searle, *Rediscovery,* for his view of the unconscious, see pp. 155–56. A similar view is taken by Galen Strawson in *Mental Reality* (Cambridge, MA: MIT Press, 1995): 'the only distinctively mental phenomena are the phenomena of conscious experience' (p. xi).

of the mental. If we take this view, then we must reject the distinction implicit in McGinn's, Rorty's and Wilkes's remarks, that the phenomenal is one thing, the intentional another. Whatever the fate of qualia, we must accept that all mental states are permeated with intentionality, and characterizing their phenomenal character – giving a phenomenology – can be achieved by characterizing their intentionality.[46]

Brentano's view was that the science of psychology should be distinguished from both physiology and philosophy, not by its methods, but by its subject-matter. These days, it is less common for there to be serious dispute among psychologists about the subject-matter of psychology. But there is perhaps more disagreement in today's philosophy of mind about what its subject-matter is, and in some cases

---

[46] For some different approaches to the same idea, compare M. G. F. Martin, 'Setting Things Before the Mind', this volume; and Gregory McCulloch, 'Intentionality and Interpretation', this volume. My remarks in this last section are highly speculative, and raise many issues which demand further elaboration. One question is whether the suggested 'unification' of the phenomena of mind by the concept of intentionality can be achieved within the weak intentionalist picture I defend here. For if one allows that the existence of non-intentional phenomenal properties (qualia) is compatible with the intentionality of all mental states, then it appears as if a question can be raised for weak intentionalism which recapitulates the question I am raising for the McGinn/Rorty picture. More needs to be said about non-intentional properties in order to assess the force of this question. Here I am indebted to participants in the discussion at the Royal Institute of Philosophy meeting, and especially to Paul Boghossian.

there is even disagreement about whether it has one. Those who find this situation unacceptable may wish to reconsider the popular rejection of Brentano's thesis that intentionality is the mark of the mental, and therefore the subject-matter of the philosophy of mind.

Intentionality and Interpretation

GREGORY McCULLOCH

I

According to Brentano in a much-quoted passage,

> Every psychological phenomenon is characterized by...
> intentional inherent existence of ... an object... In the
> idea something is conceived, in the judgement something
> is recognized or discovered, in loving loved, in hating
> hated, in desiring desired, and so on.[1]

This is a doctrine about the nature of thought or cognition,
and some would say that the matters it raises have only fairly
recently come to be directly engaged by mainstream philosophers of the analytical tradition. For analytical philosophy's approach to the question of intentionality has tended
to be routed through concern with *linguistic behaviour*, its
interpretation and its logical and semantic analysis. The
depth of this concern with language is, if anything, emphasized when we consider more recent attempts by heirs of the

---

Thanks to Tim Crane and Chris Hookway for valuable comments on an
earlier draft.

[1] F. Brentano, *Psychology from an Empirical Standpoint*, ed. L. McAlister,
trans. A. Rancurello, D. B. Terrell, and L. McAlister (New York:
Humanities Press, 1973), p. 88.

398

analytical tradition to approach the question of intentionality more directly, missing out the trip through linguistic behaviour. According to one very influential version of this tendency, the problem of intentionality is still to do with the properties of linguistic structures, only now not public, spoken linguistic structures, but systems of mental representations in the brain.[2] The tendency to miss out the trip through public language reflects, in part, a reaction against behaviourism and in favour of mentalism: just as one of the principal causes for the longevity of the result of the 'linguistic turn' was undoubtedly the influence of behaviourism on analytical philosophy of mind. I think the mentalists are right to be anti-behaviouristic, but that their forerunners were also right to focus on the interpretation of linguistic behaviour when approaching cognition in general and intentionality in particular. By the same token, then, there has usually been something wrong with analytical approaches in this area: too much behaviourism, or too little concern with linguistic behaviour. In this paper I want to recommend a more balanced approach, building on themes from Quine and Davidson.

II

A behaviouristic starting point is explicit in the Quine of *Word and Object.*

> one is ready to say of the domestic situation in all
> positivistic reasonableness that if two speakers match in

[2] For example, see H. Field, 'Mental Representation', *Erkenntnis* 13 (1978), 9–61 J. Fodor, *Psychosemantics* (Cambridge, MA: MIT Press, 1987).

all dispositions to verbal behavior there is no sense in
imagining semantic differences between them.[3]

Consequently, he focuses on *radical translation*, on how a
field linguist might penetrate an unknown tongue with no
established links with her own. The reason is that 'all the
objective data [the linguist] has to go on are the forces
impinging on the natives' surfaces, and the observable
behaviour, verbal and otherwise, of the native'.[4] The behaviourism is notably radical: the idea is to make independent
sense, in terms of these 'objective data', of mentalistic
notions such as meaning, belief, intentional object. Quine's
thesis of the indeterminacy of translation then amounts to
the view that no such independent sense can be made:

> the relativity to non-unique systems of analytical
> hypotheses invests not only translational synonymy but
> intentional notions generally.[5]

For example, the 'objective data' will support nothing better
than stimulus meaning, and terms can be stimulus-
synonymous without even being co-extensive, much less
intuitively synonymous: thus, according to Quine, 'rabbit'
and 'undetached rabbit-part'. He later dubbed this phenomenon the *inscrutability of reference* (later still, the indeterminacy of reference),[6] and given his behaviourism it entails

---

[3] W. V. Quine, *Word and Object* (Cambridge, MA: MIT Press, 1960),
p. 79.

[4] Ibid., p. 28.   [5] Ibid., p. 221.

[6] For 'inscrutability' see W. V. Quine, *Ontological Relativity and Other
Essays* (New York: Columbia University Press, 1969), p. 37; and for

the *impotence of intentionality*. If conceiving is, at bottom, a matter of linguistic and other behaviour, then problems with reference *just are* problems with conceiving, and Brentano goes beyond the Quinean 'objective data' when saying 'in the idea something is conceived'. For Quine, the 'something' is neither rabbit, nor undetached rabbit-part, nor any other determined thing. One can no more direct attention at rabbits than use words to refer to them, and in his own words:

> the arbitrariness of reading our objectifications into the heathen speech reflects not so much the inscrutability of the heathen mind, as that there is nothing to scrute.[7]

Nor are things any better, from Brentano's point of view, if we draw the Quinean moral that inscrutability of reference delivers ontological relativity: the idea that ontological questions only make sense relative to this or that scheme. There is no mention of relativity in Brentano's thesis as stated, and we shall see there is no evident sense in applying the relativity point to the thesis correctly construed.

Davidson, we know, self-consciously departs from the Quine of *Word and Object* over a number of central matters.[8] In particular, he is explicitly anti-behaviourist, claiming that behaviour is no more than 'the main evidential

---

'indeterminacy' W. V. Quine, *Pursuit of Truth* (Cambridge, MA: Harvard University Press, revised edition 1992), p. 50.

[7] Quine, *Ontological Relativity*, p. 5.

[8] Indeed, later Quine seems to move significantly towards Davidson: see, e.g. Quine, *Pursuit of Truth*, §29.

basis of attributions of belief and desire'.[9] He also denies that mentalistic notions, to be made respectable, need to be reduced to non-mentalistic ones. In this connection he drops Quine's notions of assent and dissent, and introduces the more mentalistic one of *holding true*. He finds no use for stimulus meanings, instead matching utterances with ordinary worldly conditions. He rejects theorizing in terms of translation, using a more demanding notion of structure-revealing interpretation: although he retains Quine's concern with the radical case, and I shall be much concerned with this important point. He doubts whether the scope for indeterminacy in semantics is as wide as Quine suggests. But despite all this, Davidson's approach to intentionality is very close indeed to Quine's. First, he argues for the inscrutability of reference:

> suppose every object has one and only one shadow... On a first theory, we take 'Wilt' to refer to Wilt and the predicate 'is tall' to refer to tall things; on the second theory, we take 'Wilt' to refer to the shadow of Wilt and 'is tall' to refer to the shadows of tall things. The first theory tells us that the sentence 'Wilt is tall' is true if and only if Wilt is tall; the second theory tells us that 'Wilt is tall' is true if and only if the shadow of Wilt is the shadow of a tall thing. The truth conditions are clearly equivalent... What matters is that what causes the response or attitude of the speaker is an objective situation or event, and that the response or attitude is

---

[9] See D. Davidson, *Inquiries into Truth and Interpretation* (Oxford: Oxford University Press, 1984), p. 160.

directed to a sentence or the utterance of a sentence. As long as we hold to this, there can be no relevant evidence on the basis of which to choose between theories and their permutations.[10]

Given Davidson's anti-behaviourism, commitment to the inscrutability of reference does not directly yield the impotence of intentionality: but armed with other Davidsonian themes, we soon get there. For he claims that there is no general grip to be had on the content of speakers' beliefs except through an account of what their words mean. On the Davidsonian approach, held-true sentences are matched with worldly conditions, and if the theory that supplies the matching satisfies certain constraints, these conditions are deemed the truth-conditions of the utterances. The utterances may then normally be taken as expressions of belief with those same truth-conditions, since it is assumed that speakers usually hold-true a sentence on the basis of a true belief (the principle of charity). Any potential for permutation in the apparatus that supplies the truth-conditions of utterances thus carries over to belief, at least in the case of language users and beliefs expressible in language. But then Davidson denies beliefs to non-linguistic creatures.[11] And although his argument seems independent of the main body of his doctrines, overall we confront a position on which inscrutability of reference comports with impotence of intentionality. The problem over whether I am *talking* about

[10] Ibid., pp. 230–1.
[11] Ibid., Essay 11; also D. Davidson, 'Rational Animals', in *Actions and Events*, ed. E. Lepore and B. McLaughlin (Oxford: Blackwell, 1985).

Wilt yields a parallel problem over whether I am *thinking* about him, over whether I can direct my attention at him. In the idea Wilt is no more (and no less) conceived than Wilt's shadow. Davidson regards this as an acceptable result:

> Indeterminacy of meaning or translation does not represent a failure to capture significant distinctions; it marks the fact that certain apparent distinctions are not significant.[12]

III

One might suspect, in the light of the striking closeness to Quine, that Davidson's anti-behaviourism is only skin-deep. One could then go on to defend Brentano and the doctrine of intentionality by attacking the behaviourism, the message being that cognition can only be accommodated by mentalism. This could mean dropping the concern with linguistic behaviour, and focusing instead on a notion of mental representation presumed to underlie it, resulting in a version of *behaviour-rejecting mentalism*: a view which denies bodily behaviour any essential role in thought or cognition. According to a behaviour-rejecting mentalist, an appropriately stimulated and sustained *ab initio* vat-brain could have the same cognitive properties as I do as I sit here now. Thus Fodor:

> If you imagine a brain in a vat that's hooked up to *this* world, and hooked up in *just* the same way one's own

---

[12] Davidson, *Inquiries,* p. 154.

> brain is, then – of course – that brain shares one's
> thought-contents. . .[13]

As we shall see, there are signs of (unstable) behaviour-rejecting mentalism in Davidson. Nevertheless, moving from Davidson-*qua*-lover-of-linguistic-behaviour to behaviour-rejecting mentalism involves taking a lot of steps: more than I think justifiable, for reasons some of which will emerge. So I want to recommend a non-behaviouristic defence of Brentano, against the impotence claim, which is much more accommodating to Davidson's over-arching concern with linguistic behaviour and interpretation, as well as to other broadly Davidsonian themes. This involves recommending *behaviour-embracing mentalism,* according to which embodiment and bodily behaviour are essential aspects – though not sufficient conditions – of thought and cognition.[14] To make the argument, we need to begin with two doctrines common to Quine and Davidson. One is obviously not behaviouristic, the other not obviously so. These doctrines are (1) the primacy of sentences, and (2) the primacy of the radical case.

1. *The primacy of sentences.* On Quine's account, stimulus meaning approximates most nearly to meaning as intuitively

---

[13] Fodor, *Psychosemantics,* p. 52. Note that there is some absurdity in suggesting that disembodied brain could be hooked up to the world in *just* the way that an embodied brain is. This is not as trivial a point as it may look, given the possibility of behaviour-embracing mentalism (for which see immediately below).

[14] See G. McCulloch, *The Mind and Its World* (London: Routledge, 1995), chapters 5–8.

conceived in the case of *observation sentences*, those 'occasion sentences whose stimulus meanings vary none under the influence of collateral information... These are the occasion sentences that wear their meanings on their sleeves.'[15] Other sentences do less well, but indeterminacy attributable to the inscrutability of reference does not appear until sentences are broken into terms. Davidson also homes in on sentences:

> the evidence available [for a theory of interpretation] is just that speakers of the language to be interpreted hold various sentences to be true at certain times and under specified circumstances.[16]

As well as reflecting these philosophers' concern to give empirical substance to their accounts of language, these claims also highlight their view that sentences are in some sense primary. At its most innocent this derives from the centrality of inference and truth to any viable classical account of logical structure, and reflects also the observation, in Dummett's words, that 'we cannot ... do what Wittgenstein called "make a move in the language game" without, in effect, using a sentence'.[17] Given this, subsentential semantic notions like reference and satisfaction come out as derivative, their utility exhausted by the role

[15] Quine, *Word and Object*, p. 42. Occasion sentences are those which 'command assent or dissent only if queried after an appropriate prompting stimulation' (pp. 35–6).

[16] Davidson, *Inquiries*, p. 135.

[17] M. Dummett, *Frege: Philosophy of Language* (London: Duckworth, 1973), p. 3.

they play in helping systematize what Quine calls 'the inter-animation of sentences'. As he puts it in a fairly recent paper on Davidson:

> On the one hand there is the set of theoretical sentences ... On the other hand, there is the observation sentence ... subject to a verdict by dint of sensory stimulation. Where complexity comes is in the relation of the set of theoretical sentences to the observation sentence. They are connected by a network of intervening sentences, variously linked in logical and psychological ways. It is only here that we have to pry into sentences and take notice of ... objective reference, as Davidson well argued...[18]

Once the focus shifts away from language as logician's abstraction to language as revealed in linguistic behaviour, the primacy of sentences quite smoothly transposes into the primacy of speech acts (more accurately, of assertion: or – given that it is thought we are ultimately supposed to be dealing with – judgement). And this much, so far, is not to be quibbled with. But problems threaten when it is combined with the doctrine of the primacy of the radical case.

2. *The primacy of the radical case.* As remarked, Quine's focus on radical translation is a device to make graphic behaviouristic assumptions. As also remarked, Davidson drops translation and moves to interpretation, but retains the focus on the radical case. Given that he cannot offer

---

[18] W. V. Quine, 'Events and Reification', in *Actions and Events,* ed. Lepore and McLaughlin, p. 169; cf. Quine, *Pursuit of Truth,* chapter 2.

Quine's behaviouristic motivation, what does he offer instead? He writes:

> I propose to call a theory a theory of meaning for a natural language L if it is such that (a) knowledge of the theory suffices for understanding the utterances of speakers of L and (b) the theory can be given empirical application by appeal to evidence described without using linguistic concepts, or at least without using concepts specific to the sentences and words of L. The first condition indicates the nature of the question; the second requires that it not be begged.[19]

Given his aim to 'understand semantic concepts in the light of others',[20] we need to exclude certain linguistic notions from the characterisation of the evidence for this or that interpretation. Clearly, focusing on the radical case is a way of doing this, and so it would not be easy to pin underlying or vestigial behaviourism on Davidson here. Any quasi-reductionist ambition, howsoever mild, might reasonably make use of the radical case. Whether even mild quasi-reductionism can be warranted in the philosophy of thought is another matter to which we shall return.

First, though, we need to have before us a key Davidsonian argument that inscrutability of reference is inevitable once a focus on the radical case is added to the doctrine of the primacy of sentences. It turns on the fact that while the primacy of sentences merely entails that sub-sentential semantic notions are derivative, adding the

---

[19] Davidson, *Inquiries*, p. 215.   [20] Ibid., p. 219.

primacy of the radical case converts this into the stronger idea that they are theoretical, 'non-observational' notions, whose role in saving the phenomena of sentence-production exhausts their empirical reality. Thus Davidson:

> I suggest that words, meanings of words, reference and satisfaction are posits we need to implement a theory of truth. They serve this purpose without needing independent confirmation or empirical basis.[21]

Given the focus on the radical case, all the evidence there is relates to the production of sentences in observable circumstances; and sub-sentential semantics is then, according to Davidson, in the same boat as theories about microscopic physical structure: 'we explain macroscopic phenomena by postulating an unobserved fine structure'.[22] So: the idea is that primacy of sentences *plus* the radical case makes sub-sentential semantics theoretical, leaving room for permutations at the sub-sentential level which equally well save the observable phenomena. That's inscrutability of reference, and impotence of intentionality seems to follow on given the general plan of tying cognition essentially to linguistic behaviour in Davidson's manner.

But think of the charge often levelled against Quine that he without good reason converts underdetermination into indeterminacy where translation is concerned. Now think of Davidson's analogy between physical and sub-sentential structure. The initial claim is that empirical or evidential reality is exhausted by a range of phenomena

---

[21] Ibid., p. 222.   [22] Ibid.

(macrophysical, linguistic) which can then be held fixed while the 'theoretical' story is permuted. But in the micro-physical case, this certainly only reflects underdetermina-tion, and there is no demonstration here that the whole reality of the microphysical is exhausted by its empirical reality. So why not take the same line in the linguistic case, and say that there is more to the reality of sub-sentential semantics than is given by what Davidson offers as its empirical reality? Such a move is exactly what one expects a behaviour-rejecting mentalist to make: beneath the overt production of sentences lies a cognitive mechanism that determines what is left underdetermined by correlation of sentences with observable states of affairs.[23] Now in Quine's case, the reply to this is straightforward: to make the move is to abandon his axiomatic behaviourism, according to which the reality of 'theoretical' posits precisely *is* exhausted by their empirical reality:

> Language is a social art which we all acquire on the evidence solely of other people's overt behavior under publicly recognizable circumstances. Meanings, therefore, those very models of mental entities, end up as grist for the behaviorist's mill.

[23] This appears to be the suggestion in J. Searle, 'Indeterminacy, Empiricism and the First Person', *Journal of Philosophy* 84 (1987), cf. Quine, *Ontological Relativity*, pp. 28–9. There are similarities between Searle's diagnosis of what drives Quine and Davidson towards indeterminacy, and the one offered in the present lecture. But for a very big difference in the countersuggestions offered, see section V below. Thanks here to Barry C. Smith.

> In psychology one may or may not be a behaviorist,
> but in linguistics one has no choice ... There is nothing
> in linguistic meaning beyond what is to be gleaned from
> overt behavior in observable circumstances.[24]

But the straight Quinean answer is not available to the anti-behaviourist in Davidson: so we need from him a different reason why empirical reality should be taken to exhaust the whole of reality where sub-sentential semantics is concerned. Having noted this absolutely crucial point, however, I shall delay further discussion of it for a short while. But we shall see that there is a major fault line in Davidson's position on account of this matter.

IV

I first want to counter a strong impression sometimes given by Davidson that his inscrutability and impotence result is entailed by the primacy of sentences doctrine alone. As Dummett has argued:

> Since it is only by means of a sentence that we may
> perform a linguistic act ... the possession of sense by a
> word cannot consist in anything else but its being
> governed by a rule which partially specifies the sense of
> sentences containing it. If this is so, then, on pain of
> circularity, the general notion of the sense possessed by a
> sentence must be capable of being explained without

---

[24] Quine, *Ontological Relativity,* p. 26 and *Pursuit of Truth,* pp. 37–8, respectively.

reference to the notion of the senses of constituent words. . .[25]

Sentence-meaning is primary when it comes to explaining what it is for words to have the sense they do, even though word-meaning is primary in another way: 'we *derive* our knowledge of the sense of any given sentence from our previous knowledge of the senses of the words that compose it. . .'[26] There is no commitment here to the idea that sub-sentential semantics concerns the theoretical or non-observational, much less the indeterminate. To see this, we need only consider a kind of approach which combines a Fregean truth-conditional account of sentence-meaning with an ideational conception of word-understanding. On this approach, one would understand 'the cat is on the mat' in virtue of the ideas one associated with 'cat', 'mat' etc., even though the semantic complexity of the signifying words could only be fully explained in terms of the sentence's truth conditions. If the ideas here are construed in the traditional style as objects of introspection or inner perception then there is no danger that they would be merely theoretical or non-observational, at least from the first-person point of view: while any supposed problems from the third-person point of view would naturally be regarded, in the first instance anyway, as epistemological, and hence as indicating underdetermination rather than indeterminacy. Now such an approach is, of course, hopeless for a whole variety of reasons. But it is not true that the key problem is a question-

[25] Dummett, *Frege*, pp. 4–5.   [26] Ibid., p. 5; emphasis added.

begging failure to theorize in terms of the radical case. So here we have the primacy of sentences without inscrutability of reference and impotence of intentionality. In the cat-idea *cats* are conceived.

To take this admittedly hopeless line is not to revert to what Davidson criticizes as the Building Block theory, which tries to explain directly the referential properties of sub-sentential expressions and then to characterize truth and other sentential semantic notions on this basis. Davidson gives a lightning historical sketch of that approach, and concludes that:

> as the problems become clearer and the methods more sophisticated, behaviourists and others who would give a radical analysis of language and communication have given up the building block approach in favour of an approach that makes the sentence the focus of empirical interpretation. And surely this is what we should expect. Words have no function save as they play a role in sentences. . .[27]

But the problem with this passage is that it deals simultaneously with two issues: (1) the question whether sentential semantics is prior to sub-sentential; and (2) the proposal to give a 'radical analysis of language and communication'. Perhaps sentences are prior but there is something wrong with the idea of radical analysis. Dropping it would not then equate with reverting to the Building Block theory. In other words: one might join Davidson in rejecting the ambition of

---

[27] Davidson, *Inquiries,* p. 220

defining truth in terms of independently understood sub-sentential reference etc., without thinking that linguistic concepts can be understood in the light of non-linguistic ones, which is what 'radical analysis' means here. It may be that, historically, the two projects – defining truth, 'reducing' semantics – have gone together: but there is clear blue logical water between them.

V

So I want to leave unquestioned the primacy of sentences doctrine and suggest instead that there *is* something wrong with the idea of 'radical analysis'. The impotence of inten-tionality result looks as straightforward a *reductio* of an approach to thought as one could imagine.[28] For present purposes, the key point here is that thinking, conceiving, doubting and so on can occur as *conscious* (and sharable) phenomena: there is such a thing as having direct conscious awareness as such of a piece of contentful thought, either one's own or someone else's. Content can be as much a constituent of the stream of consciousness – whatever *that* means – as itches or patches of red. Thus one may con-sciously feel an itch, 'see red', or suddenly think (or hear someone say) *that the cat is on the mat.* In the last kind of case, the propositional content figures in the same conscious domain as itches or flashes of red. Moreover, unsurprisingly, the content appears as structured appropriately: this is why

---

[28] Compare Searle, 'Indeterminacy', 124–7, 136–7.

one can intelligibly and consciously go on to infer *that there are cats*. In the context of all this – which was certainly Brentano's context – the claim that cat-thoughts have cats as intentional objects is not part of some underdetermined or relativized theoretical structure for delivering a theory of interpretation for 'cat'-utterances. Rather, it is an aspect of phenomenological analysis, part of the enterprise of saying what our conscious life is like in itself. That we can direct our thought and talk at cats rather than undetached cat-parts, not relative to this or that scheme imposed by someone else from outside but period, is a highly salient feature of this life. Any account of thought which denies this is simply, *literally*, failing to save the phenomena.

This is not to say that focusing on interpretation and linguistic behaviour is a mistake. On the contrary: If content-bearing states can be conscious, then at least part of knowing the consciousness of another falls under the general heading of knowing their intentional states. And to know an intentional state *as* the intentional state it is involves knowing it as the state *that thus and so*, i.e. involves knowing its content. So the enterprise of gathering knowledge about the consciousness of subjects overlaps with the overall project of interpreting them: of making sense of their behaviour, linguistic and otherwise, by e.g. seeing what they are doing and hearing what they are saying, and ascribing beliefs, desires and other intentional states to them. Knowing what it is like to be someone involves being able to interpret or understand them for oneself. It follows that a complete – that is phenomenologically adequate – 'account' of their conscious life must be *interpretational*: any 'account' of their consciousness which did not enable us to interpret them would thereby be incomplete, since it would not tell us what it is like to be them. This aspect of their phenomenology would be missing.[29]

All of this should make it plain that to emphasize the phenomenology of content is not to revert to a version of the traditional ideationism mentioned above, or to accept what Quine calls 'the myth of a museum in which the exhibits are meanings and the words are labels',[30] or to fall into the temptation warned against in this passage from Davidson:

> Perhaps someone ... will be tempted to say, 'But at least the speaker knows what he is referring to.' One should stand firm against this thought. The semantic features of language are public features. What no-one can, in the nature of the case, figure out from the totality of the relevant evidence cannot be part of meaning. And since every speaker must, in some dim sense at least, know this, he cannot even intend to use his words with a unique reference, for he knows that there is no way for his words to convey this reference to another.[31]

We do not need to make these mistakes because the point about the phenomenology of content does not concern the Cartesian theatre, but rather the interpersonal facts involved in consciously thinking, understanding and communicating. More generally, it is not even primarily a point about the

---

[29] For much more on this, see G. McCulloch, 'Bipartism and the Phenomenology of Content' (forthcoming).
[30] Quine, *Ontological Relativity*, p. 27.   [31] Davidson, *Inquiries*, p. 235.

first-person case,[32] but is equally a point about the public practice of understanding each other. In a recent discussion of what he calls 'understanding experience', Galen Strawson cites an excellent statement of this part of the matter from Schopenhauer:

> While another person is speaking, do we at once translate his speech into pictures of the imagination that instantaneously flash upon us and are arranged, linked, formed, and coloured according to the words that stream forth, and to their grammatical inflexions? What a tumult there would be in our heads while we listened to a speech or read a book! This is not what happens at all. The meaning of the speech is immediately grasped, accurately and clearly apprehended, without as a rule any conceptions of fancy being mixed up with it.[33]

Meaning figures in phenomenology not only in the first-person case, as when one is thinking consciously, but also in the third-person case, as when someone is speaking and one is aware of what they are saying (as when one interprets them success-fully). It figures there directly, unmediated, but there is no need to claim that we are infallible detectors of meaning, our own or those of others: we can certainly misinterpret (hear the wrong meaning), and whatever has ultimately to be said about privil-eged first-person knowledge, there are well-known problems with making too much of it. But we should maintain that meanings, others' as well as our own, can figure as integral

[32] *Pace* Searle, 'Indeterminacy', 126, 126–7, 141, 145.

[33] G. Strawson, *Mental Reality* (Cambridge, MA: MIT Press, 1994), p. 7, n4.

components of our conscious life. Moreover, these are indeed public features of the use of language, since the point is that public matters like speech, interpretation and communication are themselves fundamentally conscious phenomena. What I think is often what I consciously put into words; and suitable audiences frequently hear *that same thing*.

To say all this is to stand on its head Davidson's reasoning in the last passage quoted from him. Speakers have a very strong conviction that they *can* intend to use their words with a unique reference or intentional object, and that there are situations in which their words *do* convey this reference to another. Given also the point that meanings can be phenomenologically available, speakers have, if anything, more than a dim knowledge that 'what no-one can, in the nature of the case, figure out from the totality of the relevant evidence cannot be part of meaning'. So the correct conclusion to draw is that it is Davidson's conception of the relevant evidence that is suspect. His focus on the radical case simply excludes some of the evidence that is available to speakers when they understand one another's utterances: it excludes the phenomenology of thought and communication.

This now puts us in a position to see fairly easily why Davidson, despite his anti-behaviourism, moves directly from underdetermination to indeterminacy in the case of sub-sentential semantic reality. The answer lies in the passage under discussion, and specifically in this part of it:

> The semantic features of language are public features. What no-one can, in the nature of the case, figure out from the totality of the relevant evidence cannot be part of meaning.

This, I suggest, amounts to an *acknowledgement*, howsoever mishandled, that meanings are manifest: that the kind of content aimed at by a theory of interpretation is a phenomenological notion, something that can, for example, be directly seen and heard in the behaviour, linguistic and otherwise, of speakers. (Earlier, we encountered what amounts to a rather similar acknowledgement in Quine, when we quoted him as saying that 'There is nothing in linguistic meaning beyond what is to be gleaned from overt behaviour in observable circumstances.') Now if meaning is, indeed, a phenomenological notion, then of course there is a sense in which sub-sentential semantic reality *is* exhausted by its empirical reality, by what is available to our ordinary observations of the personal realm. I hear you say that the cat is on the mat, and *thereby* am (defeasibly) aware that you are directing your thinking at cats. However, if Davidson is to avoid Quine's radically *behaviouristic* conception of what it is for empirical reality to exhaust the whole of sub-sentential semantic reality, then he has to move to a richer conception of the empirical reality. In theorizing in terms of the radical case, he is trying to keep the empirical base thin in order to leave room for 'radical analysis'. But this procedure is in severe tension with the claim that *meanings* (rather than behaviouristic surrogates) are manifest. Yet only something like this claim – which he anyway rather appears to accept – could protect him from the charge of an unargued (or behaviouristic) slide from underdetermination to indeterminacy. So something has to give. If Davidson really is to occupy *principled* space between Quine's behaviourism, and a behaviour-rejecting mentalism that acquiesces in underdetermination but jibs at indeterminacy, albeit at the cost of trying to locate the essential determining facts behind linguistic behaviour, then the thin empirical base has to go. And it takes the notion of 'radical analysis', the primacy of the radical case, with it.[34]

It is very important to get this point right.[35] The temptation is to retort that what I am calling the phenomenological availability of meaning and intentionality boils down to something like: speakers evince beliefs or so-called knowledge about what their words and sentences mean; so, of course, one is inclined to make utterances such as '"cat" as we use it refers to cats, not to undetached cat-parts'. But if that is all the point comes to, then there is a simple Davidsonian reply: namely, such utterances are as open to the permutation trick as any others, so that although on one theory 'refers' refers to reference, on another it refers to p-reference, where for 'cat' to p-refer to cats is for it to refer to undetached cat-parts.

In reply: It is question-begging to assert that the point about phenomenology 'boils down to' the fact that

---

[34] This is not to say that reflection on the radical case has no merit at all. On the contrary, I think it can be used to make plausible the central insight of the *Verstehen* tradition that knowledge of minds as minds is fundamentally different from knowledge of body: see the brief mention of the epistemological Real Distinction in section VII below; also G. McCulloch, 'An Essentially Dramatic Idiom: Quine and the Attitudes' (forthcoming).

[35] Thanks here to my colleagues Harold Noonan and Jose Zalabardo.

speakers evince beliefs or so-called knowledge and make utterances about the meanings of their words, all of which are open to the permutation point. That should be, at best, the result of an argument that starts with the need for 'radical analysis' and ends with the inscrutibility of reference and the impotence of intentionality (somehow one needs to have moved from points about the artificially constructed radical case to a generalization that embraces the home case). But the present argument concerns the initial propriety of aiming for 'radical analysis' and its concomitant thin empirical base. If we do not make Quine's behaviouristic assumptions, it is not a *datum* that 'radical analysis' should be undertaken. On the contrary: I am claiming as a datum that in the course of our conscious, communal mental life we direct our thoughts upon objects, unrelativized, in the way claimed by Brentano. If this fact cannot be coped with by attempts at 'radical analysis', then so much the worse for concern with the radical case. As for my claim about what is a datum: assessment of that has to be left as an exercise for the reader. Do you find yourself now and again directing your attention at cats? Do you sometimes hear other people talking about cats? Or what?

VI

Naturally, a lot can be said about Davidson's analogy between sub-sentential semantics and the microphysical. But here I shall make two comments.

Suppose first that the analogy is strong. Then it is curious that Davidson should be so keen on 'radical analysis'. Even if, in the physical case, there is something relatively theory-neutral, a shadow of what traditional empiricism saw as the evidential basis of physical science, few would accept that this shadow exhausts the actual observational or phenomenological domain of scientific data. A lot of our ordinary observational classification of the passing show is not theoretically innocent: yet this is where the evidence for the underlying microphysical reality is gathered. This practically undeniable fact that theory taints the evidence gives rise to well-known problems: nevertheless, practically undeniable fact it is. Why should things be any different in the theory of meaning? Why shouldn't the way people appear to us be 'tainted' by semantic reality in just the same fashion? And if so, then oddly enough one might draw support here, from Davidson's own analogy with the scientific case, for the richer conception of the empirical reality of sub-sentential semantics canvassed above. The call for 'radical analysis' in the physical domain would be nothing less than a plea for a very unappealing empiricism. Why should this be any more appealing in the theory of meaning?

All of that, of course, is a standard response for behaviour-rejecting mentalists, who hold that genuine semantic reality is 'underlying' in the same way that microphysical reality is. But I am interested in offering Davidson a different thought, based on the idea that the analogy between sub-sentential semantics and the microphysical is weak (to say the least): a thought that is more in keeping with his own mis-handled point that meanings are manifest, part of the phenomenological domain.

It is not bold or interesting to complain that Quine's conception of 'the objective data' is tendentious: that is just another way of saying that it is behaviouristic, and therefore inadequate to its domain. The foregoing points about the phenomenology of content can then be seen as supporting the idea that adequate conceptions of thought require mentalism. But a lot here depends on what you mean by 'mentalism'. Behaviourism, at least when considered as an ideology as opposed to a methodology, centres on the determination to root out of our conception of the mind any suggestion of the occult. In practice this meant the elimination of mentalistic vocabulary or, at least, of any connotation such vocabulary may have of the inner, essentially private, or hidden. In so far as this ideology was part of a general positivism, it is not surprising that the mentalistic backlash should have involved the idea that mental reality is essentially a matter of the 'theoretical' underlying causes of behaviour – i.e. be behaviour-rejecting. But there is middle ground. I have claimed, in effect, that the 'behaviouristic' aspects of Davidson's account, evinced by its closeness to Quine's on many matters of substance, are a due if blurred reflection of the important point that meaning is a phenomenological notion. Equally, we might say that the incompatibility between this idea and Davidson's hope for 'radical analysis' reflects an aspect of mentalism: it reflects at least the thought that no adequate treatment of intentional matters can dispense with mentalistic, intentional vocabulary (something that Davidson himself accepts: for more on which, see below). All of this leaves in the air to what extent this vocabulary carries connotations of the inner causes of behaviour. But it is clear that one can make something of the thought that it does without going the whole behaviour-rejecting hog and regarding intentional reality as essentially 'theoretical'. Perhaps the distinction between genuine performance and mere simulation turns on the question of etiology. But it does not follow from this that such necessary conditions of cognition are also sufficient. And although I don't have the space to argue the point here, I think it can be shown that behaviour-rejecting mentalists, who make this sufficiency claim, are as unable to accommodate the phenomenology of content as those who theorize in terms of the radical case.[36] Quickly: think of the version of the ideational account of understanding sketched in section IV. I said there that the unavailability of ideas from the third-person point of view would naturally be regarded as epistemological. But, of course, things are much worse than that, as anyone knows who has considered the question of grafting a theory of communication on to such an account. The 'subjective' drops out as irrelevant: and nothing changes if we replace subjective items as traditionally conceived with expressions from the language of thought. The point is that since communication is both a public event and a sharing of thoughts, the bearers of thought-content themselves *have to be* public. That is one reason why Quine and Davidson are quite right to focus on linguistic behaviour when approaching the

---

[36] McCulloch, *The Mind and Its World,* chapters 5–8, and G. McCulloch, *From Malicious Demon to Evil Scientist: How Much World Does a Mind Need?* (Inaugural Lecture, University of Birmingham, 1997)

matter of intentionality. Where they go wrong is to focus on the radical case, since that simply washes away the public facts, the phenomenology, that they set out, insightfully, to capture. What is *really* required here, I am claiming, is behaviour-embracing mentalism: that is what the phenomenological facts dictate. And to say all this just is to say that the analogy between sub-sentential semantics and the microphysical is weak, or much worse.

VII

The foregoing has been critical of a salient aspect of Davidson's approach. So it is instructive and rather satisfying to note how easy it is to excise this aspect without warping the rest. One searches very hard to see why he follows Quine over the radical case. We noted a brief mention of not begging questions above, and the following passage actually contains an explicit argument:

> 'Theory of meaning' is not a technical term, but a gesture in the direction of a family of problems ... Central among the problems is the task of explaining language and communication by appeal to simpler, or at any rate different, concepts. It is natural to believe this is possible because linguistic phenomena are patently supervenient on non-linguistic phenomena.[37]

But the spirit of this passage is strangely counter to that of the following one on anomalous monism:

[37] Davidson, *Inquiries,* p. 215.

> Although the position I describe denies that there are
> psychophysical laws, it is consistent with the view that
> mental characteristics are in some sense ... supervenient
> on physical characteristics ... Dependence or
> supervenience of this kind does not entail reductibility
> through law or definition...[38]

The argument in the first passage is also weak, for reasons
given in this continuation of the second:

> if [supervenience did entail reducibility], we could reduce
> moral properties to descriptive, and this there is good
> reason to *believe* cannot be done.[39]

Furthermore, Davidson is quite emphatic that the mental
and the physical are fundamentally separate, answerable to
their own 'disparate commitments'.[40] What he appears to
gesture at hereabouts is some version of what I have elsewhere called the epistemological Real Distinction,[41] the central claim of the *Verstehen* tradition that knowledge of
minds as minds is fundamentally different from knowledge
of body. Here is what looks like a commitment:

> When we attribute a belief, a desire, a goal, an intention
> or a meaning to an agent, we necessarily operate within a
> system of concepts in part determined by the structure of

---

[38] D. Davidson, *Essays on Actions and Events* (Oxford: Oxford University
Press, 1980), p. 214.

[39] Ibid.   [40] Ibid., p. 222.

[41] McCulloch, *From Malicious Demon to Evil Scientist.*

426

> the beliefs and desires of the agent himself... this feature
> has no counterpart in the world of physics.[42]

Now all of this is entirely in keeping with Davidson's focus on *interpretation*, as well as the principle of charity and his truth-theoretic approach to meaning. More to the point, none of it is touched if the commitment to 'radical analysis' is abandoned. So why should Davidson have followed Quine so closely over the matter of the radical case, given that his arguments for so doing, such as they are, are weak, and the rest of his position does not require it? Summing up in 'Reply to Foster', he wrote that

> My way of trying to give an account of language and
> meaning makes essential use of such concepts as those of
> belief and intention, and I do not believe it is possible to
> reduce these notions to anything more scientific or
> behaviouristic. What I have tried to do is give an account
> of meaning (interpretation) that makes no essential use
> of unexplained *linguistic* concepts.[43]

Given his views about the tight interdependency between thought and talk, it is strange that he should discriminate them so emphatically. We should, of course, remember that the notion of irreducible belief and intention he accepts, thanks to his focus on the radical case, is infected by the impotence of intentionality and so somewhat removed from the pre-theoretical. What he claims to be irreducible is not what we think we have before the arguments for inscrutability of reference swing in. But this makes it even more

[42] Davidson, *Essays,* p. 230.   [43] Davidson, *Inquines,* p. 176.

mysterious why he should see such a large gulf between the mental and the linguistic. Anyway, for what it is worth, I suspect the following. In rejecting Quine's behaviourism, Davidson more or less unthinkingly moves to behaviour-rejecting mentalism, which involves regarding cognition as essentially a matter of what happens 'behind' behaviour. Then even given his claim that thought requires talk, the fact still remains that linguistic behaviour is not, in itself, essentially mental, even though the capacity to exhibit it is held necessary to the having of beliefs and similar cognitive states. Talk is fundamentally distinct from though fundamentally involved with thought. And *because* this is behav-iour-*rejecting* mentalism, talk must derive its 'intentional' or semantic properties from the underlying mental reality it purportedly reveals. Hence it is 'natural' (his word) to think that *linguistic* semantic concepts can be explained in terms of mental ones.

If that is right, then it is Davidson's unthinking recoil to behaviour-rejecting mentalism that leads him to keep in place the aim for 'radical analysis' even after Quinean behaviourism has been rejected. In fact, given the general point raised above about how theory infects evidence, this kind of mentalism does not sit easily with the idea of 'radical analysis', so the resulting position is unstable. But much more importantly, neither 'radical analysis' (I have argued here) nor behaviour-rejecting mentalism (I have argued elsewhere) can accommodate the phenomen-ology of content: and this is a much deeper point than the observation that theory infects evidence. So a much more promising tack is to drop the aim for 'radical analysis', and to persevere with the remaining bulk of Davidson's position as an articulation of a kind of behaviour-embracing mentalism, on which semantic reality is located in the public, phenomenological domain, the impotence of intentionality is avoided – and proper sense can be made of the point that meaning is manifest.

Externalism and Norms

CYNTHIA MACDONALD

W e think that certain of our mental states represent the world around us, and represent it in determinate ways. My perception that there is salt in the pot before me, for example, represents my immediate environment as containing a certain object, a pot, with a certain kind of substance, salt, in it. My belief that salt dissolves in water represents something in the world around me, namely salt, as having a certain observational property, that of dissolving. But what exactly is the relation between such states and the world beyond the surfaces of our skins? Specifically, what exactly is the relation between the *contents* of those states, and the world beyond our bodies?

I believe that the correct view of the relation between certain mental contents, the contents of at least some of our intentional states, and the world beyond our bodies is an *externalist* one. Crudely, externalism is the view that certain of our intentional states, states such as beliefs

I would like to thank Graham Macdonald, Graham Bird, Anthony O'Hear, Michael Martin, Scott Sturgeon, Jan Bransen and Marc Slors for comments and discussion of issues in this paper.

and desires, have contents that are *world-involving*.[1] Less crudely, it is the view that certain intentional states of persons, states such as beliefs and desires, have contentful natures that are individuation-dependent on factors beyond their bodies. My belief that salt dissolves in water, has a content, *that salt dissolves in water*, that is individuation-dependent on a certain substance in the world beyond my body, namely, salt.

The roots of externalism lie in the work of Hilary Putnam, who was concerned to show something, not specifically about the nature of mental states, but about the nature of meaning.[2] He argued that one's meaning what one does by a natural kind word, although intuitively a state of mind, is world-involving. It is world-involving because it is determined in part by the actual, empirically discoverable nature of something in the world external to one's body. So a person's meaning some-thing by a natural kind word cannot be determined independ-ently of that person's relation to the physical world around them.

Putnam reinforced this claim by invoking what is by now the familiar strategy of the twin earth thought experiments. These experiments invite us to suppose that the environments of two individuals might differ in certain ways while all the 'within-the-body' physical and phenomenological (or 'felt') facts about those individuals remain invariant. In that case, Putnam argued, the meanings of the words in those individuals' mouths would

---

[1] The term is Philip Pettit's and John McDowell's. See their 'Introduction' to *Subject, Thought, and Context*, ed. P. Pettit and J. McDowell (Oxford: Oxford University Press, 1986), pp. 1–15.

[2] See 'The Meaning of "Meaning"', in *Mind, Language, and Reality*, vol. 2 Cambridge University Press, 1975), pp. 215–71.

also vary: these within-the-body twins would then mean different things by their (indistinguishable) utterances.

Tyler Burge took the moral of the twin earth thought experiments one step further.[3] He argued that since, when a person is sincere, what she says is what she believes, the Putnam conclusion about meaning carries over to intentional states such as beliefs and desires. Burge argued that the twin earth thought experiments not only show that meaning is (partly) an external phenomenon, but that mental states like beliefs and desires, whose contents are typically specified by means of words whose meanings are determined by factors external to persons' bodies, are also partly external phenomena. Just as my twin and I might mean different things by our indistinguishable utterances of 'there is salt in the pot' because of differences in the chemical constitutions of superficially and phenomenologically indistinguishable substances to which we are related in our respective environments, so too might my twin and I think different thoughts when we think thoughts with those propositional contents.

The twin earth thought experiments have been used by Burge and others to support the externalist view that certain intentional states have contentful natures that are individuation-dependent on factors external to the bodies of persons who undergo them. Put like this, it may make look

---

[3] See, for example, 'Individualism and the Mental', in *Midwest Studies in Philosophy* 4 (Minneapolis: University of Minnesota Press, 1979), pp. 73–121; 'Other Bodies', in *Thought and Object: Essays on Intentionality*, ed. A. Woodfield (Oxford: Oxford University Press, 1982), pp. 97–120, and 'Individualism and Psychology', *The Philosophical Review* 95 (1986), 3–45.

as though there is one single, clear formulation of externalism and that there is agreement amongst externalists about what it entails with regard to the existence of objects beyond the bodies of persons who undergo intentional states with representational contents. But this is so far from being the case that part of my aim in this paper is to disentangle some of the different formulations and associated commitments of the view from others, in order to fix on what I take to be a central commitment common to all of them and to defend that commitment.

Externalist theses can be strong or weak, and they can be strong or weak in different kinds of ways. However, most theses apply in the first instance to contentful intentional types or kinds, such as the kind, *thinks that salt dissolves in water*. Many thinkers can think thoughts with this content, and when they do they think thoughts that fall under a single contentful kind.[4]

---

[4] See, for example, Burge, 'Individualism and Psychology', Jerry Fodor, 'Individualism and Supervenience', *Proceedings of the Aristotelian Society,* Supplementary Volume 60 (1986), 235–62, *Psychosemantics* (Cambridge, MA: MIT Press, 1986), and 'A Modal Argument for Narrow Content', *Journal of Philosophy* 88 (1991), and Gregory McCulloch, *The Mind and Its World* (London: Routledge, 1995). Many who are externalists with regard to contentful intentional kinds also endorse externalism with regard to individual states or events that fall under, or are of those kinds. Tyler Burge is one notable example; he is what might be called a *token* externalist as well as a *type* externalist (see 'Individualism and the Mental', and 'Individualism and Psychology', note 7). Token externalism is the view that the natures of individual intentional mental *events* or *states* are individuation-dependent on factors beyond persons' bodies. They are so because they are individuated by the contentful types or kinds under which they fall, which themselves are individuation-dependent on factors beyond persons' bodies.

It is this version of externalism that I wish to concentrate on in the remaining sections of this paper. In section I below, I briefly outline a small number of type or content externalist theses, in order to fix on a core commitment that they share. I then formulate type externalism in these terms. Then, in section II, I focus on a debate between

Since to be a mental event is to be an event of a contentful kind, and since contentful kinds are individuation-dependent on factors external to persons' bodies, mental events are themselves individuation-dependent on factors external to persons' bodies.

Despite this natural association of type with token externalism, it is possible to be a type externalist without embracing token externalism, and *vice versa*. Both of these possibilities have been argued for, and in my opinion both positions are defensible. In particular, the combination of type externalism and token internalism is defensible. Whether one is a token as well as a type externalist depends on whether one thinks that it is of the essence of any mental event which is of a contentful type that it be of a contentful type. This is not a question about the truth of the claim that, necessarily, each event that has intentional content has intentional content. That claim is obviously and uncontroversially true. It is a question, rather, about the truth of the claim that necessarily, each event that has intentional content *necessarily* has intentional content. And this claim is not obviously and uncontroversially true. Whether it is true depends on the truth of other views. For instance, it depends on whether non-reductive physicalism is true and contingent. If it is, then token externalism is false, since non-reductive physicalism is committed to the view that the essences of mental events are physical, not mental. It may be true that mental events, *qua* mental, cannot be individuated independently of the contentful types or kinds under which they fall; but it does not follow that these events cannot be individuated independently of the contentful kinds under which they fall. For that depends on whether these events are essentially mental events.

434

two very well-known adversaries, Tyler Burge and Jerry Fodor. This debate concerns the truth of anti-individualism, which differs from externalism in that it concerns how mental kinds are to be taxonomized *for the purposes of a scientific psychology*. However, the debate is instructive, since it helps to identify the *source* of individualism; of why both externalists and anti-individualists disagree with individualists with regard to the core commitment articulated in section I. Then, in section III, I defend Burge by anchoring the source of type externalism in a very general but distinctive argument, one that relies on the rationalistic normativity of the psychological domain. My defence trades on likenesses between psychological explanation and functional explanation in biology. If the defence succeeds, it succeeds equally for externalism and anti-individualism. Finally, in section IV, I conclude with some remarks about the consequences of this particular form of externalism.

I Varieties of Type Externalism

There is a central claim that almost all of the varieties of content externalism share, which concerns the dependency of contentful kinds on conditions or factors in the environment in which subjects are embedded.[5] To see this, we need

---

[5] McGinn (*Mental Content* (Oxford: Oxford University Press, 1989)) is an exception. He distinguishes between what he calls 'strong' and 'weak' externalism, and argues for the latter and against the former. By 'strong' externalism, McGinn means one which takes content-individuation to require the existence, in the environment in which a thinker is situated, of some object or objects external to the thinker's body. McGinn rejects this view, but endorses the weaker externalist view that

consider only a few of the ways in which type externalism is typically expressed.

Externalism is often expressed in terms of some kind of supervenience claim regarding the contentful natures of certain intentional types.[6] Broadly speaking, the

content-individuation requires the existence, in the world of the thinker, of some object or objects beyond that thinker's body.

This departure from most other externalism means that McGinn is not prepared to rest the truth of falsity of externalism on the existence of twin earth examples. Thus, he says:

> it understates the case to express the upshot of twin earth reflections as inconsistent with methodological solipsism, since those reflections imply strong externalism, not just weak. Such understatement can be misleading if it encourages the idea that the inapplicability of twin earth arguments to certain cases shows that internalism is true in those cases.
>
> You can be a weak externalist about a certain kind of content, and so reject methodological solipsism, and yet deny vehemently that a twin earth case can be given for the content at issue: that is in fact my position about certain kinds of content, as will become apparent. (*Mental Content*, p. 9, n. 13).

If McGinn is right, then the truth or falsity of externalism is not decided by whether twin earth examples exist: although the existence of a twin earth example may be decisive for externalism with regard to certain contents, other contents may be externalistically individuated even when a twin earth example is not forthcoming. Although I do not subscribe to McGinn's brand of externalism, I agree with him that the truth or falsity of the thesis is not anchored in the twin earth examples. However, because his version of externalism departs markedly from most others, I set it aside for present purposes.

[6] See, for example, Martin Davies, 'Aims and Claims of Externalist Arguments', *Philosophical Issues* 4 (1993), 227–149, where externalist theses are explicitly formulated in these terms. Also, see Brian McLaughlin and Michael Tye, 'Externalism, Twin-Earth, and

claim is that such types weakly (in the case of the twin earth thought experiments) or strongly (for thought experiments involving other possible worlds) supervene on factors beyond the bodies of persons.[7] However, this claim can itself be interpreted in a number of ways. The reason is that supervenience is a name for a very general co-variance relation, one which states that things cannot differ (or vary) in one respect without differing (or varying) in another, and this covers many different types of case.[8] What is related by supervenience, and how it is related, can differ greatly from case to case; and the strength of that relation may vary also, in accordance with variation in the objects related and the nature of the relation. All of this will make a difference to how the claim of supervenience is to be understood, and whether it is likely to be true in any particular case. In short, supervenience itself is a name for a class of theses that may

Self-knowledge', in *Knowing Our Own Minds,* ed. C. Wright, B. Smith, and C. Macdonald (Oxford: Oxford University Press, forthcoming), note 39, where externalism is formulated in terms of supervenience, and Burge, 'Individualism and Psychology', where individualism is formulated in terms of supervenience, externalism being the negation of that thesis.

[7] The Putnam twin earth thought experiments concern weak supervenience, since Putnam envisaged twin earth as being a planet in our own universe, and so in the same possible world. Twins are members of different linguistic communities, but communities within the same possible world.

[8] See Frank Jackson, 'Armchair Metaphysics', in *Philosophy in Mind: The Place of Philosophy in the Study of Mind,* ed. M. Michael and J. O'Leary-Hawthorne (Dordrecht: Kluwer Academic Publishers, 1994), pp. 23–42, who characterizes supervenience in similar terms, as lack of independent variation.

concern different objects, different kinds of relations between them, and different strengths of relations, each thesis itself requiring independent explanation and defence.[9]

[9] For example, there are supervenience relations between logically or conceptually related properties, such as being coloured and being red, supervenience relations between what we might call 'metaphysically' related properties, such as moral or aesthetic properties and psychological ones, or psychological properties and physical ones, and supervenience relations between causally related properties, such as those that figure in causal laws. All of these conform to the formula that is thought to characterize supervenience relations generally, namely, no change in supervenient property without a change in subvenient property. So no psychological change without a physical change, no aesthetic change without a physical change, no change in effect property without a change in cause property. But the relations are really very different in these different types of cases. Although they all involve a relation between properties, they differ in the types of properties related, and they differ in the kind of relation that is thought to hold between them. Other theses differ from these in relating, not properties, but regions of worlds or worlds themselves, or events or states.

Global supervenience claims typically concern worlds or regions of worlds. See, for example, Terence Horgan, 'Supervenience and Microphysics', *Pacific Philosophical Quarterly* 63 (1983), 29–43.

Matters are more complicated still, since the strength of the dependency relations associated with these different kinds of supervenience relations also varies considerably. For example, the dependency relation associated with being coloured and being red is said to be logically or conceptually necessary. But this is not so for the relation that is thought to hold between moral and aesthetic properties and psychological properties, or between moral and aesthetic properties and physical properties. Here the relation seems to be weaker than one of logical-cum-conceptual necessity. It seems, rather, to be either metaphysically necessary, where this is understood not to require conceptual necessity, or physically necessary, a necessity that is weaker still, requiring only compatibility with the existing laws of nature in this world.

Given this variety, one cannot expect there to be just one externalist thesis associated with any given claim of supervenience. And indeed there is not. Some have held that externalism commits one to the view that contentful intentional properties, properties associated with contentful kinds such as *thinks that salt dissolves in water,* actually *entail* the existence of objects or kinds of objects in the world beyond the skins of persons.[10] This, it is said, is because externalism is committed

---

[10] See, for example, Martin Davies, 'Externalism, Architecturalism, and Epistemic Warrant', in *Knowing Our Own Minds,* ed. Wright et al., and B. McLaughlin and M. Tye, 'Externalism, Twin-Earth, and Self-Knowledge', same volume. The twin earth thought experiments are standardly construed as supporting conceptually necessary externalist theses. This is what lies behind arguments of the kind that Michael McKinsey has advanced to show that externalism is incompatible with privileged access, or authoritative self-knowledge. His argument depends on externalism being committed to the claim that it is a conceptual truth that, for some thought content, *C,* which has externalistic individuation conditions (such as *that water is transparent),* it is a conceptual truth that if one is thinking that *C,* then *P,* where *P* is a proposition that cannot be known *a priori* (such as *water exists).* See Michael McKinsey, 'Anti-individualism and Privileged Access', *Analysis* 51 (1991), 9–16. For a reply which denies that externalism is committed to such a claim, see Anthony Brueckner, 'What an Anti-individualist Knows *A priori*', *Analysis* 52 (1992), 111–18. But many externalist theses do not purport to be conceptually necessary. See, for example, Fred Dretske, *Knowledge and the Flow of Information,* (Cambridge: MA: MIT Press, 1980) and *Explaining Behaviour: Reasons in a World of Causes* (Cambridge, MA: MIT Press, 1988), Ruth Millikan, *Language, Thought and Other Biological Categories* (Cambridge, MA: MIT Press, 1984), David Papineau, *Reality and Representation* (Oxford: Basil Blackwell, 1987), and Fodor, *Psychosemantics.* There are differences between the view known as anti-individualism and externalism. Fodor, for example, explicitly distinguishes the two, and claims that externalism is true, but anti-individualism is not (see 'A Modal Argument for Narrow Content').

to the claim that it is a *conceptual* truth that, for some propositional content C (such as *that salt dissolves in water*), and some proposition, P, not knowable *a priori* (such as *salt exists*), if a thinker knows that C, then P. Thus, for example, externalism is committed to the claim that it is a conceptual truth that if a thinker is thinking that water is transparent, then water exists.[11] If this is so, then it must be conceptually necessary that contentful properties supervene on factors beyond the bodies of subjects that undergo states with those properties.

Others deny that externalism is committed to anything as strong as this claim.[12] Although it requires that the contents of certain intentional states be *object-dependent*, this is not a matter that can be known *a priori*, since one cannot know *a priori* that certain concepts, or propositional

---

Externalism is a view about how the contents of intentional states, states with propositional content, are correctly individuated. Anti-individualism, on the other hand, is a view about how the contents of intentional states are, or should be, individuated *for the purposes of a scientific psychology,* i.e. for the purposes of (causal) explanation in psychology. The distinction between externalism and anti-individualism raises important questions about the nature of psychological explanation and the nature of scientific explanation and taxonomy in general. However, these issues are largely irrelevant to the present discussion, and so the distinction will not play a role in the argument to be developed.

[11] McLaughlin and Tye ('Externalism') have pointed out that no type externalist seems actually to have held a view this strong. Brueckner ('What an Anti-individualist Knows'), in his reply to McKinsey ('Anti-individualism') (whose argument is directed at Burge), points out that Burge (in 'Other Bodies') actually argues against this view.

[12] Burge ('Other Bodies') is one. See also Fodor (*Psychosemantics*), Millikan (*Language, Thought, and Other Biological Categories*), Papineau (*Reality and Representation*), and Dretske (*Knowledge and the Flow of Information* and *Explaining Behaviour*).

contents, are object-dependent. This seems especially plausible in the case of natural kind contents.[13]

Still others claim that externalism commits one to
something stronger than a mere claim of object-dependency
but weaker than a claim of conceptual entailment, since it
requires dependency on objects with which persons causally
interact in their environments.[14] Teleological externalist
theses, which require that content supervenes on the causal
history of subjects and their interactions with objects in their
environments, are theses of this kind. These are very different kinds of theses than either of the two just mentioned,

[13] The argument is this. Whether a concept is a natural kind concept
cannot be known *a priori,* since it cannot be known *a priori* that there
are natural kinds (and according to at least one version of externalism
there can be no natural kind concepts without natural kinds). This can
only be known *a posteriori,* if at all, since whether or not there are
natural kinds is an empirical matter. But if it cannot be known *a priori*
that the concept of salt is a natural kind concept because it is not
knowable *a priori* that there are natural kinds, then it cannot be a
conceptual truth that if one is thinking that water dissolves in water,
then salt exists. See Brueckner, 'What an Anti-individualist Knows'.

[14] I am thinking of Millikan, *Language, Thought, and other Biological
Categories,* Dretske, *Knowledge and the Flow of Information* and
Explaining Behaviour, Jerry Fodor, *Psychosemantics,* and Papineau,
Reality and Representation. It is difficult to know where to place
McGinn (*Mental Content*). On the one hand, he rejects the
requirement of causal interaction with instances of the natural kind by
individuals who possess concepts of that kind (and in this he commits
himself to a thesis weaker than Millikan's and others), and on the other
he seems to think that a thinker's thinking such contents *conceptually*
entails that objects exist beyond the bodies of subjects who think them.
For more on this, see McLaughlin and Tye, 'Externalism'.

and failure to distinguish them can only lead to confusion about the basic commitments of externalism and about whether externalism is itself a plausible or implausible doctrine.

These people disagree about the strength of the relation between the subvenient and the supervenient in externalist theses. Others disagree about the *sorts* of objects related. Externalists may take their commitment to externalism to entail the existence primarily of individual things, corresponding to the contents of singular thoughts such as the thought that Cicero was a Roman orator, or demonstrative thoughts such as the thought that this computer has a coloured monitor.[15] Others may take the view to entail the existence of natural kinds of things, such as tigers, salt and water (corresponding to natural kind thoughts), but not necessarily to any individual instances of such kinds.[16] Others still may take the view to entail the existence of both natural kinds and instances of such kinds with which persons who undergo thoughts with contents that are individuation-dependent on such kinds interact causally.[17] Finally(!), still others may take the view to entail the existence of artefactual kinds, such as sofas and chairs (corresponding

[15] See John McDowell, 'On the Sense and Reference of a Proper Name', *Mind* 86 (1977), and Gareth Evans, 'Understanding Demonstratives', in *Meaning and Understanding*, ed. H. Parret and J. Bouveresse (Berlin: W. De Gruyter, 1981), pp. 280–303, and *The Varieties of Reference* (Oxford: Clarendon Press, 1982), chapters 4–8.

[16] See McGinn, *Mental Content*.

[17] See Putnam, 'The Meaning of "Meaning"'.

to thoughts concerning socially determined kinds).[18] Since these views are compatible with one another, externalists may take the view to commit them to some combination of the above commitments.

Despite all of these differences, however, type or content externalists are united in denying that the contentful nature of any intentional kind supervenes only on factors within the bodies of the subjects that undergo states of that kind. So all forms of externalism are committed to some kind of supervenience claim with regard to certain contentful intentional types. The claim is that certain intentional contents supervene on factors beyond person's bodies, in the sense that subjects' intentional states can vary or change with regard to their contents without varying with regard to all of their intrinsic physical properties.[19] Given the variation amongst externalists in what factors these may be, this claim is best formulated in terms of the negation of an *individualist* supervenience thesis. And since variation in supervenient properties requires variation in subvenient ones, so that sameness with regard to subvenient properties prohibits the possibility of difference with regard to the

---

[18] See Burge, 'Individualism and the Mental'.

[19] I leave open the issue of whether such variation would entail variation in phenomenological, or 'felt' properties. It may be that variation in factors beyond the body of an individual would affect not only contentful states such as beliefs and thoughts, but also sensation states such as perceptual experiences. This is so, for example, for externalists who think that there is no non-conceptual content (see, for example, John McDowell, *Mind and World* (Oxford: Oxford University Press, 1995)).

supervenient ones, we can formulate the negation of that thesis as follows:

1. It is not (conceptually, metaphysically, physically) necessary that, for any two individuals x and y and any contentful property M, if x and y are indiscernible with regard to all of their intrinsic physical properties P, then x and y are indiscernible with regard to M.

Or,

2. It is (conceptually, metaphysically, physically) possible that, for any two individuals x and y and any contentful property M, x and y are indiscernible with regard to all of their intrinsic physical properties P, but discernible with regard to M.

What this says is that it is possible for two individuals to be the same with regard to their intrinsic physical properties but different with regard to their contentful mental properties. Short of a specific form of dualism, namely an internalist one, this possibility can only be because the natures of contentful kinds depend on factors or conditions external to the bodies of persons who undergo states of those kinds.[20]

---

[20] One might think that dualism alone is sufficient to account for the truth of this claim. However, dualism is silent on the internalism/externalism issue. It is consistent with dualism that mental contents should be individuation-dependent on factors external to the bodies of thinkers (and so external to the mind). See McCulloch, *The Mind and Its World,* p. 227, note 5.

Versions of externalism that are articulated in terms of this general supervenience claim are sometimes called *modal externalist theses.*[21] These are concerned with the existence of twin earth examples. Since the twin earth examples make explicit the dependency of contentful kinds on factors or conditions external to subject's bodies, implicit in supervenience formulations of externalism is a claim which is sometimes called *constitutive externalism.* This is the claim that the correct philosophical account of the natures of certain contentful types takes them to have natures that depend on factors or conditions that exist beyond the bodies of individual subjects that undergo states of those kinds.[22]

---

[21] This is Davies's terminology. See 'Aims and Claims of Externalist Arguments', p. 227-8. See also his 'Externalism, Architecturalism, and Epistemic Warrant'.

[22] As Martin Davies puts it, constitutive externalism says that

> the most fundamental philosophical account of what it is for a person or animal to be in the mental states in question does advert to the individual's physical or social environment, and not only to what is going on within the spatial and temporal boundaries of the creature. ('Aims and Claims of Externalist Arguments', 230).

Davies correctly points out that one can establish a constitutive externalist thesis by establishing that modal *individualism* is false, i.e. that the supervenience claim (1) stated above is true, but that one cannot establish modal externalism just by establishing that constitutive externalism is true. It may be, for example, that although constitutive externalism is true, modal externalism is false because there is a necessary connection between subjects' intrinsic physical properties and factors or conditions beyond that subjects' bodies, so that an environment in which the contents of subjects' intentional

Constitutive externalism is the view I want to defend. Although it is a common strategy to employ the twin earth examples to establish it, I want to defend the view in a more direct way. The twin earth examples are best viewed as a kind of counterfactual test of the truth or otherwise of constitutive externalism. This test is meant to flesh out and validate intuitions about the object-dependence of contentful kinds. However, the test is only as persuasive as the intuitions that prompt it. If one is inclined to think that mental contents are object-dependent, then one will be inclined to accept that the twin earth examples are really possible and that they establish such object-dependence. If on the other hand, one is inclined to think that mental contents are not object-dependent, then one will be inclined to think either that the twin earth examples are not possible or that they do not show that mental contents are object-dependent.[23]

---

states varied would necessarily be an environment in which their intrinsic physical properties also varied.

[23] This emerges in debates such as that between Burge and Fodor concerning the truth or falsity of anti-individualism. Burge argues that attention to actual descriptive and explanatory practices in psychology reveals that the taxonomy of both intentional and nonintentionally described behaviour and the taxonomy of intentional states to be non-individualistic. For the interpretation of these practices fails to respect local supervenience, and this is supported by the twin earth thought experiments. However, his arguments for anti-individualism, based on these arguments, have been charged with presuming the truth of anti-individualism. In a similar vein, Burge effectively accuses Fodor's arguments for individualism, which also make use of twin earth thought experiments, of presuming the truth of individualism. Fodor

I want, therefore, to ground the intuitions on which that test is based in certain features of actions and their explanation, where the relevant actions are ones based on perception. Like Burge, I see the source of externalism as lying in our actual descriptive and explanatory practices. And I believe that attention to these practices can help to explain certain of our intuitions in the twin earth cases. But the argument for externalism can be mounted

argues that since whether or not twins have type-identical states depends on whether they have the same causal powers, and since sameness and difference of causal powers must be assessed across contexts rather than within them (casual power being a counterfactual notion), whether twins have type-identical intentional states depends on whether their states have the same causal powers across contexts. Burge agrees, but argues that twin earth considerations cannot determine and distinguish causal powers of intentional kinds because one cannot decide which contexts are relevant for determining and distinguishing causal powers without making assumptions about the kinds in question. To suppose that the actual environment external to subjects' bodies is not relevant to determining causal powers, and so taxonomy of contentful kinds, is already to assume individualism. The moral for the twin earth thought experiments is that they play a more peripheral role in adjudicating between individualism and anti-individualism. The reason is that their employment is evidently not independent of individualistic/anti-individualistic assumptions. See the debate between Burge and Fodor in *Philosophy of Psychology: Debates on Psychological Explanation*, (ed.) C. Macdonald and G. Macdonald (Oxford: Basil Blackwell, 1995), containing Burge's 'Individualism and Psychology' and Fodor's 'A Modal Argument for Narrow Content', with a commissioned reply by Burge.

447

independently of the twin earth cases. So our intuitions concerning externalism can be vindicated without appeal to them.

The argument that I develop specifically concerns thoughts and other intentional states whose contents, widely construed, concern natural kinds, such as salt and water.[24] I believe that it can be generalized to other sorts of case, but I shall not attempt that here.

II   The Source of Externalism

It is common in debates between externalists and individualists for both parties to appeal to behavioural considerations in support of their claims about the individuation of contentful kinds. But it is important to see how this appeal is put to work in arguments for and against externalism, and how little it establishes in the way of externalist or individualist conclusions.

---

[24] In fact, nothing in the argument to follow requires commitment to any doctrine about natural kinds, even though the examples concern what many would consider to be natural kinds. Natural kinds are typically employed in twin earth thought experiments in order to bolster the view that twin earth twins might have thoughts that are distinct despite the phenomenological indistinguishability of the objects or substances to which their thoughts relate in their respective environments. However, the thesis that is being defended here is constitutive externalism, not twin earth externalism. Further, the examples on which the argument is mounted make reference only to the observable effects on normal observers of objects in their environments.

Consider, for example, the debate between Tyler Burge and Jerry Fodor. Burge maintains that explanatory practices in psychology supports externalism/anti-individualism because the explananda in many cases, when they are behaviour, are commonly and clearly understood to be behaviour, relationally understood as involving relations between organisms and their environments.[25] Thus, he appeals to the fact that one distinguishes a heart from a waste pump by its biological function in the organisms in which it performs its function, which cannot be determined to be what it is independently of the causal history of its ancestors in organisms of the same and similar kinds. Its function cannot be specified independently of relations it bears to its surrounding environment, and the way it is embedded in that environment.

However, Fodor does not deny that many of the behaviours in which intentional creatures engage, intentionally described, are to be understood as involving relations between organisms and their environments. What he denies is that such relations are *relevant* to the *taxonomy* of intentional content, at least for the purposes of causal explanation employing such content. They are not relevant because they do not make a difference to the causal powers of contentful kinds. And the individuation of contentful kinds is sensitive only to their causal powers. Thus, he reasons that because twin earth twins are molecular duplicates and so their actual

[25] See 'Individualism and Psychology', and 'Intentional Properties and Causation', in *Philosophy of Psychology*, ed. Macdonald and Macdonald, pp. 226–35.

and counterfactual behaviours are identical in relevant respects, the causal powers of their mental states are identical in relevant respects. They therefore belong to the same natural kind of purposes of psychological explanation, and individualism is true.[26]

Fodor recognizes that this argument can be turned on its head simply by denying that the actual and counterfactual behaviours of me and my twin are identical in relevant respects. After all, when I am thirsty, I reach for water, whereas when my twin is thirsty, she reaches for twater.[27] Since the behaviours are not identical, neither are the causal powers of the mental states which explain them. Inasmuch as externalists and individualists are agreed that differences in behaviour, non-intentionally described, are not what is at issue, but rather differences in behaviour, *intentionally* described, it seems that this argument for individualism does not go through.

Fodor, however, is not perturbed by this. He argues that the question of whether the relevant intentional kinds of twins are the same is a matter of their causal potentialities and that this is to be determined, not *within* contexts, but *across* them. So, for example, the fact that my beliefs on earth cause me to drink water whereas my twin's on twin earth cause her to drink twater does not show that these beliefs have distinct causal potentialities. What is relevant is

---

[26] Fodor, 'A Modal Argument for Narrow Content'. Fodor has since given up his commitment to narrow content. See *The Elm and The Expert* (Cambridge, MA: MIT Press, 1994).

[27] See Burge, 'Individualism and Psychology'.

whether my twin's beliefs *would* cause her to drink water on earth and whether my beliefs *would* cause me to drink twater on twin earth. By this (cross-context counterfactual) criterion, the causal potentialities of our beliefs are the same and the beliefs are type-identical.

This response doesn't quite work, since it is still vulnerable to the charge that when I utter the words 'Gimme water' on earth, I get what I ask for, but when I utter the words 'gimme water' on twin earth, I do not get what I ask for. Similarly for my twin. Our behaviours, intentionally described as water/twater requests, do not have the same causal powers, even across contexts.

Fodor attempts to patch the criterion up by providing a general condition on when differences in properties of causes are differences in causal powers. His claim is that differences in properties of causes are differences in causal powers when those properties are *not conceptually connected* to the effect properties for which they are responsible. By these lights, such differences as there are in intentional behaviour between me and my twin cannot be attributable to differences in the contentful properties of the states which cause that behaviour, widely construed as beliefs about water and beliefs about twater. For those properties are conceptually connected to the properties of the behaviour which makes them intentional, i.e. actions, namely, water requests and twater requests. My water requests and your twater requests may differ, but this difference in behaviour does not mark a difference in content between my water beliefs and your twater beliefs, since the contentful properties of these beliefs, widely construed as beliefs about water and beliefs about twater, are conceptually connected to the behaviour those beliefs cause.

What this debate between Fodor and Burge brings out clearly is that one can agree (1) that intentional content is to be taxonomized by its relation to behaviour, (2) that behaviour is decisive in determining the truth or falsity of externalism and (3) that behaviour is to be taxonomized for psychological purposes intentionally in ways that involve relations between organisms and their environment, and yet (4) *still* disagree about whether externalism is true or false. Burge and Fodor agree on all of these points, and even on the further two points that (5) mental kinds are to be taxonomized in terms of their causal powers for the purposes of psychological explanation and (6) psychological explanation is causal explanation. But despite all of this agreement, they disagree about whether externalism is true.

What this shows, I think, is that the truth or falsity of externalism, inasmuch as it turns on the broad/narrow content distinction, depends on the issue of the explanatory efficacy of broad or wide content. That is to say, it depends on the issue of whether, in at least some cases of the explanation of action, the contentful kinds implicated in such explanations, to do their explanatory work, must be individuated widely, i.e. by relation to factors that exist beyond the surfaces of the bodies of organisms who undergo states of these contentful kinds. Burge thinks they must because individuation of contentful kinds is individuation by causal powers, but this is not independent of assumptions about the kinds in question. Contentful kinds, like biological-functional kinds, are not only causally but conceptually connected with their effect properties. So the taxonomy of the cause properties is not independent of conceptual connections with their effect properties.[28]

In Burge's view, this makes psychological explanation, like functional explanation in biology, explanation which is causal but which breaches the 'Humean' requirement of connecting effects with causes non-conceptually.[29] Burge acknowledges that it breaches this requirement, but does not see that it presents any problem for the view that psychological explanation is causal explanation, since he rejects the 'Humean' requirement.

Fodor, on the other hand, thinks that the contentful kinds implicated in the explanation of intentional behaviour or action need to be individuated narrowly, i.e. individualistically. This is because, although he agrees with Burge that individuation of contentful kinds is individuation by causal

---

[28] Thus he claims,

> One could plausibly claim that it is a conceptual truth that hearts differ from twin waste-pumps in that they pump blood. One could plausibly claim that it is conceptually necessary that if something is a heart, then when functioning normally, it pumps blood.
> ('Intentional Properties and Causation', p. 233).

[29] According to Burge, that is. See 'Intentional Properties and Causation'. In this Burge concurs with Neander ('Functions as Selected Effects: The Conceptual Analyst's Defense', *Philosophy of Science* 58 (1991), 168–84.). But note that Millikan (*Language, Thought, and Other Biological Categories*) denies that there are such conceptual connections between functional properties and the effect properties to which their taxonomy is sensitive. Similarly for intentional properties.

powers, he accepts the Humean requirement that causes and effects must be individuated in terms of properties that are conceptually independent of one another if the cause properties are to be genuinely causally potent with regard to their effect properties and psychological explanation is to be genuinely causal explanation. Since psychological explanation is genuine causal explanation, it too must meet this requirement. By that standard, widely individuated content gets ruled out from being genuinely causally potent, hence genuinely explanatorily potent.

So the crucial issue that divides Burge and Fodor is whether the explanatory potency of intentional kinds requires that such kinds meet the Humean requirement on causal explanation of being conceptually independent of their effect properties. I think that Burge is correct in his claim that psychological explanation, explanation of actions by means of states with intentional content, works by way of broadly conceptual connections between explanans property and explanandum property. Such contentful properties do their explanatory work because they have causal powers which relate them conceptually to their effect properties.

However, unlike Burge, I believe that attention to the ways in which psychological explanation is like explanation in functional biology shows it to be of a distinctive, normative noncausal type. Moreover, I think that by attending to the ways in which contentful properties are like biological-functional ones, and unlike physical ones, it is possible to mount an argument for externalism that does not lead to the kind of stalemate that seems to be the inevitable result of debates between externalists like Burge and individualists like Fodor.

The dispute is between those who agree that taxonomy of contentful properties is taxonomy by causal powers but disagree about whether this supports externalism because they disagree about whether such taxonomy meets the Humean requirement that for a property to be a distinctive causal power, it must be contingently or non-conceptually related to its effect property. But this dispute seems to me to be unresolvable within the narrow confines of externalism. It simply relocates the disagreement in the issue of whether psychological explanation is like functional explanation in biology or like causal explanation in such sciences as physics. However, one needs a principled reason for adjudicating between these two alternatives.

I want to try to provide that principled reason by showing that and how the explanation of action by intentional content is like functional explanation in biology in a certain important respect. First, I shall mount the argument. Then I will locate the source of the externalist commitment, and indicate how like it is to the source of externalism in functional biology.

III An Argument for Externalism

I begin with the observation that the truth or otherwise of externalism does not depend on whether the explananda of psychological explanations are actions construed widely or actions construed narrowly (but intentionally). As the debate between Burge and Fodor illustrates, one can agree with an externalist that the explananda of psychological explanations are actions, widely construed, and disagree about whether this shows externalism to be true. However, I think it plausible that contentful states are employed as explanantia of both sorts of actions. Sometimes, for example, we may wish to explain why a subject washes her clothing with water (rather than with sand, or with Coca-Cola), where what seems to need explaining is why she engages in a particular *type* of action with regard to a particular object or type of object. But there are other cases where what we wish to explain is not why a subject engages in a certain type of action with respect to a particular object or type of object, but where we simply wish to explain why that subject engages in actions of a particular type at all. Sometimes, for example, we may want to explain why a subject eats every day, or goes to bed at night, where the actions that serve as explananda are actions, narrowly construed. It may be that a subject cannot eat without eating something, but *what* is eaten is not what one wants to explain. What one wants to explain is the *activity* of eating, or the *activity* of washing, itself. Phenomena like these are actions, narrowly construed.

Narrow actions seem to be just the sort of phenomena whose explanation would only require narrow content, if any phenomena are. So let us concentrate for the moment on actions, narrowly construed. If the explanation of even these cannot be effected without appeal to wide content, then externalism will have been vindicated.

Narrow-act explanation seems to require no mention of any particular object, or of any of a range of objects, on which such actions depend. Because of this, the states which explain and make intelligible such behaviour also seem to be capable of doing so by means of narrow content. That such actions can be construed individualistically evidently supports the view that the contentful kinds that are required to explain them by making them intelligible can also be construed individualistically. For if their taxonomy does not depend on the existence of any particular object or range of objects, then they can evidently be made intelligible, or explained, by means of contents that also do not depend on the existence of any particular object or range of objects.

This idea can be further supported by a twin earth thought experiment. Consider Sue, who washes with water, and her twin, who washes with twater. Although the activity of washing requires that there be *something* that one washes with, the activity itself, *what* Sue and her twin do with the respective stuff, is the *same kind of thing*. Since the activities are the same, it is plausible to hold that so too are the contentful kinds which explain them.

I do not think, however, that this establishes individualism. The reason is that the individuation of actions, narrowly construed, can only take place against the background of wide-act individuation; and wide acts are only made intelligible by states with wide content.

Actions are not only purposeful; at least sometimes they involve interaction with objects. Further, when these actions are successful, that they are object-involving is not an accidental feature of them. If such actions were not at least sometimes non-accidentally object-involving, they could not be purposeful. But if they could not be purposeful, they could not be actions at all.

The point here is not that there must be successful actions if there are to be actions at all. It is true that actions, in being purposeful movements, *aim* at success. But this is consistent with the possibility that no action is actually successful; that creatures should regularly fail to succeed at what they aim to accomplish by moving their bodies in various ways.

So it is not a necessary, but a contingent matter that there are successful actions in the world. It is a contingent matter that there are objects in the world with which human beings engage, and it is a contingent matter that by engaging with these objects they are both changed by and change the world. But that there are such objects with which human beings engage, and that they at least sometimes do so successfully, is, I take it, common ground between externalists and individualists.

Given that there are successful actions in the world, intentions that engage with the world are required to make them intelligible. Without such intentions, one cannot make intelligible the non-accidental connection between action and object when an action is successful. This is because without intentions that engage with the world, there is an explanatory gap which leaves it mysterious why that connection is non-accidental. One makes it intelligible by citing intentions concerning objects that match the objects with which subjects non-accidentally engage in their behaviour. The connection between purpose and the world beyond the body is required because successful object-involving action is non-accidentally successful. Wide content is needed to explain successful action, which happens to, but need not, occur.

Think, now, of Sue, who washes every day. We, who want to make intelligible that activity, explain it in terms of her desire to make herself clean and her belief that by washing she will make herself clean. However, that belief and desire will only serve to explain her activity against the background of assumptions she has about the sorts of stuff that makes things clean. For not every substance is such that it can make things clean. Water can make things clean. Sand can make things clean. But Coca-Cola cannot make things clean. Nor can tar, mud or hydrochloric acid.

In short, the intelligibility of *what* one is doing, narrowly construed as a successful activity, takes place against the background of assumptions about what it is *appropriate* to do it *with*. One does not make intelligible Sue's activity of washing every day just by mentioning her desire to make herself clean and her belief that by washing she will make herself clean. Her activity simply does not count as an activity of washing if she does it with mud, or with Coca-Cola, or with tar. And here I mean: *successful* activity. Her movements may be the movements of someone who takes herself to be washing. But movements are not actions; and their classification as actions, even narrowly construed, depends on what the appropriate objects are towards which they are directed. One's actions being the successful actions they are *depends* on the appropriateness of such objects to them.

So narrow-act taxonomy is made intelligible against the background of wide-act taxonomy, taxonomy which is object-dependent at least to the extent that it requires appropriate objects in the environment in which agents are embedded towards which they can successfully act. And given that this is so, the explanation of even narrow acts by states with narrow content is made intelligible against the background of explanation of wide acts by states with wide or broad content. Sue's activity of washing herself is made intelligible by her desire to make herself clean and her belief that by washing she will make herself clean, only if she also has beliefs about what it is appropriate to wash with. Her success in *washing* depends on this. That is to say, her *washing* depends on this, since the taxonomy of her behaviour, narrowly construed, is not independent of what objects are appropriate to wash *with*.

Even her unsuccessful attempts at washing, using inappropriate substances such as tar or mud, require this. For her unsuccessful attempts are ones in which she mistakenly *takes herself* to be washing. But if she takes herself to be washing, then she takes herself to be doing what agents do when they wash. Sue can only be mistaken about whether she is washing if she has correct beliefs about the washing, which require beliefs about what it is appropriate to wash with.

These observations about successful actions and appropriate objects may seem insufficient to establish externalism. For externalism requires that the contents of at least some intentional states be individuation-dependent on factors beyond their bodies. Sue's water content must be a *water* content, not just a content that depends on the existence of some substance or other. And it is not clear that appeal to successful actions towards appropriate objects establishes such dependence.

Consider Sue's twin. She successfully does with twater what Sue does with water. And twater is, on *twin* earth, appropriate to wash with. On twin earth, twater gets things clean. Appeal to considerations about successful actions towards appropriate objects fails to discriminate between Sue's behaviour and her twin's behaviour, narrowly construed. Does this not show that the dependency of actions and intentional content on appropriate objects is insufficient to discriminate between water and twater contents, so that individualism is still viable?

One cannot respond to this by saying that whether an object is appropriate for a given activity depends on its empirically discoverable nature. The problem that the twin earth examples pose is that although water and twater have *different* natures, both are appropriate to wash with. So it looks as though such differences as there are between their natures cannot make a difference to the determination of intentional content.

The problem arises because the twin earth examples are designed to keep firmly in place the ordinary, day-to-day role that certain objects, substances or phenomena beyond persons' bodies play in their activities and, correspondingly, in their thoughts, while varying in their natures in ways that are hidden to the naked eye. Since our day-to-day activities can be and often are insensitive to such differences in the natures of things that do not manifest themselves to the naked eye, it is not surprising that water and twater should play the same (narrow) role in Sue's and her twin's day-to-day activities.

However, I think that externalism can be defended in the face of this. The twin earth examples are effectively tests of antecedently held intuitions, as I have said. How they are to be interpreted, and what they establish, depends on the intuitions that prompt them. The intuition that the argument for externalism just given set out to defend is that water contents are *water* contents because our day-to-day descriptive and explanatory practices can only intelligibly explain subjects' successful actions, even narrowly construed, against the background of successful actions which take water as an appropriate object, where these explanations require the employment of contents that are *water* contents. Water actions are made intelligible by states with *water* contents. Unsuccessful attempts at water actions that take objects other than water are made intelligible in part by states with *water* contents.

It is true that on twin earth, it is stipulated that twater plays the role in twin-earthians' day-to-day life that water plays on earth. Why then do Sue and her twin think thoughts with different contents? Because whether Sue's thoughts are *water* thoughts depends on her actual behaviour, in the actual context in which she is situated. Her counterfactual behaviour – what she would do in other circumstances, and in other environments – depends on this. If she were to be transported to twin earth, what would she do? She would wash with twater, drink twater, and so on. But it would not be appropriate *for her* to do so.

Why? Because appropriateness is context-dependent, and the organism is part of the context.[30] Sue's

---

[30] Two objections might arise here. One is that what is appropriate behaviour towards an object depends in part on how the type of object involved in that type of behaviour is specified, and that, specified more generally (say, as 'the thirst-quenching, odourless, transparent, colourless liquid'), twater is appropriate for Sue to wash with, because on twin earth, the stuff which satisfies that description gets things clean. The other objection is that appropriate behaviour must be, as the functional behaviour is, capable of allowing for novelty in the range of objects to which such behaviour can become adapted. Creatures move around and may, in new environments, encounter objects of kinds that are distinct from those of the kinds to which their behaviours were initially adapted. It may thus be accidental that these objects serve the needs for which the behaviours were initially selected. Still, engaging with them might prove to be beneficial for these creatures, and so it may be functional for them to behave in the same way towards these new items as they did towards the old ones.

Consider the first objection. Suppose that we are concerned to specify the function of the frog's tongue-flicking behaviour. On one view, the function is to catch small dark moving things. On another, it is to catch frog-food. How we specify the object toward which the frog behaves matters because it makes a difference to whether the frog is functioning biologically normally rather than malfunctioning when it flicks its tongue at black spots in its visual field.

Similarly, it might be argued, for Sue and water/twater. On one view, appropriate behaviour for Sue is behaviour towards water. On another, it is behaviour towards the thirst-quenching, odourless, transparent, colourless liquid. How we specify the object towards which Sue behaves matters here too because it makes a difference to whether Sue is behaving appropriately when she washes with twater.

Indeterminacy of function-specification is a problem in an environment where both specifications apply precisely because of its consequences for what would count as malfunctioning behaviour. And it is a problem in Sue's environment, since both ways of specifying water are satisfied by water. However, the considerations that may lead one to think that the correct specification of the frog's behaviour is the more general one do not apply with equal force to Sue's behaviour.

In the case of the frog, the inclination to specify its functional behaviour as frog-food catching behaviour seems poorly motivated in the light of the fact that the frog's perceptual system seems to be sensitive only to small dark moving things in its environment. To attribute more specificity in functional behaviour to the frog than this would require us to view the frog as capable of seeing small dark moving things as frog-food. But nothing in its behaviour gives us good reason to suppose that the frog has this capacity.

The situation is different for Sue and water. The frog's environment contains many things which count both as frog-food and also as small, dark and moving. However, Sue's environment does not contain many stuffs that are phenomenologically indistinguishable from water. Whereas in its actual environment, the frog flicks its tongue at many small, dark, moving things which may not be frog-food, Sue does not in her actual environment wash with many thirst-quenching, odourless, transparent, colourless liquids which may not be water. Whereas, in the case of the frog, we see no reason to specify its behaviour in the more specific way, in the case of Sue, we have no motivation for specifying her behaviour in the more general way. It all depends on the organism and what is in its actual environment.

So, in the case of Sue, unlike the case of the frog, we do have a reason to specify her behaviour as appropriate behaviour towards water. And so we have a reason for taking her behaviour on twin earth towards twater to be inappropriate, although intelligible. We can make sense of such inappropriate behaviour because, although the environment of twin earth happens to cooperate with Sue, that it does is an accident.

Now consider the second objection. Suppose that the correct way to specify the function of the frog's tongue-flicking behaviour is in terms of its goal in catching frog-food. Still, it might be argued, different things in different environments might count as frog-food. Thus, suppose that the frog were to be placed in a new environment, one where creatures of a different type than those to which the frog's tongue-flicking behaviour was originally adapted nevertheless served to nourish the frog. Would it not then be functional for the frog to flick its tongue at these different creatures?

I want to say here that the behaviour in the new environment, however beneficial to the organism it may be, is not thereby functional for the frog. The reason is that whether a behaviour is functional depends on the types of objects to which the behaviour was initially adapted. It was frog-food, not small dark moving things, to which the frog's behaviour was initially adapted, and for which that behaviour was selected. It was *creatures* of a certain type to which that type of behaviour was initially adapted and for which that behaviour was selected. So it was frog-food of a certain kind to which the frog's behaviour was initially adapted and for which that behaviour was selected. And that is why it is functional for the frog to flick its tongue now in the presence of that kind of frog food. That different organisms in another environment nourish the frog, so that the its tongue-flicking behaviour in those circumstances is beneficial for the frog, is fortuitous. It is just good luck for the frog that its new environment obliges its need for nourishment by supplying different, but satisfying creatures for it to eat. (See Ruth Millikan, 'Compare and Contrast Dretske, Fodor, and Millikan on Teleosemantics', in *White Queen Psychology and Other Essays for Alice* (Cambridge, MA: MIT Press, 1993), pp. 123–33, especially 125–31.) Happy coincidence between producer and consumer does not thereby make for functional behaviour. Similarly for Sue's behaviour towards twater.

It does not follow from this that the frog's functional behaviour cannot be adapted to new things, and that these things cannot come to figure in the process by which a type of behaviour or trait is selected. They can. And those that do will thereby figure in the specification of objects towards which that type of behaviour is functional. But that they are objects towards which a type of behaviour is functional depends on their role in the selection process, and not vice versa. Similarly for Sue and her appropriate behaviour towards water.

465

behaviour is appropriate on earth because of the beneficial effects washing with water has in that environment. But on twin earth those beneficial effects are *accidental* for Sue: on twin earth it is an accident that twater is appropriate for Sue to wash with. It is no accident that on twin earth twater is appropriate to wash with for *twin earthians.* And so it is no accident that Sue's twin acts in ways made intelligible to twin earthians by twater contents. But Sue's actions will not be made intelligible by beliefs and desires of hers with twater contents – not, at least, independently of the fact that Sue's actions are based on misperceptions of twater as water. Given that Sue thinks water thoughts and given that such differences as there are between water and twater do not manifest themselves in the day-to-day role that these substances play in the activities of agents on earth and on twin earth, it is not surprising that Sue should wash with twater. It is not surprising; but nor is it true that Sue's act of washing on twin earth is made intelligible independently of her water thoughts.[31]

In responding to these objections in this way I am presuming a particular view of biological function, namely a causal-historical view, such as that advocated by Millikan in *Language, Thought, and Other Biological Categories.* It contrasts with ahistorical accounts, such as propensity accounts (see John Bigelow and Robert Pargetter, 'Functions', *Journal of Philosophy* 84 (1987), 181–96).

[31] As Burge puts the point,

Imagine that a heart and an organ that pumps digestive waste (from a completely different evolutionary scheme) were physically indistinguishable up to their boundaries. Clearly they would be of two different biological kinds, with different causal powers, on any conception of causal power that would be relevant to biological

Is this response question-begging against the individualist, whose criterion for the taxonomy of behaviour and intentional content is counterfactual? I do not think so, and the reason connects the taxonomy of psychological kinds firmly to the taxonomy of functional kinds in biology. In biology, the taxonomy of functional kinds is both teleological and what one might call 'effect-sensitive' in a normative sense of the term. The camouflaging behaviour of this chameleon is camouflaging behaviour, not because it has camouflaging effects in *this* chameleon, nor even because it tends to have camouflaging effects in the majority of chameleons. It is camouflaging behaviour in this chameleon because this type of behaviour had camouflaging effects in a sufficient number of its ancestors to lead to the proliferation of chameleons which displayed that behaviour. That type of behaviour exists *in order* to have camouflaging effects in this and other chameleons, whether it does so or not. And it exists in order to have such effects precisely

taxonomy. Judging the heart's causal powers presupposes that it is connected to a particular type of bodily environment, with a particular sort of function in that environment. One cannot count being connected to such a body to pump blood as just one of many contexts that the heart might be in, if one wants to understand the range of its biologically relevant causal powers. It would show a serious misconception of biological kinds to argue that the causal powers and taxonomically relevant effects of the heart and its physical twin are the same because if one hooked up the waste pump to the heart's body, it would pump blood and cause the blood vessels to dilate; and that if one hooked the heart to the waste pump's body, it would move waste. ('Intentional Causation and Psychology', p. 227) because its presence in ancestors led to the survival and so to the proliferation of chameleons which displayed this behaviour. Similarly for the deer's flight behaviour, the bee's dancing behaviour, and so on.

In biology, teleology arises from the working of natural selection on instances of physico-chemical properties of organisms.[32] Turning green in this environment just in this chameleon's camouflaging itself given that it inhabits a green environment and that instances of this type of behaviour in this chameleon's ancestors helped them to avoid predators and so to aid survival and proliferation of descendants. It is the success of instances of certain types of behaviours in the past that gives rise to teleology in functions, and this teleology persists even when the effects which instances of such behaviour now have regularly fail to occur. Causes are *designed* to bring out certain effects, even when they do not. Still the functional pattern remains, and still the chameleon displays such behaviour, *in order* to have camouflaging effects.

So in biology, certain types of behaviour too *aim* at success: their having teleology just in their aiming at success. To be a functional kind just is to aim at success, and this makes functional behaviour very like action in this respect. In biology, the fit between behaviour and environment is non-accidental when successful because the cause – say, the

---

[32] This is the view of biological-functional kinds advocated by Millikan in numerous works. See particularly *Language, Thought, and Other Biological Categories,* and *White Queen Psychology and Other Essays for Alice.* It is a causal-historical (in contrast to a propensity) account of biological function.

chameleon's turning green – is designed to have a certain (functional) effect, namely, to match the colour of the environment. So too in the domain of intentional psychology. In successful action, the fit between behaviour and environment is non-accidental when successful because the cause – contentful intentional states – is designed to have a certain (purposeful) effect. The source of the design in the two cases may not be the same, since in biology it is brought about by the process of natural selection. But the design itself – that the cause exists in order to bring out a certain type of effect – is present in both. This is what makes for teleology in biology, and it is what makes for teleology in the domain in the psychological.

If this is right, then the non-accidental fit between activity and object in actual cases of successful action is required for the taxonomy of action itself, just as the non-accidental fit between behaviour and environment in successful behaviours is required for the taxonomy of functional kinds. In the biological case, successful behaviour depends on the actual environment in which it was selected: a chameleon placed in a pink environment cannot camouflage itself.[33] And in the case of action, the success depends on there being appropriate objects toward which agents can at least sometimes act. Sue can get it wrong occasionally when she takes inappropriate substances to wash with. She can even get it wrong much of the time. But she cannot get it wrong all of the time. Beyond a certain point, we are no

---

[33] Millikan uses the term 'Normal' (with capital 'N') to distinguish the biological-normal from 'normal' in the sense of 'average' or 'usual' or 'typical'. See *Language, Thought, and Other Biological Categories*.

longer prepared to say: she washes. And getting it right or wrong means getting it right or wrong *in her environment*. And so what is appropriate is what is appropriate *in her environment*. Similarly for Sue's twin. And *this* is why a counterfactual criterion is inappropriate for the taxonomy of action and content.

In the case of biology, teleology is there because of functions, and functions arise from the workings of natural selection on instances of physico-chemical properties. Why is there teleology in the case of action? Here there is teleology because there is intentional content. Contentful kinds imbue behaviour with purpose. Behaviour counts as intentional, hence as action, only if it is caused by states with intentional content. But if so, then they aim at success precisely because their contentful causes themselves aim at success. Without teleology in the contentful cause, there is no teleology in the intended effect. This is not, of course, to say that without intentional states there would be no teleology in human behaviour. There would be teleology because human beings are biological creatures. But the teleology would not be the teleology of intentional behaviour. Movements would remain purposeful, but they would not thereby be intended, and so would not be actions.

IV   Conclusion

This completes the argument for externalism. It remains to consider some of its consequences. The externalism argued for here is distinctive in being essentially normative. The objects (etc.) upon which narrow-act taxonomy depends are ones that are *appropriate* to those actions. As I remarked at the end of the last section, this normativity lies firmly in the mind. It lies in the essentially teleological nature of contentful kinds.

However, for reasons which should be apparent from the comparison of psychological kinds with functional kinds in biology, I do not think that this teleology can exist independently of the actual environments in which agents are embedded. So what counts as an appropriate object towards which an agent can successfully act is not independent of the actual, empirically discoverable nature of that object. What makes Sue's washing with water a successful act is not independent of its being a washing with water; and water's being an appropriate object to wash with is not independent of the fact that it is, unlike hydrochloric acid, H_2O. Hydrochloric acid does not have a nature such that it is appropriate to wash with, nor does mud, nor tar. Given what has just been said, it would not be *rational* for Sue to attempt to wash with these substances. However, it would be intelligible for Sue to wash with twater on twin earth, since we can make intelligible why she might think it appropriate to do so, even though it isn't appropriate *for her.* For twater is phenomenologically indistinguishable from water and also gets things clean. Given this, it is understandable that Sue should do something that is inappropriate for her but appropriate for twin earthians. It is understandable, and perhaps also rational, in much the same way that a person who misperceives salt as sugar and pours salt in her tea can be seen to be behaving rationally because of this misperception. But is it not thereby appropriate, given that appropriateness is context-dependent and the individual is part of the context. There is slack between what is appropriate in the environment of twin earth and what is appropriate for Sue.

This is not to say that whether an object or substance is appropriate to a certain activity reduces to, or can be determined only by, its empirically discoverable nature. It is true that whether a given object or substance is appropriate for a given activity depends in part on its empirically discoverable nature; but different natures can be equally appropriate for the same type of activity. On earth it is appropriate to wash with water; but it can also be appropriate to wash with sand. Apples are appropriate objects to eat, but so are walnuts and mushrooms.

Because objects with different natures can be equally appropriate to a single activity, there is no telling in advance, there is no *a priori* limit on, what object or objects can be appropriate for a given activity. Appropriateness depends on actual effect – for example, in the case of washing, getting things clean – and this in turn depends in part on the nature of the objects with which one engages when one acts. But different objects can have the same effect. And so different objects can be appropriate for a given activity. It is appropriate to wash with water, and with sand, but not with tar, because water and sand gets things clean, but tar does not.

However, the similarity between contentful intentional kinds and functional-biological kinds ends here. Specifically, the attribution of contentful kinds is, whereas the attribution of functional kinds is not, sensitive to both the perspective of others and the perspective of the subject. This makes the norms that govern the attribution of intentional content to subjects' states answerable both to the perspective of those subjects and to the perspective of others. There is no analogue of this dual-perspective constraint on functional taxonomy in biology.

Failure to appreciate this can lead to too close an assimilation of the psychological to the biological, with undesirable consequences. For example, Ruth Millikan has claimed that because externalism is true, a subject who is ignorant of the factors that determine intentional content might fail to recognize that two beliefs with the same content have the same content, and as a result hold contradictory beliefs, one the negation of the other. Many externalists would be prepared to concede this point.[34] But she goes on to infer from this that the norms that govern rationality itself lie beyond the individual subject, in much the same way that the determinants of functional behaviour lie beyond the biological organisms that display it. She holds that externalism has the consequence that whether humans are rational is not determined by, or even partly answerable to, subject's perspectives.[35]

---

[34] See, for example, Tyler Burge, 'Intellectual Norms and the Foundations of Mind', *Journal of Philosophy* 83 (1986), 697–720.

[35] Thus she says,

> it is implicit in contemporary 'externalist' accounts of the contents of thought that what is consistent versus inconsistent, indeed, I will argue, what is rational versus irrational, is not epistemically given to the intact mind. ('White Queen Psychology', in *White Queen Psychology and Other Essays for Alice*, p. 281)

And similarly,

> If the White Queen is right, then that Alice has a coherent system of thought, that she possesses, for example, only one thought of each semantic kind, and hence that she thinks in accordance with laws, say, of rational psychology, depends on a felicitious *coordination* between Alice-the-organism and Alice's environment. It depends, in fact, on much the same kind of felicitous coordination that

But I deny that externalism has any such consequence. It is true that externalism implies that subjects
might think thoughts with contents they imperfectly grasp.
And since they might, they might mistakenly think that two
thoughts have the same content when they do not, or that
they have different contents when they do not. Fallibility in
knowledge of one's own thoughts of this kind is indeed a
consequence of externalism.

> constitutes Alice's thinkings of *true* thoughts; rationality fails to be
> in the head in the same sort of way as does truth. (Ibid., p. 285.)
>
> The illusion that modes of presentation will help save logical
> possibility also rests on a failure to see that rationality pivots
> essentially on *referential* content, or *Bedeutung*, and not at all on
> mode of presentation, that rationality cannot simply be lifted up
> and attached to mode of presentation. The capacity to reidentify
> content but only under a mode is a *restriction* on rationality, a
> lessening of rationality, not a removal of rationality into an inner
> and safer sphere. (Ibid., pp. 283–4.)

Millikan apparently thinks that *that* rationality, like content itself, is
world-involving, shows that it lies beyond the subject altogether
('rationality pivots... not at all on mode of presentation', 'rationality
fails to be in the head in the same sort of way as does truth'). I deny
that content externalism has this consequence. That rationality is
world-involving does not thereby show that it does not depend in any
way on the perspective of the subject, and so does not show that the
norms that govern rationality lie beyond the individual. That *what* is
thought about when thinking a content lies beyond the individual does
not show that *how* it is thought about is not *also* involved in thinking
rationally. The rejection of narrow content does not force one to reject
any role for the subject to play in rationality; nor is it a 'pernicious
Cartesianism' to insist on the importance of that role. Without it, it is
difficult to see why subjects should be critically reflective thinkers, and
what role critical reflection might serve in an individual's psychology.

But I do not see that the norms that govern rationality do not thereby operate 'from within' the individual subject. For these norms operate in epistemic ways, in ways that make the behaviour of agents intelligible, not only to others, but also to themselves. And it is a constraint on the attribution of content by others that such attribution respect the agent's perspective.

In short, the factors that make a certain content the content it is do not thereby determine the acceptance or rejection of that content by a subject, or the patterns of reasoning in which that subject might engage with regard to that content. Externalism a metaphysical view about the factors that help to determine intentional content. But rationality, and the norms that govern it, is an epistemological matter. So it does not follow from the fact that externalism is true, hence that the determinants of intentional content lie beyond the individual, that the determinants of reasoning and behaviour lie beyond the individual also. On the contrary, it is plausible to maintain, in the face of externalism, that these norms are accessible to and operate within the subject, and guide the very formation, rejection, and assimilation, of contentful states.[36]

---

[36] So I am recommending a combination of metaphysical externalism with regard to the determinants of intentional content and epistemological internalism with regard to the norms that govern rationality. Burge seems to pursue a similar strategy. See 'Our Entitlement to Self-Knowledge', *Proceedings of the Aristotelian Society* 96 (1996), 91–116.

Mind, World and Value

MICHAEL MORRIS

I

Naturalism is the dominant philosophy of the age. It might be characterized as the view that the only real facts are facts of natural science, or that only statements of natural science are really true. But perhaps this scientistic formulation underestimates the depth and everydayness of the dominance of naturalism. More informally, we might say that naturalism is the view that the world is a world of natural objects and natural phenomena, that the only properties of these objects are natural properties, and the relations between them are all natural relations – in short, there are only natural facts, natural truths.

There are obvious questions to be raised about the coherence of naturalism (for example: can the truth of naturalism really be supposed to be a natural truth?); but I shall not dwell on these here. I want to put naturalism into question in a different way: by suggesting an alternative to it in the philosophy of mind which is rich enough to stop naturalism seeming compulsory.

It is often simply assumed that a good account of the mind must be naturalistic. What does this rule out? Sometimes it seems to be supposed that all that is ruled out is an account which presents the mind as something *supernatural.* (A particular kind of Cartesian bogeyman will be imagined.) But this is a shallow contrast which is in danger of blinding its opponents to the strength of naturalism's own commitments. For the concept of the *supernatural* is the concept of something which is of the right general kind to be given a naturalistic explanation – for which there *ought* to be a naturalistic account – but for which no naturalistic explanation is possible, for reasons other than the mere inadequacy of the minds of the explainers. A supernatural thing is a miraculous natural thing. The supernatural is an alternative to the natural conceived of from within naturalism.

A more fundamental contrast is suggested by the thought that it is the business of natural sciences to describe how things are, and perhaps how they must inevitably be, but not how they *should* be. This ties in with Kripke's famous objection to dispositionalist accounts of meaning, that they explain what I will say rather than what I should say;[1] and with an older objection to psychologism in ethics. If this is right, what is distinctive of naturalism is that it finds no place for value in the world. The natural facts exclude facts about value; the world is value-free; natural science is dispassionate and value-neutral.

This suggestion is not uncontentious, since it rules out both a traditional kind of ethical naturalism, and an alternative (perhaps Aristotelian) conception of nature as

[1] S. Kripke, *Wittgenstein on Rules and Private Language* (Oxford: Blackwell, 1982), p. 37.

essentially value-rich.[2] But I shall adopt it here without argument, because it seems to me to provide a fair characterization at least of an orthodox kind of naturalism, and because it suggests a way of developing a clear alternative to orthodox naturalistic theories of the mind.

II

We will get a clear alternative to orthodox naturalism about the mind, if we develop an account which makes explicit reference to value. Where should we begin? We might take a hint from that thought of Kripke's: he wanted an account of meaning to explain what we *should* say, rather than what we will say. Kripke was not concerned with etiquette, but with right answers: that is, with truth. So a first suggestion might be: truth is what we should say. This is uncompelling for two reasons: first, it might sometimes be right not to say what is true (for reasons of diplomacy, or just politeness); secondly, it cannot ever be required that we should say everything that is true, because there are absurdly many truths (start with simple addition and keep going). So here is a revised suggestion: it is distinctive of truth that one should only believe something if it is true. And conversely: it seems essential to belief (as the term is used in the analytical tradition), that it is a state which one should not be in unless what is believed is true. In this way we get the beginnings of an evaluative account of truth and of the mind at the same time.

[2] See, e.g., J. McDowell, *Mind and World* (Cambridge, MA: Harvard University Press, 1994), pp. 78–84.

There will be an immediate objection: might it not be the case that it was psychologically necessary for someone to believe a falsehood? The answer to this is that is less than ideal to be in a condition in which it is psychologically necessary to believe a falsehood. So the revised suggestion could be revised again: one should be in a condition such that one only believes something if it is true. The important point is that such counter-examples do not have any tendency to show that value can be dispensed with here.

The attraction of locating the value that naturalism must miss in *truth*, specifically, is that it seems reasonable to hope that this will explain the importance of the normative in reasoning and thinking in general. Classical logic is based on the thought that truth preservation is the essence of validity. Almost every epistemology holds that what is distinctive of knowledge is that it provides some kind of guarantee of truth. The difficulty with the suggestion is that it is hard to see what kind of value truth might be: why *should* one only believe the truth? What is it about truth which matters so much?

One thought might be that the value of truth lies in the evolutionary advantage which true belief confers. An obvious difficulty is that it is hard to see why truth should be especially advantageous: indeed, it is easy enough to imagine circumstances in which false belief might help. But there is a more fundamental problem with the suggestion, for our present purposes: it hardly provides an alternative to a naturalistic account. It is not merely that evolutionary accounts are commonly championed in the name of naturalism. The important point is that an evolutionary account makes no essential appeal to value. Indeed, the whole purpose of evolutionary explanation is to show how to dispense with the value-rich conception of the world which we so easily bring to our descriptions of nature.[3] (It is tempting to suppose that, by a kind of reversal of the general tendency of evolutionary explanation, evolutionary theories of the mind have seemed attractive just because they have appeared to *license* an appeal to value; whereas in fact they undermine it.)

Another suggestion might be this: the truth of one's beliefs is essential for successful action. There are a number of difficulties with this. First, this account cannot be deep enough. For successful action is presumably just action which achieves what one wants: we seem to need to appeal to an unexamined notion of desire. Secondly, it is not obviously true that the truth of one's beliefs is necessary for one to achieve what one wants: convenient accidents would do as well. Thirdly, the truth of our beliefs cannot have a merely instrumental value in the satisfaction of our desires: for without any true beliefs it is hard to see what content our desires could have at all. Fourthly, action is only a part of the range of behaviour in which belief can be manifest, and in which the truth of our beliefs seems to matter.

Noticing the uncritical use of the notion of desire in this last suggestion might prompt us to wonder whether we could offer an explicitly evaluative account of desire to

---

[3] For support for this point, see J. Fodor, 'A Theory of Content, I' in his *A Theory of Content* (Cambridge, MA: MIT Press, 1990), p. 79.

parallel the evaluative account of belief which was offered before. And we can. For it is surely true that one should only desire something if it is good, or at least not bad. There are two clear differences between this account of desire and the corresponding account of belief. First, this connection with value does not suffice to single out desire: for it is also true that one should only approve of something, or hope for something, or wish for something, or like something, or enjoy something, or be pleased at something, if the something is good, or at least not bad. Further distinctions between all these attitudes need to be drawn. The second difference between the account of desire and the account of belief lies in the nature of the value which is appealed to. In the case of desire, it seems clearly to be a kind of value which is at least continuous with the moral. It may not be appropriate to describe every issue about what one should want as a moral issue, particularly if the concept of the moral is reserved for a particular kind of social institution; but it seems clear that the question of what one should want will always fall within the range of that larger question, which has been taken to be the founding question of moral philosophy, of how one should live.[4] This provides us with a contrast between true belief and good desire which should enable us to get clearer about the value of truth.

---

[4] In this respect I am distancing myself from Kant, who held that there was a fundamental distinction between moral motivation and desire. It is unclear how Kant could accommodate the notion of what one should want.

481

But this link with the moral is likely to frighten some enough to drive them to an alternative account of the difference between beliefs and desires, in terms of 'direction of fit'. Here is Platts providing an orthodox characterization (even though he is not sympathetic to the view himself):

> Beliefs aim at the true, and their being true is their fitting the world; falsity is a decisive failing in a belief, and false beliefs should be discarded; beliefs should be changed to fit the world, not vice versa. Desires aim at realisation, and their realisation is the world fitting with them; the fact that the indicative content of a desire is not realised in the world is not yet a failing *in the desire*, and not yet a reason to discard the desire; the world, crudely, should be changed to fit with our desires, not vice versa.[5]

The first sentence provides a characterization of belief entirely in accord with the suggestion I have offered. The account of desire which follows is just false, however. Desires do not aim at realization. Only the person whose desires they are aims at their realization. But this is just to say that she *desires* their realization. And since their realization *is* just the object of the desires, this amounts to no more than saying that she desires what she desires,[6] which

---

[5] M. Platts, *Ways of Meaning* (London: Routledge and Kegan Paul, 1979), pp. 256-7.

[6] Someone may suspect that this argument involves a fallacious application of Leibniz's Law within an intensional context. I think there is no fallacy: the realization of a desire must be thought by the desirer to be the object of the desire.

provides no account of desire. And it is false that the world should be changed to fit with our desires: if our desires are wicked, the world should not be changed to fit with them. Anyone tempted by the first sentence of Platts' characterization should realize that a truly comparable account of desire would be the one I have offered. And this will only suggest that there is a difference in 'fit' (though hardly *direction* of fit) if desiring what is good is not counted as fitting the world; which will only be if the world is not allowed to contain values; that is, if we accept an orthodox naturalism.

Moral evaluation is largely concerned with behaviour in the widest possible sense: actions, certainly, but also certain kinds of non-intentional response, and certain tendencies of character. These are things that are characteristically explained by means of beliefs, desires, hopes, wishes and all the other propositional attitudes. (The concentration on action in moral theory matches the concentration on desire among 'motivational' attitudes in the philosophy of mind.) How does the moral (when it is clearly moral) evaluation of behaviour relate to the motivational attitudes of the person whose behaviour it is?

The simple answer is that the moral evaluation of behaviour is just the evaluation of the motivational attitudes which explain the behaviour. An action is good insofar as it manifests a good desire. A glance is kind and considerate insofar as the thought 'behind' it is kind and considerate. A decision is morally good insofar as it is made for the right reasons. This conflicts, of course, with familiar consequentialist ways of evaluating behaviour; but the contrast with consequentialism is one which we will want to maintain in the construction of an alternative to naturalism. Evaluating behaviour simply in terms of its consequences, whether actual or merely likely, is no longer to think of behaviour as a special category, the object of a special kind of evaluation. Behaviour becomes just another causal factor, of no evaluative interest in itself. This attitude to behaviour is hard to square with the alternative to naturalism which I am suggesting. For the suggestion is precisely that what is distinctive of the mind, and hence of behaviour (as opposed to mere movement), is that it can only be understood in terms of value.

Once we see that the evaluation of motivational attitudes is the same as the (moral) evaluation of the behaviour which they explain, we can give a characterization of an evaluative approach to the mind which makes it vivid. Behaviour simply strikes us as being appropriate for such evaluation.[7] We simply see affection in a touch, cruelty in a sneer, aggression and despair in a slouch. Any sensitive description of behaviour must bring out more clearly what there is to be admired, what to be loved, what to be feared, what to be hated, what to be pitied in it: a sensitive characterization may not make unambiguous evaluation any easier, but it will make clearer what is at issue in the evaluation of it.

---

[7] The idea of such rich perception is to be found in many places in McDowell's work: e.g. 'On "The Reality of the Past"', in Action and Interpretation, ed. C. Hookway and P. Pettit (Cambridge: Cambridge University Press, 1978), p. 140.

484

If the evaluation of motivational attitudes is the same as the moral evaluation of the behaviour which they explain, it should also be true that the evaluation of beliefs, as true and false, is the same as a kind of evaluation of the behaviour which they explain. And we might hope that the evaluative approach to belief might be made vivid in the appropriate evaluation of behaviour. Here is a simple example. Someone walks upstairs reading a magazine. At the top she takes one step too many and stumbles. The stumble is comic and pathetic. This shows that the person thought there was another step. This belief was false. The falsity is manifest to us in the ludicrousness of the stumble: finding it ludicrous just is acknowledging the falsity of the belief which it manifests.

This shows the nature of the value of truth in belief. If a belief is false, then the behaviour which depends on it is in a certain sense empty, or pathetic, or futile: it is, as it were, all for nothing. Our sense of the comic and the tragic often depends upon this. It may be, of course, that the person gets what she wants, luckily, anyway. But this does not detract from, even if it compensates for, the foolishness created by false belief.

Here we can see the truth or falsity of belief in behaviour. But what is the belief itself? If someone acts on the belief that p, one will be able to recognize what she does as foolish or otherwise according to whether or not it is false that p. As a provisional suggestion, I propose the simplest possible extrapolation of this as an account of belief: someone believes that p at a certain time just in case it is legitimate, in virtue of how she is at that time, to count what she does as foolish or otherwise according to whether or not it is false that p.[8] This does not mean that whatever she does at that time *must* be evaluated according to whether or not it is false that p; not even if her action is of a general type which might be explained by the belief that p. It means, simply, that if we were to assess what she does in these terms, we would be considering her on her own terms. Someone may complain that it is now very uncertain whether or not someone believes something if she is not acting on that belief. But this is an unreasonable complaint: it often is uncertain whether someone believes something if she is not acting on that belief. Did you believe that 'consequence' is a longer word than 'theory' before I mentioned it?

An account in the same style can be provided for desire. If someone acts on a certain want, then what she does is bad or otherwise, according to whether or not what she wants is bad. And the simple proposal is: someone has a desire at a certain time just in case it is legitimate, in virtue of how she is at that time, to count what she does as bad or otherwise according to whether or not that is a bad thing to want.

Here we have the skeleton of an evaluative conception of mind. We can now paste on some flesh, before concluding with some obvious worries.

---

[8] This definition is provisional because it does not yet secure the right degree of intensionality for belief contexts. There are several possible revisions, one of which is suggested in my *The Good and the True* (Oxford: Oxford University Press, 1992), chapters 12–13.

III

The character of this explicitly evaluative conception of the mind is most clearly seen in the account it provides of the kind of explanation which is given when we explain behaviour in terms of states of mind. The dominant view of this kind of explanation is that it is a species of causal explanation. This dominance is not surprising: causal explanation is what natural sciences – in particular physics – are peculiarly suited to provide, and the conception of the world as the world of natural science is the dominant conception.[9] But for all its dominance, the view has no compelling arguments to support it.

There has been no significant advance on Davidson's two considerations in favour of the causal theory.[10] One is that unless we suppose that beliefs and desires (for example) *cause* behaviour, we cannot make sense of the difference between doing something *because* one has a certain belief, and merely doing it *while* having that belief. But although this is a reasonable *ad hominem* objection to some particular (rather vague) accounts of this kind of explanation – which was actually Davidson's original point – there is no ground for proposing it as a general claim: I shall suggest a different way of marking the

---

[9] Peacocke actually defines naturalism about explanation as the view that 'any explanation of an event or temporal state of affairs is a causal explanation': *A Study of Concepts* (Cambridge, MA: MIT Press, 1992), p. 127.

[10] D. Davidson, 'Actions, Reasons, Causes', in his *Essays on Actions and Events* (Oxford: Oxford University Press, 1980).

distinction. (And in fact, as I shall argue, there is room for doubt about whether Davidson's version of the theory actually does provide an account of that 'because'.) The second of Davidson's considerations might be thought to support the first: we have no better model of the explanatory connection than the familiar causal one, so we should adopt the causal one. This argument (if it deserves the title) is doubly parasitic on the dominance of naturalism. First, in that naturalism makes the causal account seem the natural choice. Secondly, in the basic assumption that any model is better than none: this is legitimate only when the adoption of the model plays an instrumental role in the pursuit of some further project, as in the technological application of science; not when the goal is just the understanding provided by that model itself, unless we suppose – as some versions of naturalism indeed do – that all such understanding must have a merely instrumental value. In any case, this second consideration of Davidson's is vulnerable to the provision of an alternative model; which I shall supply.

The causal theory typically brings with it a certain conception of the nature of the behaviour which states of mind are cited to explain, as well as a particular view of the nature of the explanation involved. It may be that not every causal theorist has felt committed to these things: I suspect that that is because the consequences of adopting a causal theory have not been thoroughly thought through. But my concern is to present what is distinctive about an explicitly evaluative approach to the mind; and for this it is enough to contrast it with the views typically associated with the causal theory.

The causal theory is typically associated with a restrictive conception of the behaviour which states of mind are cited to explain: in the simplest case, the behaviour is thought of as just bodily movement. The restrictiveness follows from a certain (natural, and Humean) conception of causation: the nature of the cause is not intrinsic to the effect. It is possible to know everything about the intrinsic nature of an effect without being able to infer from that anything about the intrinsic nature of its cause.[11] If we apply this principle to the case of explanation by means of states of mind, then we have to suppose that the behaviour which states of mind are cited to explain does not in itself require that it be explicable in terms of states of mind. Putting it crudely, the behaviour is not intrinsically *behaviour* at all: it is movement, perhaps, or something else whose intrinsic nature is characterizable without recourse to any mental terms. We then count it as behaviour in virtue of having found something mental to be its cause.

It is perhaps this commitment of the natural conception of causation which leads to the view that states of mind are hidden from us, and cannot be seen in behaviour. Any view which supposes that the mind lies somehow *behind* the behaviourism seems to be a distinctly causal view, and it certainly requires that states of mind are not unproblematically visible in behaviour.

A similar result is reached from the thought that causes bring about events, or happenings (causes make

---

[11] This notion of intrinsicness is here left unexplained. It needs to be explained as part of a fuller account of causation.

things happen). To see something as a happening is to bring it under a general scientific view of the world. To say that actions are events is to say that there is nothing in their intrinsic character which sets them apart from the world of natural occurrences.[12] Actions then become events with a particular distinctive kind of cause; but as events, they are intrinsically on a par with earthquakes, punctures and the gradual decay of buildings. To think of actions as events is to think of them as intrinsically (that is, in respect of their intrinsic nature) agentless.

Any causal theory which accepts this sterilization of behaviour (and I suspect that all should, if there is to be any point in insisting that causes are involved) is led to an odd conclusion. The theory aims to provide an analysis of a certain explanatory relationship, between states of mind and behaviour. But what it suggests is a more fundamental description of that relationship – that it holds between states of mind and certain happenings or events – which would never normally be recognized as a description of that relationship at all. If anyone were to say that a particular state of mind made something happen, the something would not be the kind of thing we explain by means of belief in the basic examples of the kind of explanation we are concerned with. (Consider, for example: 'The managing director's uncritical

---

[12] Davidson's philosophical-logical argument for the claim that actions are events (which is questionable anyway) does not actually require more than that actions be entities of a much more general sort, over which one can quantify. See his 'The Logical Form of Action Sentences', in *Essays on Actions and Events.*

confidence in the value of its product made the company collapse.')

A similar forgetting of what the causal account was designed to explain is evident in another feature of many versions of the causal theory. In Davidson's account, for example, the status of states of mind as causes of the events which are described as actions is ensured only by the fact that both states of mind (or 'mental events', if you prefer) and actions are physical events, and as physical events fall under genuine 'homonomic' causal laws.[13] The problem with this is that the causal account is supposed to be an account of the 'because' in such claims as 'She winced because she thought the gas was about to light'; and this 'because' is vindicated, if it is, by the fact that this thought, described as a thought with that content, is explanatory of the behaviour described as behaviour. If one were to appeal here to the familiar Davidsonian separation between causal relations and causal explanation,[14] that would serve only to emphasize the fact that this version of the causal theory fails to explain what it was designed to explain.

A similar difficulty infects certain traditional computational versions of functionalism. One argument for a representational theory of mind has been that it is not content which is causally efficacious in computational

[13] See Davidson, 'Mental Events', in *Essays on Actions and Events*.
[14] See Davidson, 'Causal Relations', in *Essays on Actions and Events*.

491

systems, but the non-intentional properties of the bearers of that content.[15] But this, once again, is just to deny the genuine explanatoriness of those features whose presumed genuine explanatoriness led us to a causal theory in the first place. The theory undercuts its own motivation.

An obvious response to this is to liberalize the conception of causal efficacy which creates the problems. If this goes far enough, it will be unclear what point there is in insisting that the explanatory connection between states of mind and behaviour is causal. And the central motivational difficulty remains: it is unclear how calling the connection causal helps us to understand what is explanatory about it. At this point it is hard to find any reason to adopt a causal theory of the mind apart from a blanket commitment to naturalism.

A generally naturalistic conception of the kind of explanation involved here is evident when it is characterized as 'folk psychology'. The picture is of a primitive people's first attempt at science. The offensive condescension of this view is acknowledged in the amendment of the label to 'commonsense psychology', but the naturalistic commitment of the original description is left unrevised. To count the claim that a certain person maintained a cheerful demeanour because she thought it would cause most irritation as *psychological* at all is already to count terms like 'thought' and 'desire' as theoretical terms of a commonsense science, and their subject matter as one in which science

---

[15] See, e.g., J. Fodor, 'Fodor's Guide to Mental Representation', in his *A Theory of Content*, 19–24.

alone can provide authoritative advances in understanding. The idea will typically be that the concepts of thought and desire are integral to a project which is fundamentally oriented towards prediction, just as the physical sciences are. Insofar as the project is oriented towards prediction, its value will primarily be instrumental, although we can become interested in thoughts and feelings for their own sake – out of curiosity, for example.

This psychological conception of our understanding of each other is required, I think, by the causal theory of the explanation of behaviour; but not conversely.[16] For there can be instrumentalism in psychology, just as in any scientific field (even if its coherence in psychology is open to doubt); and an instrumentalist account might be seen as an alternative to, rather than as an analysis of, causal explanations in the field in question.

[16] I here blithely ignore the debate about 'simulation' accounts of our ascription of propositional attitudes. (See J. Heal, 'Replication and Functionalism', in *Language, Mind and Logic*, ed. J. Butterfield (Cambridge: Cambridge University Press, 1986).) There are two reasons for not considering it here. First, it is unclear to me that the 'simulation' or 'replication' theory offers a radically different account of the nature of states of mind from that provided by an explicitly theoretical conception, rather than simply a different account of the way we usually think about them. (What is it that is simulated, after all?) Secondly, Heal herself accepts (see, e.g., J. Heal, 'Simulation and Cognitive Penetrability', *Mind and Language* 11 (1996), 48) that a 'simulation' account of our thinking about other people's minds is not incompatible with our having a 'prototheory' of the mind; which is enough to bring the 'simulation' account within the scope of the characterization of typical naturalistic theories provided in the text.

Here is a quick sketch, then, of the kind of view of the explanation of behaviour which will be congenial to naturalism. When we say what someone thinks or wants, we are adopting an attitude to them which is fundamentally theoretical, and the terms we use are constrained fundamentally by their efficiency in the prediction of behaviour. On the dominant view, we are concerned with the diagnosis of the causes of events which are not in themselves intrinsically mental, but which we can come to see as mental in virtue of finding that they have mental causes, or which we initially presume to be mental in the expectation of finding that they have mental causes. Quite what role the content of thoughts and desires has in this explanation is left obscure.

IV

The account of the explanation of behaviour suggested by an explicitly evaluative approach differs from this in every particular. In the first place, it is hard to see how it can be causal.[17] Recall that I suggested that for someone to believe something at a particular time is simply for it to be legitimate at that time to count what she does as foolish if what she believes is false. There is surely no conception of causal relevance so relaxed as to permit *its being legitimate to count what she does as foolish if something is false* to qualify as

---

[17] A more direct argument against the causal account, on the ground that it is incompatible with freedom, is provided in my *The Good and the True*, chapter 8.

causally relevant to someone's doing something. But this disqualification brings immediate advantages.

To begin with, much of the motivation for the sterilization of behaviour is removed. Behaviour does not need to be thought of as in itself neutral with respect to whether it is the behaviour of a thinking agent. Nor need it be supposed to be just a matter of happenings. We should think of it as essentially and intrinsically value-rich. It is of the very nature of behaviour that something rides on it, that it is capable of being foolish or wicked. This is, of course, how it strikes us, and how we always describe it. We see gestures as tentative, gentle, bold and rough: these categorizations demand our evaluation. It is not that there need be any simple correspondence between one particular adjective and approval, or between another and disapproval: it is rather that they are categories for which it is essential that value is an issue. Within an evaluative conception of the mind, this is to say that the behaviour itself is intrinsically the behaviour of a thinking agent: the beliefs and desires which may be cited in explanation of the behaviour are internal to the behaviour itself.

This seems to entitle us to say that what people think and feel, and that they think and feel at all, is in principle simply perceptible in their behaviour.[18] There are two principal reasons for resisting this: acceptance of a causal theory of the mind; and a certain view of the kinds of things which are in principle available to perception. The

[18] This conception is to be found in McDowell: see footnote 7 above.

first reason has been removed, and the second surely depends upon a restriction of what is strictly perceivable which is traceable through the empiricists to Descartes, and seems ultimately to depend upon naturalism. But the significance for our present purposes of recognizing that thoughts and feelings can be in principle simply perceptible lies not in the response it provides to the supposed problem of other minds, but in the space it leaves for the explanation of behaviour in terms of states of mind.

To say that it is in principle possible simply to perceive what someone thinks and feels is not to say that it is always in fact possible, or that it is impossible to be mistaken about someone's motives. We can still find room for the idea that someone's thoughts may be hidden from us: what we cannot do is think that they are altogether *behind* their behaviour. And, of course, there is room for informative explanation of another's behaviour in terms of her states of mind only insofar as we can be ignorant of them. In the cases where we offer an interpretation of another, what is generally perceived is just that the person has behaved – that is, that she has some motive or other. What we supply is just an account of what the motive is.

How is this explanatory? One requirement of explanation in general is that it meet something like the following counterfactual condition: if what we offer as explanation had not been true, there would not have been the thing we are trying to explain.[19] In our case, we want

---

[19] We should therefore doubt the adequacy of counterfactual analyses of causation, if we accept that there are non-causal explanations. But this

something like this to be true: if she hadn't believed that, she wouldn't have done that. (I say 'something like this', because there is dispute about exactly which counterfactuals we should insist on.) There are two ways in which we can achieve this within a non-causal, non-naturalistic conception of the mind.

First, and most simply, if someone does something *because* she believes something, the belief is intrinsic to the behaviour. There would not have been this behaviour without that belief, because without that belief whatever was done would not have been this behaviour. When we explain why someone has done something, we are revealing the character of the behaviour itself. The explicitly evaluative account I have been sketching makes it easy to see how this can be. It is essential to what people do, if it is to be behaviour at all, rather than mere happenings, that there is something at stake in it. That is, it is essential to it, that there is an issue of whether it is foolish or bad. For it to be foolish is for it to have been done on the basis of a false belief; for it to be bad is for it to have been done on the basis of a bad desire.

'On the basis of': this marks the asymmetry between state of mind and behaviour which secures the direction of explanation (and gives the causal theory its opening). For although there could not have been the behaviour without the belief, there could have been the belief without the behaviour. All that is required for someone to have a belief

does not undermine the main purpose of counterfactual analyses, which is to distinguish between explanatory and non-explanatory relations in cases where causation is the only realistic candidate.

497

at a particular time is that it should be legitimate at that time to count what she does as foolish or not, according to whether or not what is believed is false. No particular piece of behaviour is required for this, even if it is perhaps plausible that some appropriate behaviour or other is necessary. And this now makes room for the contrast which Davidson was concerned to emphasize: someone can have a particular belief or desire, and do something of a kind which would be appropriate for that belief or desire, without doing it *because* of that belief or desire. The right explanatory connection is only in place when the behaviour is itself properly assessed or foolish or bad, or otherwise, in terms of that belief or desire.

There is another way in which something like the claim that she would not have done that if she had not believed that can be true. I have suggested that the particular behaviour could not have been done without that belief because the belief is essential to the behaviour. But often, in asserting such counterfactuals, we are concerned not with particular pieces of behaviour, but with behaviour of a certain type. When I say, 'He would not have run if he hadn't seen the bus', I am not concerned to insist just that there would not have been *that* running if he had not seen the bus. I am now explaining the fact that he ran at all. Does this provide any basis for a causal theory?

Not at all. The claim that he would not have run if he hadn't seen the bus rests on two underlying claims:

1. He would not have run if he hadn't had reason to;
2. He would not have had reason to run if he hadn't seen the bus.

Presumably (2) is true in virtue of the nature of the circumstances and the person's general state of mind. It is (1) which contains the link between reason and types of behaviour. The causal theory, of course, holds that it is a causal counterfactual. But a non-naturalistic account can suggest, on the contrary, that it is true simply because running is a type of *behaviour*. It is distinctive of behaviour, as opposed to mere occurrences, that it is done for a reason. Which is to say, on the explicitly evaluative conception, it is intrinsic to it that there is an issue of non-foolishness and virtue in it.

The evaluative approach provides an altogether different account of the kind of understanding we get from explanations of behaviour from that offered within the dominant naturalistic tradition. In the first place, it does not suppose that explaining another's behaviour has merely instrumental value. It is difficult to see anything but instrumental value in the kind of explanation which the naturalistic tradition thinks is involved. The emphasis is often explicitly on prediction (notice how often the real importance of explaining other people's behaviour is said to reside in the possibility of such things as making appointments). And the point of prediction is generally to be able to do something about the predicted outcome.

In contrast with this, the point of the explanation of behaviour on the alternative account which I am outlining is just to understand other people. The evaluative account makes a distinctive claim about what it is to understand others: it is a matter of getting clear about the basis on which it is legitimate to evaluate what they do. But this is not to make understanding others a matter of instrumental value for the larger purpose of commending or criticizing them. For the values we bring to the understanding of others are themselves liable to be revised in the light of that understanding: for example, we can come to see a point in doing something which we had not previously seen. In general, the evaluative account has the Kantian virtue of treating people as people, rather than as objects whose movements need to be negotiated in the course of our own independent projects in 'getting around the world'.[20]

There is no difficulty at all in understanding how it is that the content of states of mind can be explanatory. What is explained when we explain behaviour is just what has to be the case for the behaviour to be decent and not foolish. This is to understand the nature of the behaviour. And it is also to give the content of the states of mind which inform the behaviour.

It is not just the content of states of mind in any old sense of 'content' which is essential to the explanation of behaviour on the evaluative conception of the mind: truth conditions are essential. There is therefore no tendency at all for considerations to do with the explanation of behaviour to draw us towards 'internalism' about content, or towards a bifurcation of content into the 'broad' and the 'narrow', or the universal as opposed to the singular.[21] On a naturalistic

---

[20] Although this conception of the fundamental task for human beings (or any cognitive creature) is widespread, we should note how contentious it is: it seems already to presuppose naturalism.

[21] For a classic statement of a view which distinguishes between 'broad' and 'narrow' content, see C. McGinn, 'The Structure of Content', in

view of the explanation of behaviour, by contrast, some such tendency seems almost irresistible.

The issue can be clarified by considering the counter-factuals which are held to be presupposed by a claim such as that he ran because he saw the bus. How are we to understand 'He would not have run if he had not seen the bus'? If our concern is with prediction, we cannot restrict our attention just to whether this person would have run *in these circumstances* if he had not seen the bus. We will want to be able to generalize: we will hope to be able to predict running in general. In pursuit of this goal, we will notice that is not strictly necessary for such running that the person be motivated by a belief with precisely the content that the bus was there already. Similar beliefs about taxis, trains or any other mode of transport would motivate very similar running. And although the belief that the relevant transporter was there then is no doubt relevant to explaining why the person ran *in that direction* and *at that time*, we can imagine very similar beliefs motivating similar runnings at different times. The pressure towards generalizing to a uniform abstraction from specific content, or narrowing down to a basic common core of content, seems irresistible. But this is only because a general concern with prediction makes us interested in similar behaviour in similar circumstances. If we are interested just in understanding people in a way which privots on evaluation,

Thought and Object, ed. A. Woodfield (Oxford: Oxford University Press, 1982). For the view that thoughts are essentially individuated by universal features, see S. Blackburn, *Spreading the Word* (Oxford: Oxford University Press, 1984), chapter 9.

there is no pressure to widen our gaze to include all other circumstances: what we want to know is precisely why that person did that then. We therefore understand the counter-factual, 'He would not have run if he had not seen the bus', as being to be evaluated against the background of this person's state of mind at the time. And this means that the explana-toriness of truth-conditional content can remain integral to the evaluative theory's account of states of mind.

The explicitly evaluative conception of the mind turns out to be thoroughly anti-Cartesian in two respects. First, in making states of mind intrinsic to behaviour, and therefore in principle, even if not inevitably, perceptible in behaviour, it prevents the traditional problem of other minds from getting going at all. Secondly, in making states of mind essentially world-involving, it prevents traditional scepticism about the 'external' world from arising. (I refer to these problems in their 'traditional' form, with reason: it is another question whether every version of other-minds or external-world scepticism is undercut by these moves.) But although it brings with it these epistemological benefits, the reasons I have been advancing for considering an evaluative conception of the mind have had nothing to do with epistemology: the task has simply been to provide a non-naturalistic account of the explanation of behaviour, using the typical awkwardness of naturalistic accounts as a clue to their replacement.

V

What is it to have a mind, then? The suggestion is that it is for there to be an issue of right and wrong, strictly and literally, in what one does. There is an obvious worry about this: it is that the view is behaviouristic, since it requires that there be something one does if one is to have a mind.

The charge of behaviourism is worrying only to the extent that behaviourism is a bad thing. Whether behaviourism is a bad thing depends chiefly on the conception of behaviour which informs it. The principal tradition of philosophical behaviourism arose alongside logical positivism. Its concern was to replace an unscientific or pseudo-scientific psychology. What seemed to be needed was an approach which treated the field of psychology as consisting of unquestionably natural phenomena, and which eradicated mystery-mongering by insisting on empirical testability. These two requirements define the conception of behaviour which informs traditional behaviourism. On the one hand, behaviour is thought of as essentially a type of occurrence: it is therefore not something which is intrinsically mental at all. On the other hand, behaviour is thought of as essentially publicly observable. Any behaviourism which supposes that states of mind require at least a disposition to produce behaviour which meets either of these descriptions seems to be denying what is most important about the mind.

Neither condition is required for the evaluative conception of the mind which I have been developing. The rejection of the first condition is integral to its opposition to naturalism. And adherence to the second condition is simply of no interest to the evaluative conception. It is true that states of mind are counted intrinsic to behaviour. And since some behaviour is observable, there is no reason in principle why states of mind should not be directly perceptible. But the fact that some behaviour is observable does not mean that behaviour is essentially observable; or that there is a special relationship between states of mind and publicly observable behaviour. The crucial relationship is between states of mind and what someone may do because of her states of mind. Anything which is properly explicable by appeal to states of mind can count as behaviour, as far as the evaluative conception is concerned. This means that mental acts are included in behaviour. No doubt these can sometimes be observed: it is easy to think of visible decisions, for example. But there is no reason why they should be open to public view, and often they are not.[22]

Is the evaluative conception behaviourist, then? Not as behaviourism is traditionally understood; so not in any way which permits there to be an easy objection.

There will remain those, however, who will find even mental behaviour too active to be essential to having a mind. The core of mentality, it might be said, is experience, where experience is supposed to be not itself active.[23] Experiences, someone might say, just happen to one.[24] The difficulty with any such view is to understand why what I experience must be something to me. The evaluative conception is the result of accepting a fundamentally Kantian

---

[22] The resulting view of behaviour is very like that advocated by G. Strawson in *Mental Reality* (Cambridge, MA: MIT Press, 1994), chapter 10, though Strawson's general account of mind is very different from mine.

[23] This is Strawson's view: see *Mental Reality*, p. 315 (but passim too).

[24] Strawson seems to be tempted by this: see ibid., p. 303.

answer to that question. What I experience is something to me only insofar as I take it in some way or other. But to take it in some way is already to do something which might be admired or regretted, as an object of pity or congratulation.

This is the deep way in which the evaluative conception differs from naturalism. To think of the world as a world of natural objects and natural phenomena is to think of it as the counterpart to Hume's faculty or 'reason'. Hume's 'reason' is an essentially disengaged and dispassionate faculty. It is supposed to 'discover objects as they stand in nature, without addition or diminution'. It is supposed to be the fundamental, and truly revealing, stance towards reality; the deliverances of 'taste' merely 'gild' or 'stain' what it shows.[25] According to the evaluative account, there can be no such thing as Hume's 'reason'. Experience is never disengaged or dispassionate. The evaluatively neutral view is not basic, but reached by abstraction from our fundamental engagement with the world. Once we see this, we have undermined the basic presumption of naturalism.

[25] D. Hume, *Enquiry concerning the Principles of Morals*, ed. L. Selby-Bigge; 3rd edition, ed. P. Nidditch (Oxford: Oxford University Press, 1975), p. 294.

Mind, Knowledge and Reality: Themes from Kant

QUASSIM CASSAM

I

According to what might be described as 'humanist' approaches to epistemology, the fundamental task of epistemology is to investigate the nature, scope and origins of human knowledge. Evidently, what we can know depends upon the nature of our cognitive faculties, including our senses and our understanding.[1] Since there may be significant differences between human cognitive faculties and those of other beings, it would seem that an investigation of the nature, scope and origins of human knowledge must therefore concern itself, in the first instance, with uncovering the structure and operations of the human cognitive apparatus. The most influential versions of humanism in epistemology have also been inclined to insist both that it is contingent that our cognitive faculties are as they are, and that an investigation of these faculties must be largely empirical. An empirical investigation is to be understood, very

I am grateful to P. F. Strawson for his comments on an earlier version of this paper.

[1] I take it that a cognitive faculty is one the proper exercise of which is necessary for the acquisition of knowledge.

roughly, as one which relies upon observation and experiment, and to describe such an investigation as naturalistic is to draw attention to the fact that it is presupposed by humanism that the faculties being investigated are a part of the natural world, the world of space, time and causal law.

Locke's *Essay*[2] and Hume's *Treatise*[3] are arguably the most distinguished examples of works whose approaches to epistemology are, in these terms, 'humanist'. To begin with, the *Essay* is *An Essay Concerning* Human *Understanding*, and the *Treatise* is *A Treatise of* Human *Nature*. As Nidditch remarks in connection with the *Essay*, the epithet 'human' is intended by Locke to make it clear that the work is about 'man and not about the understanding belonging to God, angelic spirits, or intellectual corporeal beings, infinitely different from those of our little spot of Earth elsewhere in the universe'.[4] Thus, Locke writes in the opening chapter of the *Essay* that his purpose is to 'inquire into the Original, Certainty, and Extent of humane Knowledge; together, with the Grounds and Degrees of Belief, Opinion, and Assent', and that it will suffice for this purpose to 'consider the discerning Faculties of a Man, as they are employ'd about the Objects, which they have to do with'.[5] In a related passage in his introduction to the *Treatise*, Hume maintains that all the sciences have a greater

---

[2] John Locke, *An Essay Concerning Human Understanding*, ed. P. H. Nidditch (Oxford: Clarendon Press, 1975)

[3] David Hume, *A Treatise of Human Nature*, ed. L. A. Selby-Bigge (Oxford: Clarendon Press, 1978).

[4] Foreword to Locke's *Essay*, p. xxiii.   [5] *Essay*, I.i.2.

or lesser relation to human nature since 'they lie under the cognizance of men, and are judged by their powers and faculties'.[6] Given that 'the science of man is the only solid foundation for the other sciences... the only solid foundation we can give to this science itself must be laid on experience and observation'.[7]

What is the alternative to regarding an empirical investigation of the discerning faculties of human beings as foundational for epistemology? The obvious alternative is what might be called 'universalism'. For the universalist, it is the proper business of epistemology to give an account of the conditions of *any* knowledge or, perhaps, any *empirical* knowledge of reality. There is nothing in the concept of empirical knowledge which would justify the stipulation that only human beings are capable of such knowledge, so arriving at an understanding of the peculiarities of the human cognitive apparatus cannot be as important for the universalist as it is for the humanist. Instead, universalism might hold that an account of the conditions of empirical knowledge must be grounded in an analysis of concepts such as those of knowledge, belief and justification. For example, if it is a conceptual truth that fulfilment of some condition C is necessary for empirical knowledge of reality, then the cognitive faculties of any beings, including human beings, who are capable of empirical knowledge of reality must be so structured as to enable them to fulfil condition C. If it turns out that only beings whose cognitive faculties are similar to ours

[6] *Treatise*, p. xv.   [7] Ibid., p. xvi.

can fulfil condition C, this would be an important discovery, but it would still not be a reason to accept a definition of the concept of empirical knowledge which has built into it the stipulation that only members of a particular animal species are capable of such knowledge. The key to universalism, therefore, is its insistence that epistemology must concern itself with the uncovering of conditions of knowledge which are universal in scope, conditions which must be fulfilled by any knowing subject, human or otherwise.

It is far from obvious that humanism and universalism are mutually exclusive.[8] Indeed one of my aims here will be to look in some detail at a position which combines elements of humanism and universalism in its account of the conditions of empirical knowledge. Before saying more about this 'mixed' position, however, it would be worth remarking that the distinction between humanism and universalism also has a bearing on our understanding of the subject matter of the philosophy of mind. The philosophy of mind is, presumably, concerned with the nature of mind, but it would be natural to ask *whose* mind or what *kind* of mind is at issue here.[9] The humanist in the philosophy of mind is someone who thinks that the primary concern

---

[8] In his Introduction to *Epistemology and Cognition* (Cambridge, MA: Harvard University Press, 1986), Alvin I. Goldman defends a conception of epistemology which combines elements of what I am calling 'universalism' and 'humanism', though Goldman's label for humanist epistemology is 'psychologistic epistemology'.

[9] Colin McGinn presses these questions in *The Character of Mind* (Oxford: Oxford University Press, 1982), pp. 1-4.

of what is generally known as the philosophy of mind is, and ought to be, with the nature of the human mind. Human minds are not the only minds that there are, but the philosophy of mind is only concerned with non-human minds to the extent that they are like human minds. In contrast, the universalist is someone who thinks that the philosophy of mind ought to concern itself with what might be called 'mind in general'[10] or 'mind as such'.[11] For the universalist, human and non-human minds are all instances of mind in general, and this means that theories of mentality which only address the human case are guilty of an unwarranted parochialism.[12]

These remarks might prompt the thought that the contrast between humanism and universalism in the philosophy of mind is a false one since, as Wittgenstein puts it, 'it is only of a living human being and what resembles (behaves like) a living human being one can say: it has sensations; it sees; is blind; hears; is deaf; is conscious or unconscious'.[13] This anthropocentric approach to the mind maintains that what the universalist calls 'mind as such' is simply an abstraction from certain abilities and dispositions

---

[10] McGinn, *The Character of Mind*, p. 2.

[11] W. H. Walsh, *Kant's Criticism of Metaphysics* (Edinburgh: Edinburgh University Press, 1975), p. 89.

[12] For example, McGinn claims in *The Character of Mind*, p. 1, that 'it is frequently a good test of a theory of some mental phenomenon to ask whether the proposed theory would be applicable to *all* actual and possible creatures exemplifying that phenomenon'.

[13] L. Wittgenstein, *Philosophical Investigations*, translated by G. E. M. Anscombe (Oxford: Basil Blackwell, 1978), section 281.

possessed by live human beings,[14] so one should not follow the universalist in representing the humanist's investigation of the human cognitive apparatus as something which falls short of the proper business of giving an account of the nature of mind as such. Rather, once it is recognized that all minds must be conceived of on an analogy with our own, an investigation of 'our' cognitive faculties may be seen as deepening our understanding of mind as such. By the same token, if all minds must be conceived of on an analogy with our own, then one should also refuse to follow Locke and other humanists in contrasting the human understanding with other types of understanding that might be fundamentally different from ours.

I will have more to say in due course about anthropocentrism, but the next section will be concerned with an epistemological position which combines elements of humanism and universalism, while apparently distancing itself from anything recognizable as anthropocentrism. The position which I have in mind is one which is suggested by Kant's discussion in the *Critique of Pure Reason* of what he refers to as '*a priori* conditions of the possibility of experience' (A94/B126).[15] It is true that Kant himself does not employ the terminology of humanism and universalism. Instead, he sets out to defend transcendental idealism, the view that space and time are merely the forms of our sensibility rather than conditions of objects as they are in

---

[14] Cf. Walsh, *Kant's Criticism of Metaphysics,* pp. 251–2, and Q. Cassam, *Self and World* (Oxford: Clarendon Press, 1997), pp. 12–21.

[15] All references in this form are to Norman Kemp Smith's translation of *Kant's Critique of Pure Reason* (London: Macmillan, 1929).

themselves, and to distinguish his conception of the *a priori* or necessary conditions of the possibility of experience from the subjectivist thesis that such conditions are merely subjectively necessary. Nevertheless, it will emerge that there is a close connection between, on the one hand, Kant's humanism and his transcendental idealism, and, on the other, between his universalism and his opposition to subjectivism, a position which he associates with Hume. One of my aims in what follows will be to explore these connections.

While transcendental idealism may be a position for which few late twentieth-century epistemologists and philosophers of mind have much sympathy, it would be a mistake to conclude that Kant's position is of merely historical interest. Quite apart from the intrinsic interest of the proposal that humanism and idealism are linked in the way that Kant suggests, questions about the appropriate balance between universalism and humanism remain of fundamental importance for our understanding of knowledge and mind. Whether or not Kant's deep and subtle account of these matters is ultimately acceptable, it is not one which one can afford to ignore if one has ever been struck by the difficulty of giving a straight answer to the question of what the philosophy of mind is about. Thus, the issues which I propose to address are these: first, does Kant's conception of the status and origins of his *a priori* conditions of the possibility of experience constitute a stable and coherent combination of humanism and universalism? Secondly, what is the bearing of Kant's theory of *a priori* conditions on the dispute between transcendental idealism and what he calls transcendental realism? My own view is that the first of these questions should be answered in the negative, and that the most attractive position in connection with the second question is one which combines a form of universalism with transcendental realism, the view that space and time are conditions of the possibility of things in themselves *as well as* conditions of our sensible awareness of empirical reality.

II

A priori conditions of the possibility of experience are necessary conditions of the possibility of experience. Experience, for Kant, is a form of empirical knowledge. So *a priori* conditions of the possibility of experience may be understood as necessary conditions of the possibility of empirical knowledge. Empirical knowledge of an object is represented by Kant as involving two factors, 'first, the concept, through which an object in general is thought ... and secondly, the intuition, through which it is given' (B146). At this stage, an 'object' may simply be understood as a particular instance of a general concept.[16] The concepts which the understanding must employ in thinking or conceptualizing objects of (sensible) intuition are the Kantian 'categories', which include those of substance and causality. Intuitions are singular and immediate representations of particulars which are given to us by means of sensibility. Sensibility is 'the capacity (receptivity) for receiving representations through the mode in which we are affected by

---

[16] This is the less 'weighty' of the two senses of 'object' which P. F. Strawson distinguishes in *The Bounds of Sense: An Essay on Kant's Critique of Pure Reason* (London: Methuen & Co. Ltd., 1966), pp. 72–3.

objects' (A19/B33). In the Transcendental Aesthetic, Kant argues that space and time are the 'two original forms of sensibility' (A41/B58), that is, 'necessary conditions under which alone objects can be for us objects of the senses' (A28-9). Thus, space and time might be described as the sensible conditions of empirical knowledge and the categories as its intellectual conditions.[17]

While this way of representing Kant's position is undoubtedly along the right lines, it is incomplete in at least one important respect, for it fails to make anything of the fact that Kant is not even-handed in his treatment of the sensible and intellectual conditions of our knowledge. With regard to space, Kant insists that it is 'solely from the human standpoint that we can speak of space, of extended things, etc.' (A26/B42). There are two closely related points being made here. The first is that space does not represent any property of things in themselves; it is *merely* a subjective condition of sensibility. The second is that 'we cannot judge in regard to the intuition of other thinking beings, whether they are bound by the same conditions as those which limit our intuition and which for us are universally valid' (A27/B43). In other words, we are only entitled to assert that space and time are the necessary conditions of *human* awareness of particularity. To the extent that Kant is only concerned in the Transcendental Aesthetic with the conditions of human awareness of particularity, his account of the original forms

---

[17] This way of putting things is suggested by Henry Allison in *Kant's Transcendental Idealism: An Interpretation and Defense* (New Haven: Yale University Press, 1983), chapters 5 and 6.

of sensibility is humanist rather than universalist, though he would have insisted that his investigation of these forms is *a priori* rather empirical or naturalistic. A universalist about the forms of sensibility would be someone who maintains that spatio-temporal intuition is a necessary condition of any empirical knowledge of objects, but Kant leaves open the possibility that spatio-temporal awareness is a mode of perceiving which is 'peculiar to us, and not necessarily shared in by every being, though, certainly, by every human being' (A42/B59). As for the link between humanism and transcendental idealism, the very fact that Kant expressed his idealism by saying that it is solely from the human standpoint that we can speak of space suggests that he saw the two as closely connected, though the precise nature of this connection has yet to be explained.

Kant's account of the status of the categories is very different. It is true that the categories are said to have their 'first seeds and dispositions in the human understanding' (A66/B91), but he also insists that they relate 'to objects of intuition in general, whether that intuition be our own or any other, provided only it be sensible' (B150). In other words, the categories are not just concepts which we humans must employ in order to conceptualize the objects of our spatio-temporal sensible intuition, but also concepts which must be employed by any discursive intellect in thinking the objects of its sensibility, spatio-temporal or otherwise.[18] The

---

[18] A discursive understanding is characterized by Kant as one whose knowledge must be 'by means of concepts' (A68/B93). He adds that 'the only use which the understanding can make of these concepts is to

primordial being – God – would have no use for the categories, since divine intuition would be 'intellectual' rather than sensible, but this is compatible with maintaining that the categories are the universal and necessary conditions of any *empirical* knowledge of objects, any knowledge the acquisition of which involves the exercise of sensibility. So the most striking difference between Kant's theory of the categories and his theory of the forms of our sensibility is that the former is universalist in its orientation,[19] whereas the latter has much more in common with the humanist tradition.

My question is whether Kant's conception of the status and origins of his *a priori* conditions of the possibility of experience constitutes a stable and coherent combination of humanism and universalism. In the light of what has just been said about the respects in which Kant is a humanist and the respects in which he is a universalist, it should now be clear that this extremely general question can now be broken down into a series of rather more precise sub-questions. With regard to the theory of sensibility, the most pressing sub-questions would appear to be these:

judge by means of them' (ibid.). As W. H. Walsh remarks, it was Kant's consistent doctrine that 'the categories were by no means peculiar to human nature, but were involved in discursive thinking as such' (*Reason and Experience* (Oxford: Clarendon Press, 1947), pp. 163–4).

[19] To the extent that Kant's account of the role of the categories is an important element of his 'transcendental psychology', its universalist orientation is not brought out by Patricia Kitcher's characterization of transcendental psychology as seeking 'to determine the necessary and universal elements of human cognition' (*Kant's Transcendental Psychology* (Oxford: Oxford University Press 1990), p. 19).

S1. Are there good grounds for thinking that space and time are necessary conditions of human awareness of objects which would not also be good grounds for thinking that space and time are necessary conditions of any sensible awareness of objects?

S2. To the extent that the Transcendental Aesthetic is an investigation of *our* mode of perceiving objects, how can it be anything other than an *empirical* investigation of contingent aspects of the functioning of the human cognitive apparatus?

S3. What exactly is the relationship between the claim that it is solely from the human standpoint that we can speak of space and the thesis that space is transcendentally ideal?

The point of these questions is this: if, in connection with (SI), it turns out that the only legitimate grounds for thinking that space and time are necessary conditions of human awareness of particularity would also be grounds for thinking that they are necessary conditions of any sensible awareness of particularity, then the thesis that it is solely from the human standpoint that we can speak of space is open to question. Yet, as is suggested by Kant's response to (S3), the loss of this thesis would amount to the loss of an important element of the case for transcendental idealism. As for (S2), Kant is apparently prepared to grant that it is contingent that space and time are the forms of our sensibility.[20] In that case, it might be wondered whether he is

---

[20] Strawson reads Kant in this way in 'Kant's New Foundations of Metaphysics', in *Entity and Identity and Other Essays* (Oxford: Clarendon Press, 1997), pp. 237–8. He quotes B145–6 in support of this

right to be so resistant to the idea that his investigation of these contingent aspects of the human cognitive apparatus can only properly be read as an empirical investigation. Yet, Kant's conception of the relationship between his theory of mind and the theories of more straightforward humanists such as Locke and Hume makes it very important for him to resist any such account of the nature of his investigation.

With regard to Kant's theory of understanding, it is the humanist rather than the universalist who may have doubts on this score. Among the questions which will need to be addressed in this connection are these:

U1. If, as Kant insists, we know nothing but our mode of perceiving objects, then should he not also have insisted that we know nothing but our mode of thinking objects of sensible intuition, and that the categories can only be known by us to represent the intellectual conditions of human knowledge of objects rather than conditions of all discursive thinking?

U2. What kind of investigation would be required to demonstrate that the categories relate to objects of sensible intuition in general, whether that intuition be our own or any other?

U3. How can concepts which, by Kant's own lights, have their first seeds and dispositions in the *human*

---

reading. For a more detailed discussion on Kant's position on this question, see Lorne Falkenstein, *Kant's Intuitionism: A Commentary on the Transcendental Aesthetic* (Toronto: University of Toronto Press, 1995), pp. 193–200.

understanding have the universal scope which Kant claims for the categories?

The point of these questions, then, is to suggest that Kant should have been as modest about the status of his theory of understanding as he was about the status of his theory of sensibility. Like Locke, he should have refrained from making claims about the intellectual faculties of finite thinking beings other than man.

One way of working up to a detailed consideration of these questions would be to look more closely at the notion of an *a priori* condition. So far, I have said that *a priori* conditions are necessary conditions of the possibility of experience, but it might be wondered what kind of necessity this is supposed to be. On one view, *a priori* conditions are subjectively necessary conditions. I will refer to this view as *subjectivism*. On another view, they are what Henry Allison calls 'epistemic conditions'.[21] I will refer to this view as *idealism* about *a priori* conditions. A third view, which I will refer to as *realism*, would be that *a priori* conditions are objectively necessary conditions of the possibility of experience. Subjectivism and idealism are both humanist rather than universalist, whereas realism's conception of *a priori* conditions is universalist rather than humanist. With regard to the dispute between transcendental realism and transcendental idealism, it should come as no surprise that idealism about *a priori* conditions goes with transcendental idealism and that realism about *a priori* conditions goes with

[21] See Kant's *Transcendental Idealism,* 10–13.

transcendental realism. The position of the subjectivist on this question is less clear, though it will eventually emerge that subjectivism is at least compatible with transcendental realism.

Kant's own conception of *a priori* conditions is idealist rather than subjectivist or realist. My claim will be that idealism fails to provide satisfactory answers to the questions outlined above. I will also argue that most of Kant's objections to subjectivism and realism are misguided. The failure of these objections is due, in part, to the fact that Kant's attempt to combine elements of humanism and universalism results in a position which is fundamentally unstable. To this extent, it remains unclear how the Kantian programme in epistemology is to be understood. While Kant's objections to subjectivism are largely misguided, my own position is not subjectivist. Instead, I will be arguing that the best position in this area is realism, and that this has important consequences for our understanding of the nature of epistemology and the philosophy of mind.

III

What would it be for a condition of human knowledge to be merely subjectively necessary? To regard a condition as merely subjectively necessary is to regard it as grounded in contingent, empirically discoverable facts about the structure or constitution of our – that is, human – cognitive faculties. This is the sense in which subjectivism is a form of humanism. Suppose, for example, that our senses are so constituted as to restrict us to the perception of objects with spatial properties. If this is a contingent, empirically discoverable fact about the constitution of what Kant refers to as our 'faculty of sensible intuition', then it is subjectively necessary that for an object O to be perceivable, and hence knowable, by us, O must be spatial. This might be described as an *intuition version* of the subjectivist view.[22] An example of a *concept version* of subjectivism would be this: suppose that our understanding is so constituted as to make it impossible for us to think of objects of experience unless they are, and are thought of by us as being, causally ordered. In that case, it is subjectively necessary that for objects to be thinkable, and hence knowable, by us, they must be causally ordered and must be represented as such. This would be an example of a subjective necessity, as long as it is assumed that this fact about the structure of our faculty of understanding is empirically discoverable.

If there is one thing that is clear about Kant's position, it is that he did not accept that *a priori* conditions are merely subjectively necessary. His explicit objection to subjectivism is that it amounts to a form of scepticism. The sense in which the subjectivist is a sceptic is supposed to be this: if all we can say is that our senses are so constituted as to restrict us to the perception of objects in space, then this is simply a fact about us, from which nothing follows about the nature of the objects themselves. By the same token, if all we can say is that we are so constituted as to be incapable of thinking of given representations other than as causally

---

[22] Paul Guyer appears to attribute this version of subjectivism to Kant in *Kant and the Claims of Knowledge* (Cambridge: Cambridge University Press, 1987), p. 367.

connected, we would not be able to say that 'the effect is connected with the cause in the object'. This, Kant continues, 'is exactly what the sceptic most desires' (B168).

On the face of it, this objection to subjectivism is mistaken. To say that we are limited to perceiving objects with some property P is not just to make a claim about the perceiving subject; it is also to make a claim about how *objects* must be if they are to be perceivable by us. So if O is an object that is perceivable by us, then O must have the property P. On this reading, the judgement that any possible object of human sense-perception must have the property P is, in Broad's terminology, 'transcendentally *a priori*', one which is 'entailed by certain very general facts about the way in which human minds work'.[23] The fact that transcendentally *a priori* judgements are grounded in such facts would arguably be one good reason for insisting, in response to (S1), that O's possession of P might be a necessary condition of *our* awareness of O without being a necessary condition of *any* sensible awareness of it. Moreover, the claim that O would not be perceivable by us if it lacked the property P is independent of any commitment to the idea that O's possession of P is something for which 'we' are responsible; it can be true both that P is a mind-independent property of O, and that our ability to perceive O is conditional upon its possession of P.[24] So the subjectivist should argue, in

[23] C. D. Broad, *Kant: An Introduction*, edited by C. Lewy (Cambridge: Cambridge University Press, 1978), p. 7.

[24] This is the moral of Ross Harrison's important paper on 'Transcendental Arguments and Idealism', in *Idealism Past and*

response to (S3), that even if space and time are specifically human conditions of object-awareness, it does not follow that 'if the subject, or even the subjective constitution of the senses in general, be removed ... space and time themselves, would vanish' (A42/B59).

This might prompt the thought that the sense in which subjectivism is what the sceptic most desires is not that it creates an unbridgeable gap between mind and world, but that it fails to establish the 'objective validity' of the categories and of the concepts of space and time. To establish the objective validity of the categories would be to show that they 'furnish conditions of the possibility of all knowledge of objects' (A89–90/B122). If the need for us to employ categories in thinking objects of sensible intuition is simply a reflection of the peculiar constitution of the human understanding, on what basis can the subjectivist claim that they furnish conditions of the possibility of all knowledge of objects? The subjectivist will not be troubled by this question. To begin with, Kant himself describes the concepts of space and time as objectively valid (A87/B120) despite the fact that he does not regard himself as entitled to assert that spatio-temporal awareness is a necessary condition of any sensible awareness of objects. For the subjectivist, the moral is that Kant was not entitled to assert that the categories are conditions of any discursive thinking, any more than he would have been within his rights to claim that space and time are conditions of any sensible awareness of objects.

Present, ed. G. Vesey, Royal Institute of Philosophy Lecture Series 13 (Cambridge: Cambridge University Press, 1982).

This is the essence of subjectivism's response to (U1). This response to (U1) means that (U2) lapses. As for (U3), the subjectivist will maintain that Kant simply fails to recognize the tension between his own conception of the human origins of the categories and his universalist conception of their scope.

A somewhat different interpretation of Kant's objection to subjectivism would be that while it is perfectly legitimate to represent very general facts about the way in which human minds work as the basis of *a priori* conditions, it is not legitimate for the subjectivist to represent these facts as empirically discoverable. The underlying point here is presumably that an investigation of *a priori* conditions must itself be *a priori*. The difficulty with this objection is brought to light by (S2). As has already been remarked, Kant is in agreement with the subjectivist that it is contingent that our cognitive faculties are as they are. In other words, while it is necessary that space and time are the conditions of human awareness of particularity, it is not necessary that they have this status.[25] If, however, the truths about our cognitive faculties upon which Kantian *a priori* conditions are grounded are in themselves contingent, then it is far from obvious how our knowledge of such truths could be

---

[25] As Falkenstein puts it, Kant's view is that it is a 'contingent truth that, for us, space is a *necessary* ground of outer appearances' (*Kant's Intuitionism,* 199). The related idea that some necessary or 'eternal' truths are only contingently necessary has also been attributed to Descartes. See Edwin Curley, 'Descartes on the Creation of Eternal Truths', *Philosophical Review* 93/4 (October 1984), 569–97.

anything other than empirical. For Kant, 'any knowledge that professes to hold *a priori* lays claim to be regarded as absolutely necessary' (Axv), but his own assertions about the constitution of our faculty of intuition do not lay claim to be regarded as absolutely necessary. In that case, it can scarcely be a good objection to subjectivism to point out that it represents subjectively necessary conditions as a reflection of facts about our cognitive apparatus that are empirically knowable, since, by Kant's own lights, we cannot have *a priori* knowledge of a contingent truth.

So much, then, for Kant's objections to subjectivism. In the light of these difficulties, it would be worth considering the possibility that *a priori* conditions are what Allison calls 'epistemic conditions'. An epistemic condition is an 'objectivating' condition, 'one that is necessary for the representation of an object or objective state of affairs'.[26] What makes this position idealist is its distinctive conception of the scope and origins of epistemic conditions. With regard to the scope of epistemic conditions, Allison's thesis is that they 'express the universal and necessary conditions in terms of which alone the human mind is capable of recognizing something as an object at all'.[27] To the extent that epistemic conditions are specifically human conditions of object-awareness, they might be described as being species-specific in scope. With regard to the origins or basis of epistemic conditions, the proposal is that they 'reflect the structure and

---

[26] *Kant's Transcendental Idealism,* 10.   [27] Ibid., p. 9.

operations of the human mind'[28] rather than the nature of objects as they are in themselves. In this sense, epistemic conditions are species-specific in origin. Since epistemic conditions are species-specific both in scope and in origin, Allison's account is humanist rather than universalist. On the other hand, it is also supposed to be quite different from subjectivism. A subjectively necessary condition is merely psychological, that is, 'a propensity or mechanism of the mind which governs belief and belief acquisition'.[29] The alleged difference between epistemic conditions and psychological conditions is that the latter have no objectivating function and so lack objective validity.

Does idealism provide a satisfactory response to (SI)? In defence of Kant's theory of space, Allison argues that

> in order to be aware of things as numerically distinct from one another, it is necessary to be aware, not only of their qualitative differences, but also of the fact that they are located in different places. In other words, the representation of place, and therefore of space, functions within human experience as a necessary condition of the possibility of distinguishing objects from one another . . . it is not a logically necessary condition. There is no contradiction in the thought that there might be some other, nonspatial mode of awareness of numerical diversity; we simply do not know what such a mode of awareness would be like.[30]

[28] Henry Allison, 'Transcendental Idealism: A Retrospective', in *Idealism and Freedom: Essays on Kant's Theoretical and Practical Philosophy* (Cambridge: Cambridge University Press, 1996), pp. 4–5.

[29] Ibid., p. 4.   [30] Kant's *Transcendental Idealism*, pp. 83–4.

The difficulty with this passage is that it is extremely unclear what work the qualification 'human' is supposed to be doing in its second sentence. On the face of it, the best possible case for saying that spatial awareness is a necessary condition of awareness of things as numerically distinct from one another is that we can make nothing of the idea of non-spatial awareness of numerical diversity. To the extent, however, that nothing can be made of the idea of non-spatial awareness of numerical diversity, this would appear to constitute a case for saying that spatial awareness must function within any sensible experience as the form of awareness of particularity. Perhaps the 'must' in this formulation is not, as Allison insists, a strictly logical 'must', but it is still plausible that the connection between spatial awareness and awareness of numerical diversity is either valid for all sensible cognition or it is not genuinely necessary. Unless what is at issue is a merely psychological necessity, it makes no sense to suppose that a genuinely necessary condition of the possibility of experience might turn out only to be necessary for human beings, *qua* members of a particular animal species. To the extent, therefore, that the point of the reference to human experience in Allison's second sentence is to imply that spatial awareness is, or might be, a species-specific condition of awareness of particularity, it is not justified by the best case for his opening sentence. So idealism fails to provide a satisfactory response to (S1).

It might be objected that this line of argument ignores the simplest and most obvious case for insisting that the sensible conditions of human knowledge are species-specific in scope. It has just been argued that the best way of explaining the peculiarly intimate connection that obtains between spatial awareness and awareness of particularity would be to point out that nothing can be made of the idea of non-spatial awareness of numerical diversity. To say this, however, is simply to say that we can make nothing of this idea, and this only goes to show, at best, that we cannot imagine being aware of particularity other than in spatial form. To conclude that spatial awareness is a necessary condition of *any* awareness of numerical diversity would be grossly to exaggerate the importance of our imaginative limitations.

Later I will argue that this attempt to explain the force of the thesis that epistemic conditions are species-specific in scopes is unsuccessful. First, there are other matters to consider. With regard to (S2), the idealist must insist, on pain of undermining the distinction between idealism and subjectivism, that his investigation of the forms of human sensibility is not an empirical investigation. The difficulty with this, however, is that it is far from obvious that the idealist has a coherent alternative to the subjectivist's conception of the status of Kant's inquiry. The natural alternative would be to think of Kant's investigation as broadly conceptual or analytical, but if spatial awareness is a *conceptually* necessary condition of the possibility of awareness of particularity, then it would seem that it must be a conceptually necessary condition of *any* sensible awareness of particularity. Since it is quite mysterious how a conceptually necessary condition of awareness of numerical diversity could only be valid for human cognition, it is the thesis that space is a species-specific conditions of empirical knowledge which is one against under threat.

What is the relationship between the thesis that space is a species-specific condition of human knowledge, and the transcendental idealist thesis that space does not represent any property of things in themselves? For the idealist, the connection might be something like the following: if space is only a necessary condition of human awareness rather than a necessary condition of any sensible awareness of objects, then it cannot also be a property of objects or things as they are in themselves. The spatial perspective would simply be *our* perspective on the world, a mode of representing objects which is peculiar to us, and properties which are simply a reflection of the constitution of our faculty of intuition cannot properly be attributed to the world as it is in itself. Things in themselves are things considered independently of the subjective conditions of human sensibility, so if space and time are such conditions, then spatial and temporal predicates cannot meaningfully be ascribed to things as they are in themselves.

This response to (S3) raises the following question: in arguing from the premise that space is only a condition of human awareness of objects to the conclusion that spatial predicates cannot properly be ascribed to things as they are in themselves, is the idealist not guilty of begging the question against transcendental realism? According to transcendental realism, things in themselves are spatial, and this means that spatial awareness is not just a subjective condition of human sensibility but a necessary condition of any empirical knowledge of objects. Thus, according to transcendental realism, one would only have grounds for thinking that space is merely a condition of human awareness rather than of any sensible awareness of objects if one is *already* persuaded of the non-spatiality of things as they are in themselves. It would appear, therefore, that the thesis that space is a species-specific condition of awareness of particularity cannot be regarded as a non-question-begging premise in an argument for transcendental idealism. By the same token, however, the thesis that things as they are in themselves are spatial can hardly be regarded as a non-question-begging premise in an argument against the idealist's conception of the scope of epistemic conditions. The idealist is hardly likely to accept that his humanist conception of the scope of epistemic conditions is inadequate *because* things as they are in themselves are spatial, any more than the realist is likely to accept that spatial predicates cannot meaningfully be ascribed to things as they are in themselves *because* epistemic conditions are merely subjective.

At this point, it might seem that the idealist and realist have reached a stand-off, with each accusing the other of begging the question. I will have more to say about this apparent stand-off when I give a more detailed account of realism about *a priori* conditions, but first there is another objection to idealism to discuss. So far, I have represented transcendental idealism as relying upon the thesis that epistemic conditions are species-specific in scope, but it is not clear that this thesis is faithful to Kant. To begin with, I have already remarked that Kant does not represent the categories as species-specific conditions of knowledge. One reaction to this observation would be to argue, in response to (U1), that Kant was wrong to be a universalist about the categories, but this attempt to bring Kant's theory of understanding into line with his theory of sensibility is arguably guilty of misunderstanding the latter. For while Kant does say that it is solely from the human standpoint that we can speak of space, he adds that spatio-temporal intuition 'need not be limited to human sensibility. It may be that all finite, thinking beings necessarily agree with man in this respect, although we are not in a position to judge whether this is actually so' (B72). If all finite, thinking beings necessarily agree with man in this respect, then spatio-temporal intuition is not a species-specific condition of sensibility. To the extent that Kant is agnostic on the question of whether space and time are species-specific conditions of sensibility, it would not bring his theory of understanding into line with his theory of sensibility to insist upon the species-specificity of the categories as conditions of knowledge.

By the same token, it might be held to be a misunderstanding of Allison to represent him as maintaining that epistemic conditions are species-specific in scope. It might be argued, instead, that the point of the qualification 'human' in his account of epistemic conditions is to mark a distinction between *finite* cognition and the 'standard of cognition theoretically achievable by an "absolute" or "infinite" intellect'.[31] With regard to the representation of space, therefore, the claim is that it constitutes a universal and necessary condition in terms of which alone *any finite intelligent* being is capable of recognizing something as an object. A finite intelligent being is one whose intuition is sensible

---

[31] Ibid., p. 19

and whose understanding is discursive. Since any knowledge that involves the exercise of sensibility is empirical knowledge, finite cognition is empirical cognition. So the claim that a given condition is a necessary condition of all finite cognition amounts to the claim that it is a necessary condition of any empirical knowledge of objects, and this is precisely what the universalist wishes to maintain.

Since humanism about the conditions of sensibility has so far been represented as holding the key to transcendental idealism, what would remain of idealism once it is conceded that space, time, and the categories are not just conditions of human knowledge but conditions of any empirical knowledge of objects? One response to this question would be to argue that idealism remains a distinctive position as along as it continues to insist that *a priori* or epistemic conditions are species-specific in origin. In other words, the fact that space, time and the categories are universal conditions of empirical knowledge is to be seen as a reflection of the 'cognitive structure of the human mind'[32] rather than the nature of things as they are in themselves. Presumably, the cognitive structure of the human mind consists in the fact that space and time are the forms of human sensibility and that the categories are the rules of our understanding. On this reading, Kant's agnosticism about the scope of space and time as conditions of sensibility is not essential to his idealism; what is essential is his conception of the human origins of *a priori* conditions.

[32] Ibid., p. 29.

At this point, however, a generalized version of (U3) becomes especially pressing, for it might be wondered how conditions which are universal in scope can still be species-specific in origin. The difficulty is that unless all finite minds are assumed to be like human minds, it cannot coherently be supposed that the cognitive structure of the *human* mind is the source of conditions which bind *all* finite minds that are capable of empirical knowledge of objects. Given the assumption that finite intelligent minds might be of very many different types, the cognitive structure of the human mind can surely only be the source of epistemic conditions understood as the universal and necessary conditions of *human* cognition. So if, as Kant says, the categories have their first seeds and dispositions in the human understanding, then he is not entitled to regard them as universal in scope. If they are universal in scope, then it is not the human understanding that is the source of the categories, but the Understanding in a more generic sense. More generally, *a priori* conditions which are truly universal in scope must be seen as reflecting the structure of 'mind as such' rather than the cognitive structure of the human mind.

There are several difficulties with this proposal. The first is that it remains to be seen whether anything can be made of the notion of 'mind as such'. The second is that very little remains of idealism about *a priori* conditions once it is accepted that such conditions are not only universal in scope but also that they are not species-specific in origin. In the light of these difficulties, it might be worth exploring the anthropocentric position outlined above. Anthropocentrism, it will be recalled, is the view that all minds must be conceived of on an analogy with our own, and that what the universalist calls 'mind as such' is nothing more than an abstraction from certain abilities and dispositions that are possessed by live human beings. As Jonathan Lear puts it, in connection with what he takes to be Wittgenstein's conception of mind, anthropocentrism in its strongest form maintains that 'the concept of being minded in any way at all is that of being minded as we are'.[33] Given this conception of mindedness, it is no longer mysterious how the structure of the human mind can be the source of *a priori* conditions which are universal in scope. If the concept of being minded in any way at all is that of being minded as we are, then the conditions of empirical knowledge which bind human minds must also bind all minds which must be conceived of on an analogy with human minds, that is to say, all minds.

This attempt to make something of the suggestion that non-species-specific *a priori* conditions might still be grounded in the structure of the human mind is only as good as the case for anthropocentrism. A non-anthropocentric, 'objective' conception of mind would be one which insists, with Nagel, that 'we must think of mind as a phenomenon to which the human case is not necessarily central, even though our minds are at the center of our world'.[34] Human minds are instances of mind in general, but what entitles us to regard ourselves as the central instances? To this it might be replied, on behalf of anthropocentrism, that

---

[33] 'The Disappearing "We"', *Proceedings of the Aristotelian Society*, Supplementary Volume 58 (1984), 233.

[34] Thomas Nagel, *The View Front Nowhere* (Oxford: Oxford University Press, 1986), p. 18.

for something to be a mind at all it must be interpretable by us, and that we can only interpret minds which resemble our own. Presumably, however, someone who is opposed to anthropocentrism will reject this argument on the grounds that its assumption that mindedness requires interpretability *by us* presupposes, and so is not an argument for, the notion that mind is a phenomenon to which the human case is necessarily central.

Fortunately, it is not necessary to resolve this dispute here since it is clear that Kant's conception of mind is not anthropocentric. Far from accepting that all minds must be like human minds, Kant repeatedly contrasts our minds and the distinctively human perspective on reality with the minds and perspectives of beings who might be very different from ourselves.[35] One contrast is that between human mindedness and the mindedness of the primordial being, whose intuition would be intellectual rather than sensible. Another contrast is that between ourselves and other finite thinking beings whose sensibility might be, for all we know, non-spatio-temporal. If Kant were to accept the anthropocentric proposal that these contrasts are in some way illegitimate, he would hardly have chosen to express his idealism by saying that space is something which we can only speak of from the *human* standpoint, and that we cannot judge in regard to the intuition of other thinking beings whether they are bound by the same conditions as those which limit *our* intuition. Unlike Wittgenstein, therefore, Kant does not

[35] This aspect of Kant's position is rightly emphasized by Lear in 'The Disappearing "We"', 232.

accept that the concept of being minded in any way at all is that of being minded as we are. So while it is arguable that anthropocentrism is itself a form of idealism, it is not idealism in Kant's sense.

The position, then, is this: idealism was introduced as the view that *a priori* or epistemic conditions are species-specific in both scope and origin. It was then argued that idealism fails to give a satisfactory explanation of how *a priori* conditions can be species-specific in scope, since the considerations which support the view that space, time and the categories are the universal and necessary conditions of human cognition also support the view that they are among the universal and necessary conditions of all empirical knowledge. An attempt was then made to preserve something of the spirit of idealism about epistemic conditions by arguing that even if such conditions are universal in scope, they might nevertheless reflect the cognitive structure of the human mind. It was then argued that this hybrid position is unsatisfactory, and that Kantian idealism about *a priori* conditions is not helped by an anthropocentric conception of mind. In the light of these difficulties with idealism, the time has come to explore the prospects for realism. In the course of this exploration, I will return to what was referred to above as the simplest and most obvious idealist case for insisting that the conditions of human knowledge are species-specific in scope, namely, the idea that so-called epistemic conditions can only be a reflection of human imaginative limitations.

Realism is the view that *a priori* conditions of the possibility of experience or empirical knowledge are objectively necessary conditions of the possibility of experience or empirical knowledge. To regard *a priori* conditions as objectively necessary is to regard them as universal in scope – that is, as necessary conditions of *any* empirical knowledge of objects – and as reflecting the nature of the objects of empirical knowledge as they are in themselves. These two aspects of realism are connected in the following way: *a priori* conditions are universal in scope *because* they must be faithful to the character of things in themselves. The underlying point here is that conditions which have no objective basis, in the sense that they do not accurately reflect the character or constitution of reality as it is in itself, could not properly be described as conditions under which *knowledge* of reality is possible. On the other hand, conditions which *are* objectively based must be universal in scope, since conditions which reflect the nature of things as they are in themselves are, precisely, conditions which are not grounded in the peculiarities of the human cognitive apparatus.

The attractions of realism, together with some of its limitations, may be brought out by examining P. F. Strawson's writings on Kant. Strawson represents Kant as pushing to the limit the distinction between intuitions and concepts, 'trying to extract as much as he can of the *a priori* conditions of empirical knowledge or experience from a consideration merely of one half of the distinction, namely, the necessity of bringing particular objects of experience – whatever the forms of particularity may be – under general concepts'.[36] The bringing of objects under concepts is

[36] *The Bounds of Sense*, pp. 77–8.

identical with the making of judgements about objects, and it is 'an analytic truth that the judgement involves concepts, that concepts are such as to be applicable or inapplicable to one or more instances, that judgements or propositions are capable of truth or falsity'.[37] The problem with Kant's position is that reflection on the conditions of making objective judgements seems unlikely to 'yield much of a harvest in the way of categories',[38] but there is a relatively simple way of dealing with this difficulty. For we are creatures whose intellects are discursive and whose intuition is sensible; such creatures must

> in judgement, employ and apply general concepts to the objects of sensible intuition; the very notion of the generality of a concept implies the possibility of numerically distinguishable individual objects falling under one and the same concept; and once granted that objects are themselves spatio-temporal, then space and time provide the uniquely necessary media for the realization of this possibility in sensible intuition of objects.[39]

This account has a two important consequences. The first, which distinguishes realism from subjectivism as well as idealism, is that spatio-temporal intuition now appears as 'a uniquely fundamental and necessary *condition* of *any*

---

[37] Strawson, 'Sensibility, Understanding, and the Doctrine of Synthesis: Comments on Henrich and Guyer', in *Kant's Transcendental Deductions: The Three 'Critiques' and the 'Opus postumum'*, ed. E. Förster (Stanford: Stanford University Press, 1989), p. 71.

[38] *The Bounds of Sense*, p. 81.

[39] Strawson, 'Kant's New Foundations of Metaphysics', pp. 239-40.

empirical knowledge of objects'.[40] The second is that once objects of experience are assumed to be spatio-temporal, there are indeed particular ways in which we must conceive of them if we are to be able to make objective judgements about them; specifically, such objects must be conceived of as space-occupying substances that are subject to causal law, and this is the best that can be done to explain the status of the categories of substance and causality as *a priori* conditions of empirical knowledge.[41]

There can be little doubt that Strawson's account if *a priori* conditions is realist rather than idealist or subjectivist. Strawsonian *a priori* conditions are universal in scope, and they are grounded in the supposed nature of things in themselves, as well as certain analytic truths about the nature of judgement and of concepts. The crucial difference between Strawson and Kant is that Strawson is a transcendental realist about space and time, for it is the assumption that objects are in themselves spatio-temporal which underpins the Strawsonian derivation of the categories of substance and causality and its universalism about the necessary conditions of empirical knowledge. This version of realism yields the following responses to the questions outlined above. With regard to (S1), Strawson's universalism and his transcendental realism clearly commit him to answering this question in the negative. This also means that (S3) lapses, since it is *not* solely from the human standpoint that we can speak of space. In connection with

[40] Ibid., p. 240.   [41] Cf. *The Bounds of Sense,* pp. 82–5.

(S2) and (U2), Strawsonian *a priori* conditions are supposedly analytically or conceptually necessary conditions, so the realist's investigation of sensibility and understanding must be conceptual rather than empirical or psychological. This is the essence of realism's disagreement with subjectivism. Given certain assumptions about the nature of things in themselves, it is not contingent that we have 'just the forms and functions of judgement and just the spatial and temporal forms of intuition that we do have'.[42] Unlike Kant, therefore, Strawson is not faced with the difficulty of explaining how it is possible to have *a priori* knowledge of allegedly contingent aspects of the functioning of the human cognitive apparatus.

With respect to (U1), the fact that the employment of categories such as those of substance and causality is a conceptually necessary condition of the possibility of making judgements about spatio-temporal objects is not in itself a reason for maintaining that the categories are necessary conditions of all discursive thinking, unless it is also assumed that the making of judgements about spatio-temporal objects is a necessary condition of discursive thinking. Whether or not such an assumption would be defensible, it might be enough for the purposes of realism about *a priori* conditions that the categories can be known, on broadly conceptual grounds, to represent the universal intellectual conditions of empirical knowledge of a unified spatio-temporal world. Since the categories are, in this sense,

---

[42] Strawson, 'Kant's New Foundations of Metaphysics', p. 237.

universal in scope, there is no reason to suppose, in connection with (U3), that they have their first seeds and dispositions in the human understanding rather than in reflection on the conceptually necessary conditions of the possibility of experience of an objective and spatio-temporally unitary world.

The most serious objection to realism, at least in its Strawsonian form, is that it begs the central question in its dispute with idealism. *Once granted* that objects are themselves spatio-temporal, there might indeed be a case for maintaining that spatio-temporal intuition is a uniquely fundamental and necessary condition of any empirical knowledge of objects, but in a dispute between realism and transcendental idealism, such an assumption about things as they are in themselves is surely not one to which the realist is entitled without a great deal of further work. The question, then, is whether realism has an argument for the thesis that objects are in themselves spatio-temporal, or whether this thesis functions as an unargued premise in realism's defence of its distinctive conception of the scope and basis of *a priori* conditions. In the absence of an argument for transcendental realism about space and time, idealism about *a priori* conditions is still in play.

At this point, the realist might proceed as follows: 'objects', it will be recalled, are to be understood as particular instances of general concepts, and the basis of the assumption that objects are in themselves spatio-temporal is that 'spatio-temporal position provides the fundamental ground of distinction between one particular item and another of the same general type, hence the fundamental ground of identity of particular items'.[43] Once granted that spatio-temporal position provides the fundamental ground of identity of particular items, it must also be granted that such items are in themselves spatio-temporal. So far from functioning as an unargued premise in the context of realism about *a priori* conditions, this thesis about the nature of objects as they are in themselves is supported by realism's theory of identity. As well as calling transcendental idealism into question, this theory also undermines subjectivism about *a priori* conditions. If spatio-temporal position provides the fundamental ground of identity of particular items, then the need for us to perceive the world as spatio-temporal cannot properly be seen as nothing more than a reflection of contingent, empirically discoverable facts about the constitution of our faculty of intuition.

This argument for realism about *a priori* conditions is unlikely to convince the transcendental idealist. Kant had no difficulty accepting that 'difference of locations, without any further conditions, makes the plurality and distinction of objects, as appearances' (A272/B328), but he disputed the assertion that this tells us anything about the nature of objects *as they are in themselves.* For Strawson, the thought (T) that there might be general concepts such that 'we could encounter and distinguish *in experience* different particular instances of those concepts, and yet such that their instances were not spatio-temporal things at all', is a thought which 'leaves us quite blank',[44] but this still leaves the idealist with

---

[43] *The Bounds of Sense,* p. 49.

[44] P. F. Strawson, *Subject and Predicate in Logic and Grammar* (London: Methuen & Co. Ltd., 1974), p. 16.

a certain amount of room for manoeuvre. In the first place, it might be claimed that it fails to exclude the possibility that 'the things which we intuit are not in themselves what we intuit them as being; (A42/B59). In the second place, to say that (T) leaves us blank is to make a point about our imaginative limitations, and there is a quite general question about the legitimacy of taking our imaginative limitations as a reliable guide to the nature of reality as it is in itself.

The second of these points leads back to the simplest and most obvious case for idealism about *a priori* conditions. For when realism claims that *a priori* conditions are grounded in the nature of reality as it is in itself, the idealist will want to know the basis upon which the realist claims an insight into the character of things in themselves. The fact that (T) leaves us blank does not entitle us to draw any conclusions about things in themselves since the world as it is in itself is not limited by what we humans can conceive of. Realism is only entitled to regard the conditions which it identifies as objectively necessary given certain assumptions about reality as it is in itself, but the mind-independence of reality as it is in itself means that any attempt to argue for these assumptions on the basis of our alleged imaginative limitations is mistaken in principle. Since the thesis that reality as it is in itself is spatio-temporal is one for which the realist lacks an adequate defence, the most that can be concluded from the discussion of (T) is that spatio-temporal intuition is *for us* a condition of empirical knowledge.

In response to this argument, the realist should concede that there is, in principle, a gap between claims about what we can and cannot conceive of and claims about how the world is in itself, but insist that it would be inappropriate to regard our inability to make anything of (T) *simply* as a reflection of how things are with us. According to the realist, to suppose that this inability has no bearing at all on the nature of things in themselves is to be committed to what can only be described as a form of scepticism about reason. Just as scepticism about the senses questions the ability of our senses to deliver knowledge of mind-independent reality, so scepticism about reason questions the ability of rational reflection concerning the fundamental ground of identity of particular items to deliver knowledge of the nature of such items as they are in themselves. In reply, it needs to be pointed out that while there may be no absolute guarantee that rational reflection is a reliable guide to how the world is in itself, the validity of assumption that we *are* estranged from reality to the extent implied by the sceptic is, to say the least, no more obvious than that of the assumption that reality is, in Craig's words, 'transparent to our faculties'.[45] The initial idealist argument against realism was that the latter's conception of the nature and status of *a priori* conditions rests upon an unargued realism about space and time, but it should now be clear this is not a charge that can be made to stick. It is one thing to say that the considerations to which realism appeals in support of its

---

[45] Edward Craig, 'Arithmetic and Fact', in *Exercises in Analysis: Essays by Students of Casimer Lewy*, ed. I. Hacking (Cambridge: Cambridge University Press, 1985), p. 91.

conception of reality as it is in itself are not sceptic-proof, but this is not to say that these considerations do not even amount to an argument.

The current state of play might be summarized as follows: when it is claimed that a given condition (C) is an objectively necessary condition of empirical knowledge, it needs to be explained both what makes it the case that (C) is such a condition and how we can know that (C) has this status. If (C) is an *a priori* condition in virtue of certain truths about the nature of the objects of our knowledge as they are in themselves, or in virtue of analytic truths concerning the nature of judgement or concepts, then it would seem that *knowledge* that (C) is an *a priori* condition requires *knowledge* of those truths in virtue of which (C) is an *a priori* condition. According to one version of realism, knowledge of these truths is made possible by rational reflection. The idealist is, in effect, someone who questions the ability of rational reflection to account for knowledge of *a priori* conditions that are objectively necessary and universal in scope, but there are now two things to be said in response to idealism. First, even if it has succeeded in identifying an epistemological problem for realism, the moral is not that genuinely *a priori* conditions are species-specific in scope; the moral is that we do not know which conditions are genuinely *a priori*. Secondly, by associating itself with scepticism about reason, idealism lays itself open to the charge of paying an unacceptably high price for its anti-realism. To mistrust reason is to mistrust a basic cognitive faculty, and if reason or rational reflection cannot even provide us with knowledge of the objectively or analytically necessary conditions of judgement, then there seems no reason to trust any of our basic cognitive faculties.[46]

While these considerations help to bring out the unattractiveness of some anti-realist arguments, they fail to address several residual anxieties about realism. One has to do with the role of realism in Kantian epistemology. On one interpretation, a major element of Kantian epistemology is the devising of anti-sceptical transcendental arguments. Suppose that P is a proposition about mind-independent reality, and that it is in question whether we can know that P is true. A transcendental argument responds to the sceptic about P by arguing that the truth of P is a necessary condition of something which is not and cannot coherently be doubted by the sceptic, namely, experience. On the face of it, the necessary conditions of the possibility of experience which figure in the minor premises of transcendental arguments are precisely the *a priori* conditions that are at issue between realism, idealism and subjectivism. Suppose, then, that one's interest in the nature and basis of *a priori* conditions is the result of an interest in the anti-sceptical potential of transcendental arguments. Realism would then face the objection that in conceiving of *a priori* conditions as objectively necessary conditions, it renders transcendental arguments wholly superfluous in its dispute with scepticism. For, to the extent that objectively necessary conditions are

[46] These remarks are only intended to give a very rough indication of how an effective response to scepticism about reason might go. On their own, they are unlikely to persuade those who question the ability of rational reflection to deliver knowledge of things in themselves.

grounded in propositions about mind-independent reality which we can know to be true on the basis of rational reflection, it would seem that the same rational reflection ought to be capable of providing us with knowledge of the truth of those propositions about mind-independent reality which are disputed by the sceptic. The difficulty, in other words, is that as long as rational reflection is a self-sufficient source of knowledge of things as they are in themselves, there is no need for the epistemological reassurance allegedly promised by transcendental arguments. If, on the other hand, rational reflection cannot tell us about mind-independent reality, then it cannot tell us which conditions of the possibility of experience are objectively necessary. In that case, it is difficult to understand how transcendental arguments can carry much weight against scepticism, since the sceptic will claim that we have no insight into the necessary conditions of the possibility of experience.

There are several things that might be said in response to this anxiety about realism. It might be held, for example, that it is enough for the purposes of transcendental arguments that the *a priori* conditions to which they appeal are *in fact* faithful to how things are in themselves. Once it is conceded that transcendental arguments do not presuppose *knowledge* of those truths about things in themselves in virtue of which their minor premises are objectively necessary, there is no need to try to account for the possibility of such knowledge in terms of rational reflection. It would also be worth remarking that if the minor premise of a transcendental argument is analytic, then its epistemological standing ought to be no more problematic than the epistemological standing of any analytic judgement.[47] While it may not be analytic that things in themselves are spatio-temporal or that spatio-temporal intuition is a necessary condition of empirical knowledge, this is not a reason for the realist not to attempt to construct transcendental arguments which exploit *a priori* conditions that *are* objectively necessary in virtue of being analytic.[48] Finally, the capacity of rational reflection to deliver knowledge of the objectively necessary condition that figures in the minor premise of a given transcendental argument is no guarantee of its ability to disarm the specific version of scepticism that is the target of that argument. So even if the minor premise of a transcendental argument presupposes the kind of knowledge of how things are in themselves that is the product of rational reflection, this need not render the argument superfluous as long as the proposition about things in themselves which underpins the realist's *a priori* condition is not the very proposition about mind-independent reality that is under sceptical attack.

Each of these responses to the first residual anxiety about realism deserves to be examined in greater detail than is possible here, but it is important not to exaggerate the significance of this discussion. The most that the first anxiety

---

[47] This is, of course, not to suggest that the epistemological standing of analytic knowledge is wholly unproblematic.

[48] One question for someone who argues in this way is whether, as has so far been assumed, analytically necessary conditions are, in the realist's sense, objectively necessary conditions. I will not pursue this difficult issue here.

shows is that a certain kind of realism about *a priori* conditions raises a question about the role of transcendental arguments in Kantian epistemology, but it is not obvious that an interest in the nature and scope of *a priori* conditions needs to be motivated by an interest in the anti-sceptical potential of transcendental arguments. Nevertheless, the kind of realist who is not preoccupied by scepticism, and who thinks that rational reflection is potentially a source of knowledge of things as they are in themselves, is still under an obligation to say more about the nature of rational reflection and its alleged ability to provide an insight into the objectively necessary conditions of the possibility of experience. The second residual anxiety about realism, then, is that its epistemology is incomplete in certain important respects.

Despite these reservations, realism remains the most attractive of the three positions considered above. The capacity of rational reflection to yield knowledge of the objectively necessary conditions of the possibility of experience is certainly something which needs explaining, but it would be unwise for the idealist to attempt to make too much of this gap in realism's epistemology. For acceptance of the thesis that *a priori* conditions are epistemic conditions rather than objectively necessary conditions would still leave one with the task of explaining how knowledge of epistemic conditions is possible, and this is arguably as difficult a task for idealism as the corresponding task for realism. If epistemic conditions reflect the cognitive structure of the mind, then knowledge of epistemic conditions is presumably a form of self-knowledge, but it would be a mistake to suppose that the relevant form of self-knowledge is any easier to account for than our knowledge of objectively necessary conditions. When it comes to developing a credible epistemology of *a priori* conditions, both realism and idealism have more work to do, but the reason for preferring realism is that it is the only position which does justice to the point that the conditions of empirical knowledge must reflect the nature of the *objects* of empirical knowledge as they are in themselves, and cannot simply be a reflection of the structure of *our* cognitive faculties. Idealism is unacceptable because it fails to respect this fundamental point, and fails to demonstrate that this is a point which does not deserve to be respected.

IV

I began by contrasting humanism and universalism in epistemology, and by suggesting that this contrast also has a bearing on our understanding of the subject matter of the philosophy of mind. In epistemology, the universalist is someone who thinks that the theory of knowledge must concern itself with the uncovering of conditions of empirical knowledge which are universal in scope, conditions which must be fulfilled by any knowing subject, human or otherwise. Similarly, a universalist philosopher of mind is one who maintains that the philosophy of mind must concern itself not just with the human mind but with the nature of mind as such. How are these two versions of universalism related, and what is to be made of the notion of 'mind as such'? Realism suggests the following response to those questions: if 'mind as such' is understood as the *knowing* mind, then one way of arriving at an understanding of its nature would be to arrive at an understanding of the conditions that must be fulfilled by any mind, human or otherwise, which is capable of empirical knowledge. These are precisely the conditions which interest the universalist epistemologist.

Suppose, next, that realism is right to insist that it is in virtue of their objective basis that the *a priori* conditions of empirical knowledge are universal in scope. In that case, an account of mind as such must, as Locke might have said, take into consideration the inherent nature of the objects which knowing minds have to do with. This is not to suggest that the peculiarities of the human cognitive apparatus should be of no interest to the universalist. It is to suggest, however, that knowledge of the structure of mind as such cannot be detached from knowledge of the world in which knowing minds, including human minds, are embedded.

The Modality of Freedom

CHRISTOPHER PEACOCKE

I   The Problem as an Instance of the Integration Challenge

The classical problem of free will is one instance of the Integration Challenge. The Integration Challenge in its general form is that of reconciling our metaphysics of any given area with our epistemology for that same area. In the case of free will, the challenge is that of reconciling our seeming first-person knowledge of our exercise of free thought, deliberation, choice and action with a description of what is really going on in the world as characterized in terms of causation, determination, explanation and causal possibility.

There are at least six general theoretical options to be considered whenever we are faced with a philosophical problem which is an instance of the Integration Challenge. These options divide into two groups. Each of the two groups comprises three of the six options. The first group contains the conservative options of (i) providing an

Versions of this material were also presented in colloquia at Columbia University and the University of Connecticut, Storrs. I thank Akeel Bilgrami, Paul Boghossian, Tyler Burge, John Collins, Paul Horwich, Kirstie Laird, Michael Martin, Ruth Millikan and Stephen Schiffer for comments and discussion, and the Leverhulme Trust for time.

improved metaphysics which meets the challenge; (ii) providing an improved epistemology; and (iii) providing an improved conception of the relations between the appropriate metaphysics and epistemology. These options are evidently not exclusive of each other. Each of these options aims at head-on reconciliation. The options are conservative in the sense that proper, successful development of one of these options will attribute some truth condition to the problematic sentences, and will explain how we can come to know that they obtain, when we do. In the case of free will, development of one of these options will involve attributing to a sentence such as 'He chose freely' a truth condition which aims to be a correct elucidation of what that sentence states, and which is knowably true pretty much in the cases, and in the ways, we normally take it to be. Of course development of these options may not be conservative of philosophical theory. Highly revisionary, innovative theory may be required to develop the options in this first group. It is rather our pretheoretical views of which options in this first set aim to be conservative.

The second, revisionary group of options includes the option (iv) of offering some cleansed or reduced truth condition for the problematic sentences, a truth condition which captures some but not all of what we ordinarily mean by the problematic sentences, but which is purged of those features which were preventing integration. The next member of the second group is option (v), under which no truth condition is assigned to the problematic sentences: rather, under this option, some role of the problematic sentences in our assertoric, inferential or social practices is described, a role which is made rational or at least explained by something other than that role's being justified by the sentences' truth conditions. Finally in this group is option (vi), which claims that the relevant concepts expressed in the problematic sentences are quite incoherent, in such a way that not even options (iv) and (v) are available. The options in this group are each radical in the sense that they can only be rationally endorsed by someone who thinks that it is impossible to give a truth condition for the problematic sentences which both captures their pretheoretical meaning, and for which the Integration Challenge can be met.

Such has been the recalcitrance of the problem of free will that the topic is perhaps the only one on which each of the more radical revisionary options have been endorsed by some recent thinker or other. The views of Peter Strawson[1] and Christine Korsgaard[2] are examples of the fifth option. Galen Strawson is one of those endorsing the sixth in print,[3] and others endorse it in conversation. It is also of particular pertinence to the problem of free will that the distinction between conservative options and the radical option (iv) may be very hard to apply in some examples. If a concept is widely and firmly associated with some

---

[1] P. Strawson, 'Freedom and Resentment', in *Freedom and Resentment and Other Essays* (London: Methuen, 1974).

[2] C. Korsgaard, 'Creating Kingdom of Ends: Reciprocity and Responsibility in Personal Relations', in *Creating the Kingdom of Ends* (Cambridge: Cambridge University Press, 1996).

[3] G. Strawson, 'The Impossibility of Moral Responsibility', *Philosophical Studies* 75 (1994), 5-24.

misconception or incorrect articulation, there may be some indeterminacy on the issue of whether some theoretical proposal about an underlying truth condition is or is not conservative of our pretheoretical conceptions – that is, on the issue of whether the proposal is really a case of (i) or a case of (iv).

My plan of action in this paper is first to articulate some aspects of our intuitive notion of freedom in decision, actions and thoughts. Then I will attempt an account of 'could have done otherwise' which seems to meet the Integration Challenge by building a theory which is either conservative or at worst indeterminate as between conservatism and a form of case (iv). I will try to respond to those arguments which have pressured others, in the case of free will, into the revisionary options (v) or (vi), or into competing conservative conceptions. In terms of the traditional labels, the conservative conception I will be advocating is compatibilist, but it is of a rather different stripe of compatibilism than that made familiar by G.E. Moore.[4]

My own view is that we should aim, if at all possible, for an account which gives a genuine and satisfiable truth condition for an attribution of freedom. Though the point would be disputed by some distinguished writers – to whose views I will turn later on – it seems to me implausible that an attribution of freedom involves no factual as opposed to practical commitments; or that it involves on the factual side nothing going beyond the immediate phenomenology

---

[4] G. E. Moore, *Ethics* (London: Oxford University Press, 1947), chapter 6.

of decision-taking. Consider one of Penfield's experiments, in which Penfield inserts an electrode into patient's brain, and fires it. As a result, the patient says he has spontaneously taken the decision to do something. I doubt anyone would happily classify this as a free decision, even though it may have the phenomenology of one. In more ordinary cases, we can make sense of suggestion that our decisions in some area are really the result of some neurosis, and that our decisions are thus not freely made. It needs empirical investigation to confirm or refute any such hypothesis. It cannot be ruled out just by first-person consciousness of the decision taker.

It may be said the existence of factual commitments in an attribution of freedom is consistent with a non-truth-conditional view (that is, with option (v)). It is just that there are certain conditions – manipulation by others, neuroses, which are on a list sufficient for legitimate assertion that the agent is not freely thinking, deciding or acting. It seems, though, prima facie implausible that our understanding of a predication 'x is deciding freely' involves tacit knowledge of a mere list, and nothing more. We seem to have an open-ended ability to classify new examples as free or unfree, in a way going beyond anything which could be captured by a list of cases. We had a general conception of free decision prior to any theory of neuroses, and then applied that conception in classifying a new case, once neurosis had been identified. I doubt whether something so important to us as freedom could ever be captured by a list of conditions which do not have some deeper unifying characteristic.

I am then aiming to give a metaphysical account of freedom, in the belief that this is the first step we need to take if we are ever to meet the Integration Challenge for attributions of freedom. It is impossible within the ambit of a paper to address all of the issues which could be raised for the position I will be developing. To identify a potentially occupiable position in logical space will be my main task. Of some of those who attempted to give metaphysical accounts, Nietzsche wrote:

> The desire for 'freedom of the will' in the superlative, metaphysical sense, such as still holds sway, unfortunately, in the minds of the half-educated, the desire to bear the entire and ultimate responsibility for one's actions oneself, and to absolve God, the world, ancestors, chance, and society, therefrom, involves nothing less than to be precisely this *causa sui,* and, with more than Münchausen daring, to pull oneself up into existence by the hair, out of the slough of nothingness[5].

The metaphysical account I will be offering will be less than a 'superlative' metaphysical sense of the sort Nietzsche has in his sights. Something less than the superlative may suffice, however, consistently with recognition of those truths Nietzsche is emphasizing.

II   An Intuitive Characterization of Freedom

The concept of freedom is organized around the notion of a person being free with respect to a factor. Such a factor

---

[5] F. Nietzsche, *Beyond Good and Evil*, trans. H. Zimmern (Buffalo, NY: Prometheus Books, 1989), section 2.

might be either a prima facie reason for decision one way rather than another, or it might be some other factor which may influence one's decision in some wholly nonrational fashion. To be a thinker who is free with respect to a factor is to have the capacity to reflect on that factor and to decide effectively whether to let that factor influence one, and if so in what way. The claim that the heroin addict is not free, without assistance, not to act on his desire for the substance is the claim that he does not, unaided, have the capacity not to act on that desire.

There are nonrational influences on choices which cannot be regarded as the operation of any kind of prima facie reason. Consider an agent who has to appoint one out of several candidates to some post. When comparing two candidates for a position, one of whom has been interviewed, and given a favourable impression, and the other of whom is known only from his CV, many people give, and indeed are aware that they give, undue weight to the favourable impression left by the interviewed candidate. It is an empirical question whether the appointing person has the capacity to overcome this tendency, that is, whether he is free with respect to it. When it is operative, this tendency need not be operating as any kind of prima facie reason within the agent's deliberation.

Given this characterization of freedom with respect to a factor, we can go on to say that a person is free with respect to a range of factors if he is free with respect to each one of them. Similarly, one person is more free than a second person if the range of factors with respect to which the first is free properly includes those with respect to which the second is free.

One feature of this initial, intuitive characterization of freedom with respect to a factor is that it makes clear one of the links between conceptualization and freedom. We can deliberate only about what we can think about. A thinker must conceptualize some factor before it can enter his rational – or irrational – deliberations about whether it should influence him, and if so in which way. New theoretical knowledge, framed in concepts which are also new, may identify new factors in our decision-taking. It will again be an empirical question which of these newly identified factors are ones with respect to which we are free. In some cases the new theory may entail that we are not free in some range of our activities. But only when we have properly conceptualized the factors influencing us will there be any chance of our being, or becoming, free with respect to them.

Another feature of the characterization of freedom with respect to a factor is that it applies to thought too. On this characterization, a thinker can be free with respect to the factors which may be influential when he is making up his mind what to think or judge. The capacity effectively to give weight to some prima facie reasons, and none to others, or to block otherwise influential nonrational factors, is one that can be present in making judgements just as it is present in taking practical decisions. My own view is that this is no accident, for judging just is one species of action.

There are necessarily certain limits to freedom in the case of thought. The rational thinker who accepts that all Fs are Gs is not free to judge that something is both F and not-G. This point cannot be dismissed by the observation that we should distinguish causal from rational determination. We should of course distinguish them. Many theorists of concepts would, however, insist that a proper theory of possession of, for instance, logical concepts entails that certain states of acceptance stand in causal relations to other content-involving states, including relations of production and exclusion. It is partially constitutive of a concept's being that of universal quantification that a thinker rejects the thought that all Fs are Gs when he comes to accept that something is both F and not-G. However, the apparent loss of freedom such theories entail should not be thought of as something to be regretted. If certain combinations of thoughts cannot be simultaneously accepted, as a consequence of a philosophical account of the possession of particular concepts involved, then there is, on a priori philosophical grounds, no possibility of still employing those concepts whilst not being subject to those constraints. Losing the capacity to think certain thoughts is not a way of increasing freedom. In fact one paragraph back, we were noting just the contrary.

It is a consequence of this intuitive characterization of freedom that an animal without the capacity to think of itself as influenced by a range of factors will not be free with respect to them. Nor does the definition make it suffice for freedom with respect to a range of factors that the agent has higher-order attitudes about those factors, or about his own attitudes to them. An agent may have second-order attitudes which cause first-order attitudes, and thereby influence his actions. Such is the case of the Puritan who has a second-order desire not to act on certain of his first-order desires. If our Puritan is not capable of preventing those second-order attitudes from influencing him, he is not free with respect to them, or with respect to the relevant first-order desires.

To have, for any given factor that may influence one, the capacity to decide effectively whether to let it influence one is to be distinguished from the following capacity: the capacity to decide, for all the factors which may influence one, whether to let all of them influence one. To suppose that the first capacity requires the second is analogous to moving from the premise that one has, for each book in the British Library, time to read it before one dies, to the conclusion that one has time to read them all before one dies. Actually, it is worse than that transition, for the conclusion, in the case of factors that may influence one, is incoherent, and not merely, in Russell's phrase, a medical impossibility. Whatever process takes place of scrutinizing and weighting factors which may influence one, once a decision is made, there is always something left unscrutinized, on pain of the task being uncompletable. Such scrutiny is, in the phrase Ryle memorably used to describe the impossibility of a certain kind of self-prediction, 'logically condemned to eternal penultimacy'.[6] The point applies also to the nonrational factors influencing the choice of which of several prima facie reasons is to be operative with one, if there is some explanation of why the agent makes the decision he does. Whatever the nonrational factors that affect that final choice, they will not themselves have been the subject of a decision on whether they should be influential.

---

[6] G. Ryle, *The Concept of Mind* (London: Penguin, 1963), p. 186.

A fully rational and free thinker does not need to aim at the incoherent goal of scrutinizing everything that may influence a decision. If a thinker is entitled to believe that further proper scrutiny of rational and nonrational factors will not affect the direction of his decision – is entitled to believe that his decision is *stable* as we may call it – then he can rationally cease the process of scrutiny.

III   'Could have done otherwise': The Closeness Account

When the intuitive description of being free with respect to a particular factor applies to a person, it will be true that the subject could have let the factor influence him, and could equally not have let it influence him. Whatever he decided, he could have decided and done otherwise. Accounts of the nature of the modality in 'he could have done otherwise' offered hitherto by compatibilists, and in particular the account offered by Moore, have been found very unconvincing by incompatibilists. I find them unconvincing too. Some have tended to move from this point in the discussion, together with the non-negotiability of some form of modal requirement in our ordinary conception of freedom, to an incompatabilist conclusion. That was certainly how I myself thought for many years. But I have come to think that there is a compatibilist option which has been overlooked, and this section is devoted to developing it.

Suppose you travel on a train through the Channel Tunnel, and there is a fire in the engine. Suppose also that the only reason that the fire does not spread poisonous smoke through the ventilation system is that some luggage, which could easily have been placed in a different configuration, happens to set up a draught which diverts the smoke from the ventilation system. It is true to say of this situation that there could easily have been a fatal accident. This is the kind of 'could have' with which we are concerned when assessing safety. It also seems that this species of possibility is compatible with determinism. If it were determined, on this particular occasion, that the luggage be stored in that configuration, perhaps because of the particular practices of the individual baggage-handlers on duty that day, that is not enough to establish that that particular journey was safe – to establish that, in the particular sense with which we are concerned, there could not easily have been an accident. Intuitively, only small variations from the actual conditions, small variations which there is no occasion-independent mechanism preventing, would have resulted in an accident. Happily favourable initial conditions are not sufficient for safety, nor do they imply that there is no kind of possibility under which an accident was possible.

The relevant kind of possibility is one under which something's being not possible means that in a certain way one can *rely* on its not obtaining. Another area in which we employ this kind of modality is epistemology. It would be widely agreed that if someone is in a region where there are, to use the time-worn example, unbeknownst to him, many convincing barn-facades scattered through the countryside, he cannot learn that something is a barn just by looking at it. This correct verdict on the case is unaltered if we lived in a deterministic, Newtonian universe, so that it is determined that it is a barn, and not a barn-facade, that he is now seeing. The method of taking such perceptual experiences at face value still cannot be relied upon in those circumstances. If conditions had been only slightly different – for instance, if our subject had turned left rather than right at the last junction – he would have been confronted with a barn-facade rather than a barn, and the method would have led him into error. We can hear some species of possibility in the statement 'The method could have led him into error' on which it is true, even in a deterministic world.

Let us call the kind of possibility involved in the safety and in the knowledge examples 'closeness possibility'. Closeness evidently needs elucidation, but a great deal of what I have to suggest involves only the existence of such a kind of possibility, and is independent of particular analyses. So for the present, let us just specify that we are concerned with the kind of possibility involved in those examples, whatever its proper elucidation may be.

A closeness elucidation of freedom could then be offered. It states that someone is free to F just in case

    a. he could (closeness possibility) try to F, and
    b. he would F if he tried to.

Clause (b) may be negotiable down to 'he might F, if he were to try to'. There are some arguments for the stronger versions: it may be said that when only the weaker conditions are met, it is true only that the agent is free to try. There might also be some indeterminacy in the ordinary meaning; in any case, the difference will not be crucial to the issues

I will be discussing. The position I will propose could equally be developed using the weaker version.

So, according to the closeness elucidation, I am free to act on (free with respect to) a prima facie reason on which I do not in fact act, if (a) it could easily have been the case that I try to act on it, and (b) if I had tried to act on it, I would have succeeded in bringing about that for which it is a prima facie reason. The friend of the closeness elucidation will say that it is because we take it that this condition is fulfilled with respect to a particular factor that we count a particular person as free with respect to it. By contrast, it is not true of the kleptomaniac wandering in the department store that it could easily be the case that she does not steal some object within her grasp. Our conception of kleptomania is that of a state which, when someone is in it, it is a prima facie law that the person will steal when the opportunity arises, and this state is not one which, when in the department store at least, she could easily rid herself of.

The closeness account is a compatibilist account. It is, though, noteworthy that there are three points on which it actually agrees with the criticisms which incompatibilists have levelled against other compatibilist attempts at elucidation.

1. Successive generations of thinkers have complained against early Moore-style compatibilist accounts of freedom which say that 'He was free to F' means only that 'If had tried to F, he would have' (or perhaps with 'choose' instead of 'try'). The entirely compelling objection, voiced

by A. Campbell Garnett,[7] accepted by Moore,[8] and also emphasized by Chisholm[9] and Wiggins,[10] is that one is not free to F if one is not free to try F, or is not free to choose to F. Berlin gives some further history of the point.[11] Far from being an objection to the closeness elucidation, however, the point which all these thinkers rightly insisted upon is entailed by the closeness elucidation. The closeness elucidation entails that if there is no close world in which the subject tries to F, then he is not free to F. The point that one must be free to try to F if one is to be free to F is, then, not the exclusive property of incompatibilist positions. Its soundness can equally be explained on a properly marshalled compatibilist position which appeals to closeness.

2. A second point on which the closeness theorist will agree with a classical incompatibilist criticism of other compatibilist positions is this. Excusing conditions, the closeness theorist will insist, do not have to reduce merely to an unexplained list, with no underlying principle of

---

[7] A. C. Garnett, 'Moore's Theory of Moral Freedom and Responsibility', in *The Philosophy of G. E. Moore*, Volume I, ed. P. A. Schilpp (La Salle, IL: Open Court, 1968).

[8] G. E. Moore, 'A Reply to My Critics', in *The Philosophy of G. E. Moore*, ed. P. A. Schilpp, Volume II, (La Salle, IL: Open Court, 1968).

[9] R. Chisholm, 'Human Freedom and the Seif', in *Free Will*, ed. G. Watson (Oxford: Oxford University Press, 1989), esp. Chapter 4.

[10] D. Wiggins, 'Towards a Reasonable Libertarianism', in *Needs, Values, and Truth* (Oxford: Blackwell, 1987).

[11] I. Berlin, 'From Hope and Fear Set Free', in *Concepts and Categories: Philosophical Essays*, ed. H. Hardy (Oxford: Oxford University Press, 1980).

unification. One class of excusing conditions will be unified by the condition that each is one whose obtaining implies that there is no close world in which the agent tries to act in the relevant way. On this approach, one will distinguish between those cases in which the excuse really does involve a lack of freedom, from those in which the subject is free to act, but the costs of acting are too high. Here I am in agreement with Williams.[12]

3. The modality involved in freedom, on the closeness account, is not merely epistemic. It is metaphysical. Closeness possibilities do not have to align in any straightforward way with epistemic possibilities. It may seem, from the best available information, that something could easily have been the case, when in fact because of some hitherto undiscovered scientific principles and other conditions which could not easily have been different, it could not easily have been the case. The converse is possible too: it may be that, unbeknownst to us, the earth could easily have been destroyed by a passing asteroid a century ago. Similarly, chaos theory in effect shows that many conditions which one might have thought could not easily have obtained in fact could have come about with only tiny changes from the way the actual world is. So, when incompatibilists object to those compatibilists who offer merely epistemic elucidations of 'could have done otherwise', our closeness compatibilist will agree.

[12] B. Williams, 'How Free Does the Will Need to Be?' in *Making Sense of Humanity and Other Philosophical Papers* (Cambridge: Cambridge University Press, 1995), p. 4.

What is the relation between the notion of a close possibility which I have been using, and the *closer than* relation which is used in some possible-worlds semantics for counterfactuals? It should not be assumed that the notion of closeness I have been using is simply the positive form of some concept whose comparative is the *closer than* relation used in some possible-worlds semantics, not even under the supposition that some such semantics is correct. Suppose for present purposes that Lewis's semantics for counterfactuals is correct[13]. (We could equally make the corresponding points for Stalnaker's treatment[14].) So that we have a notation which does not encourage any begging of the question, let us indicate the three-place relation used in Lewis's semantics with the expression 'world u is L-closer to world w than is world v'. Lewis's semantics states that an arbitrary counterfactual 'If A were to be the case, then C would be the case' is true at w iff some (accessible) world in which A and C are true is L-closer to w than any world in which A and $\neg$C are true. (A person could agree to this without accepting Lewis's own philosophical theory of the nature of the three-place relation *L-closer* (u,v,w).) Now let us return to consider the unsafe, but causally determined, train trip. Suppose that we also hold the following principles, which may be found tempting: (a) that backtracking counterfactuals ('If I were to strike the match now, something in the past would be different') are false; (b) that close worlds contain no violations of laws of nature. If we

[13] D. Lewis, *Counterfactuals* (Oxford: Blackwell, 1973).

[14] R. Stalnaker, 'A Theory of Conditionals', in *Studies in Logical Theory*, ed. N. Rescher (Oxford: Blackwell, 1968).

agree that there is a close possibility that there is a fire on the train, then any world-history in which this close possibility is embedded must have at some point a different past from that of our actual world, given the supposition of determinism (and no violations of the laws). If this world were an L-close world, there is a danger that some backtracking counterfactuals will then be counted as true in cases in which they are not true. One way (though not the only way) out of this is to distinguish sharply between the closeness property I have been discussing, and any positive form derived from the relation of L-closeness. The matter could be given extensive separate discussion. At any rate, the important point for present purposes is that the notion of closeness I am using is introduced by way of the examples of our apparent use of it. Any connections between the notion so introduced and the relation *L-closer*(u,v,w) and others needed in modal semantics would need to be established by further argument.

IV   A Puzzling Inference

We can clarify the closeness conception by considering a puzzle. The puzzle concerns a certain form of inference. Suppose someone is not free to be not-F, and it's causally (nomologically) necessary that if he is F then he is also G. Does it follow that he is not free to be not-G? We can abbreviate the inference in question thus:

(1) ¬free ¬F
(2) causally necessary (if F, then G)

(3) ¬free¬G.

The puzzle emerges if we raise the question: is this inference, which I label '(L)', valid on the closeness conception of freedom? It may strike one as valid. It may also appear that there is a sound argument from the semantics of 'is free to' on the closeness conception to the validity of (L). The argument would run thus. It seems reasonable to suppose that laws of the actual world are also laws of close worlds. If that is so, then premise (2) of argument (L) implies that in any close world in which our agent is F, he's also G. Now suppose, contrary to the conclusion (3), that our agent were free to be ¬G. By the closeness account, this implies that there is a close world in which he tries to be ¬G. It would certainly be puzzling if under this approach to freedom, none of the close worlds in which he tries to be ¬G is one in which he succeeds. By (2), any close world in which he so tries and succeeds in being ¬G will also be one in which he is ¬F. Won't he then be free to be ¬F, simply by trying to be ¬F by in turn trying to be ¬G? This then contradicts (1). So, it may seem from the semantics, the argument-schema (L) must be valid.

So far, no puzzle. The puzzle emerges only when we add that (L) is very close to, indeed something which has an instance, the form of argument classically used by libertarians, and by incompatibilists, in attempts to establish that freedom conflicts with determinism (van Inwagen;[15] Wiggins[16]). Yet the closeness conception was put forward

[15] P. van Inwagen, 'A Formal Approach to the Problem of Free Will and Determinism', *Theoria* 40 (1974), 9–22. 'The Incompatibility of Free Will and Determinism', *Philosophical Studies* 27 (1975), 185–99.
[16] Wiggins, 'Towards a Reasonable Libertarianism'.

as a compatibilist elucidation of freedom. So somewhere on this short journey, a mistake must have been made, maybe more than one. What is it, or what are they?

An analogue of (L) is indeed valid for some intuitive notion of determination. If we substitute 'determined' for '¬free¬', then I have no quarrel with the validity of the resulting schema. The same applies if we substitute a specifically determinism-related 'open' for 'free'. However, in offering a compatibilist elucidation of freedom, we will be developing an approach on which those substituted notions are distinguished from what they are replacing. We will be in agreement with David Lewis's point that not all ways of being determined not to do something are ways which amount to inability to do it.[17] And indeed, (L) in its original form, a schema involving the notion of freedom, is in fact invalid.

Consider an instance of (L), as incompatibilists commonly do, in which 'F' is replaced by some predication about some time t, and G about some later time t+n, and the operator 'is free to' is in both (1) and (3) understood as concerning the later time t+n. That is, we are considering the case:

(1a) He is not free at t + n to be ¬F at t

(2a) Causally necessary (if he's F at t, then he's G at t + n)

(3a) He is not free at t + n to be ¬G at t + n.

An agent is not free to change the past. That is uncontroversial on the intuitive understanding of freedom. It is also the verdict

---

[17] D. Lewis, 'Are We Free to Break the Laws?' in *Philosophical Papers, Volume II* (New York: Oxford University Press, 1986), p. 292.

of the closeness elucidation, since an agent's being free to change the past would require its being true that if the agent tried to, he would – and of course he wouldn't. (No doubt the agent is free in some sense to have had a different past, but this just means that in the past, he was free to have acted differently.) So (1a) is true. We can suppose G chosen so that (2a) is also true. Nonetheless (3a) may still be false. It is false if there is a close world in which he tries to be ¬G at t+n, and if it is true that were he to try to be ¬G at t+n, he would succeed. Nothing in the premises (1a) and (2a) rules out the holding of those two conditions. A close world in which he is G at t+n, and which has the same laws as the actual world, must of course have a different past from the actual world. But nothing in the premises (1a) and (2a) rules out the existence of such a world, and nor do the other requirements on close worlds.

The fallacy in the semantic argument occurred when it said 'Won't [the agent] then be free to be ¬F, simply by trying to be ¬F by in turn trying to be ¬G?' The answer to the quoted question is negative, in the case in which trying to be ¬G involves the agent's trying to bring about the truth of some proposition about a time earlier than that of his attempt, where the proposition is false of that earlier time.

I am developing a treatment of the case on which it matters that some close worlds are worlds in which the past is different from the way it actually is. The intuitive examples by which we introduced closeness possibilities should make us recognise that. We said that the following combination is coherent: the train trip is not safe, even when it is determined from fortunate initial conditions that there will not be an accident. If lack of safety consists in the closeness of a world in which there is an accident, then that close world must be one whose initial conditions are also different from those of the actual world, if it has the same laws as the actual world. We could make a corresponding point about lack of reliability in the knowledge example.

So, on this treatment, the holding of

(4)   the agent is not free at t+n to be ¬F at t.

does not imply that

there is at t+n no world close at t+n at which he is

(5)   F at t.

There may be such a close world. The closeness account provides for at least two different ways in which a statement of inability (or more strictly, unfreedom) may be true. First, it may be true because there simply is at t+n no close world in which he tries to do the thing and succeeds (or perhaps he can't even try). This is the case which includes my current, and no doubt permanent, inability to jump 8 feet high. The second way a statement of inability may be false is this: although there are close worlds in which the agent has the property in question, the counterfactual 'if he were to try to have the property, he would have it' is false. This applies to any case in which the property concerns a time prior to t+n, and is one the agent did not in fact have at t+n. (I return at the end of section V to address those incompatibilists who think this sort of defence weakens the compatibilist's position.)

A less general form of inference (L+) is valid on the closeness conception, the form in which the time indices in F and G are the same. This instance of (L+) is a valid argument:

(1b) He is not free at t + n not to keep the air pressure in the cabin constant.

$\left(2b\right)$ It's causally necessary that if he keeps the air pressure constant,

the temperature stays contant.

$$\left(L+\right)$$

$\left(3b\right)$ He's not free to vary the temperature in the cabin

Suppose, once again, that (3b) were false – that our agent is free to vary the temperature. Then we ask the question 'Won't he then be free not to keep the air pressure constant simply by trying to make it vary by varying the temperature?' Here the answer to the quoted question is affirmative. A close world in which he tries to vary the temperature and succeeds will also be one in which he varies the pressure, if the world has the same laws as the actual world. ((2b) assumes that we are outside the range in which the cabin blows up with increasing pressure.) The form (L+), unlike the more general (L), is valid. Its validity may help to explain the attraction of (L) to some incompatibilists. On the present theory, though, it cannot justify that attraction.

V   Elaboration of the Closeness Conception

Kant claims that 'we must necessarily attribute to every rational being who has a will also the idea of freedom, under which only can such a being act'.[18] Does a rational being also

---

[18] I. Kant, *Ethical Philosophy*, trans. J. Ellington (Indianapolis: Hackett, 1994), Grounding 488 on Akademie pagination.

act under the idea of freedom as the closeness conception elucidates freedom? It seems that we do act under the idea that in engaging in ordinary practical deliberation, the options we are considering are ones that we could try or decide to act on, and be effective in so acting or deciding. The 'could' in this claim seems to me to be the 'could' with a closeness elucidation. Suppose there is no close possibility in which we realize options other than the one actually chosen. I noted earlier that for the closeness 'could have', there is a correlative 'reliably', of such a kind that 'there is a close possibility that p' is equivalent to 'not reliably $\neg$p'. If there is no close possibility in which we realize options other than the one actually chosen, that is equivalent to its reliably being the case that we don't realize those other options. (This of course doesn't mean that the actual deliberation isn't causally effective.) It seems to me that ordinary rational deliberation about a range of options presupposes that those options are ones the deliberator could realize, where this is the 'could' of closeness possibility. A rational deliberator who became convinced that a certain subset of his apparent options are ones which he could not, in any close possible world, realize cannot rationally continue to include them in the range of options about which he is deliberating.

It also seems to me that we want it to be the case that, over a certain range, we could try to act on desires or values other than those which were in fact operative with us on a particular occasion, and be effective in doing so. Freedom with respect to a factor can be something worth having. The qualification 'over a certain range' also matters.

I would rather be of a psychological make-up of such a sort that there is no close world in which I can even bring myself to try to act cruelly, for instance.

What is involved in properly assessing which worlds are close to a given world? What is the right way to assess whether there is a close possibility that a person, object or system of things be other than it actually is? Three kinds of factor should enter the assessment.

i. The *ceteris paribus* laws of a given world w are preserved at worlds which are close to w. That is, they are preserved as *ceteris paribus* laws. In worlds close to the actual world, it is also true that *ceteris paribus* a rise in interest rates in a country produces an inflow of capital to that country, true that *ceteris paribus* meandering rivers erode their outer banks, and so forth. There is no close possibility of something which involves violation of a *ceteris paribus* law, that is, involves failure of a law in conditions which there is not some independent reason, of a sort which would apply equally in the actual world, for declaring that other things are not equal.

ii. We have a conception of some properties and relations of a given system of objects at a given time as being much more robust than others, and these, again *ceteris paribus,* are also preserved as properties and relations of that system, at that time, in close worlds. Precisely what we aim to put in place in making the train safe are devices which, for instance, detect smoke, insulate from heat or will not shatter dangerously, in a wide variety of conditions. (This is closely related to Nancy Cartwright's notion of an object's having a certain capacity).[19]

iii. Assessment of which possibilities are close depends not only on the factors (i) and (ii), but also on what, contingently, is the case outside the system for which close possibilities are in question. Consider again, for instance, whether the earth could easily have been destroyed in the last century by some collision with some other massive object in space. This question cannot be answered just by considering the *ceteris paribus* laws describing the stability of orbits in the solar system and the robustness of the arrangement of most the solar system's into planets and a sun. Whether a collision is a close possibility depends also on whether comets or asteroids far away in time and space from the earth in the nineteenth century could easily have traced a somewhat different course, and eventually have collided with the earth in that century. If there were no such heavenly bodies anywhere near the regions they would have occupied for a collision to occur, and there could not easily have been, then our intuitive verdict would be that there could not easily have been a collision.

One proper way, then, to make it plausible that there is a close possibility in which a given object F at t is to make it plausible that (a) a little before t, some small difference from the actual world could obtain, a variation which some *ceteris paribus* law implies is sufficient for the

---

[19] N. Cartwright, *Nature's Capacities and Their Measurement* (Oxford: Oxford University Press, 1989), esp. Chapter 4.

object's being F, and (b) that there would in those circumstances be no changes in the robust conditions which undermine the applicability of the *ceteris paribus* law. There are negative existentials in these conditions, so a certain open-endedness is present. In general such claims of close possibilities will be potentially open to undermining by the discovery that some unobvious, robust conditions were preventing the earlier condition from holding. Equally they could be undermined by the discovery that it is much easier than was previously thought for the conditions under which things are no longer equal to obtain.

Whether an object which is not actually F could easily have been F can vary with time. Such time-dependent variation is precisely what we are aiming to achieve when we try to make our trains safe, try to cure kleptomaniacs or try to make our belief-forming methods more reliable means of reaching the truth. Correspondingly, a notion of 'could have chosen otherwise' explained in terms of closeness will be significantly time-relative. What could easily happen to a train may vary over time; what a person is capable of choosing may change over time. The notion of freedom identified by the closeness conception is genuinely historical, a function of the agent's situation at the time. There is also a relativity to circumstances: the full form is the four-place *x is free to F in circumstances C at time t.*

Since closeness is evidently a matter of degree, the closeness elucidation makes freedom a matter of degree. Is this a problem? No doubt freedom is commonly thought to be a matter of degree, and we use the comparative and superlative forms. Abraham Pais, in his celebrated biography of Einstein, writes: 'Were I asked for a one-sentence biography of Einstein, I would say, "He was the freest man I have ever known".'[20] However, the common conception of freedom as a matter of degree, to which comparatives and superlatives can legitimately be applied, is arguably concerned just with the *range* of factors with respect to which a person is free. The freer person is free with respect to a wider range of factors. It is not so clear that the ordinary conception allows that freedom with respect to a given factor can be a matter of degree, or may have borderline cases, or can admit of an intelligible comparative. Yet the closeness account is committed to all of these.

The closeness theorist should reply that it can sometimes come as a surprise which concepts admit of degree, and correspondingly exhibit a certain sort of borderline case. Let us take one of our parallel cases again. The factors which underlie knowledge of a given proposition, as opposed to how knowledgeable someone is, may seem initially not to be a matter of degree. Yet one can be forced to soften such a position by examples. There is a spectrum of cases, perhaps many spectra, which show that the factors which underlie knowledge are matters of degree. Consider our subject who believes 'That's a barn', when taking his visual experience at face value. He does not know it to be a barn, even when he is seeing a barn, if there are barn-facades scattered around nearby. But of course the barn-facades might not have been installed, and he still not know, if there had merely been

[20] A. Pais, 'Subtle is the Lord. . .' *The Science and the Life of Albert Einstein* (Oxford: Oxford University Press, 1982), p. vii.

a delay in installing them, so that he could easily at that time not have been in a facade-free environment. Or we can consider the case in which they were installed somewhere else altogether, but the film director had still been considering our believer's location as a filming site; or the case in which he was still choosing between installing barn-facades and real barns, and had not yet selected a site; or the case in which he was deliberating between filming only in a studio, and filming in some countryside somewhere or other... and so forth. As we know from much reflection on vagueness, we cannot avoid this element of degree by moving from a requirement 'no close worlds of such-and-such a kind' to 'no *definitely* close worlds of such-and-such a kind'. 'Definitely close' seems to display the same problematic phenomena, the borderline cases and the like. I think that, contrary to first appearances, the factors which underlie knowledge of a given proposition is to be classified with other predicates which are, apparently, matters of degree. The closeness theorist will say the same of being free with respect to a given factor. Further on, I will offer some independent evidence for this position.

Alternatively it may be objected that the closeness possibilities I have been identifying may be real enough, but that I have not shown that they are under the agent's control. What might be meant by this, and what does the objector want? The complaint should not be that on the closeness conception, which of various close possibilities is realized does not depend on the agent's choice or decision. That would be false: on the closeness conception, what the agent does causally depends upon his decision (a standard compatibilist remark). The closeness possibilities which the present position identifies as crucial to freedom have the feature that the agent could try to realize them, and would succeed if he were to try. What more could be required for the possibilities to be under the agent's control? The objector may rather be concerned that there is nothing in the closeness conception which entails that it is indeterminate, prior to the agent's making a choice, which course of action he will pursue. The closeness conception is at least in the target area of that remark, for indeed it has been put forward as a compatibilist view. This last construal of the objection is just a classic statement of the incompatibilist intuition, and I will consider it in section VII.

How does the closeness conception compare with some other recent compatibilist elaborations of freedom? By addressing this question, we can reach a better articulation of what distinguishes the closeness conception. David Lewis presents a classic compatibilist position in his 'Are We Free to Break the Laws?'[21] Suppose I am free to go to the meeting, but do not in fact go. Lewis highlights the distinction between (a) my doing something such that, were I to do it, either it or one of its effects would be a breaking of an actual law, (b) my doing something such that, were I to do it, some or other earlier small miracle would have occurred. Lewis's points are that it is (a) which would have to be involved in a freedom to break the laws, and that nothing in his position commits him to (a). On Lewis's own theory of counter-factuals, it is only (b) which is entailed by my freedom to go to the meeting. On that theory, if I were to go to the meeting, some or other small 'divergence' miracle would have occurred earlier. I think that Lewis's response to van Inwagen-style incompatibilism is the right one for someone who accepts all of the Lewisian approach to counterfactuals – the full Lewisian, as we can call him.

There is indeed a position in logical space which combines the full Lewisian view with the closeness analysis of freedom which I have been presenting. Under this combination, the role of the closeness analysis is to state the conditions which some event, in a non-actual possible world, of my going to the meeting must satisfy in order for it to be true in the actual world that I am free to go to the meeting. It is, however, very important that the closeness analysis is quite independent of any commitment to the full Lewisian treatment of counterfactuals, with its reliance on his particular theory of the counterfactually significant similarity relations between worlds.

In particular, the closeness elucidation can also be accepted in combination with Jackson's theory of counterfactuals.[22] On Jackson's approach, a sequential counterfactual 'if it were to be the case that p at t, then it would be the case that q at $t+n$' is true iff q is true at $t+n$ in all p-worlds meeting the following three conditions. First, their causal laws at and after t are the same as those of the actual world. Second, their time-slices at t are most similar in matters of particular fact to ours. Third, they are identical in matters of particular fact to the actual world prior to t. Jackson

[22] F. Jackson, 'A Causal Theory of Counterfactuals', *Australasian Journal of Philosophy* 55 (1977), 3–21.

emphasizes that on his theory, nonvacuous and empirical sequential counterfactuals are true only if there are appropriately sustaining laws. Similarity not based on laws cannot sustain such counterfactuals.

Still, even the combination of the closeness conception of freedom and the Jacksonian treatment of counterfactuals may be thought to have unacceptable consequences. Must it not still be involved with miracles in the worlds that verify the counterfactuals? In particular, if I do not in fact leave for the meeting at 8.00 p.m., must not this combination count the following counterfactual as true. 'If I were to leave for the meeting at 8.00 p.m., then some miracle would have occurred in the period of time up to 8.00 p.m.'? Must not something have gone wrong in a compatibilist account of freedom which, if freedom exists, is committed to the nearby possibility of small miracles?

I argue that there is no commitment, provided the case for the closeness elucidation of freedom is properly marshalled. We should distinguish very sharply between counterfactuals of the form

> If it were to be the case that p at $t+n$, then it would have been the case that q at the earlier time t

and conditionals of the form

> If it were to be the case that p at $t+n$, then that could only be because q was the case at the earlier time t

or of the form

> If it had been the case that p at $t+n$, then it would have had to be the case that q at the earlier time t.

Though counterfactuals of the first of these three forms – the back-trackers – are sometimes regarded as mere terminological variants of the latter 'could only' and 'would have to have' conditionals, as by Bennett,[23] it seems to me that they have a quite different meaning. Let us call a nonvacuous, empirical backtracking counterfactual with a consequent which is false with respect to the actual world a *threatening* backtracker. It seems to me that the defender of the combination I am advocating should insist that threatening back-trackers are true only if there is backwards causal influence. That is what assertion of the threatening back-trackers would properly be used to express.

The defender of the present combination can and should agree with the truth of such conditionals as 'If I were to leave for the meeting at 8.00 p.m. (which I am not), then that could only be because [or: then it would have to have been the case that] some conditions earlier were different from those which actually obtain.' The worlds which verify *these* conditionals do not involve the occurrence of any miracles (however small).

This combination differs also from the positions offered to the compatibilist in other recent discussions. In his valuable book *The Metaphysics of Free Will*,[24] John Martin Fischer considers how the compatibilist might respond to the challenge that an agent cannot do something

---

[23] J. Bennett, 'Counterfactuals and Temporal Direction', *Philosophical Review* 93 (1984), 57–91.

[24] J. M. Fischer, *The Metaphysics of Free Will: An Essay on Control* (Oxford: Blackwell, 1994).

of which it is true that were he to do it, the past would have been different (his principle '(Fpnc)', p. 79). Fischer offers the compatibilist a position on which in certain examples both a 'can' claim is true, and so too are certain backtrackers. He considers a seadog who would never go sailing at noon unless the weather forecast earlier in the morning had been favourable. Fischer (p. 91) says the compatibilist can say, even after an unfavourable weather forecast, both that the seadog can go sailing, and that 'if the seadog were to go sailing at noon, the past would have been different from what it actually is' (p. 91). On the combination I am proposing, though, since there is no real possibility of backward causal influence, such backtrackers are never true. No correct position can require their truth. It is rather the 'could only have been because...' and 'would have to have been because...' conditionals which are true in the Fischerian examples. Their truth does not involve any denial of the fixity of the past. (In effect, this is to suggest that Fischer's (Fpnc) principle, in which the 'nc' indicates the claim that it is a non-causal principle, is in fact causal after all.)

How then does the combination I am favouring respond to Fischer's 'Basic Version' of incompatibilism (pp. 87–94), the principle that 'an agent can do X only if his doing X can be an extension of the actual past, holding the laws fixed'? (Fischer, p. 88, also cites Ginet.)[25] On one intuitive understanding of the phrase, the closeness account does give an account of what is involved in an agent, with

[25] C. Ginet, *On Action* (Cambridge: Cambridge University Press, 1990).

her actual past, being free to do X. Her actual past is highly relevant, since it determines whether she is in a state which prevents there from being any close world in which she tries to do X (or any close world in which she tries and succeeds). Fischer would protest, though, that that intuitive construal is not what he means. What he means by the Basic Version is that an agent can at t do X only if there is a possible world coinciding at all times prior to t with the actual world, with the same laws as the actual world, and in which the agent at t does X. This, though, seems to be too strong as a necessary condition of possibility at t, even outside cases of agency. In our example of the deterministic world in which at t our subject sees a barn, we emphasized that there is a sense in which that subject could at t have been seeing a barn-facade. In that example, there is no possible world coinciding at all times prior to t with the world there envisaged as actual, with the same laws envisaged as actual there, and in which the agent is not seeing a barn. Nonetheless, it seems that there is some sense in which our subject could have been seeing a barn-facade; and that is why he does not count as knowing that there is a barn in front of him. On the way I have been developing the closeness conception, corresponding points hold for the 'could have' involved in freedom.

VI   Non-Theoretical Construals of Freedom

I now turn to consider some options I've implicitly rejected in putting forward the closeness conception. I will consider in a little more detail views that construe ascriptions of freedom or responsibility as a manifestation, perhaps an expression, of a practical attitude, rather than of a theoretical belief which might be false. This is the kind of position famously associated with Peter Strawson, but a position of this general character is developed in detail, with great resourcefulness, by Christine Korsgaard, in the title essay of her collection *Creating the Kingdom of Ends*.[26] She writes 'Responsibility is construed practically by those who think that holding someone responsible is adopting an attitude towards her, or, much better, placing yourself in a relationship with her' (p. 198). She contrasts the practical construal she favours with one on which 'Deciding whether to hold someone responsible is a matter of assessing the facts; it is a matter of arriving at a belief about her' (p. 197). Korsgaard's view is that the practical rather than the theoretical construal of responsibility 'is implicit in our actual practices' (p. 197). I want to consider briefly the phenomena she cites in support of that, and to argue that those phenomena can be explained on a theoretical conception of freedom and responsibility.

1. On Korsgaard's practical conception, there is, she notes, some distance between the practical issue of whether to hold someone responsible and the question of whether he acted voluntarily (p. 198). She writes 'there is neither need nor reason to... say that people under severe emotional stress *cannot* control themselves. We do not need to understand a form of debilitation as a form of impossibility in order to make allowances for it; we need only to

---

[26] Korsgaard, *Creating the Kingdom of Ends*, pp. 188–221.

know what it is like.' (p. 198) This seems to me intuitively correct. But it is also to be counted as correct on the closeness view. It will, on that view, be a matter of degree how easy it is to overcome some factor which, unless one makes some effort, will cause one's actions. It may be easy, somewhat hard, hard, ... through to extremely difficult to overcome it. These distinctions in degree correspond to differences in how close are the worlds in which one does overcome it, the more difficult cases being less close (though still close enough for the agent to be free to overcome it). A theoretical construal of freedom with respect to a factor does not need to, and should not, take it as an all-or-nothing matter. In sum, what we earlier raised as an objection to the closeness account, its recognition of degrees of freedom with respect to a factor, should properly be counted as a virtue of the approach.

2. Korsgaard also very acutely notices that 'it may be perfectly reasonable for me to hold someone responsible for an attitude or an action, while at the same time acknowledging that it is just as reasonable for someone else not to hold the same person responsible for the very same attitude or action. Perhaps it is reasonable for *you* to forgive or overlook our friend's distrustful behavior on the grounds that he has suffered so much heartbreak, but not for me, *not* because I fail to appreciate how hurt he has been, but because I am the woman whose loving conduct is always met with distrust' (p. 199). Korsgaard gives this as an example of a possibility 'that would not make sense if responsibility were a fact about the person'

(p. 199). But it seems to me that the theoretical view can accommodate this phenomenon too, provided that it recognizes differences in degree of difficulty in carrying through an action the agent is free to perform. The different relations in which two people may stand to the agent – in Korsgaard's example, one being an outside observer, the other engaging in loving conduct towards the agent – may generate different entitlements or legitimate expectations in the degree of effort they can properly demand of the agent in overcoming difficulties in pursuing a course of action, before they forgive or overlook some of the agent's behaviour. It seems to me that Korsgaard is right to say that the loving woman has a right to require more than the disinterested observer of the situation may reasonably expect. What I cannot see is that the phenomenon is inexplicable on the theoretical conception of freedom. It is the different relations to the agent which are generating the differences in legitimate expectations. The example does not force us to say inconsistent things about the factual issue of the freedom of the agent.

3. I am much less sure than Korsgaard that there is so tight a connection between one's placing oneself in a relationship with someone, and attributions of responsibility and freedom. She discusses the reciprocity and openness involved in close friendship, and ways in which this may be abused. As she notes, we may eventually 'write someone off', and in extreme cases cease to have reactive attitudes to them altogether (p. 200). Yet it is not at all clear to me that this must involve thinking of this other

person as unfree or as not responsible, as opposed to just being awful, manipulative or utterly egocentric. These latter characteristics seem to me, unfortunately, to be compatible with freedom.

VII   Libertarianism

Russell at one point in *Human Knowledge: Its Scope and Limits* wrote:

> Perhaps in the brain the unstable equilibrium is so delicate that the difference between two possible occurrences in one atom suffices to produce macroscopic differences in the movements of muscles. And since, according to quantum physics, there are no physical laws to determine which of several possible transitions an atom will undergo, we may imagine that, in a brain the choice between possible transitions is determined by a psychological cause called 'volition'. All this is possible, but no more than possible.[27]

I want to introduce an issue by the apposite comment made on this by a distinguished libertarian, David Wiggins, who wonders 'Could not the incidence of human acts of "volition" upon quantum phenomena upset the probability distributions postulated by the quantum theory?'[28] Wiggins also observes that if the volitions were postulated to have some immaterially realized source (perhaps to connect them

---

[27] B. Russell, *Human Knowledge: Its Scope and Limits* (London: Routledge, 1992), Part I, chapter 5, pp. 55–6.

[28] Wiggins, 'Towards a Reasonable Libertarianism', p. 292.

with the agent's character) the theory would be unacceptably Cartesian; he writes that 'We need not trace free actions back to volitions construed as little pushes aimed from outside the physical world' (p. 292).

It seems to me, however, there is a problem lurking here for the libertarian conception of freedom which can be formulated in a way quite independent of any commitment to Cartesian mythology. The assumption required for formulation of the problem is rather the non-Cartesian principle that mental events and states supervene on physical states and events (not necessarily restricted, in fact necessarily not restricted, to physical states of the brain given externalist theories of content). Suppose an agent has a choice between an action-type A and an action-type B, and suppose that he cannot do both. Let S_A be the set of physical states on which his choosing A would supervene, and let S_B be the set of physical states on which his choosing B would supervene. Just before the moment of choice, his being in some or other state in S_A and his being in some or other state in S_B each have certain probabilities. (The probabilities cannot be calculated in practice.) If the libertarian theory is that the subject's complete freedom to choose either A or B implies that it is completely indeterminate which he will choose, then won't the libertarian theory imply that an agent with this freedom can make either choice with whatever frequency he pleases? Cannot a collection of agents, similarly situated, make either choice with whatever frequency they please? That would then eventually conflict with the probabilities and frequencies implied by quantum mechanics. This means that the original point, rightly raised by

Wiggins against the conception Russell described, applies equally against a range of libertarian views. It is not only volitional theories and Cartesian variants thereof which are vulnerable to the objection.

It is worth noting that only supervenience has been employed in this argument. There has been no commitment to token-identity theories, nor even to the existence of realization or constitution relations between mental events and physical events.

I am inclined to draw from these reflections three points. The first is that a probabilistic micro-theory is just as threatening as classical determinism to the existence of freedom as conceived by libertarians.

Second, these reflections also make me wonder whether a libertarian theory will not have to be non-naturalistic to a degree that its proponents may not have envisaged.

Third, if neither deterministic nor indeterministic physical theories of the sort we currently have can be squared with the libertarian elucidation of freedom, it must follow that either we are not free, or the libertarian elucidation is incorrect.

This is a kind of modern fork against the libertarian, though it does not involve quite the same conclusions and commitments as Hume's fork. What I have said does suggest that any form of physical theory will be problematic for the libertarian, at least given supervenience. But, unlike Hume, I do not conclude that freedom requires determinism (all to the good, since there is evidence that determinism is false). My own view is that, even on a nondeterministic conception of causal explanation, when it comes to free choices, there are cases and cases in respect of the classification of the choice as rationally caused and explained. Sometimes a free choice is rationally caused and fully rationally explained, of course. But sometimes it is part of the nature of the case that it is not. Consider for instance someone in the position of Buridan's ass, making a choice between two exactly equally attractive options, with no reason to choose one over the other. Unlike Buridan's ass, we do succeed in choosing; but the rational agent may in such a case have no reason for plumping for the one he actually selects. The choice between it and its equivalent alternative is not one which falls within the ambit of rational psychological explanation. Any explanation there is will be, at best, subpersonal. But the choice can nevertheless be a free one. My view, in short, is that freedom does not require determinism, and does not require indeterminism either.

What then produces the illusion, if it is an illusion, that freedom requires indeterminism? One source is the genuine recognition that there is a 'could have done otherwise' requirement, when that recognition is combined with the belief that only an indeterministic construal of the modality can be given. I have tried to give an alternative construal of the modality. I think, though, that part of the explanation of the illusion may also be the fact that when an agent is presented with various prima facie reasons for different courses of action, there is apparently no *ceteris paribus* psychological law of commonsense psychology about which he will choose, not even when he has deliberated and found one of the courses best all things considered.

All kinds of impulsive, and/or weak-willed, but nevertheless free, choices may be made by the agent. Since there is no such psychological law, and we also consider the alternatives between which the agent is deliberating to be genuinely open to her, it may be tempting to conclude that there is no law at all explaining her choice. Put like that, though, any such conclusion would be a *nonsequitur*. It would be entirely consistent with those premises that there is some other kind of *ceteris paribus,* and perhaps probabilistic, law which, in the circumstances in which the agent is placed, explains the choice under its intentional description. It may be anything ranging from the subpersonal-computational, or the psycho-analytic, to the sociological or the economic. All our premises said is that there is no *ceteris paribus* psychological law of commonsense psychology.

VIII   Concluding Remarks

As you might expect, I am inclined to present the closeness account as a form of the very first of the six theoretical possibilities I distinguished when there is trouble squaring the metaphysics and the epistemology in a given domain. The closeness account of freedom seems to be an account of the metaphysics of freedom which makes freedom an intelligible possibility, and makes the distinction between the cases in which an agent is free to F, and those in which he is not, an empirical matter. To this, it may be objected that some intrinsically problematic conception of freedom is inextricably entwined in our normal thought and practices, and that because this is so, the closeness account must rather be revisionary. The objection is that the closeness conception is rather an example of the fourth of the six options I identified, the option in which we offer a surrogate rather than a full-width truth-condition for statements of the problematic kind.

My immediate reaction to this objection is one which, despite our disagreement on the correct positive account, I share with Peter Strawson, when he writes that 'the idea that an entire range of emotions which pervade our personal and social lives as thoroughly as those in question should be thus linked to a condition which cannot be coherently described has a degree of implausibility which it would be difficult to rival'.[29] It may help to consider a parallel. Suppose we had a benighted community which believed in an extreme form of absolute space, and with it a distinction between absolute rest and absolute motion. This would certainly be a case in which the integration of the metaphysics and the epistemology would present severe (I would say insuperable) problems. Suppose we point out to members of this community that cases in which they speak of absolute rest really involve rest relative to some specified object or array of objects, and that is how the truth conditions of their statements about absolute rest and motion should be given. Would it be right for members of this community to object that the truth-conditions we propose would really be revisionary, would be an example of case (iv) rather than case (i), and thus not really capturing what they meant? Well, our proposal

---

[29] P. Strawson, 'Replies', in *Philosophical Subjects*, Z. Van Straaten (Oxford: Oxford University Press, 1980), p. 265.

would certainly be revisionary of a misconception of the nature of what they call rest, or motion, *sans phrase*. Maybe the misconception is indeed so inextricably involved in their thought that they would not know what to say in their old vocabulary once the situation is pointed out to them. What is clear, however, is that it would be futile in the spatial case to hope for a *better* solution than that we have offered them.

Now no one could honestly say that the case of freedom is as clear as that of absolute location. Whatever one's favoured solution, philosophical humility is the only appropriate mode in which to present it, in the face of the tremendous difficulty and recalcitrance of the problem of freedom. I do, though, want to suggest one similarity between the case of freedom and this spatial example. I suspect that we cannot coherently have more than the closeness account offers; while to settle for less seems to leave us in the rather queasy position of engaging in practices without entitlement. To establish that that suspicion is correct, much further argument would be needed. But if it can be established, then the closeness account would be something with which it would be reasonable to rest content.

Dualism in Action

JENNIFER HORNSBY

W e know what one dualist account of human action looks like, because Descartes gave us one. I want to explore the extent to which present-day accounts of physical action are vulnerable to the charges that may be made against Descartes's dualist account. I once put forward an account of human action, and I have always maintained that my view about the basic shape of a correct 'theory of action' can be combined with a thoroughgoing opposition to dualism. But the possibility of the combination has been doubted,[1] and it will remain doubtful until we have a better understanding of what makes an account objectionably dualistic. In this paper, I hope to deflect some of the criticisms aimed against what I shall call my account,[2] and to

---

[1] The account I gave in *Actions* (London: Routledge and Kegan Paul, 1980) has often been accused of Cartesianism: there are more details in section V, and see note 30 *infra*.

[2] I speak of 'my account' for the sake of having an easy label for what I defend. Despite the label, I do not mean to suggest either that it originates with me, or that it is the whole of an account of anything. Brian O'Shaughnessy defended something similar in *The Will* (2 vols., Cambridge: Cambridge University Press, 1980). The details of what I call 'my account' are to be understood as those of *Actions*. (I think that

show that when they are turned onto their proper path their actual target is some physicalist accounts.

I shall have to rely on one intuitive understanding of physical action here. According to this, where there is a physical action, a person moves, and there is a psychological explanation of a certain sort of something that she thereby does. This takes it for granted that human agency is evinced when someone does something intentionally,[3] and that when people do things by moving their bodies, they are involved in events.[4] Using this conception, and assuming a certain account of events' individuation,[5] one can say that any action is some person's moving her body (usually her moving of a bit of it). This understanding will serve in the

avoiding Cartesianism requires rejection of some of what O'Shaughnessy said in support of his account: see note 23 *infra*.)

[3] The general idea that there is human agency when a person intentionally does something is relatively uncontroversial. It can be sustained by seeing what sort of trio the concepts of *belief*, *desire* and *intention* form, and thus what kind of psychological explanation an action explanation is.

[4] Some resist the assumption that an action is ever an event. Resistance may stem from the thought that actions should not be reckoned among 'mere happenings'. I hope that it will become clear why, on my own view, there could be no reason to treat actions as 'mere happenings'.

[5] See e.g. D. Davidson, 'Agency', in *Agent, Action and Reason*, ed. R. Binkley et al. (Toronto: Toronto University Press, 1971); repr. In his *Essays on Actions and Events* (Oxford: Clarendon Press, 1980), pp. 43–61.

present context, because the debates about action which are of concern here take place in the domain that it carves out.[6]

I   Dualism vs. Physicalism

Before I come to allegations of dualism made against accounts of action, I should say something about what dualism itself amounts to. I think that in the present state of play, many philosophers have an inadequate conception of this.

Naturally enough, dualism is contrasted with physicalism.[7] We know that there are various versions of

---

[6] When actions are defined by reference to a class of physical events, the general idea of human agency is restricted in two different ways. (A) Left out from the account are things that fall into an intuitive category of the mental. Consider mental arithmetic; or consider the view that agency is evinced whenever there is an exercise of practical reason. (B) Left out from the account are things people intentionally do, the doings of which are not events. Consider an occasion on which a intentionally fails to greet b, and on which we might be apt to say that a did nothing, or say that nothing happened. Here a's intentionally not greeting b may be thought not to be an event; and, if it is not, then we have an example of agency – according to the intuitive conception of agency – but we do not have an action – not according to the restrictive conception of actions.

For present purposes, it need not be a question whether restrictions (A) and (B) ought to be lifted by a correct conception of agency, because charges of dualism are faced by accounts of action which impose the restrictions and deal with 'physical actions'.

[7] Throughout, I use 'physicalism' as the name of a kind of monism. I might have used the word 'materialism', or, introducing another bone of contention, 'naturalism', instead.

physicalism advocated in the philosophy of mind. For a start, there is the mild sort – so called token-token identities physicalism – and the stronger sort – so-called type-type identities physicalism. And then there are versions of physicalism which hold that composition or constitution, rather than identity, is the relation holding between mental and physical states and events. Whatever the details, it can seem as if we might put physicalist doctrines onto some sort of scale – a scale on which dualism might be supposed to feature at the opposite pole, as it were, from the strongest physicalist doctrine. It seems, then, as though we could ask a person: 'How physicalist are you?' One possible answer would be 'Not at all'; and then, if this were the right way to think about things, we could place the person as a dualist. But this cannot be the right account of the matter. If dualists are to be contrasted with physicalists, then that is not because they reject rather a lot of the doctrine which we have come to associate with 'physicalism' at the end of the twentieth century. Dualists are distinguished from physicalists inasmuch as a dualist answers *Two* to a certain question, to which any monist – including a physicalist – answers *One*. The question to which Descartes's answer of *Two* earns him the title of dualist is the question 'How many sorts of substance inhabit the world?'

Not only is he a dualist, but also (what matters here) Descartes's account of action is dualistic in a straightforward and obvious sense. It is true that when *res cogitans* first appears in the Second Meditation, 'it is in the strict sense only a thing that *thinks*': 'I am a mind or intelligence or intellect or reason', Descartes says. But Descartes widens 'thought' to include volitional, as well as intellectual, activity. 'What is a thing that thinks?', he asks; and answers 'A thing that doubts, understands, affirms, denies, *is willing* or *is unwilling*.'[8] Volitions, in which a *res cogitans* participates insofar as it 'is willing', belong to substances which are entirely separate, and radically different in their nature, from any bodies.

Let us call such substances 'souls'.[9] Then one disavows dualism of Descartes's sort by saying that there are no such things as souls. In that case there cannot be any need to locate oneself on any scale of 'physicalism' in order to avoid dualism. But by the same token, there must be more to Descartes's way of thinking about persons than is elicited in contrasting it with contemporary physicalists' ways of thinking. We are often encouraged to think that 'Cartesianism' still rears its ugly head. From a variety of sources, we are familiar with attacks on the idea of mental states as inner, private states whose content can be specified

[8] My italics. Descartes actually adds imagining and having sensory perceptions onto this list of attributes characterizing a soul, but these come (by the *Sixth Meditation*) to be treated in a special category of their own, so that Descartes's account of perception is not straightforwardly dualist. See John Cottingham, 'Cartesian Trialism', *Mind* XCIV, No. 374 (April 1985), 218–230. The question how straightforwardly dualist Descartes's account of action is comes up in Appendix B.

[9] I use 'souls' throughout to stand for what Descartes called sometimes 'esprit' (or 'mens'), at other times 'âme' (or 'anima'). We are familiar enough with 'minds' used as a *façon de parler*, supposed to make no commitment to non-physical substances, that 'souls' serves better to register such commitment.

without appeal to anything outside the consciousness of the person whose states they are: these are attacks on Cartesianism.[10] Cartesianism is arguably implicit in Descartes's method, and is usually supposed to be secured by substance dualism of Descartes's sort. But if charges of Cartesianism are still with us today, it seems that Cartesianism cannot actually require substance dualism of Descartes's sort.

One can see that contemporary physicalist ortho-doxy might not be proof against Cartesianism by noticing an ambiguity in 'substance dualism'. Substance dualism is often understood as the doctrine that mind and body are two different *kinds* of substance – so that, in the terminology being used here to register Descartes's view, there are souls as well as bodies, souls being of a different kind from physical things.[11] But substance dualism might be under-stood more broadly – as the doctrine that a mind, whatever kind of thing it may be, is a substance different from any

---

[10] By 'Cartesianism', I mean a conception of mind which, for instance, has been to be the butt of many of Wittgenstein's remarks. Assuming that a doctrine of substance dualism of Descartes's kind is to be avoided, I want to encourage the thought that some of its errors may actually attach to a Cartesianism which it brings with it, and which may attach also to other doctrines.

[11] The matter is more complicated than this allows, because Descartes, though he thought that individual souls were substances, took individual bodies to be modifications of stuff, not substances proper. (Those who speak of Descartes simply as a mind/matter dualist ignore his different treatments of individuals in the realm of mind and individuals in the realm of matter. And I too ignore them *pro hac vice*.)

animal body. In this broader sense, substance dualism is compatible with versions of physicalism. Indeed any physicalist who tells us that minds are *brains* would seem now to be a substance dualist (no matter what he has to say about states and events).[12] Underlying substance dualism in the broad sense is the idea that those persisting things which have mental properties are separable from all such things as lack mental properties (no matter whether the things have mental properties are actually physical things). This idea does not require *souls* to be present in the world. And it may be that some of the hostility to Cartesianism is not hostility to souls as such, but is directed towards treatments of the mental as a self-standing, inner realm. One does not automatically escape such treatments by adopting the tenets of contemporary physicalist orthodoxy.

Two possibilities have emerged here. First, it may be that one can be anti-Cartesian without endorsing any orthodox physicalist doctrine. Secondly, it may be that some of those who go in for orthodox physicalist doctrine are still Cartesian. I myself think that both of these possibilities are

---

[12] I make the assumption here that brains are substances. In the literature on personal identity, one sometimes encounters the claim that persons are brains; those who advance it do not intend to deny that persons are substances (in the relevant sense). Presumably those who say that minds are brains (who are rather more numerous than those who say that persons are brains) do not have their own special understanding of 'brain'. And we do not need Descartes's demanding notion of a substance to understand substance dualism in the broad sense (or even in the narrow one: see note 11 *supra*): 'persisting things' might serve for 'substances' here.

actual. At any rate, you will need to appreciate them both in order to understand how it can be that, in resisting the charge that my own account of action lines up with Descartes's, I should avoid endorsing any of the going versions of physicalism.

II   A Very Short History of Action Theory

We can look at a very truncated history of action theory in order to reveal where questions about Cartesianism impinge upon debates about action.

This should start with Descartes. We have seen already that he thought that volition is a faculty of souls. Here is what he said about the soul's production of movements.[13]

> The soul has its main seat in the little gland which is in
> the middle of the brain, from where it radiates
> throughout the rest of the body by means of the animal
> spirits, the nerves, and even the blood... [T]he machine
> of the body is made [so that]... this gland's being moved
> by the soul drives the surrounding spirits into the pores
> of the brain, which conduct them through the nerves into
> the muscles, by means of which it causes them to move
> the members [of the body].

Only the dualism here needs emphasizing now. The human body is one thing, a machine whose members are caused to move by muscles which (*via* the spirits) are driven by the

---

[13] *The Passions of the Soul,* Article 34.

gland wherein the soul resides. The soul itself is another thing: intellectual and volitional properties attach to it. The resulting picture of human action has been called volitionism. According to this, where there is an action:

> A soul's volition IS CAUSALLY RESPONSIBLE FOR a movement of a body

In order to move to contemporary debate, we need to skip three hundred years. This takes us to recent opposition to volitionism. The anti-volitionists of the 1950s and 1960s thought it an error to suppose that the question 'What makes a bodily movement voluntary?' should receive a causal answer.[14] They wanted to avoid the soul and its modes of affecting things; and they thought that these could be avoided if causal connections were left out of an account of the explanatory relations involved in understanding what people do. Their opposition to volitionism, then, was anti-causalist.

In the 1960s, the tide turned. Donald Davidson's paper 'Actions, Reasons and Causes' was largely responsible for that.[15] Nowadays this paper is read as providing arguments for a particular causal thesis, rather than as reacting

---

[14] This is not a question that Descartes himself ever attempted to answer. But it is plausible that the attractions of a volitionism like Descartes's may have derived from thinking that *having a mental cause* could serve to distinguish the bodily movements that occur when there is voluntary (or intentional) action from all other bodily movements.

[15] *Journal of Philosphy* 60 (1963); repr. in his *Essays* 3–19, and in *The Philosophy of Action* ed. A. Mele (Oxford: Oxford University Press, 1997), pp. 27–41.

specifically against the anti-causalism of the anti-volitionists. But situating it by reference to the thinking which prevailed when it was written, we can be aware of the care which Davidson took to avoid any events that might have been supposed to play the causal role that volitions play in Descartes's picture. Davidson thought that there is no need for any volitional items in order for causality to have its rightful place in an account of action. (His view was, and is, that beliefs and desires cause actions.[16]) Although the anti-causalism which Davidson was reacting against was popular at one time, it is not very popular any longer:[17] our powers as agents surely are power to change things; it can seem absurd to suppose that we might capture the idea of human agency without treating human beings as part of the causal world within which they operate. If Davidson showed that we can have causation on the scene without volitions there, then he might seem to have put an end to the debate about volitionism.

---

[16] I criticized this view in 'Agency and Causal Explanation', in *Mental Causation*, ed. J. Heil and A. Mele (Oxford: Clarendon Press, 1993); repr. in *The Philosophy of Action*, and in my *Simple Mindedness: A Defense of Naive Naturalism in the Philosophy of Mind* (Cambridge, MA: Harvard University Press, 1997). The criticisms leave intact a broadly causal picture of human action by allowing that one can provide a causal explanation of what an agent does by saying what her reasons for doing it were. (Although this leaves me opposed to the anti-causalists, I object not only to Davidson's version, but also to all of the usual versions, of causalism: see section V1 *infra*.)

[17] Although it is still defended: see Michael Morris, in this volume.

There must be more to be said, however. We can pose questions which are simply not addressed in Davidson's account. In the first place, there are other concepts than 'belief' and 'desire' which apparently have a peculiar relation to action; and we can ask how those concepts fit in. Secondly, Davidson spoke to the causation of *actions,* not the causation of the *bodily movements* of Descartes's picture; and we can ask about this – about such events as arms' going up, movements of lips, or whatever.[18] Action theory of the 1970s and 1980s provided accounts which attempted to answer questions of these two sorts, by

[18] At least it is natural to suppose (i) that the phrase 'bodily movements' subsumes events such as these, and (ii) that these events are not actions (where an action is an event of someone's intentionally doing something). I used to say that 'bodily movement' is ambiguous – so that it could mean either (say) the movement of a person's arm or a person's moving her arm (*Actions*, chapter 1). But I now think that I was over-generous to my opponents when I suggested that their claim that actions are movements relied upon an ambiguity. The verb 'move' is ambiguous, of course – between transitive and intransitive occurrences: 'move' plays different roles in 'She moved her arm' (where it is a transitive verb) and in 'her arm moved' (where it is intransitive). But this ambiguity appears not to carry over to the nominal 'movement'. When a trace of the transitive verb occurs in a description of an event, we have (say) 'a person's moving her leg', and it is not evident that the word 'movement' can serve for this. If it cannot serve, then it would take a serious argument to show that a hand's going up (which is a bodily movement) is the same event as a person's raising her hand (which is apparently not a *movement*). Someone equipped with such an argument will say – as Davidson and others do – that actions just are bodily movements. But the arguments seem to me ill-motivated: see section V *infra*.

going into detail about the relations between the various events that happen when someone moves her body and thereby does something intentionally. The account I defended myself exploits a connection between what is done *intentionally* by an agent (i.e. what may be explained by allusion to what she wants and what she thinks) and what the agent *tries to* do:

> (T) She V-d intentionally → she tried to V

In the presence of the understanding of *an action* that we are working with (*sc.* an event of a person's doing something intentionally), (T) ensures that every action is a person's trying to do something. Allowing, then, that in the case of physical action, it is because she is trying to do something that a person's body moves, one reaches an account which can be summarized thus:

> A person's trying to do something is CAUSALLY RESPONSIBLE FOR a movement of her body...

Evidently this account is readily associated with Descartes's: at first blush it might seem simply to rename Descartes's volitions using 'trying to —'. It could appear, then, as if the result of filling in a causalist account were to return one to the very volitionism that the anti-causalists had reacted against. But I think that this is a false appearance. And I want to free myself from guilt by association. So I shall defend (T) against charges of Cartesianism (section III).[19]

---

[19] Since delivering the lecture on which the present paper is based, I have come across *Descartes' Dualism*, by Gordon Baker and Katherine J.

And I shall show how superficial the similarity is between Descartes's account and the one I have just summarized ('my account': see note 2 *supra*).

III   The Import of Thesis (T)

By introducing 'try to', (T) brings in antecedents of bodily movements which fall into an intuitively mental category. So my account's seeming similarity with Descartes's appears to come in through its endorsement of (T). I need to explain why (T) should not be thought responsible for any items' being conceived of in Descartes's way.

Notice, first, that it is not only someone who accepts (T) who might have to guard against objections of Cartesianism. (T) makes a very general claim about what is required to do something intentionally.[20] But even someone who rejects this general claim will surely accept that there

Morris (London: Routledge, 1996), in which the authors argue that Descartes did not hold the doctrine (sc. 'Cartesian Dualism') which contemporary philosophers attribute to him. If they are right, then we may be less well placed than I suppose we are to base knowledge of a dualist account of action on our understanding of Descartes. I have responded by adding Appendix B.

[20] (T) is to be read as a schema: in any instance 'V' is to be replaced by a verb, and the tense of the verb at its left-hand-side occurrence is to match the tense introduced into the 'try to' that occurs before the verb's infinitive occurrence on the right-hand-side.

'My account' actually requires only that whenever there is an action, there is *at least one* thing that the agent intentionally does which is something she tries to do (at least one substitutend for 'V' gives a truth). My 'quick and simple' argument (*infra*) suggests that agents try are occasions when a person moves her body in trying to do something or other. On such occasions at least, a movement of a bit of the person's body arguably depends upon her trying to do whatever it is.[21] Suppose, for example, that someone moves her fingers against the keyboard trying to type a '£' sign, but because the key has been reassigned she actually types an '@'. Her finger's movement then depends upon her trying to type a '£' sign. If there were objections to the very idea that the movement of a person's body might depend upon her trying to do something, then the objections would apply in this case. And this means that a charge of dualism (if such a charge can really be made) is likely to be made in particular cases even if it is denied that 'try to' has the pervasive application which someone who endorses (T) believes that it does. The crucial questions here do not turn upon the correctness of (T).

Notice, secondly, that even though we are making a general assumption that actions require bodily movements, and (T)'s claim in respect of actions is very general, (T) does *not* make a claim about moving the body. You might hold that a person moves her body whenever there is a physical action of her doing something, and hold (as (T) says) that a person tries to do everything she intentionally does. That does not amount to your holding that people try to *move*

---

to do *everything* they intentionally do; but this fully general claim, which schema (T) catches, actually need not be at issue.

[21] An argument would require the distinctness of actions (e.g. her depressing the key marked '£') and bodily movements (e.g. her finger's moving against the key). Cf. note 18 *supra*.

their bodies whenever they do something intentionally. For it might be that people's intentions sometimes take off at points beyond their bodies. (T) can be acceptable, then, even where it is denied that something an agent always does is to try to move her body. Endorsing (T) does not force one to speculate about what it is to move the body.

Notice, thirdly, that someone who accepts (T) will think that nearly all of the things that agents try to do are things that they actually succeed in doing; and that even where an agent fails to do something that she tries to do, she usually succeeds in doing *something* (there is something else she does – other than what she tries to do). Thus an ordinary case of someone's trying to do something, whether successful or not, is just an ordinary case of action. (T) should not lead anyone to believe in things called 'mere tryings'.[22]

By accepting (T) and a claim about the causal dependence of agents' effects in the world upon events in which agents participate, one arrives at a quite natural

---

[22] When 'tryings' (simply) are spoken of, people conjure up a picture of 'mere tryings': they forget the adverbial characters of 'try to'. (See my 'Reasons for Trying', *Journal of Philosophical Research* 20 (1995), 525–39.) It is hard to find a natural terminological policy which enables one both to speak generally and to avoid the misleading impression that there might be 'mere tryings'. The policy I have adopted here where the context allows is to use 'try-to' (rather than just 'try') for shorthand, and to use 'try to —' as a sort of schematic verb: the intention is to keep it in mind that to try is always to try to do something.

There is a particular case where 'mere tryings' have seemed to be in question – the case of an agent who tries to do something actually does nothing. I discuss this in Appendix A: On Landry's Patient.

account of the difference between successful and unsuccessful attempts. Thus: someone who tries-to-have-an-effect-and-succeeds is someone who participates in an event which has some result she intended, whereas someone who tries-to-have-an-effect-and-fails is someone who participates in an event which doesn't have some result she intended. On this account, 'try to —' appears as a sort of common denominator, which is present both in intentional doings and in unsuccessful tryings. But those who have their doubts about (T) will wonder why 'try to' should be supposed to have any application at all when an agent actually *does* what she means to. The doubters may think that anyone committed to 'try to''s having such a pervasive application as (T) suggests must have been involved in a search for a common denominator – a sort of search which prescinds from the world surrounding the agent and considers only the agent herself and how things might have seemed to her. Well, it is certainly true that philosophers have given arguments for (T) in which such considerations are very much to the fore.[23] But there is a quick and simple argument for it which

---

[23] In volume II of *The Will* (Cambridge: Cambridge University Press, 1980), O'Shaughnessy announces that a Gricean argument supports the claim about 'trying to' which he and I accept. But he proceeds to give (among others) an argument from illusion, whose tenor is certainly Cartesian. Suffice it here to say that I do not think a defence of (T) (still less of the weaker claim which is really at issue: see note 20 *supra*) need advert to 'trying to do seeming Ø', or take a view on the 'epistemological status of bodily tryings'. A properly Gricean argument can certainly be much simpler than O'Shaughnessy's argument from illusion: see note 24 *infra*.

requires no speculations about the phenomenology. All that this argument needs is that 'try to do something' can be glossed as 'do what one can to do the thing'. The agent who is influenced by having a reason to do something does what she can to do it. But what one does for a reason, one does intentionally. And in doing what one can to do something, one tries to do it. So agents try to do what they intentionally do.

This argument will be too quick to satisfy.[24] But my purpose is not to vindicate the account I outlined, but only to distance it from Descartes's. It is enough here to say that (T) will seem plausible only when it is understood that it can be true that someone tries to do something without the fact that she tries to do it being at all a usual or useful thing for anyone to say or to think. Usually, of course, people simply *can* do the things which they do-what-they-can to-do. Otherwise life would consist mainly of frustrated attempts. That is why there is usually no point in thinking of the person who has *done* what she set out to do as having done what she *could*. Certainly there is no need for the agent herself to think of herself as trying to do that which (in fact) she tries to do. So (T) need not be responsible for the musings of those philosophers who conceive of 'tryings'

---

[24] A Gricean argument which I stated in my *Actions*, pp. 34–5 (which is an argument from ignorance, rather than an argument from illusion) also seeks to show that the background facts which conduce to an instance of 'She V-d intentionally' suffice for the relevant instance of 'She tried to V'.

(as they call them – cf. note 22) exclusively from the standpoint of the agent.

These points all help to show that (T) is not an accomplice in Cartesianism. But they do not speak directly to the similarity of my account and Descartes's. What I shall do next is to consider lines of objection which might be thought to have application equally to both accounts. I hope to show that their proper target is Descartes's account alone (sections IV and V).

IV   A Mysterious Gulf?

In Gilbert Ryle's description of Descartes's account, 'mental thrusts, which are not movements of matter in space, can cause muscles to contract'; and mental thrusts work 'in some way, which must remain forever mysterious'.[25] Ryle is one of the anti-causalist anti-volitionists. He wanted to know how something purely mental could have a causal influence in the material world where muscles contract. How is the gulf between mind and matter bridged?

Descartes for his part saw no problem here. He once said 'if "corporeal" is taken to mean anything that can in anyway affect a body, then mind too must be called "corporeal" in this sense'.[26] Of course, we are unlikely to be much impressed by this: a philosopher who tells us, as Descartes did, that the properties of thought and of

---

[25] Gilbert Ryle, *The Concept of Mind* (London: Hutchinson, 1949), pp. 62.

[26] Letter to Hyperaspistes, August 1641, at 112 in *Descartes' Philosophical Letters*, tr. and ed. Anthony Kenny (Oxford: Clarendon Press, 1970).

extension are mutually incompatible can hardly be entitled to claim that there is any sense in which a thinking thing 'must be called "corporeal"'. But the possibility of using the claim in response to Ryle shows that an objection of 'mental thrusts' on its own is only as powerful as the very familiar general objection to Descartes's sort of substance dualism – the objection which says that souls, being of a different kind from physical things, are alien to the world of causes and effects.

Descartes hoped that his detractors might be persuaded to stop thinking of volitions as alien to movements by constructing a category, the 'corporeal', to which volitions and movements both belong. Evidently an analogous step could be taken in respect of my account if it seemed to need defence. In order to demonstrate that there is a category to which events of trying-to and movements both belong, one could say that an event of a person's trying to do something is, in some sense, physical. That would be enough to put any version of the familiar general objection to Descartes to rest. But Ryle's objection is actually more powerful than this allows. To see this, imagine someone who says that she can only conceive of electrochemical impulses as 'thrusts', and that she is puzzled about how their causing muscles to contract could illuminate human action. No doubt one sort of difficulty is alleviated if she is brought to see that there is a level of physical description which subsumes both the electrochemical and the mechanical. But even when the operation of neural transmission is made to seem unmysterious to her, she is not helped in understanding what a person's intentionally doing something consists in. If you hope to be better placed to understand those powers of persons which allow them to get things done by moving their bodies, then you would seem to be no better served by an account of neural transmission than by an account of a gland's being moved by a soul.

Descartes's elaborate story (quoted above, invoking the animal spirits) is presumably meant to help us to understand the rational soul's active powers. The problem which Descartes faces and which could never be solved by calling the soul corporeal begins to emerge when we consider that story. In order for the soul's action to be found intelligible, the goings on around the pineal gland must be related to an understanding of human agency. The soul is a rational being, having intentional states. So we can ask Descartes: *What* does it will? The answer to this cannot be *that the pineal gland moves*. For a rational soul need not concern itself with the gland (just as ordinary active people need not concern themselves with neural transmission). It must be, then, that a soul is supposed to will (say) *that a finger moves*. But in that case the soul seems to have a magical power – the sort of power that we should attribute to a person if we could believe that she could directly move something remote from her. This is why Descartes's account of ordinary physical agency has been said to involve psychokinesis.[27] The only thing that a soul can move *directly* is the pineal gland. But we can understand a rational being's capacity to move x *in*directly, only by thinking of it as having knowledge of how

[27] See Bernard Williams, *Descartes* (Harmondsworth: Penguin, 1978), pp. 288–92.

x can be affected by something that it can move directly.[28] The trouble then is that souls do *not* have knowledge of how glands have to be affected for body parts to move, so that we lack any understanding of how something placed as the Cartesian soul is could be in a position to move (say) the little finger of a certain body. This remains, as Ryle said, 'forever mysterious'.

The mystery here is created by the situation of the soul, and is independent of its non-physical nature. And my own account would introduce a mystery if 'try to —' were taken to apply to something that lacks capacities for movement. But there is no possible basis for supposing that 'try to —' could apply to something lacking such capacities.[29] When accounts like mine are described, one often finds that 'try to —' is applied to *nothing*: philosophers often speak simply of 'tryings' – as if these might be unowned and (as it were) free-floating events. But of course what has to be meant by 'a trying', in any particular case, is someone's trying to do some particular thing. In my account, then,

---

[28] To use the terminology of *basicness*: everything an agent has it in her power to do is either something basic, or requires knowledge of how nonbasic things can be done by doing basic ones. The relevant notion of basicness here is a teleological one: see my *Actions*, Chapter 6. (I put the matter slightly differently from Williams *Descartes*, thinking as I do that a teleological notion of basicness is different from a causal one.)

[29] In my *Actions*, I claimed that 'actions [and thus events of trying-to] occur inside the body'. The claim is misleading at best. But notice now that the idea was never that there is something inside the body to which predications of 'trying to —' attach. And see further the end of Appendix A *infra*.

there is a place for things to which we actually predicate 'try to —'. Such things are human beings, whom we can readily conceive as having capacities to move their bodies. In order to conceive of them thus, we have only to think of ourselves, and to hold fast to the truth that there are no souls that our selves are.

Whereas human agents are lost sight of in Descartes's picture of human action, they feature in mine. One can think that a person's action requires an event of her trying to do something without thinking of the person as composed from a proper part which tries. The claim that a person's trying to do something is distinct from her body's moving does not involve one in the idea that a person can be decomposed into a thing that tries and a body.

V   A Mysterious Inner Realm?

A different sort of Cartesian malady has been thought to afflict my account. The allegation is not that I am involved in a distinction between mental and physical substances, but that I am involved nonetheless in a distinction which was bound to be present in Descartes, given his separating of souls from bodies. The distinction now is between a mental realm – wherein events of people trying to do things, or of souls' willing things may be supposed to occur – and a physical realm – wherein bodies move. In consequence of my holding that an agent's trying to do something results in a bit of her body's moving, it has been said that I am (i) Cartesian, and (ii) 'a mental action theorist'; and it has been said that, on my account of them, actions (a) are not 'overt',

(b) are identified with 'purely mental acts of will', and (c) have their 'essence located in the will'.[30] The critics who say these things recognize that even when persons are not problematically decomposed, the phenomenon of agency may still be. (Even where substance dualism is absent, Cartesian thinking may still be present – as we saw in section I.) Certainly, if these things were true, there would be more of an affinity between Descartes's account and mine than I have just allowed.

In fact the allegations bring to light a difference between Descartes and me. I say that a person's trying to do something is an action (*is* her doing something that she does intentionally),[31] whereas Descartes does not say that a soul's volition *is* an action. There is thus no question on my account, as there is on Descartes's, of an action's being

---

[30] See (i) R. A. Duff, *Intention, Agency and Criminal Liability: Philosophy of Action and the Criminal Law* (Oxford: Blackwell, 1990); (ii) Myles Brand, *Intending and Acting: Towards a Naturalized Action Theory* (Cambridge, MA: MIT Press, 1984), and Michael Moore, *Act and Crime: The Philosophy of Action and its Implications for Criminal Law Intending* (Oxford: Oxford University Press, 1993); (a) Brand; (b) Bill Brewer, 'The Integration of Spatial Vision and Action', in *Spatial Representation,* ed. Naomi Eilan, Rosaleen McCarthy and Bill Brewer, (Oxford and Cambridge, Ma: Blackwell, 1993), pp. 294–316; (c) Duff, *Intention.*

[31] If there are cases in which a person tries in vain to move a part of her body, then the claim here is not a universal one. For present purposes, it makes no odds whether one accepts that there are such cases: the claim might be that where someone tries to do something *and* thereby intentionally does something, her trying to do the thing is her doing it. I discuss vain attempts to move the body in Appendix A.

'partly in the mental realm', 'partly in the physical'.[32] Still, this difference by itself will not impress the critics. For they think that a problem is exposed in my account as soon as a distinction between mental and physical is registered there. 'Even if actions themselves do not straddle the mental/physical divide,' they may say, 'it is objectionable that an account of action should straddle it. And as for actions themselves, these should be located firmly in the physical realm, not a mysterious inner one.'

To get to the bottom of the objections envisaged here, we need to know why a claim of identities of actions with events of trying-to should be thought to make actions 'mental' and to place them beyond what is 'overt'. Suppose that you accept such identities – you accept, say, that her hitting the ball into the net was her trying to make a winning shot. Will you be led to say that her action of hitting the ball into the net must really be mental (seeing that is is describable using the word 'try')? Would you not rather say that her trying to make a winning shot must be physical (seeing that it is describable using the word 'hit')? You might equally well say either of these things. The claim of an identity of a putatively mental item (a person's trying to do something) with a putatively physical one (an action) might just as well

---

[32] Descartes might have said that a volition is *part* of an action, the other part being a bodily movement. Not talking the explicit event language, Descartes did not in fact address questions about parthood. But some contemporary philosophers are explicit about actions having both mental and physical proper parts, taking this to be a *sine qua non* of action's psychophysical character.

be taken to reveal the physical character of the putatively mental item as the mental character of the putatively physical one.

The objections can now be seen to rely upon the idea that a distinction between mental and physical corresponds to an actual division in the spatio-temporal world. If there were such a division, then no doubt one would be obliged to answer questions about which side of it actions, events of trying-to, and bodily movements fall on. But an event describable using both a piece of mental vocabulary ('try to —') and a piece of physical vocabulary ('hitting'), since it can equally well be said either to be mental or to be physical, might perfectly well be said to be both mental and physical. So the question 'Mental *or* physical?' has to be refused. The distinction between mental and physical does not partition the events that there are. And the assumption that there are boundaries in space between mental events and physical events must be rejected. Once the split between the soul and body has been renounced, there is no real divide for an account of action to straddle.

If an assumption of a spatial mental/physical divide is made, then denying that actions are bodily movements appears to exclude them from the physical world. If an action is not a bodily movement but is someone's trying to do something, then, thinking of it with the putative divide in place, one conceives of it as hidden from view, as something which somehow initiates movements of a body. Actions then belong to a mysterious inner realm, separate from the outer realm inhabited by people's bodies. But when the assumption is rejected, there is no reason to think that actions belong *anywhere* in a picture containing the putative divide.

Recognizing the identity of actions with events of trying-to helps to show (as we saw) that an intuitive distinction between mental and physical is inimical to such a divide. Refusing the identity of actions with bodily movements (we can now see) cannot create the mysterious realm which the divide introduces. For suppose that one really did have to say that actions, being causally anterior to bodily movements, must take up residence in a mysterious inner realm. Would it not then be in exactly such a realm that beliefs and desires were located by theorists who identify actions with bodily movements and who say that actions are caused by beliefs and desires? (Presumably beliefs and desires would be supposed to fall on the mental side of any mental/physical divide.) It is true that such theorists usually claim that the beliefs and desires which they take to cause actions are components of the same natural world as the physical things which they take all movements to be. But they are not entitled to such a claim if there is a problem with the idea that exercises of our powers as agents can be revealed in the items alongside which bodily movements are classified when the putative mental/physical divide does its work.

There is a genuine difficulty about bringing events which are the doings of sentient beings who do things for reasons into relation with events conceived as on the farther side of a mental/physical divide. And bodily movements are often thought of as belonging on the farther side by philosophers: the claim that actions are bodily movements is often glossed as the claim that they are 'mere movements of the body', or that they are 'no more than bodily movements'.[33] Bodily movements then come to be assimilated to items which might be there even if there were no persons whose bodies they were movements of. It is this assimilation, rather than anything in my account, which is the source of the genuine difficulty. If a difficulty sprang simply from denying that actions can be identified with bodily movements, then we should expect it to go away as soon as the identity was asserted. But in the presence of the difficulty, the step of identifying actions with bodily movements seems like subterfuge. The problem is to understand how a person's role in getting done the things that she does for reasons could be a matter of her operating on inanimate nature. The problem cannot be made to go away by declaring that an action (a person's doing whatever it is when she does something for a reason) is itself the operation of inanimate nature.

A typical action theorist of today sees no problem at this point. Just as Descartes was content to call souls corporeal 'in a sense', in order to ensure that we should not have to think of causal transactions across alien kinds, so a typical action theorist of today is content with a homogeneous conception of those events which occupy the spatio-temporal world and participate there in causal relations. (Such a conception informs orthodox physicalism, as we shall see.) But perhaps even a typical action theorist has an

---

[33] See Davidson, 'Agency', at p. 59 in reprinted version; and Moore, *Act and Crime*, at p. 83, who announces that 'actions are no more than bodily movements' is a 'reductive' thesis.

inchoate sense of the problem. At least if he does, that would explain why it should be thought that distinguishing actions from bodily movements is tantamount to relegating actions to a mysterious inner realm (or to denying that they are 'overt', or to locating 'their essence in the will').

The problem, as I have said, arises from supposing that the bodily movements that there are when there are actions might be located in a world bereft of beings who do things for reasons – a world where so-called 'mere movements of bodies' belong. The supposition prevents one from treating movements in such a way that they can be rightly related to the agents who produce them. (And it makes no difference to this whether or not one says that bodily movements are the same as actions.) Those who make the supposition may see a point, as Descartes did, in calling a human body 'a machine'. They may forget that Descartes can be faulted for his assumption that corporeal substance excludes the features of thinking beings as much as for his more familiar assumption that the bearers of mental properties are not the sort of things to which physical properties attach.[34]

Ryle's objection to Descartes was that souls cannot be rightly related to what they are supposed to act upon.

---

[34] Descartes's belief in souls is normally thought of as arrived as through the introspective route he took in the *Meditations*. But part of his reason for attaching mental properties to a soul was a difficulty he thought he saw about attaching them to a substance whose principles of operation are purely mechanistic. See 'Descartes, Rorty and the Mind-Body Fiction', repr. in *Simple Mindedness*, pp. 24–41.

I said that the Rylean objection can be seen not to touch my account once it is allowed that a human being is not detachable from an event which is her trying to do something. In allowing this, one rejects a Cartesian conception of people's possession of (intuitively) mental properties. What I say now is that the objection of a mysterious inner realm will present itself unless it is allowed that human beings are the bodily beings they are, and that the movements which they make are theirs. In allowing this, one rejects a Cartesian conception of people's possession of (intuitively) physical properties.

VI   Mental Causation: Dualism and Physicalism in Action

I hope to have shown that there are no Cartesian assumptions in my account of action (section III), and that if there seem to be, that is because others read them in to it (section V). I want to suggest in conclusion that it is actually the orthodox physicalists' treatment of action, not mine, which is really aligned with Descartes's.

The similarity of my account to Descartes's is partly to be blamed on their common focus of attention – on the agent's body. But notice that there are different reasons for this narrow focus. The reason for the apparent shortsightedness of my own account is simply a desire to generalize. If one hopes to say anything general about physical action, it is no good having one's sights on the world surrounding agents, because there are so many things of such various sorts that agents do. The thread running through them all is that the agent has to move to do them, and that is how the focus comes to be turned towards the agent's body. (The outlook of my own account is actually broader than the narrow focus suggests, because the things that agents can try to do are as many and various as the things they do.[35] The point emerged in section III: my account does not deal only with people moving their bodies, but covers also all the more interesting things that they do.) In Descartes's account, attention to the agent's body has a different rationale. When the soul has been introduced, we are owed some account of its doings, and given the soul's situation, the close-up story of the production of movements is bound to be told. Descartes cannot simply acknowledge, as I do, a kind of being that has basic capacities of movement.

But here the similarity, such as it is, shows up. Although I acknowledge that human beings have capacities of movement, I nevertheless discern a sort of causal complexity in exercises of those capacities. Human beings are complex beings; some of the events in which they participate depend causally upon others. The dependencies in the case of action, are dependencies of movements of parts of agents' bodies upon events of their trying to do things. So I think, as Descartes does, that when there is an action, a movement of the agent's body can be seen to depend causally upon something which is (intuitively) mental.

---

[35] There are plenty of substitutes for 'something' in 'the agent's trying to do something', plenty of verbs besides 'move the body' which can replace 'V' in (T); and (T) introduces the agent's trying to do any of the things which she does intentionally.

This may be put in slightly different terms: both Descartes and I think that action involves 'mental causation'. Put in these terms, what I have been trying to establish, in order to show that the similarity does not go deep, is how very differently Descartes and I treat 'mental causation'. Since nearly everyone accepts that action involves 'mental causation', what distinguishes Descartes from me is something of which nearly everyone must take a view.[36] 'Mental causation' has been of great concern recently, especially among orthodox physicalists.[37]

None of the claims of orthodox physicalism was required to avoid Ryle's objection of a mysterious gulf. We

---

[36] I say *'nearly* everyone' to allow for the anti-causalists (see section II *supra*). The treatment of mental causation is a question for all causalists. It might seem that there is a special question for Descartes and me, because we accept (what many don't) that the agent's body is a locus of 'mental causation'. (Many think that one has to look to actions' antecedents – to what occurs before anything bodily – in order to find anything which is both psychologically describable and causally operative.) Still, we saw in section III that even someone who rejects my general claims about action may accept that there are occasions when a person moves her body therein trying to do something. So perhaps nearly everyone accepts that the agent's body is *sometimes* a locus of mental causation. That would ensure that there is in fact no special question for Descartes and me. But however this may be, nearly everyone allows that there is 'mental causation'.

[37] And it has been the topic of a massive literature: see, e.g., the papers in *Mental Causation,* ed. Heil and Meie. I attach scare quotes to 'mental causation', being reluctant to think of the causal dependencies which correspond to persons' causal complexity as marking out any *kind* of causation: see note 40 *infra.*

saw that this objection is avoided by insisting on the sameness of that which tries to do something and that whose parts it can move. The movements which are caught up in the understanding of such a thing – of a human being – are then individuated as events in which someone's participation is crucial, and not as the subject matter of physics or of any other Science. Bodily movements are physical of course. But the sense of 'physical' in which it is obvious that they are physical is not that which has informed the recent debate on 'mental causation'.

Most contemporary philosophers think that physicalism requires one to be able to see the mental's causal operation as an example of the world's working causally in such a way as to reflect its law-like workings. Their treatments of 'mental causation' encourage one to take the close-up view of the agent which Descartes took. They may say that events of trying-to, if they are causally responsible for movements of bodies, are, or are constituted by, 'brain events'. But an objection of Cartesianism arises however this is interpreted.

If a brain event is something in which a brain participates, then the orthodox physicalist tells us that the causal transitions involved in human action are transitions between brain and body. In that case he accepts a version of substance dualism in the broad sense identified in section I. We saw in section IV that the principal objection to Descartes does not actually depend upon the nature of the soul; and this means that if one thinks of a person's trying to do something as the brain's doing something, one renders physical action mysterious as Descartes did. There is a kind of causal dependence encountered when effects are produced by a being with contentful States (a being that can will something, or try to do something); and this kind of dependence is not found intelligible when causal properties are attributed to something located inside a body.

The other possibility is that calling something a brain event is a matter of locating it in the domain of neurophysiology (rather than of thinking of it specifically as the brain's doing something). Brain events in this case are among the flux of events in nature, unowned and free-floating, as it were; and the causal connections which are examples of 'mental causation' are discoverable without finding something to which 'try to —' can be predicated. But this is equally problematic. We have seen that the items of Descartes's story – the volitions which belong to souls, and the movements which belong to mind-excluding substances – are foreign to a proper account of physical action. Equally foreign must be the unowned and free-floating events. For the underlying difficulty is to think about the production of bodily movements as human action even when the causes of those movements are supposed to be identifiable without making reference to any bodily being. If one takes bodily movements to be robust presences 'in the physical world', then, in searching for their antecedents with the agent removed from the scene, one thinks of inner items, and then one may conjure up an inner realm for those items to inhabit. Here a Cartesian difficulty stems from attempting to find what are actually changes in a rational being inside a world which one had hoped to conceive of as physical in some exacting sense. The orthodox physicalist, in avoiding the mysterious gulf, puts herself under pressure to introduce the spurious divide between mental and physical.[38]

The problem here, for the orthodox physicalist, is the one we saw in section V – about understanding how causal transactions in inanimate nature could account for a person's role in getting done the things that she does for reasons. Causal dependencies which reflect the causal complexity of a human being are not examples of the world's working causally in such a way as to reflect its law-like workings. The phenomenon of 'mental causation', in which human beings show up as causally complex beings, cannot consist in pairs of particulars standing in a relation of causation as this is typically conceptualized by philosophers.[39] So the dependencies encountered in human agency are not the 'physical causation' to which orthodox physicalists have wanted to assimilate 'mental causation'.[40]

---

[38] Cf. John McDowell, *Mind and World* (Cambridge, MA: Harvard University Press, 1994), at p. 90. Put in the terms that McDowell takes from Sellars, what the present paper argues is that human physical action is situated in the space of reasons, where the space of reasons is to be contrasted not with the space of causes but with nomological space (and where the space of reasons, evidently, is not the space just of cognition).

[39] For reasons to reject the typical conceptualization, see Helen Steward's arguments against what she calls the network model of causation in her *Ontology of Mind: Events, States and Processes* (Oxford: Clarendon Press, 1997).

[40] In 'The Mental Causation Debate,' *Aristotelian Society Supplementary Volume* 69 (1995), 211–36, Tim Crane argues that the dominant contemporary versions of physicalism implicitly reject the assumption of 'homogeneity' – the assumption 'that mental and physical causation

We saw in section I that someone might be anti-Cartesian without endorsing any orthodox physicalist doctrine, and that someone might be a Cartesian orthodox physicalist. What we see now is that endorsing physicalist doctrine is actually just a way of being Cartesian. Orthodox physicalisms's attitude to causation is a source of Cartesian thinking.

are the same kind of relation'. It seems then that I am on the side of contemporary physicalists in my treatment of mental causation. Well, I am more than happy to acknowledge Crane's point that there is a homogeneity assumption which provokes contemporary physicalist treatments of mental causation but which they find themselves forced to abandon. (I take their abandonment of the assumption to be symptomatic of a problem which is inherent in the orthodoxy and which I have tried to expose here.) But it would be an oversimplification of my own view to say that mental and physical causation are different kinds of relation. It is rather that we have to stop thinking that all causation can be understood by reference to the going model of 'physical causation' (cf. Steward, *Ontology,* and my 'Causation in Intuitive Physics and in Commonsense Psychology', in *Simple Mindedness,* pp. 185–94); and that we have to allow for the species of intelligibility that is peculiar to rational sentient beings.

I should note that my arguments here – about treating events of trying-to as brain events – are directly addressed to a version of physicalism which does not flout the homogeneity assumption as Crane sets things up. But when I say that it is part of the orthodoxy that one must be able to see the mental's causal operation as an example of the world's working causally in such a way as to *reflect* its law-like workings, I intend to speak to other versions of physicalism, including what Crane calls 'the constitution view'.

I thank Paul Boghossian, David Papineau, Scott Sturgeon, and (especially) Tim Crane (who prompted me to re-read his 'Mental Causation Debate') for questions asked after the lecture on which this paper is based.

Appendix A: On Landry's Patient

In defending (T) against charges of Cartesianism, I pointed out that a person's trying to do something can usually be identified with an action. But if there are cases in which a person tries in vain to move a part of her body, then a person can try to do something without there being an action of hers. It has been thought objectionable that I should allow such cases. Bill Brewer puts an objection to my account of action, saying that 'the subject is distanced from movement in her body in such a way as to threaten her status as agent'.[41]

The case to which Brewer and others speak is the case of Landry's patient. The patient had lost all sensation in one arm. When his eyes were closed, he was told to raise his arm; unknown to him, his arm was held down – it was prevented from rising; and when he opened his eyes, he was surprised to find that it had not risen. It seems natural to say that, although he didn't raise his arm, he tried to.

It may be that in contemplating Landry's patient, one starts to think in phenomenological terms about events describable using the word 'try': one thinks that it must have seemed to the patient just as it would have seemed if he had moved his arm (if the arm, in which he had no sensation, had not been prevented from rising); and then one may start to think of events of trying to do things under the aspect of seemings. But in fact one does not need to focus on the phenomenology to judge that the patient tried to move his arm. The judgment might be based on knowledge that he is obedient to instructions: obedient as he is, he does what he can to raise his arm when told to do so; and his belief that he has raised his arm, evinced in his surprise that it had not moved, is then a further piece of evidence that he tried to raise it.

It is not that we should necessarily go wrong if we considered how things seemed to the patient. But there is no reason to think that we must be working with some purely phenomenological notion when we think of Landry's patient as having *tried* to raise his arm. And of course it cannot be right generally to think about events of trying-to as seemings.

---

[41] Brewer, 'Integration', p. 306.

(We could not have acquired the concept of trying to if we had had only phenomenology to work with.) We must not forget what an extraordinary epistemic and practical situation Landry's patient was in: he was not allowed to see; he was proprioceptively incapacitated; and his movements were obstructed. We can agree with Brewer that 'his status as agent is threatened'. Thoughts that we have about his case cannot be expected to generalize to other cases. Landry's patient's failed attempt is at least as unsuited to providing a model for action as the case of a false belief is unsuited to providing a model for knowledge.

Still if we do accept that Landry's patient did try to move his arm, then the account I gave in section III, of the difference between successful and unsuccessful attempts, applies in this case. Thus: a person's trying to raise her arm is her raising it if is it causally responsible for her arm's rising, but is her unsuccessfully trying to raise it if no event of her arm's rising ensues. It is this to which Brewer really objects. Brewer wants to be able to say that someone's unsuccessfully trying to raise her arm is of a fundamentally different kind from her raising it. And he suggests that we need a 'disjunctive conception of tryings'. The trouble is that a disjunctive conception of tryings seems quite implausible in general. Remember the case of the typist who typed an '@' sign when the key had been reassigned. Is her moving her finger against the keyboard of a fundamentally different kind from the kind it is of when the key has not been reassigned and she actually types a '£' sign? Surely not.

I believe that it is a disjunctive conception of bodily movements, not of events of trying-to, that we need if we want, as Brewer and I both do, to keep the subject in touch with movements of her body. (Such a conception is implicit in what I have said at section V and echoed in section VI *supra,* and it is explicit in my writing elsewhere.[42])

Landry's patient's case was one of the things that encouraged me to say (as I did once upon a time, cf. note 29 *supra)* that actions occur inside the body. That claim, though misleading at best, need not be Cartesian, because it could be that predictions belong properly to a whole

---

[42] 'PostScript' to 'Bodily Movements, Actions and Epistemology', in *Simple Mindedness.*

substance, even where the events whose occurrence actually makes those predictions true are locatable in a volume smaller than the whole substance. Consider: when I varnish the table, the event of its coming to be shiny is plausibly located at the surface of the table, even though being shiny is a property that the table comes to have. (This is only analogous in some respects of course. And one will not see the point in such an analogy until one has rid oneself of the orthodox physicalists' way of thinking about causation.)

Appendix B: On *Descartes' Dualism*

The distinction I made in section I, between dualism and Cartesianism, is different from the distinction Baker and Morris make between Descartes's dualism and Cartesian dualism.[43] 'Cartesian dualism' in the sense of Baker and Morris is certainly Cartesian; the argument of their book is that Descartes did not hold the doctrine known as, and criticized as, Cartesian dualism. Here I make some remarks about how Baker and Morris's challenge to the nowadays usual reading of Descartes might affect what I say.

Baker and Morris's distinction shows that we can understand 'Cartesianism' if we know only the recent secondary literature. And for the argument of my paper, it would not matter if no-one actually held the views I attribute to Descartes (so long as they are wrong, and they line up more with orthodox physicalists' views than with mine). But I am inclined to think that the historical Descartes actually has slightly more in common with the Descartes to whom I attribute views than Baker and Morris would allow.

Part of Baker and Morris's attack on the idea that Descartes was a Cartesian dualist is their claim that he was neither a volitionist nor an interactionist (in the usually meant senses). They suggest that the view 'that voluntary action is to be analysed in terms of volitions that are efficient causes of bodily movements' is ascribed to Descartes without any grounds. There are three things here of which Descartes's present-day

[43] In *Descartes' Dualism*.

634

expositor might be guilty: (a) crediting Descartes with analytical ambitions, (b) assuming that the volitions of which Descartes spoke are (to put it in my terms) unowned and free floating events, (c) assuming that Descartes held that 'cause' relates volitions and movements. On (a): I have not said that Descartes attempted to analyse voluntary action (see note 14 *supra*). On (b): I have been careful (as Ryle perhaps was not) to see the volitions of which Descartes speaks as some *soul's* volitions. On (c): I have deliberately used 'is causally responsible for' (which I take to be more open-ended than 'causes') in my statement of Descartes's account. I acknowledge that there is much more to be said on the subject of Descartes and causation, and that most expositors say very little. But I do not think that there can be any doubt that Descartes took his dualism to be the upshot of a correct understanding of causal transactions in the physical world (as I contended at the end of section V). That does not establish that Descartes was an interactionist, rather than an occasionalist. (And Baker and Morris endorse Russell's claim [which certainly seems sustainable] that occasionalism is derivable from premises in Descartes.) But the question for Descartes – about how to accommodate human action in a world of bodies as he conceived them – remains, whether or not, in giving his own answer to it, Descartes resisted a crude interactionism and plumped for occasionalism.

Baker and Morris say that Descartes simply conceded that 'there *could be* no intelligible connection between soul and body' (p. 56, their italics). Well, presumably if Descartes was an occasionalist, then he might have allowed that a connection between the two was intelligible to God. And even if, as Baker and Morris say, Descartes did not expect us to understand soul/body transitions, we find Descartes trying to make them less unintelligible to us, e.g. when he says that the soul might be called corporeal. If Descartes had not been at all inclined to make any attempt to find the connection intelligible, then we should not expect to find the *Passions* passage (quoted in section II *supra*), which contains the close-up story. In any case, the stock criticism of Descartes, on which I rely, says only that the connections is not intelligible to a follower of Descartes's. (Here again there is much more to be said – now under the head of 'the substantial union of soul and body'.)

What I call volitionism can probably be attributed to Descartes simply on the basis of the passage I quoted. To the extent to which it can be shown to be doubtful that he held that account, Descartes was a less consistent philosopher of mind – albeit it a more interesting one – than is commonly supposed.

INDEX

CPSIA information can be obtained
at www.ICGtesting.com
Printed in the USA
LVHW010916050722
722697LV00008B/380

9 781009 108638